EROTIC LITERATURE IN ADAPTATION AND TRANSLATION

# LEGENDA

LEGENDA is the Modern Humanities Research Association's book imprint for new research in the Humanities. Founded in 1995 by Malcolm Bowie and others within the University of Oxford, Legenda has always been a collaborative publishing enterprise, directly governed by scholars. The Modern Humanities Research Association (MHRA) joined this collaboration in 1998, became half-owner in 2004, in partnership with Maney Publishing and then Routledge, and has since 2016 been sole owner. Titles range from medieval texts to contemporary cinema and form a widely comparative view of the modern humanities, including works on Arabic, Catalan, English, French, German, Greek, Italian, Portuguese, Russian, Spanish, and Yiddish literature. Editorial boards and committees of more than 60 leading academic specialists work in collaboration with bodies such as the Society for French Studies, the British Comparative Literature Association and the Association of Hispanists of Great Britain & Ireland.

The MHRA encourages and promotes advanced study and research in the field of the modern humanities, especially modern European languages and literature, including English, and also cinema. It aims to break down the barriers between scholars working in different disciplines and to maintain the unity of humanistic scholarship. The Association fulfils this purpose through the publication of journals, bibliographies, monographs, critical editions, and the MHRA Style Guide, and by making grants in support of research. Membership is open to all who work in the Humanities, whether independent or in a University post, and the participation of younger colleagues entering the field is especially welcomed.

ALSO PUBLISHED BY THE ASSOCIATION

*Critical Texts*
Tudor and Stuart Translations • New Translations • European Translations
MHRA Library of Medieval Welsh Literature

*MHRA Bibliographies*
Publications of the Modern Humanities Research Association

*The Annual Bibliography of English Language & Literature*
*Austrian Studies*
*Modern Language Review*
*Portuguese Studies*
*The Slavonic and East European Review*
*Working Papers in the Humanities*
*The Yearbook of English Studies*

www.mhra.org.uk
www.legendabooks.com

# TRANSCRIPT

*Transcript* publishes books about all kinds of imagining across languages, media and cultures: translations and versions, inter-cultural and multi-lingual writing, illustrations and musical settings, adaptation for theatre, film, TV and new media, creative and critical responses. We are open to studies of any combination of languages and media, in any historical moments, and are keen to reach beyond Legenda's traditional focus on modern European languages to embrace anglophone and world cultures and the classics. We are interested in innovative critical approaches: we welcome not only the most rigorous scholarship and sharpest theory, but also modes of writing that stretch or cross the boundaries of those discourses.

*Editorial Committee*
*Chair*: Matthew Reynolds (Oxford)
Robin Kirkpatrick (Cambridge)
Laura Marcus (Oxford)
Patrick McGuinness (Oxford)
Ben Morgan (Oxford)
Mohamed-Salah Omri (Oxford)
Tanya Pollard (CUNY)
Yopie Prins (Michigan)

*Advisory Board*
Jason Gaiger (Oxford)
Alessandro Grilli (Pisa)
Marina Grishakova (Tartu)
Martyn Harry (Oxford)
Linda Hutcheon (Toronto)
Calin-Andrei Mihailescu (London, Ontario)
Wen-Chin Ouyang (SOAS)
Clive Scott (UEA)
Ali Smith
Marina Warner (Birkbeck)
Shane Weller (Kent)
Stefan Willer (Berlin)

*Managing Editor*
Dr Graham Nelson
41 Wellington Square, Oxford OX1 2JF, UK

www.legendabooks.com/series/transcript

TRANSCRIPT

1. *Adapting the Canon: Translation, Visualisation, Interpretation*, edited by Ann Lewis and Silke Arnold-de Simine
2. *Adapted Voices: Transpositions of Céline's Voyage au bout de la nuit and Queneau's Zazie dans le métro*, by Armelle Blin-Rolland
3. *Zola and the Art of Television: Adaptation, Recreation, Translation*, by Kate Griffiths
4. *Comparative Encounters between Artaud, Michaux and the Zhuangzi: Rationality, Cosmology and Ethics*, by Xiaofan Amy Li
5. *Minding Borders: Resilient Divisions in Literature, the Body and the Academy*, edited by Nicola Gardini, Adriana Jacobs, Ben Morgan, Mohamed-Salah Omri and Matthew Reynolds

# Erotic Literature in Adaptation and Translation

Edited by Johannes D. Kaminski

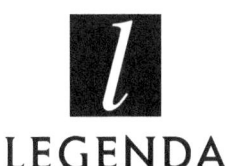

Transcript 7
Modern Humanities Research Association
2018

Published by Legenda
an imprint of the Modern Humanities Research Association
Salisbury House, Station Road, Cambridge CB1 2LA

ISBN 978-1-78188-521-5 (HB)
ISBN 978-1-78188-522-2 (PB)

First published 2018

All rights reserved. No part of this publication may be reproduced or disseminated or transmitted in any form or by any means, electronic, mechanical, photocopying, recording or otherwise, or stored in any retrieval system, or otherwise used in any manner whatsoever without written permission of the copyright owner, except in accordance with the provisions of the Copyright, Designs and Patents Act 1988, or under the terms of a licence permitting restricted copying issued in the UK by the Copyright Licensing Agency Ltd, Saffron House, 6–10 Kirby Street, London EC1N 8TS, England, or in the USA by the Copyright Clearance Center, 222 Rosewood Drive, Danvers MA 01923. Application for the written permission of the copyright owner to reproduce any part of this publication must be made by email to legenda@mhra.org.uk.

Disclaimer: Statements of fact and opinion contained in this book are those of the author and not of the editors or the Modern Humanities Research Association. The publisher makes no representation, express or implied, in respect of the accuracy of the material in this book and cannot accept any legal responsibility or liability for any errors or omissions that may be made.

Trademark notice: Product or corporate names may be trademarks or registered trademarks, and are used only for identification and explanation without intent to infringe.

© Modern Humanities Research Association 2018

Copy-Editor: Birgit Mikus

# CONTENTS

| | | |
|---|---|---|
| | *Notes on the Contributors* | ix |
| | Introduction<br>JOHANNES D. KAMINSKI | 1 |
| 1 | Translation, Ethics and Obscenity<br>THOMAS WYNN | 13 |
| 2 | The European Market for Pornography: Some French Texts in German Translation Around 1900<br>JOHANNES FRIMMEL | 33 |
| 3 | Eroticized Materiality and Postcolonial Agency in Pierre Guyotat's Algerian Works<br>DEAN A. BRINK | 43 |
| 4 | Let's Talk about Sex: How to Find Words for what You Cannot Speak of<br>STEPHANIE HEIMGARTNER | 66 |
| 5 | Seduced by Preconditions: The Eroticism of Power, Money and Love in Goethe, Sacher-Masoch and E. L. James<br>CARINA GRÖNER | 78 |
| 6 | Audio-Erotics<br>JOHANNES D. KAMINSKI | 91 |
| 7 | Erotica in Erotica: Adaptation and Somatic Translation in Late Imperial Chinese Erotic Culture<br>JIE GUO | 110 |
| 8 | National Erotics, Gender, and the Representation of Sexuality in Heian Japan (794–1185)<br>JOSHUA S. MOSTOW | 125 |
| 9 | Tragic Eroticism: or, the Silent Awakening of Meta-Pornography<br>JULIA BOOG-KAMINSKI AND KATHRIN EMEIS | 140 |
| 10 | Sensational Pain: Filming the Eroticized Trauma Narrative<br>KATIE JONES | 154 |
| 11 | From Literary Contact to Cinematic Intimacy: Patrice Chéreau Meets Hanif Kureishi<br>JULIETTE FEYEL | 172 |

12  Adapting *Jing Ping Mei*, Serializing Sex: Hong Kong's Pornographic
    Serial Melodrama                                                    186
    JIANQING CHEN

   *Index*                                                              201

# NOTES ON THE CONTRIBUTORS

JULIA BOOG-KAMINSKI holds a doctoral degree in German literature studies from Hamburg University (Germany) and is working as a Research Associate at the *IFK_ International Research Center Cultural Studies* (Austria). Recent publications include a monograph on joke structures in intercultural literature (*ANDERSSPRECHEN*, 2017).

DEAN ANTHONY BRINK is Associate Professor in the Department of Foreign Languages & Literatures, National Chiao Tung University, Hsinchu (Taiwan). His current research focuses on experimental aesthetics in contemporary poet-performance artists in North America and Taiwan. His forthcoming book is: *Japanese Poetry and Its Publics: From Colonial Taiwan to Fukushima* (Routledge, 2018).

JIANQING CHEN is a PhD candidate in Film & Media at U.C. Berkeley (United States) with a designated emphasis on critical theory. She is interested in the representation of sex and sexuality, narrative theory, and new/digital media. She has an MA in Film and Media from Columbia University (U.S.).

KATHRIN EMEIS holds a doctorate in German literature studies from Hamburg University (Germany) where she addressed the representation of teachers in contemporary German literature (published as: *Schul-Aufgabe. Der Lehrer als Figur der Krise in der deutschen Literatur zu Beginn des 21. Jahrhunderts*, 2017). Currently, she is working as a teacher for secondary education.

JULIETTE FEYEL holds a PhD in comparative literature. Her research specialises in the representations of the body and subjectivity in contemporary literature, cinema and graphic novels.

JOHANNES FRIMMEL is Lecturer in book studies (Buchwissenschaft) at the Ludwig-Maximilians-Universität Munich (Germany). He is co-editor, with Christine Haug and Anke Vogel, of a volume on erotic literature (*Erotisch-pornographische Lesestoffe*, 2015). His most recent monograph engages with the publishing industry of late nineteenth century erotic literature (*Das Geschäft mit der Unzucht*, 2018).

CARINA ULRIKA GROENER is Lecturer for German language and literature at the University of St. Gallen (Switzerland) and at the University of Konstanz (Germany).

JIE GUO is Associate Professor of comparative literature at the University of South Carolina (USA). Her research interests include the history of sexuality, gender theory, visual culture, the history of Chinese women, and Chinese literature and film. She is the Chinese translator of Judith Butler's *Undoing Gender* (2009).

STEPHANIE HEIMGARTNER is Lecturer in comparative literature at Ruhr University in Bochum, Germany. Recently, she has co-edited a volume on the reception of Dante's *Divina Commedia* (with Monika Schmitz-Emans, 2017) and one on pregnancy (with Simone Sauer-Kretschmer, 2017).

KATIE JONES is writing her PhD in comparative literature at Swansea University, United Kingdom.

JOHANNES D. KAMINSKI is Marie Skłodowska-Curie Fellow at University of Vienna (Austria) and works on German and Chinese literature, preferably in a comparative manner.

JOSHUA S. MOSTOW is Professor of Asian Studies at The University of British Columbia, Vancouver (Canada). He is the co-editor, with Norman Bryson and Maribeth Graybill, of *Gender and Power in the Japanese Visual Field* (2003), and co-author, with Asato Ikeda, of *A Third Gender: Beautiful Youths in Japanese Edo-Period Prints and Paintings (1600–1868)* (2016).

THOMAS WYNN is Professor in French literature at Durham University (United Kingdom). He specializes in eighteenth-century theatre and libertine writing.

# INTRODUCTION

*Johannes D. Kaminski*

On his wedding night, Vesperus, the hero of Li Yu's erotic masterpiece *Carnal Prayer Mat* (肉蒲團 *Rou Pu Tuan*, 1693), finds himself facing a bashful young bride. He quickly arrives at the conclusion that Yuxiang is not able to satisfy his sexual needs; her father, a venerable Confucian, has instilled her with prejudices against sensual pleasure. Vesperus is determined to challenge her perceptions. He purchases a collection of erotic images, which he intends to view alongside his inexperienced bride. 'Pulling up an easy chair, he sat down and drew her onto his lap, then opened the album and showed it to her picture by picture. This album differed from others in that the first page of each leaf contained the erotic picture and the second page a comment on it.'[1] As Vesperus convinces Yuxiang that these paintings depict perfectly natural acts, the reading experience slowly gives way to sexual intimacy. Both partners find themselves greatly rewarded: 'From that day forward they were perfectly adjusted and more deeply in love than ever.'[2]

If we apply the term 'translation' generously, the reader witnesses three stages of translation: on the level of the narration, there is the couple's corporeal translation of images into physical enactment; on the level of authorship, there is the symbolic translation of thought, images and scenes into words; and finally, on the fundamental level of linguistics, we owe thanks to Patrick Hanan for rendering the Chinese original in the English language. Hanan's 'perfect adjustment' of words allows the reader to become enamoured of a foreign text.

From a comparative perspective, the success of the couple's corporeal translation is no less startling than its linguistic rendering. Although it is easy to relate Vesperus' stance against Confucian frigidity to lewd attacks against virginal chastity, as featured in many European Enlightenment novels, the Chinese protagonist adopts a 'pedagogical' approach. Rather than using books to stimulate hetero-erotic encounters, European seducers like Samuel Richardson's Mr. B or Marquis de Sade's libertines use disguises, resort to violence or engage in lengthy philosophical discussions to manipulate their victims. Lewd books, in contrast, are considered symptoms of solitary sex only. In the Judaeo-Christian tradition, paper and ink point towards the realm of substitution, not to the joys of the bridal chamber.

In Enlightenment discourse (and beyond), symbolic representations of sex acts belong to the semantic triad of imagination, solitude and excess. As Thomas W. Laqueur demonstrates, widely read treatises like Samuel Tissot's *Onania* (1716) link masturbation to other 'dangerous' cultural techniques, such as solitary reading.[3] In allowing individuals to retreat from social control, such techniques are perceived to facilitate uncontrolled imagination and unlimited self-enjoyment. Once you engage with a book, there is no going back to the realm of the flesh. For Jean-Jacques Derrida, self-satisfaction points towards a larger mechanism at work within logocentric culture. Just as much as reading and writing, masturbation addresses the question of presence and supplementation. Commenting on Jean-Jacques Rousseau's *Confessions* (1782), Derrida makes a case for auto-eroticism, as the auto-biographer's solitary meditations enable him to recall a string of absent love objects, ranging from his mother to his nanny and his current partner. In collapsing the spacio-temporal gap between presence and absence, masturbation is understood as the purest form of sexual pleasure. This observation extends to our relationship with the world at large: 'there have never been anything but supplements, substitutive significations which could only come forth in a chain of differential references, the "real" supervening, and being added only while taking on meaning from a trace and from an invocation of the supplement, etc.'[4]

At first glance, *Carnal Prayer Mat* appears to challenge Derrida's argument. If script and representation can facilitate a heterosexual encounter rather than serving as substitution for it, the unity of presence and supplement is no longer broken. In Marquis de Sade's *Juliette* (1797–1801), Mme. Delbène raises how different cultures conceptualize sex as she encourages disciples to embrace their otherness: 'Is it not so, for example, that the same acts the Chinese do not in any sense consider inadmissible, would cause us to shudder here in France? The sooner one sets to work adopting the philosophy one intends to be guided by, the better.'[5] But does the Chinese trope of erotic *ekphrasis* really provide an alternative path to 'Western' logocentric culture? From what we learn in *Carnal Prayer Mat*, the truth is somewhat disappointing. Ultimately, Vesperus does not find happiness in an eternal state of arousal and stimulation with his wife; rather, the images and texts ignite an insatiable desire for novelty. Eventually, he finds himself disillusioned by the world of the flesh. The protagonist renounces the world and becomes a monk. For a Western reader, this decision sounds alarmingly familiar, as it recalls St. Augustine's conversion and his influential anxiety about sex.

In reading erotic literature from different cultures, the comparatist encounters many challenges: can s/he find evidence of the cultural difference which François Jullien diagnoses in much of his comparative work? Accordingly, the main task of the critic consists in highlighting the difference and making it intelligible.[6] Is s/he ready to deliver a nuanced appreciation of this difference? Or will s/he overshoot the mark by proclaiming essentialist notions of cultural otherness or universalism? Do 'Eastern' and 'Western' eroticism work similar, thus reproducing Zhang Longxi's notion of comparability?[7] In traversing broad ground, in both chronological and geographical terms, this edited volume cannot provide definitive answers, but tries to live up to Mircea Eliade's reminder that 'Western' culture must carry on conversation with the other, non-European cultures if it is not to become provincial.[8]

## Translating as 'disappearance-as-appearance'

According to Gideon Toury, translators sometimes make the 'observation that there is something "missing" in the target culture which should rather be there and which, luckily, already exists elsewhere'.[9] As a reaction to this, translated texts try to compensate for the (perceived) deficits of the target system: either through foreignization, usually in combination with footnotes or introductory commentaries, or through localization, that is, when foreign elements are replaced by more familiar concepts. By and large, criticism favours the former approach, as it helps 'to jolt the reader out of a comfortable [...] view of translations as secondary, as faint shadows of primary, vivid but lost, originals'.[10]

According to Walter Benjamin, the 'task of the translator' goes even further. As he argues with regards to Johann Heinrich Voß's renderings of Homer's epics (from Ancient Greek into German), translations can participate in the creation of 'pure language', so that 'the language imprisoned in a work'[11] can finally come into existence. Today, it is difficult to approve of Benjamin's 'messianic'[12] tone, yet we are forced to make sense of the linguistic and semantic gaps between different linguistic systems. What is more, since we no longer subscribe to a hierarchical distinction between text and image,[13] we must also evaluate media adaptations in a more dynamic manner.

A fitting characterisation of these gaps is provided by Roland Barthes's notion of 'appearance-as-disappearance': 'Is not the most erotic portion of a body where the garment gapes? [...] [T]he intermittence of skin flashing between two articles of clothing (trousers and sweater), between two edges (the open-necked shirt, the glove and the sleeve); it is this flash itself which seduces, or rather: the staging of an appearance-as-disappearance.'[14] This sequence of metaphors establishes a notion of non-linear movement which characterizes both the erotic and the 'task of the translator': just as a lover never fully absorbs the object of his desire, translations never arrive in the target language completely, but deictically point back to the source language. This metaphor, however, is not limited to realms of the erotic and language. Building on Barthes's and Umberto Eco's semiologies, researchers like José Lambert, Clem Robyns, Susan Bassnett and André Lefevere inaugurated the 'cultural turn' of translation studies by liberating the term 'translation' from its interlingual meaning only, taking place only between fixed languages and national literatures. Instead, they found it useful to extend the meaning of the term and apply it more generally to instances of semantic re-contextualisation. Translation happens once a shift occurs between competing and varying discourses and media.[15]

In light of this revaluation of the term 'translation', conventional distinctions between 'the erotic', imagined as a refined concept, and 'the pornographic', conceptualized as something racier and possibly unsettling, gain new relevance. Indicating different ends on the scale of ethical, sociological or legal acceptability, this distinction 'depends on arguments and stereotypes that are fundamentally subjective, and that are psychological, ethical, feminist, or aesthetic in nature.'[16] Or as Walter Kendrick succinctly puts it: pornography names a debate, not a thing.

Today, the conglomeration of nations that comprise our idea of 'Western civilisation' has successfully exported its 'problematic history with eroticism, pornography and obscenity'[17] by means of a culture that reaches global households irrespective of national boundaries. This problematic history is evinced by contemporary media outlets' arbitrary regulations with regards to what is considered socially acceptable and what is not: while British Film Censors established the much ridiculed 'Mull of Kintyre rule'[18] at one point, social media companies like Facebook and Instagram established their own set of rules for the publication of online content. As of 2017, posts containing nipples are offensive — but only in their photographic representation.[19] Considering the history of pornography, such exacting distinctions between acceptable erotics and the smutty nipple-bearing rest are a comparably recent phenomenon.

Rather than naming fixed genre demarcations, this dichotomy addresses debates about where the boundary between legitimate and illegitimate cultural artefacts is placed at a given point in time.[20] In some premodern societies, for example, the shock value of obscenity is directed not at public morale, but primarily used as a vehicle to attack and make fun of political and religious authorities.[21] This changed with modernity, as these authorities were pushed to the margins of the public discourse. Meanwhile, the advent of online streaming platforms has brought this debate from the censor's table to all family homes with a stable internet connection. In light of the current wave of 'hypersexualisation',[22] the old question of how to make sense of risqué material is more urgent than ever before. Is the distribution of pornography tied to the freedom of expression, like Larry Flint, the late editor of *Hustler*, would have argued? How did visual pornography come to be the considered more harmful than, say, textual representations of the act? What facilitated the mainstream success of E. L. James's bestselling *Fifty Shades* series?

Inevitably, these questions are linked to the dilemma between narratives of liberation and suppression. On the one hand, there is the contemporary tendency to bestow upon openly misogynist texts, like the Marquis de Sade's oeuvre, the title of 'world literature'. Susan Sontag argues for a neat distinction between fictional and real sexuality: 'What pornographic literature does is precisely to drive a wedge between one's existence as a full human being and one's existence as a sexual being — while in ordinary life a healthy person is one who prevents such a gap from opening up.'[23] On the other hand, there are other strata of feminist critique which beg to differ. In insisting on the interrelation between the fictional realm and the imitative instinct of its consumers, Andrea Dworkin addresses the gendered power structures of such material.[24]

Today, perhaps more than ever before, a sensible resolution of these irreconcilable positions is out of reach. Therefore, the present volume intends to interrogate the dichotomy between 'the erotic' and 'the pornographic' doggedly, but undogmatically. The authors use this terminology diversely, allowing them to find nuanced differences in a vast body of texts. The charge of pornography rings differently when describing public censorship of the book market and when addressing the ethical problem of translating a text that promotes paedophilia and murder, like the Marquis de Sade's oeuvre. While useful in individual studies, the emphatic notion of 'the erotic' remains deeply problematic in the context of transcultural analysis. In his late study *History of Sexuality* (*Histoire de la sexualité*, 1976), Michel Foucault contrasts Western *sciencia sexualis* with *ars erotica*, a cultural technique said to be practiced in Japan, China, India and the Arabic hemisphere.[25] Inevitably, the essentialism inherent in this notion continues to attract substantial criticism.

## Erotic literature as world literature

As our opening episode with Vesperus and his newlywed bride demonstrates, sexuality is a complex physiosocial phenomenon. Nonetheless, there is a common notion that 'Western civilisation' has had a particularly problematic history with sex.[26] This claim is possibly overblown and, problematically, reiterates discarded notions of the Orient as a place where sex is unrepressed and considered a natural act.[27] More so than gender demarcations and lingering colonial perceptions, the problematic nature of sex, one could argue, is the true anthropological constant. As Sontag argues, '[t]here is, demonstrably, something incorrectly designed and potentially disorienting in the human sexual capacity'.[28]

The history of erotic (or pornographic) fiction is just as promiscuous as one could expect from 'world literature'. According to David Damrosch's influential definition, it is comprised by a body of texts that 'circulate beyond their culture of origin, either in translation or in their original language'.[29] Ranging from Boccaccio's cheerful stories of adultery in the fourteenth-century collection *The Decameron* to Charlotte Roche's elaborations on female masturbation in *Wetlands* (*Feuchtgebiete*, 2008), the genre retains a timeless appeal. Including popular smut novels like the *The Lustful Turk* (1828) and George Bataille's hermetic short story *Madame Edwarda* (1941), erotic fiction caters to a broad spectrum of aesthetic preferences. And finally, from Vātsyāyana's Sanskrit poetry in the *Kama Sutra* (कामसूत्र, compiled during the 2nd century AD) to the Chinese narrative *The Plum in the Golden Vase* (金瓶梅 *Jin Ping Mei*, 1610) and to contemporary Japanese 'Boys Love' fiction, the genre defies linguistic and cultural boundaries. A minority of these books consciously form part of the genre, especially premodern non-European texts; rather, they are retrospectively attributed to it, usually by readers who never belonged to the intended audience in the first place.

While such narratives usually revolve around a shared motif, that being the sexual encounter between two or more partners (or the imagination thereof), this volume builds on a characteristic feature of erotic fiction: its transferability between different language systems and its adaptation to different media, such as illustration and film. In contrast to the astounding mobility of erotic literature across linguistic and media boundaries, existing studies tend to focus on erotic literature in isolated traditions.[30] Notable exceptions are Lynn Hunt's and Hiltrud Gnüg's studies, in which erotic fiction is understood as a European transnational enterprise.[31] In limiting their corpus to literary traditions that inherited the Greek concept of *eros*,[32] however, these volumes do not address the notable body of non-European translations that played a prominent role in the Western imagination of the Orient and the East.

Existing inquiries into adaptions of erotic literature, to image or to film, tend to focus on 'hypercanonical'[33] texts. As a consequence, a plethora of research exists on iconographic legacy of the Japanese eleventh-century text *The Tale of Genji* (源氏物語 *Genji monogatari*), an iconic text that includes erotic passages.[34] In the Western context, the eminence of D. H. Lawrence's oeuvre has drawn attention to *Lady Chatterley's Lover* (1928) and its multiple adaptations to film.[35] The most salient examples of the genre, however, are left underexploited.

This edited volume is a first attempt to bring the core texts of erotic literature to the forefront and look at their movement across linguistic and media boundaries. Not restricting themselves to their home surroundings, these texts push for adventures in adjacent territories and language systems, where they inseminate new bodies — that is, they pick up foreign tongues and forms of expression. Once they have embarked on such escapades, it can become difficult to tie promiscuous texts back to their original settings; while *The Pillow Book* (枕草子 *Makura no sōshi*, 1002) has been defaced by exoticist appropriations,[36] the Marquis de Sade's novels have attained the status of world classics. Given the arbitrariness of erotic gestures and sexual signs, however, representations of sexual experiences are highly mediated and culturally coded, presenting many difficulties for their translators. Anastasia Steele's moans ('*Whoa*')[37] are quite straight-forward, but the nosebleeds of sexually aroused anime characters,[38] for example, may leave translators baffled. It is not the intention of the present volume to provide a rule book on how to translate one cultural code into another; instead, the aim is to give prominence to the fluctuation of codes and conventions across linguistic and genre boundaries.

### The contributions

Building on the 'cultural turn' of translation studies, the articles in this volume are divided into three different parts — TEXT TO TEXT, TEXT TO IMAGE and TEXT TO FILM. The first part addresses translations into different linguistic systems and, in a broader sense, questions of aesthetic representation. In light of the recent Penguin-translation of de Sade's *The 120 Days of Sodom* (*Les Cent Vingt Journées de Sodome*, 1785), **Tom Wynn** reassesses the translational ethics of the obscene classic he rendered into English in collaboration with Will McMorran. While all established editions and translations have corrected and polished de Sade's text, their edition follows the manuscript and preserves its stylistic clumsiness. In drawing attention away from *what* is written, to *how* it was written, it encourages the reader to move outside the text to a place of conscience. Thereby, the translators hope to bring eighteenth century libertinism into alignment with the sensibilities of a twenty-first century readership. **Johannes Frimmel** looks at late nineteenth-century pornographic literature in Europe and its distribution in different language contexts. In order to guarantee absolute discretion and to make investigation difficult, these works were produced in one country and sold in another. The first European entrepreneur of pornography, the Belgian Auguste Brancart, and the Parisian bookseller 'Robert' published a multitude of clandestine works and reprints in English, French and German. Despite middle-class customers' preference for books of French origin, they placed little interest in historical context, having consumed a 'pornotopia' in which class, age and custom are dissolved by pure sex.

**Dean Brink** engages with Pierre Guyotat's Algerian works, *Tomb for 500,000 Soldiers* (*Tombeau pour cinq cent mille soldats*, 1967) and *Éden, Éden, Éden* (1970). Guyortat translates his exploration of capitalist imperialism and the postcolonial heritage of modern France into exuberant sexual imagery. This results in a phantasmagory where all boundaries start to blur: between agent and object, the human and the non-human, and between poetry and prose writing. Reading these work in English inevitably approaches incomprehensibility. **Stephanie Heimgartner**'s article looks at contemporary publishing and addresses linguistic challenges in two English-language novels and their German translations, A. L. Kennedy's *Original Bliss* (1997) and Nicholson Baker's *House of Holes* (2011). The first text recounts the impossible love story of a couple that tries to craft a non-violent, non-coercive language for their sexual wishes and physical stimulations. In translation, however, highly charged conversations lose their denotative dimension. Nicholson Baker replaces the conventional language of pornography with idiomatic expressions, cultural allusions, onomatopoeia and unconventional metaphors for sexual organs.

**Carina Gröner** analyzes how 'uncomfortable communication' is created and controlled by means of gift-giving, a cultural technique which translates discourse into sentiment and vice versa. Be it a literary product, as in Goethe's *Sorrows of Young Werther* (*Die Leiden des jungen Werthers*, 1774/87), amnesty in Leopold von Sacher-Masoch's *Katharina II* (1891) or an *Omega*-watch in James's *Fifty Shades* trilogy (2011–2012), such gifts provide blueprints for the social practice of coupling and marriage. **My own** contribution focusses on literary representations of erotic sounds and their problematic translation into different languages. Johann Wolfgang Goethe's *Wilhelm Meister's Years of Apprenticeship* (*Wilhelm Meisters Lehrjahre*, 1795/76) and *Roman Elegies* (*Römische Elegien*, 1795) are grouped alongside Li Yu's *Carnal Prayer Mat* in order to demonstrate how audio-erotics are more than a mere addition to the linguistic representation of the act. While sound is attributed an epistemologically uncertain position in both the European and the Chinese context, these literary texts reveal the 'erratic' dimension of audio-erotics. Instead of facilitating a more intimate encounter, such sound experiences dislocate the position of the written word by rendering it superfluous.

The section TEXT TO IMAGE looks at erotic texts that are accompanied by illustrations. Often, such illustrations go beyond mere duplications of content, also complementing or even substituting the narrative. **Jie Guo** engages with late imperial Chinese erotic literature, which makes frequent mention of erotica and its correct usage. The 'erotica-in-erotica' convention not only illustrates the importance of sight in achieving sexual pleasure in this cultural context, but also serves as a window onto the intimate interrelationships among forms, mediums and genres. Finally, such representations are also designed to draw the reader in: they are endowed with an extradiegetic dimension, implying identification between the viewer of these illustrations with the couple that makes use of erotic stimuli. In turn, the reader is urged to use the book as well. **Joshua Mostow** elaborates on the construction of a Japanese 'national erotics' during the Heian period. Under the stewardship of women, indigenous culture is constructed in contrast to a Chinese Other. As *The Tale of Genji* and *The Pillow Book* show, Heian culture avoids literary representations of actual sex. In the visual realm, however, *The Lotus Sutra Painted on Fans* (扇面法華経 *Senmen Hokekyō*, 1154) features a set of fascinating illustrations. Their erotic content is only represented in a coded manner: the spatial proximity of male and female figures. In spite of Heian Japan's increasing self-awareness, erotica are informed by a double binary structure in which the internalized foreign Other, China, remains part of a national identity.

**Julia Boog-Kaminski** and **Kathrin Emeis** draw our attention to the sophisticated erotic works of Georges Bataille which seek to translate the 'unsaid' into discursive speech. To this end, his 'meta-pornography' plays with intertextuality, polyphony and complex narrative means. While the short story *Madame Edwarda* tests the limits of language and experiments with punctuation, *The Tears of Eros* (*Larmes d'Éros*, 1961) is a heavily illustrated essay. The text, however, does not answer directly to the images; rather, the images are intended to expand — or even replace — scholarly discourse. The essay climaxes in an image of torture in which Bataille's key motifs, Eros and Thanatos, converge.

The third part, TEXT TO FILM, is devoted to the interrelation between literary texts and their cinematic representations. Such adaptations seek to conquer new audiences by translating texts into moving images and sound. **Katie Jones** engages in a double comparison: first, between D. M. Thomas's *The White Hotel* (1981) and Elfriede Jelinek's *The Piano Teacher* (*Die Klavierspielerin*, 1983) and, second, between the success of Michael Haneke's film production (2001) and the halted adaptation of Thomas's template. Both novels bring forwards a critique of patriarchal social and sexual oppression. If Erika Kohut suffers from her mother and her lover's cruelty, Lisa Erdmann's psyche is first split open by Sigmund Freud, the psychoanalyst, and her body eventually destroyed during the 1941 massacre of Babi Jar. By engaging in a critique of normative and generic romance, Haneke's adaptation reorients Jelinek's narrative at the expense of the broader socio-political context. *The White Hotel*, in contrast, did not lend itself to readjustments; its promiscuous style calls into question the possibility of ethical witnessing. The challenge of representing the Holocaust alongside pleasure, voyeurism and fetishism in film appears impossible to overcome.

**Juliette Feyel** compares Hanif Kureishi's novella *Intimacy* (1998) with Patrice Chéreau's film adaptation (2001). While the text is written in the form of an internal monologue and represents the male protagonist's viewpoint, Chéreau focuses on both protagonists' bashful, gradual approach and their apprehensive yet desirous gazes. Where the novel employs conflicting linguistic registers, the film shows clumsy movements and uncomfortable changes of position. Both Kureishi and Chéreau invite their readers and viewers to reflect on the struggle in which intimate relationships are entangled out of fear of intimacy. Without hiding behind long speeches, such intimacy manifests itself in sex, where lovers expose themselves to the other's gaze. For **Jianqing Chen**, the Chinese pornographic novel *The Plum in the Golden Vase* acted as an ideal template for 1970s Hong Kong porn directors, as its complex publishing history allowed the freedom to repeatedly imagine and reinterpret the original. From the seventeenth century onwards, the novel's intricate descriptions engendered racy illustrations, and the films make ample use of established visual patterns. Most notably, the cinematography dwells on serialised representations of individual sex acts rather than building up suspense for a final orgasmic explosion. This moment of deferral also extends to the relationship between literary template and different filmic versions. As the story is retold, moral attitudes and female character portraits visibly change.

## Acknowledgements

This volume would not have been possible without the generous help of the *Centre for Research in the Arts, Social Sciences and Humanities* (CRASSH) at Cambridge, where the two-day workshop that preceded this volume took place. The moral support of Simon Goldhill and Marie Lemaire facilitated the smooth operation of this risqué enterprise. We are very grateful to Ritchie Robertson and Matthew Reynolds for taking an interest in this manuscript, and to Graham Nelson whose assistance is greatly appreciated. As my former employer, Peng Hsiao-yen from *Academia Sinica* (Taipei) also facilitated the production of this volume.

Since English is only the second language of most contributors, the Tower of Babel cast a long shadow over this book project. Thanks to the watchful eye of Kirie Stromberg, our proofreader, however, the manuscript was cleansed from clumsy writing, unintended puns and Freudian slips.

Finally, I would like to express my gratitude to Julia who supported this project from the very beginning: 'hic tibi multa licet sermone latentia tecto / dicere, quae dici sentiat illa sibi'.[39]

## Bibliography

BARTHES, ROLAND, *The Pleasure of the Text*, trans. by Richard Miller (New York, NY: Hill and Wang, 1975).

BASSNETT, SUSAN and ANDRÉ LEFEVERE (eds), *Constructing Cultures* (Clevedon: Multilingual Matters, 1998).

—— *Translation, History and Culture* (London: Pinter, 1990).

BENJAMIN, WALTER, *Selected Writings*, ed. and trans. by Marcus Bullock and Michael W. Jennings, 4 vols. (Cambridge, MA: Belknap, 2002).

BRULOTTE, GAETAN and JOHN PHILIPPS, *Encyclopedia of Erotic Literature*, 2 vols (New York, NY: Routledge, 2007).

COLLIGAN, COLETTE, *The Traffic in Obscenity from Byron to Beardsley: Sexuality and Exoticism in Nineteenth-Century Print Culture* (Basingstoke: Palgrave Macmillan, 2006).

DAMROSCH, DAVID, *What is World Literature?* (Princeton, NJ: Princeton University Press, 2003).

—— 'World Literature in a Postcanonical, Hypercanonical Age', in *Comparative Literature in the Age of Globalization*, ed. by Haun Saussy (Baltimore, MD: Johns Hopkins University Press, 2006), pp. 43–53.

DERRIDA, JACQUES, *Of Grammatology*, trans. by Gayatri Chakravorty Spivak (Baltimore, MD: Johns Hopkins University Press, 1976).

*Dragon Ball*: Episode 3, dir. by Minoru Okazaki and Daisuke Nishio (Fuji Television Network, 1986–1989).
DWORKIN, ANDREA, *Pornography: Men Possessing Women* (New York, NY: Putnam, 1981).
ELIADE, MIRCEA, *Myths, Dreams and Mysteries: The Encounter between Contemporary Faiths and Archaic Realities* (London: Harvill, 1960).
FOUCAULT, MICHEL, *Histoire de la sexualité I: La Volonté de savoir* (Paris: Gallimard, 1976).
GIFFORD, PAUL, *Love, Desire and Transcendence in French Literature* (Aldershot: Ashgate, 2005).
GNÜG, HILTRUD, *Der erotische Roman: Von der Renaissance bis zur Gegenwart* (Stuttgart: Reclam, 2002).
HENTIUK, VALERIE, *Worlding Sei Sei Shônagon: The Pillow Book in Translation* (Ottawa: University of Ottawa Press, 2012), pp. 18–32.
HUANG, MARTIN W., *Desire and Fictional Narrative in Late Imperial China* (Harvard, MA: Harvard University Press, 2001).
HUNT, LYNN, 'Introduction: Obscenity and the Origins of Modernity', in *The Invention of Pornography 1500–1800*, ed. by L.H. (New York, NY: Zone Books, 1993).
—— (ed.), *The Invention of Pornography: Obscenity and the Origins of Modernity, 1500–1800* (New York, NY: Zone, 1993).
JAMES, E.L., *Fifty Shades of Grey* (London: Arrow, 2012).
JULLIEN, FRANÇOIS, *Detour and Access: Strategies of Meaning in China and Greece* (New York, NY: Zone, 2000).
—— *Le nu impossible* (Paris: Seuil, 2005).
KANG, ZHENGGUO, *Chongshen fengyuejianjian: Xing yu Zhongguo gudian wenxue* (*Reconsidering the Romantic Mirror: Sex and Classical Chinese Literature*) (Taipei: Niang chuban, 2016).
KENDRICK, WALTER, *The Secret Museum: Pornography in Modern Culture* (New York, NY: Viking, 1987).
KOZUL, MLADEN, *Le corps érotique au XVIIIe siècle: Amour, péché, maladie* (Oxford: Voltaire Foundation, 2011).
LAMBERT, JOSÉ and CLEM ROBYNS, 'Translation', in *Semiotics: A Handbook on the Sign-Theoretic Foundations of Nature and Culture*, ed. by Roland Posner et al., 4 vols (Berlin: De Gruyter, 1997) III, 3594–614.
LAQUEUR, THOMAS W., *Solitary Sex: A Cultural History of Masturbation* (New York, NY: Zone, 2003).
LEHMAN, PETER and SUSAN HUNT, *Lady Chatterley's Legacy in the Movies* (New Brunswick, NJ: Rutgers University Press, 2010).
LEVINE, SUZNNE JILL, *The Subversive Scribe: Translating Latin American Fiction* (New York, NY: Columbia University Press, 1991).
LI, YU, *The Carnal Prayer Mat (Rou Pu Tuan)*, trans. by Patrick Hanan (London: Arrow, 1990).
MACDONALD, TOM, 'A Not-So-Modest Proposal: Instragram, Free the Nipple for the Inauguration', in *Vogue*, 19.01.2017 <https://www.vogue.com/article/instagram-free-the-nipple-inauguration-day> [last retrieved 11.10.2017].
MAN, PAUL DE, '"Conclusions": Walter Benjamin's "The Task of the Translator"', *Yale French Studies*, 69 (1985), 25–46.
MICHELSON, PETER, *Speaking the Unspeakable: A Poetics of Obscenity* (New York, NY: State University of New York Press, 1993).
OVID, *Ars Amatoria*, ed. by A. S. Hollis (Oxford: Oxford University Press, 1977).
PULIN, RICHARD and MELANIE CLAUDE, 'Appearance, Intimacy Exhibition, Hyper-sexualization and Pornography', in *The Political Economy of Media and Power*, ed. by Jeffery Klaehn (New York, NY: Peter Lang, 2010), pp. 293–317.
SADE, MARQUIS DE, *Juliette: or, Vice Amply Rewarded*, trans. by Pieralessandro Casavini (New York, NY: Lancer, 1965).

SAID, EDWARD W., *Orientalism* (New York, NY: Vintage, 1979).
SHIRANE, HARUO (ed.), *Envisioning 'The Tale of Genji': Media, Gender, and Cultural Production* (New York, NY: Columbia University Press, 2008).
SONTAG, SUSAN, *Styles of Radical Will* (London: Secker & Warburg, 1969).
THOMAS, JULIA, *Pictorial Victorians: The Inscription of Values in Word and Image* (Athens, OH: Ohio University Press, 2004).
ROSE, DAVID EDWARD, *The Ethics and Politics of Pornography* (New York, NY: Palgrave 2013).
TOURY, GIDEON, *Descriptive Translation Studies — and Beyond* (Amsterdam: Benjamin, 2012).
ZHANG, LONGXI, *Allegoresis: Reading Canonical Literature East and West* (Ithaca, NY: Cornell University Press, 2005.

## Notes to the Introduction

1. Li Yu, *The Carnal Prayer Mat (Rou Pu Tuan)*, trans. by Patrick Hanan (London: Arrow, 1990), p. 32.
2. Li, *The Carnal Prayer Mat*, p. 37.
3. See Thomas W. Laqueur, *Solitary Sex: A Cultural History of Masturbation* (New York, NY: Zone, 2003), p. 191.
4. Jacques Derrida, *Of Grammatology*, trans. by Gayatri Chakravorty Spivak (Baltimore, MD: Johns Hopkins University Press, 1976), p. 159.
5. Marquis de Sade, *Juliette: or, Vice Amply Rewarded*, trans. by Pieralessandro Casavini (New York, NY: Lancer, 1965), p. 20.
6. See François Jullien, *Detour and Access: Strategies of Meaning in China and Greece* (New York, NY: Zone, 2000), pp. 33–34.
7. Zhang Longxi's comparative study of Eastern *Tao* and Western *Logos* emphasises 'the recognition of the shared, the common, and the same in the literary and critical tradition of the East and the West beyond their cultural and historical differences[.]' Zhang Longxi, *Allegoresis: Reading Canonical Literature East and West* (Ithaca, NY: Cornell University Press, 2005), pp. 30–39.
8. See Mircea Eliade, *Myths, Dreams and Mysteries: The Encounter between Contemporary Faiths and Archaic Realities* (London: Harvill, 1960), p. 232.
9. Gideon Toury, *Descriptive Translation Studies — and Beyond* (Amsterdam: Benjamin, 2012), pp. 21–22.
10. Suznne Jill Levine, *The Subversive Scribe: Translating Latin American Fiction* (New York, NY: Columbia University Press, 1991), p. 167.
11. Walter Benjamin, *Selected Writings*, ed. and trans. by Marcus Bullock and Michael W. Jennings, 4 vols. (Cambridge, MA: Belknap, 2002) I, 257.
12. Paul de Man, '"Conclusions": Walter Benjamin's "The Task of the Translator"', *Yale French Studies*, 69 (1985), 25–46 (p. 29).
13. See Julia Thomas, *Pictorial Victorians: The Inscription of Values in Word and Image* (Athens, OH: Ohio University Press, 2004), p. 9.
14. Roland Barthes, *The Pleasure of the Text*, trans. by Richard Miller (New York, NY: Hill and Wang, 1975), p. 10.
15. See José Lambert and Clem Robyns, 'Translation', in *Semiotics: A Handbook on the Sign-Theoretic Foundations of Nature and Culture*, ed. by Roland Posner et al., 4 vols (Berlin: De Gruyter, 1997) III, 3594–614; Susan Bassnett and André Lefevere (eds), *Translation, History and Culture* (London: Pinter, 1990); and Susan Bassnett and André Lefevere, *Constructing Cultures* (Clevedon: Multilingual Matters, 1998).
16. Gaetan Brulotte and John Philipps, *Encyclopedia of Erotic Literature*, 2 vols (New York, NY: Routledge, 2007), I, p. x.
17. See. Peter Michelson, *Speaking the Unspeakable: A Poetics of Obscenity* (New York, NY: State University of New York Press, 1993), p. 2.
18. If a man's penis was more elevated than the Scottish peninsula on the map, the British Film

Censors deemed the scene as inappropriate for screening. See David Edward Rose, *The Ethics and Politics of Pornography* (New York, NY: Palgrave 2013), p. 22.
19. See Tom MacDonald, 'A Not-So-Modest Proposal: Instagram, Free the Nipple for the Inauguration', in *Vogue*, 19.01.2017 <https://www.vogue.com/article/instagram-free-the-nipple-inauguration-day> [last retrieved 11.10.2017].
20. See Walter Kendrick, *The Secret Museum: Pornography in Modern Culture* (New York, NY: Viking, 1987), p. 115.
21. See Lynn Hunt, 'Introduction: Obscenity and the Origins of Modernity', in *The Invention of Pornography 1500–1800*, ed. by L.H. (New York, NY: Zone Books, 1993)
22. See Richard Pulin and Melanie Claude, 'Appearance, Intimacy Exhibition, Hypersexualization and Pornography', in *The Political Economy of Media and Power*, ed. by Jeffery Klaehn (New York, NY: Peter Lang, 2010), pp. 293–317.
23. Susan Sontag, *Styles of Radical Will* (London: Secker & Warburg, 1969), p. 58.
24. See Andrea Dworkin, *Pornography: Men Possessing Women* (New York, NY: Putnam, 1981).
25. See Michel Foucault, *Histoire de la sexualité I: La Volonté de savoir* (Paris: Gallimard, 1976), pp. 77–78.
26. Michelson, *Speaking the Unspeakable*, p. 3.
27. See Edward W. Said's elaboration on Edward William Lane's idea of the Orient: 'everything about the Orient [...] exuded dangerous sex, threatened hygiene and domestic seemliness with an excessive "freedom of intercourse".' Edward W. Said, *Orientalism* (New York, NY: Vintage, 1979), p. 167.
28. Sontag, *Styles of Radical Will*, p. 58.
29. David Damrosch, *What is World Literature?* (Princeton, NJ: Princeton University Press, 2003), p. 4.
30. For the English context cf. Colette Colligan, *The Traffic in Obscenity from Byron to Beardsley: Sexuality and Exoticism in Nineteenth-Century Print Culture* (Basingstoke: Palgrave Macmillan, 2006). For the French context see Paul Gifford, *Love, Desire and Transcendence in French Literature* (Aldershot: Ashgate, 2005) and Mladen Kozul, *Le corps érotique au XVIIIe siècle: Amour, péché, maladie* (Oxford: Voltaire Foundation, 2011). For the Chinese context: Martin W. Huang, *Desire and Fictional Narrative in Late Imperial China* (Harvard, MA: Harvard University Press, 2001) and Kang Zhengguo, *Chongshen fengyuejianjian: Xing yu Zhongguo gudian wenxue* (Reconsidering the Romantic Mirror: Sex and Classical Chinese Literature) (Taipei: Niang chuban, 2016).
31. See Lynn Hunt (ed.), *The Invention of Pornography: Obscenity and the Origins of Modernity, 1500–1800* (New York, NY: Zone, 1993); Hiltrud Gnüg, *Der erotische Roman: Von der Renaissance bis zur Gegenwart* (Stuttgart: Reclam, 2002).
32. François Jullien pointed toward the incompatibility of Chinese and Western notions of the 'erotic'; after all, the latter is informed by the Platonic idea of the self-contained body. See François Jullien, *Le nu impossible* (Paris: Seuil, 2005).
33. See David Damrosch, 'World Literature in a Postcanonical, Hypercanonical Age', in *Comparative Literature in the Age of Globalization*, ed. by Haun Saussy (Baltimore, MD: Johns Hopkins University Press, 2006), pp. 43–53 (p. 45).
34. See Haruo Shirane (ed.), *Envisioning 'The Tale of Genji': Media, Gender, and Cultural Production* (New York, NY: Columbia University Press, 2008).
35. See Peter Lehman and Susan Hunt, *Lady Chatterley's Legacy in the Movies* (New Brunswick, NJ: Rutgers University Press, 2010).
36. See Valerie Hentiuk, *Worlding Sei Sei Shônagon: The Pillow Book in Translation* (Ottawa: University of Ottawa Press, 2012), pp. 18–32.
37. E. L. James, *Fifty Shades of Grey* (London: Arrow, 2012), p. 430.
38. For example, in *Dragonball*, when Bulma lifts her skirt and two blood streams gush out of Master Roshi's nostrils. See *Dragon Ball*: Episode 3, dir. by Minoru Okazaki and Daisuke Nishio (Fuji Television Network, 1986–1989).
39. Ovid, *Ars Amatoria*, ed. by A. S. Hollis (Oxford: Oxford University Press, 1977), p. 22 (v. 569–70).

CHAPTER 1

# Translation, Ethics and Obscenity

*Thomas Wynn*

Translation has long been framed, implicitly or explicitly, as an ethical gesture. It speaks to a set of questions as to which relations, efforts and activities are valued. How does the other concern me? How should I behave to and with the other? What is my responsibility to myself, to the other, to us? How does the other constitute me as an ethical subject? Such questions, which have featured significantly in translation studies in recent years,[1] take on a different hue and a new urgency when obscene texts pass from one canon into another. An opportune moment to reassess the ethics of translation comes with the recent appearance as a Penguin Classic of the Marquis de Sade's notorious *The 120 Days of Sodom* (*Les Cent Vingt Journées de Sodome*, 1785) which I co-translated and co-edited with Will McMorran.[2]

A framework for understanding obscenity (at least in an English context) is provided by the Obscene Publications Act (1959); the test of obscenity is that 'an article shall be deemed to be obscene if its effect or (where the article comprises two or more distinct items) the effect of any one of its items is, if taken as a whole, such as to deprave and corrupt persons who are likely, having regard to all relevant circumstances, to read, see or hear the matter contained or embodied in it' (1.1). *The 120 Days of Sodom* would appear to meet this test of obscenity. The novel ostensibly aims to inflame the reader to the point of ejaculation, and its structure of increasingly depraved sexual violence exemplifies the observation by one of the novel's characters that 'One tires of the simple thing, the imagination is piqued, and the poverty of our means, the weakness of our faculties, the corruption of our minds leads us to abominations' (p. 124). The Act also notes that publication is 'justified as being for the public good' when 'it is in the interests of science, literature, art or learning, or of other objects of general concern' (4.1). An examination of the ethics of translating *The 120 Days of Sodom* needs to attend to the purpose of translating this work, whose effects might seem remote from the interests of 'science, literature, art or learning' as conventionally understood. Rather than evaluate simply whether or not *The 120 Days of Sodom* 'functions efficiently as a work of pornography',[3] it is more opportune to consider how it makes the reader of obscenity aware of his or her ethical constitution.

When Peter France suggests that 'the translator's art is in part *ethical*',[4] he recognizes that translation should be viewed from more than solely a functionalist perspective.

Maria Tymoczko concurs, arguing that translation is now 'seen as an ethical, political, and ideological activity rather than as a mechanical linguistic exercise', and that even 'when the literary art of translation is recognized as fundamental, the ideological implications of literary creativity and innovation are also sounded'.[5] She proposes that 'expansions in the field [of translation] have traced a trajectory away from technical questions about how to translate per se toward larger ethical perspectives on translating as an activity, the role of translation products in cultures, and the nature and function of specific translations'.[6] Tymoczko makes the crucial point that translation functions as 'an invisible means of cultural grounding and cultural appropriation', thereby 'serving to construct identities and affiliations'.[7] This process is not, however, always invisible or indeed unspoken; for instance, Lawrence Venuti emphasizes a resistant or 'foreignizing' approach that foregrounds cultural and linguistic difference,[8] whereas Anthony Pym draws attention to an ethics of cooperation, highlighting the translator's responsibility for fostering mutual benefit and trust.[9] This chapter aims to consider further how translation constructs 'identities and affiliations', and heeds Pym's reminder that 'whatever the translator does [...], it is always grounded in a situation'.[10] The precise means by which — and indeed the end to which — identities and affiliations are constructed must be attended to. Any discussion of translation and ethics must take into account the context in which the translator operates, who he translates for, and what his purpose is. Reflecting on my experience of preparing a new version of Sade's novel, I hope to reassess issues of complicity, subjectivity and responsibility that lie at the heart of the ethics of translation.

Susan Sontag's essay 'The World as India' (2003) provides an entry point into these issues. Sontag premises her argument on what she calls 'the evangelical incentive', in the sense that translation is above all intended to make 'better known what deserves to be better known — because it is improving, deepening, exalting; because it is an indispensable legacy from the past; because it is a contribution to knowledge, sacred or other. In a more secular register, translation was also thought to bring a benefit to the translator: translating was a valuable cognitive — and ethical — workout.'[11] For Sontag, translation is thus an ethical act of benefit to text, translator and even to the lofty concept that is 'literature':

> To translate thoughtfully, painstakingly, ingeniously, respectfully was a precise measure of the translator's fealty to the enterprise of literature itself. Choices that might be thought of as merely linguistic always imply ethical standards as well, which made the activity of translating itself the vehicle of such values as integrity, responsibility, fidelity, boldness, humility.[12]

According to Sontag's positive assessment, translation is a supremely humanist activity that benefits the individual — whether translator and/or reader (Sontag is not precise on this point): 'Literary translation, I think, is preeminently an ethical task, and one that mirrors and duplicates the role of literature itself, which is to extend our sympathies, to educate the heart and mind; to create inwardness; to secure and deepen the awareness (*with all its consequences*) that other people, people different from us, really do exist.'[13] For Sontag, translation is both a process and a product that bring disparate individuals and imaginations into contact with each other, although, as she notes, this encounter is not without consequence or, one might intuit, potential upset. Frank Furedi has recently argued that it is 'not always easy or comfortable to wrestle with the powerful creative will of the author, but this experience is in part what gives reading its compelling power.'[14] This wrestling bout between reader and author is especially intense, and the encounter of which Sontag speaks takes on a particular ethical quality, when one is in the ring with Sade.[15] What kind of 'ethical workout' does *The 120 Days of Sodom* offer? Can a novel depicting coprophagia, rape, paedophilia, torture, dismemberment, murder and cannibalism be described as 'improving, deepening, exalting'? Does translating this novel inspire noble values of 'integrity, responsibility, fidelity, boldness, humility'? And what does the reader gain from 'extend[ing] her sympathies' in this particular situation, and from 'secur[ing] and deepen[ing] the awareness (with all its consequences) that other people, people different from us, really do exist'?

Sade may now be a canonical author,[16] but he remains a divisive figure whose writings still elicit hostility. Michel Onfray, for instance, has condemned Sade and rejected claims that he might be a radical thinker,[17] and Roger Shattuck asks: 'Shall we receive among our literary classics the works of an author who desecrates and inverts every principle of human justice and decency developed over four thousand years of civilised life?'[18] One might answer Shattuck by suggesting that it is precisely Sade's unparalleled dismantling of justice and decency that makes him so compelling. But can one, indeed *should* one entirely disregard the ethical dimension of translating Sade? What is one's ethical position and purpose when translating material such as: 'A man who used to enjoy flogging the bellies of pregnant women improves on this by attaching the pregnant girl to a wheel, beneath which, strapped to an armchair and unable to move, is this girl's mother, her mouth wide open, and forced to catch in her mouth all the filth that drips from the cadaver — and the baby if she gives birth to it' (p. 388)?

In no English-language edition of Sade's work does the translator reflect on his (and it's always *his*) ethical position vis à vis the reader.[19] In fact, in their foreword to a collection of translated works by Sade, Richard Seaver and Austryn Wainhouse are concerned more with their duty towards the author than towards the reader: 'to bare Sade to the public would seem to be rendering him a disservice.'[20] This refusal to engage with ethics makes some sense if one subscribes to Roland Barthes's once innovative argument that the Sadean text is solely semiotic and not mimetic,[21] and thus to believe that, in Geoffrey Bennington words, 'the only "real" cruelty in Sade is that worked in the body of a language'.[22] But in the light of recent research by scholars like Will McMorran who address the ethical issues of reading the Sadean text,[23] it is timely to reassess what might be at stake what when Sadean obscenity is translated.

The possibility that translating Sade might be an ethically fraught exercise has been raised, though it has been left to self-identified opponents of Sade like Andrea Dworkin to point out that reading Sade in translation might not be 'improving, deepening, exalting', to return to Sontag's terms:

> In England in 1966, a twelve-year old boy and a ten-year old girl were tortured and murdered by a self-proclaimed disciple of Sade. The crimes were photographed and tape-recorded by the murderer, who played them back for pleasure. [...] A major translator into English of Sade's work in accessible mass-market editions in the United States is Richard Seaver, a respected figure in establishment publishing.[24]

Seaver is, apparently, guilty by association of the Moors Murders, committed by Ian Brady and Myra Hindley (who disappears from Dworkin's brief account). When Richard Pevear and Larissa Volokhonsky, award-winning translators of Russian classics, were asked what it was like 'living in a world of toxic narrators and tortured murderers for five years', and if they were affected personally by translating Dostoevsky, Volokhonsky professed to be unmoved: 'No. It's a professional thing.' Pevear, however, acknowledged a greater degree of creative complicity with the material:

> I think it affects me, certainly. [...] Translation isn't done by principle or by a machine. The only way you can judge what you're doing is by how it feels to you. Is that the life of it? And for that there has to be a lot of identification — not with the characters but with the art of the book, the art that went into it. You have to have that in order to choose your words. They have to feel right. It's impossible to define. Writers know this *feeling*.[25]

Pevear distinguishes himself from the content of the book (in this case, the characters), but he does identify with the art, by which one might understand the technique by which effects are created. Pym in turn recognizes that the translator might *feel* responsible for effects of the work produced, noting that 'this type of responsibility is poorly defined, awkward, often interpreted as a sort of guilt, no doubt inspired by social relationships overly loaded with moral scruples'.[26] Pym attempts to clarify the nature of this responsibility by proposing that translators are not authors (and thus taking a different position to Pevear), and that they therefore have no specific commitment to the content of the text written prior to their translation.[27] Although not responsible for the text's content, 'translators are not simple messengers. Rather than just deliver a sealed envelope, they work on information and make decisions about its presentation. They have choices, and thus responsibility.'[28] Pym concludes that translators are 'responsible for the probable effects of their translations'.[29]

This refocusing of ethical concerns from content to effect is pertinent to an analysis of *The 120 Days of Sodom*, for this is a work fundamentally concerned with obscenity's effect on the reader. The persuasive power of texts and speech is repeatedly observed in the novel: for example, the Président de Curval is described as 'the author of several works whose effects had been prodigious, and these successes, which he would constantly recall, were still among his dearest pleasures' (p. 20) ['il était auteur de plusieurs ouvrages dont les effets avaient été prodigieux et ces succès qu'il se rappellait sans cesse, étaient encore une de ses plus chères voluptés'];[30] Duclos tells of a churchman whose rhetorical skills are so effective that 'he never missed his mark — in just two hours of conversation he was sure to make a whore out of the most virtuous and most prudent of girls' (p. 112); and one character simply states, 'the story of Lucile has made me hard' (p. 247). Furthermore the novel as a whole is conceived to elicit particular responses from the reader, as the narrator explains:

> No doubt many of the various excesses you shall see depicted shall displease you, we know, but there shall be others that inflame you to the point of spilling your come, and that it is all we require — if we had not said everything, analyzed everything, how do you think we could have guessed what appeals to you? It is for you to take what you want and leave the rest — someone else shall do the same and, little by little, everything shall have found its rightful place. This is the story of a magnificent feast where 600 different dishes are offered for your delectation — do you eat them all? Of course not[.] (p. 59)

> [Sans doute beaucoup des écarts que tu vas voir peints te déplairont, on le sait, mais il s'en trouvera quelqu'uns qui t'enchanteront au point de te coûter du foutre, et voilà tout ce qui nous faut, si nous n'avions pas tout dit, tout analysé, comment voudrais-tu que nous eussions pu deviner ce qui te convient, c'est à toi à les prendre et à laisser le reste, un autre en fera autant, et petit à petit, tout aura trouvé sa place. C'est ici l'histoire d'un magnifique repas où 600 plats divers s'offrent à ton appétit, les manges-tu tous, non sans doute[.]][31]

Following Pym, the translator may not be committed to the novel's obscene contents but he is committed to stimulating certain responses from the reader; and while the narrator indicates that the reader's perhaps involuntary and unanticipated pleasure precludes any criticism of the author for having presented these passions, the translator cannot deny all responsibility for the effects potentially due to the linguistic choices he makes. With such effects in mind, is it possible to recuperate translating 'the most impure tale ever written since the world began' as 'an ethical task', to return to Sontag's term?

An ethical reading of obscenity is predicated on the multi-faceted and shifting nature of that reading. Nancy Huston has written of the two simultaneous and superimposed readings she experiences when faced with those often pornographic texts that tell of an innocent girl's fall into sex work; firstly, the Propp-like intellectual reading that identifies this genre's variable and invariable elements, and secondly the moral and subjective reading in which she identifies with the female character.[32] As with works of other genres, erotic novels provoke multiple readings, for they do not serve one end and one end only, and this is especially the case with eighteenth-century texts that combine sexuality, politics and philosophy.[33] Sontag has argued that the pornographic imagination 'has the power to ingest and metamorphose and translate all concerns that are fed into it, reducing everything into the one negotiable currency of the erotic imperative';[34] and while the narrator of *The 120 Days of Sodom* indeed states that his purpose is to 'inflame you to the point of spilling your come', he does not limit the scope of the book — whose '600 different dishes' elicit a host of other responses such as laughter, curiosity, disgust, horror, boredom, pity and confusion — just because 'many of the various excesses you shall see depicted shall displease you'. *Contra* Sontag's reductive position that presumes a shared economy ('one negotiable currency'), this excessive Sadean text does not truncate its effects to the erotic imperative, and instead it privileges idiosyncratic, often surprising affective responses.

This affective engagement is, as Rita Felski suggests, 'the very means by which literary works are able to reach, reorient, and even reconfigure their readers',[35] for the readers thereby not only create affiliations with others (through identification with characters), but might also accept the difference of others (through understanding that other readers will enjoy pleasures distinct from theirs). When the novel's narrator tells his reader to selectively appropriate the text, he anticipates Felski's argument that 'ethics means accepting the mysteriousness of the other, its resistance to conceptual schemes, it means learning to relinquish our own desire to know.'[36] Sade presents his readers with characters who experience a range of passions; some of these provoke pleasure, others are greeted with incomprehension or displeasure, but they merit no more critique than a shrug. One might therefore heed Felski's recommendation to pursue a 'post-suspicion' critical approach that 'delv[es] into the mysteries of our many-sided attachments to texts' in order that we might better understand the complexity of the aesthetic response that comprises perception, interpretation and affective (dis)orientation.[37] Noting that 'we can be taken hold of, possessed, invaded by a text in a way that we cannot fully control or explain and in a manner that fails to jibe with public postures or ironic dispassion or disciplinary detachment',[38] Felski reminds us of the destabilizing power of the printed word, and it is the text's ability to disrupt the reader's once-assured subjectivity on which the ethical potential of *The 120 Days of Sodom* hinges. George Steiner remarked that 'To read well is to take great risks. It is to make vulnerable our identity, our self-possession',[39] and a post-suspicion approach to Sade's novel attends to the ways in which possibly unexpected and unwanted emotions disrupt the vulnerable self, unsettling the assumptions one might have about one's own ethical position.

Webb Keane has recently posited that 'ethical life does not emerge automatically from the individual', but that it 'requires ongoing social interactions to elicit and reshape that individual as he or she matures'.[40] The ethical self does not result solely from co-operative affiliations in which sympathies are extended and honoured — it is 'inherently subject to the exigencies of interaction as well'.[41] Engaging with Sade's disturbing novel is thus ripe with ethical potential. Moving from social to literary interactions, one might suggest that the consciously vulnerable reader's willing exposure to the exigencies of *The 120 Days of Sodom* is the basis for this new episode in his or her ethical life. Keane asks: 'If people do not have the consistency of character they think they have, and if their acts are not due to the reasons they give for them, but character and action are shaped by processes that lie beyond their awareness, then what role does awareness play in ethical life?'[42] By reading *The 120 Days of Sodom* without suspicion, and by being receptive to the precise effects of the six hundred dishes, one might recognize that one's ethical persona is more pliable than perhaps otherwise hoped, or wished.[43] The translator's ethical task is to bring that recognition into focus.

Gayatri Chakvravorty Spivak considers violence to be central to the translation process (which is both linguistic and spatial) that produces the self: 'the human subject is something that will have happened [with] this shuttling translation from inside to outside, from violence to conscience: the production of the ethical subject'.⁴⁴ The content of *The 120 Days of Sodom* contributes to this shuttling effect. The novel is constructed so that the passions related by the four storytellers increase in violence as the events at Silling progress towards their bloody conclusion. Some passions seem less peculiar than others, for example, the passion 'He marries the girl, deflowers her, but he has tricked her and as soon as the deed is done he ditches her there' ['Il épouse la fille, la dépucelle, mais il l'a trompée, et dès que l'affaire est faite il la plante là'] is relatively mundane and will be familiar to any reader of Molière's *Dom Juan* (1665); it is immediately followed by the more idiosyncratic passion of 'He fucks the maiden only the moment after a man has deflowered her in front of him; he wants her cunt to be all smeared with sperm', p. 318) ['Il ne fout la pucelle qu'à l'instant d'après où un homme vient de la déflorer devant lui, il veut qu'elle ait le con tout barbouillé de sperme'].⁴⁵ While this pairing might represent a move from absorption to distance, this order may be reversed; for instance, the elaborately abject passion of 'He wants twelve whores: six young ones and six old ones, and if possible six mothers and six daughters; he gamahuches their cunts, arses and mouths; from the cunt he wants urine, from the mouth he wants saliva, and from the arse he wants farts' ['Il veut douze filles, six jeunes et six vieilles, et si cela se peut, six mères et six filles ; il leur gamahuche le con, la bouche, et le cul ; quand il en est au con, il veut de l'urine, quand il en est à la bouche il veut de la salive, et quand il en est au cul, il veut des pets'], is followed by the busy though comparatively straightforward passion of 'He employs eight women to frig him, all from different positions' (p. 321) ['Il employe huit femmes à le branler, toutes différemment postées'].⁴⁶ Depending on the reader's tastes, this rapid shifting from passion to passion might provoke the effect of 'shuttling translation' identified by Spivak, and thereby enhance the reader's self-awareness, as he or she becomes sensitive to and cognisant of his or her own constitutive desires.

Another key means by which the reader moves 'from inside to outside' is linked to the way in which he or she is positioned so as to contribute to the text's sexual violence. Due to the novel's structure, whereby obscene details may only be revealed in their rightful place, the narrator is obliged to draw a veil over certain events, which the reader might begin to imagine, such as when the Bishop 'was seen in front of everyone doing things that the order we have set ourselves still prevents us from revealing, but the sensuality of which very soon made the sperm, whose prickling was beginning to discomfort his balls, flow freely' (p. 165) ['on lui vit faire devant tout le monde des choses que l'ordre que nous nous sommes prescrit ne nous permet pas de dévoiler encore, mais dont la volupté fit très rapidement couler le sperme dont le piquotement commençait à gêner ses couilles'].⁴⁷ On occasion the reader is directly addressed, and requested to step in and complete the suggestive text:

> Adélaïde and just two of the old women, Louison and Fanchon, the wickedest of the four and the most feared by the wives, headed to the coffee room, where circumstances require us to draw a curtain across what transpired there; what is certain is that our four heroes came, and Adélaïde was allowed to go off to bed. It is for the reader to imagine the scene as he sees fit and to be so good as to let us usher him, without further delay, to Duclos's narrations. (p. 261)

> [Adélaïde et les deux seules vieilles Louison et Fanchon, les plus méchantes des quatre et les plus craintes des femmes, passèrent au salon de café, où les circonstances nous obligent de tirer le rideau sur ce qui se passa, ce qu'il y a de certain, c'est que nos quatre héros déchargèrent, et qu'on permit à Adélaïde de s'aller coucher. — C'est au lecteur à faire sa combinaison et à trouver agréable, s'il lui plaît que nous le transportions tout de suite aux narrations de Duclos.][48]

The narrator regularly feigns ignorance of the events that take place at Silling, so that the reader is again left to imagine what violence the victims suffer: '[Curval] rushed into his closet, dragging Aline along by her breast, with Sophie and Zelmire, the two girls from his harem, and Fanchon obliged to follow; we are not too sure what he did in there, but we heard a woman's piercing scream and, shortly after, the roars of his climax. He returned; Aline was crying as she held a handkerchief to her breast' (p. 214) ['il se jeta dans son cabinet en entraînant par le sein Aline, et se faisant suivre de Sophie et de Zelmire, les deux filles de son sérail, et de Fanchon. On ne sait trop ce qu'il y fit, mais on entendit un grand cri de femme, et peu après les hurlements de sa décharge, il rentra, Aline pleurait et tenait un mouchoir sur son sein'].[49] In a sense, the reader enters that closet with Curval and the women, and even lays the blow upon Aline. Again, the reader may be explicitly invited to imagine (to fantasize?) about the provocatively occluded violence (p. 206):

> Their minds inflamed by this theory, they drank a great deal and went to celebrate the orgies, concerning which our fickle libertines decided to send the children to bed and spend part of the night drinking with just the 4 old women and the 4 storytellers — and to outdo each other in venting obscenities and abominations. As there was not one among these 12 interesting characters who would not have merited the noose or the wheel several times over, I leave it to the reader to reflect and imagine what was said there. Words gave way to deeds, the Duc became inflamed, and I do not know how or why, but it was claimed that Thérèse bore the scars for some time.
>
> [Ce système ayant échauffé les têtes, on but beaucoup et fut célébrer les orgies, pour lesquels nos inconstants libertins imaginèrent de faire coucher les enfants et de passer une partie de la nuit à boire, rien qu'avec les 4 vieilles et les 4 historiennes, et de s'exhaler là à qui mieux mieux, en infamies et atrocités comme parmi ces 12 intéressantes personnes, il n'y en avait une, qui n'eût mérité la corde et la roue plusieurs fois, et je laisse au lecteur à penser et à imaginer ce qu'il y fut dit de propos ; on passe aux actions, le duc s'échauffe, et je ne sais ni pourquoi ni comment, on prétendit que Thérèse porta quelque temps les marques qu'on y mit ce soir.][50]

The reader's intended role as active participant in the creation of *The 120 Days of Sodom* could not be clearer; he or she is invited not just to imagine the violent acts, but to write the dialogue that constitutes the otherwise silenced text. The reader is not, of course, compelled to take up that intended role as active participant, nor is he or she required to identify with and then supplant the narrator; such refusal itself should also be viewed in ethical terms, for as Webb Keane observes, 'ethical development typically also entails learning discrimination, knowing what kinds of persons one does *not* want to identify with, even those to whom moral norms do not apply'.[51]

For all that the reader may at times be enjoined to enter inside the violent text, he or she is also cast outside it, a place (according to Spivak's framework) of conscience, and therefore of reflection on one's engagement with the text. Sade's original text drives 'this shuttling translation' in part by linguistic means; the strategy in translating *The 120 Days of Sodom* was to ensure that the same is true in the English version. When the narrator states that 'the time has come, friendly reader, for you to prepare your heart and mind for the most impure tale ever written since the world began, for no such book may be found among either the ancients or the moderns' ['c'est maintenant, ami lecteur, qu'il faut disposer ton cœur et ton esprit au récit le plus impur qui ait jamais été fait depuis que le monde existe, le pareil livre ne se rencontrant, ni chez les anciens, ni chez les modernes'],[52] he bases the novel's claim for exceptional status on its extreme obscenity. The narrator acknowledges literary tradition ('the ancients or the moderns') only to position the novel beyond that history, a dual temporality that is essential to any text's claim to classic status: 'On the one hand, the classic is an everlasting possession, an appeal to immortality secured by an assumed permanence of its literary qualities. On the other hand, the idea of timelessness has itself to be established by setting a frontier *within* history, a temporal limit which demonstrates a work's capacity for survival.'[53] For all that the novel transcends time, it must also speak to the reader who is located in a particular historical moment — 'the time has come, friendly reader, for you to prepare your heart and mind' — and thus a translation of Sade's novel must 'negotiate the contradiction between the two mutually oppositional sides of the classic, the timeless and the contingent'.[54]

In translating *The 120 Days of Sodom*, Will and I have not attenuated the brutality of its content; we are not border guards to a realm of literature comprising solely what Wayne Booth calls 'the good stuff',[55] nor are we shock absorbers in the way that some nineteenth- and early-twentieth century translators (or rather bowdlerisers) of classical erotica were.[56] The challenges faced by the reader of *The 120 Days of Sodom* are related primarily to violence, sexuality and morality (see Katie Jones's contribution to the present volume, Chapter 10, for a contemporary take on this dilemma). Linguistic obstacles should not be introduced in the translation when there are none in the original, for this novel is meant, after all, to be an easy read: 'following the exact description we have given him in all matters, [the reader] will now have only to follow the story, effortlessly and sensually, with nothing to confuse his understanding or trouble his memory' (p. 48) ['après l'exacte description que nous lui avons faite du tout, [notre lecteur] n'aura plus maintenant que suivre légèrement et voluptueusement sans que rien trouble son intelligence ou vienne embarrasser son mémoire'].[57]

Operating within this dual and simultaneous time scheme, whereby the atemporal and the present coincide, necessitates the description of often extreme obscenity in as timeless a language as possible, one that avoids the dual pitfalls of quaintness and the jarringly contemporary. Other translators of Sade have willingly opted for the quaint: for example, David Carter prefaces his translation of the short story *Ernestine* with the statement, 'I have endeavoured to lend a "period" feel to the English, rather than risk it sounding too modern.'[58] The risk of attempting to create a period feel is, however, that one might introduce a kind of 'faux olde worlde, eighteenth century-ese', which might act as a barrier between the reader and the text, distracting her, perhaps making her laugh when no humour is intended and thereby disturbing the particular kind of shuttling that characterises Sade's text. Wainhouse and Seaver are given to quaintness in their version of *The 120 Days of Sodom*, first published in 1966 and for fifty years the only complete English translation of the novel. For example, they translate 'Ce soir-là le duc dépucelle Sophie en con, et blasphème beaucoup'[59] as 'That evening, the Duc depucelates Sophie cuntwardly, and while doing so blasphemes considerably';[60] our version is 'That evening the Duc deflowers Sophie's cunt and blasphemes a great deal' (p. 323). Sometimes quaintness becomes coyness; Sade's text 'Il dépucelle avec un godemiché, et décharge sur l'ouverture qu'il vient de faire, sans s'introduire',[61] is given by Wainhouse and Seaver as 'This one depucelates with an artificial engine, very large, and, without introducing himself, discharges upon the hole he has cleared';[62] our version is: 'He deflowers with a dildo, and comes over the opening he has made without introducing his prick' (p. 318).

On occasion, quaintness borders on incomprehensibility. The original reads:

> On fouette Rosette ce soir-là, et Curval la dépucelle en con. On découvre ce jour-là l'intrigue d'Hercule et de Julie: elle s'était fait foutre. Quand on l'en gronde, elle répond libertinement; on la fouette extraordinairement; puis, comme elle est aimée, ainsi qu'Hercule qui s'est toujours bien conduit, on leur pardonne et on s'en amuse[.][63]

This passage is translated by Wainhouse and Seaver as:

> Rosette is flogged that evening, and Curval has her forward maidenhead. The intrigue between Hercule and Julie is brought to light; she has been having herself fucked. When scolded for her misbehavior, she replies libertinely; she is therewith whipped extraordinarily. Then, because Messieurs are fond of her, and also of Hercule, who has given yeoman service so far, they are pardoned and frolicked with.[64]

We have aimed for greater clarity:

> They flog Rosette that evening, and Curval deflowers her cunt. They discover that day the affair between Hercule and Julie — she had got herself fucked; when they scold her for it she replies like a libertine. They flog her stupendously; then, as she is well-liked — as indeed is Hercule, who has always conducted himself well — they pardon them and laugh the whole thing off. (p. 334)

Sade does on occasion use somewhat peculiar terms, and suitable English equivalents must be found or coined: thus we give 'la meilleure branleuse' as 'the finest masturbatrix' (p. 85), 'sa masculine fouetteuse' as 'his male flagellatrix' (p. 226), and '36 péteurs ou péteuses' as '36 farteurs or farteuses' (p. 273). Such terms are self-explanatory, but when Sade uses the term 'saphotiser', which we give as 'to sapphotize' (p. 320), a note explains that this is a variation or echo of the (albeit rarely used) term 'socratiser', which means to stimulate a man by inserting one's fingers into his anus (p. 409). Otherwise we have attempted in our translation to find appropriate terms that will not draw undue attention to themselves and thereby diminish the intended erotic effect for the contemporary reader. While words like 'cul' (*arse*), 'con' (*cunt*), 'vit' (*prick*) proved unproblematic, others were trickier: 'branler' occurs dozens of times in the novel, and although *wank* was our first choice, this word sounds British, and since it is used for penile, vaginal and anal acts, we have used *frig* instead. Other terms we debated were 'décharge' or 'décharger' and 'foutre': for example, Sade's text reads 'On eut beau faire, beau perdre du foutre, beau n'écrire son nom sur les billets qu'à l'instant même de la décharge',[65] which Wainhouse and Seaver give as ''Twas all in vain, in vain they spattered their fuck about, in vain they wrote their names upon the ballots at the same moment they discharged [...]'.[66] We consider that 'foutre' and 'décharger' are both better translated as *come* (not *cum*, as the register is a touch too vulgar) rather than *fuck* or *discharge*, and what one loses through repetition, one gains in transparency: 'whatever they tried, whether it was spilling their come, or waiting until very moment they came before writing the names on the ballots' (p. 37). In such instances, the reader must not be distracted by peculiar terms when the focus ought to be on the sex act, even if that scenario may be distasteful or abhorrent.

    Crucial to the reader's displacement is the fact that *The 120 Days of Sodom* is an unfinished draft. Sade may have been planning his novel as early as March 1783, but he wrote up the manuscript at great speed, working in bursts from seven to ten o'clock in the evening in his cell at the Bastille. Although Sade states at the end of the manuscript that the scroll was 'finished in 37 days' (p. 397) ['finie en 37 jours'],[67] it is clear from the abbreviated form of the novel's second, third and fourth parts, and also from the notes on the script itself that this is an incomplete draft that he intended to write up in the future: 'one of my first concerns should be to have a notebook nearby at all times [...]' (p. 316) ['un de mes premiers soins soit d'avoir toujours auprès de moi un cahier de notes'].[68] Sade recognizes that his French in this draft is not as polished as it might be, at one point instructing himself in a marginal note to 'Say this better' (p. 125), and there are indeed some linguistic slips. For example, when the Duc warns the female victims that 'the slightest offences shall immediately be met with corporal or physical punishment' (p. 56) ['les moindres fautes seront à l'instant punies de peines corporelles et afflictives'],[69] one of those adjectives is redundant. But examples of what might be considered stylistic clumsiness should not be amended, for they remind the reader that *The 120 Days of Sodom* is an unfinished work, and might thereby encourage the reader to move outside the text to a place of conscience. While some parts of the novel are polished, others are not, and these rough or rudimentary elements may draw the reader's attention away from *what* is written, to *how* it was written.[70]

    In addition to infelicities, the novel includes a number of mistakes, as Sade himself was aware: 'And as I've been unable to reread myself, this must surely be teeming with other mistakes' (p. 316) ['Et n'ayant pas pu me relire, cela doit sûrement fourmiller d'autres fautes'].[71] Like Homer, Sade nods. Mistakes include contradictory information about the site of Silling itself: initially the castle is in Switzerland (p. 32), but the location shifts, probably because Sade was writing up from a different notebook: 'To reach there one first had to get to Basel; one then crossed the Rhine, beyond which the road narrowed to such a point one had to leave the carriages behind; a little later one entered the Black Forest' (p. 43) ['Il fallait pour y parvenir arriver d'abord à Basle, on y passait certain [lieu], au de là duquel, la route se rétrécissait au point qu'il fallait quitter les voitures peu après. On entrait dans la forêt noire'].[72] Giton's age is inconsistent; at first he is thirteen years old (p. 39), but some pages later he has dropped to being twelve (p. 65). Sade is occasionally confused about who his four libertines are: for instance, when he writes 'The Président — with his troop — went and shut himself away and after half an hour, which the Bishop, Durcet and Curval, along with the remaining subjects, did not spend in prayer' (pp. 223–24) ['Le président avec sa troupe fut donc s'enfermer, et au bout d'une demi heure que l'évêque, Durcet et Curval, avec ce qui leur restait de sujets, ne passèrent pas à prier Dieu'],[73] he probably means the Duc rather than Curval, given that the Président and Curval are one and the same person. Similarly, when he writes

> They went through for coffee, served by four young subjects of the same age: Zelmire, Augustine, Zéphire and Adonis — all four of them 15 years old; the Duc thigh-fucked Augustine while tickling her anus, Curval did the same to Zelmire, the Duc to Zéphire, and the financier fucked Adonis in the mouth (p. 252)
>
> [On passa au café, servi par quatre jeunes sujets du même âge, Zelmire, Augustine, Zéphire et Adonis, tous quatre de 15 ans, le duc foutit Augustine en cuisses en lui chatouillant l'anus, Curval en fit autant à Zelmire, le due à Zéphire et le financier foutit Adonis en bouche][74]

he likely means that the Bishop enjoyed Zéphire. While one does not expect realism from *The 120 Days of Sodom*, it is notable nonetheless that even though Narcisse's testicles are cut off on 21 January (p. 380), one reads that two days later they are crushed once again. We do not correct these and other mistakes — indeed we point them out in the editorial notes to enhance the distancing effect.

Almost all editions, in every language, have modernized, corrected and therefore polished Sade's text, whereas our translation is based on Maurice Heine's edition (1931–35), which follows Sade's original manuscript and features several idiosyncrasies.[75] For instance, Sade refers to the tenth month as '$8^{ber}$', to the eleventh month as both 'novembre' and '$9^{ber}$', and to the twelfth month as both 'décembre' and '$X^{ber}$'. Such details might at first sight seem inconsequential, of little more than a curiosity to the reader: 'each shall take his turn in the following order, namely Durcet during $9^{ber}$, the Bishop during $X^{ber}$, the Président during January, and the Duc during February' (p. 49) ['chacun y passe à son tour, dans l'ordre suivant: Durcet pendant novembre, l'évêque pendant décembre, le président pendant janvier, et le duc pendant février'].[76] But in a case such as 'Duclos's one of $26^{th}$ $9^{ber}$, and Martaine's of the tenth of January, a bugger, pretends to succour the poor; he gives them provisions, but these are poisoned' (p. 366) ['Celui du 26 novembre de Duclos et du dix janvier de Marraine, lequel est bougre, fait semblant de soulager les pauvres, il leur donne des vivres, mais ils sont empoisonnés'],[77] the reader may be distracted from mass murder by typography, and one might reflect on whether doing so has ethical implications. Sade also gives numbers in words and numerals, and there appears to be no logic to Sade's choice:

> From two to three o'clock, the first two tables shall be served and shall have lunch at the same time, one in the girls' spacious quarters, the other in the little boys' quarters; the 3 kitchen maids shall serve these two tables, the first of which shall include the 8 little girls and the four old women, the second the four wives, the 8 little boys and the 4 storytellers. (p. 50)

> [de deux à trois on servira les deux premières tables qui dîneront à la même heure, l'un dans le grand appartement des filles, l'autre dans celui des petits garçons ; ce seront les 3 servantes de la cuisine qui serviront les deux tables, la première sera composée des 8 petites filles et des quatre vieilles, la seconde des quatre épouses, des 8 petits garçons et des 4 historiennes.][78]

After a momentary distraction, one might move on to considering whether these numbers have a structural or esoteric significance,[79] but a different effect may also be felt. Consider this scene, which is likely meant to be erotic:

> Hyacinthe, perhaps assisted by Nature but far more likely by the examples before him, did not touch, fondle or kiss anything other than the pretty little buttocks of his masturbatrix, and a moment later his beautiful cheeks blushed, he heaved 2 or 3 sighs and his pretty little prick sent five or six spurts of come — sweet and white as cream — 3 feet from him to land on Durcet's thigh (for he was closest to him and was having himself frigged by Narcisse as he watched the operation). (p. 269)

> [Hyacinthe aidé peut-être de la nature, mais plus certainement encore par des exemples, qu'il avait sous ses yeux, ne touche, ne manie, ne baise que les jolies petites fesses de sa branleuse, et au bout d'un instant, ses belles joues se colorèrent, il poussa 2 ou 3 soupirs, et son joli petit vit lança à 3 pieds de lui cinq ou six jets d'un petit foutre doux et blanc comme de la crème, qui vint tomber sur les cuisses de Durcet, placé le plus près de lui, et qui se faisait branler par Narcisse, en regardant l'opération.][80]

The reader might be absorbed in this description of the sex act, but the slight disturbance in the prose — triggered not only by the word 'masturbatrix' but also by the inconsistent presentation of numbers — might suffice to attenuate the intended erotic effect, and the reader may consider what the conditions and extent of his or her erotic engagement might be.

The clearest means by which the reader is displaced from the obscene activities depicted is the notes that Sade writes to himself throughout the novel. At the end of the introduction, for instance, Sade issues several instructions to himself:

> 1st must say that Hercule and Bande-au-ciel are very knavish and very ugly respectively, and that none of the 8 has ever been able to have his way with either a man or a woman.
> 2nd that the chapel serves as a latrine, and describe how it is put to this use.
> 3rd that the bawds and pimps during their expeditions were accompanied by cut-throats under their orders.
> 4th describe the servants' busts briefly and speak of Fanchon's cancer. Give a little more detail about the faces of the 16 children as well. (p. 66)

> [1. Il faut dire que Hercule et Bande-au-ciel sont l'un très mauvais sujet et l'autre fort laid, et qu'aucun des 8 n'a jamais pu jouir ni d'homme ni de femme.
>
> 2. Que la chapelle sert de garderobe et les détails d'après cet usage.
>
> 3. Que les maquerelles et les maquereaux dans leur expédition avaient avec eux des coupes-jarrets à leurs ordres.
>
> 4. Détaillez un peu les gorges des servantes, et parlez du cancer de Fanchon. Peignez aussi un peu davantage les figures des 16 enfants.][81]

These extra-diegetic notes in Sade's voice disrupt the reader's engagement, remind one that this is a work in progress, and send one shuttling from Silling (the created place) to the Bastille (the place of composition). A similar though arguably more acute effect occurs when Sade loses track of his characters: 'The same one of whom Duclos spoke on 27$^{th}$ 9$^{ber}$ and Martaine on the fourteenth of January (*check*) [...]' (p. 365) ['Le même dont a parlé Duclos le 27 9$^{bre}$ et Martaine le quatorze janvier (vérifiez)'];[82] and '[a] man of whom Martaine spoke, and who used to enjoy watching a girl fall from the top of a ladder, improves on this passion (*but check which man*)' (p. 368) ['Un homme dont Martaine a parlé et qui s'amusait à voir tomber la fille de dessus l'échelle, perfectionne ainsi sa passion (mais vérifiez lequel)'].[83] In such instances the reader might initially delve back into the events at Silling in order to trace the identity of these men, but the authorial interventions soon serve as a twitch upon the thread, pulling him or her from absorption within the diegesis to an external consciousness of the text's artifice and creation. Sometimes a number of these disruptive elements may be combined:

> The three friends — d'Aucourt, the Abbé and Després — of whom Duclos spoke on the twelfth of 9$^{ber}$ still gather together to enjoy this particular passion: they find a woman who is eight or nine months pregnant, open up her belly, tear out the baby, burn it before the mother's eyes, put in its place a pile of sulphur combined with mercury and quicksilver, which they ignite, then they sew up the belly and leave her to die in front of them in unimaginable pain as they are frigged by that girl they have with them (*check her name*). (pp. 367–68)
>
> [Les trois amis : d'Ancourt, l'abbé et Després, dont Duclos a parlé le douze 9$^{bre}$ s'amusent encore ensemble pour cette passion-ci ; ils veulent une femme grosse de huit à neuf mois, ils lui ouvrent le ventre, en arrachent l'enfant, le brûlent aux yeux de la mère, lui remettent en place dans l'estomac un paquet de souffre combiné avec le mercure et le vif argent qu'ils allument, puis ils recousent le ventre et la laissent ainsi mourir devant eux, dans des douleurs inouïes, en se faisant branler par cette fille, qu'ils ont avec eux (vérifiez le nom).][84]

The numbers are given in words yet the month appears as a numeral; there is a mistake (mercury and quicksilver are the same thing); and there is an authorial intervention. To what extent does the roughness of the text cause the reader to re-view what is presented? Is the reader's horror at this double murder attenuated by his or her consciousness of the text's unfinished nature?

In conclusion, *The 120 Days of Sodom* offers an exemplary case of the ethical problems at stake in translation. Sade, like Felski, asks for open-minded readers who will let themselves be absorbed within an obscene text, be touched in plural and unexpected ways, and forge affiliations (however fleeting) with a narrator and characters whose practices and tastes might ordinarily repulse them. Though not answerable for that obscene material, the translator is responsible for shaping the text that aims to provoke certain effects. In the light of Spivak's observation that 'violent translation [...] constitutes the subject',[85] our new translation of *The 120 Days of Sodom* asks today's readers to reflect more readily upon the constitution of their ethical identity: what draws us in, and how can we acknowledge that process? What is the extent of one's excitement, pity or disgust? At what point does one refuse complicity? If the 'unsuspicious' reader is absorbed by an obscene episode of sexual degradation or violent cruelty, only to be shuttled into conscience by particular narrative techniques or textual details, then he or she is better placed to reflect on how ethical life relies not 'only on the psychological predisposition of individuals',[86] but on desires and interactions one might otherwise ignore or disavow. Sade is a moralist, a 'strange evangelist' (p. 114) ['prédicateur étrange'][87] as one of his characters is described, and the broader relevance of the new translation *The 120 Days of Sodom* is in demonstrating that the complex ethical self is forged, not diminished, through violence. But it is for the reader, not the translator or critic, to determine the novel's precise effect, and so in the words of the novel's narrator, 'I leave it to the reader to ponder how refined the moral lesson may have been' (p. 84) ['je laisse au lecteur à penser si la morale en fut très épurée'].[88]

## Bibliography

### I. Editions and translations

CARTER, DAVID (trans.), *Virtue* (London: Hesperus Classics, 2011).
COWARD, DAVID (trans.), *The Crimes of Love* (Oxford: Oxford University Press, 2005).
FRANCESCHINA, JOHN (trans.), *Rape, Incest, Murder! The Marquis de Sade on Stage*, 3 vols (Albany, GA: BearManor Media, 2013).
MCMORRAN, WILL and THOMAS WYNN (trans.), *The 120 Days of Sodom or the School of Libertinage* (London: Penguin, 2016).
NEUGROSCHEL, JOACHIM (trans.), *Philosophy in the Boudoir, or The Immoral Mentors* (New York, NY: Penguin, 2006).
PHILLIPS, JOHN (trans.), *Justine, or the Misfortunes of Virtue* (Oxford: Oxford University Press, 2012).
SADE, DONATIEN ALPHONSE FRANÇOIS DE, *Œuvres*, ed. by Michel Delon, 3 vols (Paris: Gallimard, 1990).
SEAVER, RICHARD and AUSTRYN WAINHOUSE (eds.), *Justine, Philosophy in the Bedroom, and Other Writings* (New York, NY: Grove Press, 1965).
WAINHOUSE, AUSTRYN and RICHARD SEAVER (trans.), *The 120 Days of Sodom* (London: Arrow Books, 1990).

### II. Critical literature

APTER, EMILY, *Against World Literature: On the Politics of Untranslatability* (London: Verso, 2013).
BARTHES, ROLAND, *Sade, Fourier, Loyola* (Paris: Seuil, 1971).
BENNINGTON, GEOFFREY, 'Sade: Laying Down the Law', *Oxford Literary Review*, 6 (1984), 38–56.

BERMANN, SANDRA and MICHAEL WOOD (eds.), *Nation, Language, and the Ethics of Translation* (Princeton, NJ: Princeton University Press, 2005).
BOOTH, WAYNE C., *The Company We Keep: An Ethics of Fiction* (Berkeley, CA: University of California Press, 1988).
COHEN, JOSHUA, 'Peter Cole, The Art of Translation No. 5', *The Paris Review* 213 (2015) <http://www.theparisreview.org/interviews/6386/the-art-of-translation-no-5-peter-cole> [accessed 1 June 2016].
CRYLE, PETER, 'Taking Sade serially: *Les Cent Vingt Journées de Sodome*', in *Geometry in the Boudoir: Configurations of French Erotic Narrative* (Ithaca, NY: Cornell University Press, 1994), pp. 120–46.
DARNTON, ROBERT, *The Forbidden Best-Sellers of Pre-Revolutionary France* (New York, NY: W.W. Norton, 1995).
DELON, MICHEL, 'Sade dans la Bibliothèque de la Pléiade', in *La Fin de l'ancien régime: Sade, Rétif, Beaumarchais, Laclos*, ed. by Béatrice Didier and Jacques Neefs (Saint Denis: Presses Universitaires de Vincennes, 1991), pp. 95–102.
DWORKIN, ANDREA, *Pornography: Men Possessing Women* (London: Women's Press, 1981).
FELSKI, RITA, 'After Suspicion', *Profession* 8 (2009), 28–35.
FISCHLER, CLAUDE, 'Food, Self and Identity', *Social Science Information* 27 (1988), 275–93.
FOUGERET DE MONBRON, LOUIS-CHARLES, *Margot la ravaudeuse*, ed. and trans. by Édouard Langille (Cambridge: MHRA, 2015).
FRANCE, PETER, 'Translation: The *Serva Padrona*', *Art in Translation*, 2.2 (2010), 119–30.
FUREDI, FRANK, *Power of Reading from Socrates to Twitter* (London: Bloomsbury, 2015).
GOULEMOT, JEAN-MARIE, 'Toward a Definition of Libertine Fiction and Pornographic Novels', *Yale French Studies* 94 (1998), 133–45.
HANSFORD JOHNSON, PAMELA, *On Iniquity: Some Personal Reflections Arising out of the Moors Murder Trial* (London: Macmillan, 1967).
HULBERT, JAMES, 'The Problem of Canon Formation and the "Example" of Sade: Orthodox Exclusion and Orthodox Inclusion', *Modern Languages Studies*, 18 (1988), 120–33.
HUNNEWELL, SUSANNAH, 'Richard Pevear and Larissa Volokhonsky: The Art of Translation No. 4', *The Paris Review* 213 (2015) <http://www.theparisreview.org/interviews/6385/the-art-of-translation-no-4-richard-pevear-and-larissa-volokhonsky> [accessed 1 June 2016].
HUNT, LYNN (ed.), *The Invention of Pornography: Obscenity and the Origins of Modernity, 1500–1800* (New York, NY: Zone, 1993).
HUSTON, NANCY, *Mosaïque de la pornographie* (Paris: Éditions Payot & Rivages, 2007).
KEANE, WEBB, *Ethical Life: Its Natural and Social Histories* (Princeton, NJ: Princeton University Press, 2016).
KOZUL, MLADEN, 'L'inachèvement des *Cent Vingt Journées de Sodome* de Sade', *Cahiers d'histoire des Littératures Romanes / Romanistische Zeischrift für Literaturgeschichte*, 1–2 (1995), 60–71.
LIANERI, ALEXANDRA and VANDA ZAJKO, 'Still Being Read After So Many Years: Rethinking the Classic Through Translation', in *Translation and the Classic: Identity as Change in the History of Culture*, ed. by Alexandra Lianeri and Vanda Zajko (Oxford: Oxford University Press, 2008), pp. 1–23.
MARTY, ÉRIC, *Pourquoi le XXe siècle a-t-il pris Sade au sérieux?* (Paris: Seuil, 2011).
MCMORRAN, WILL, 'Introducing the Marquis de Sade', *Forum for Modern Language Studies*, 52 (2015), 133–51.
—— 'The Sound of Violence: Listening to Rape in Sade', in *Representing Violence in France, 1760–1820*, ed. by Thomas Wynn, *Studies on Voltaire and the Eighteenth Century* 2013:10 (Oxford: Voltaire Foundation, 2013), pp. 229–49.

Moraes, Eliane Robert, 'The Reader in the *Boudoir*', in *Sade's Sensibilities*, ed. by Kate Parker and Norbert Sclippa (Lewisburg, PA: Bucknell University Press, 2015), pp. 41–63.
O'Brien, John, 'Are we reading what Montaigne wrote?', *French Studies* 58 (2004), 527–32.
Onfray, Michel, *La Passion de la méchanceté: sur un prétendu divin marquis* (Paris: Editions Autrement, 2014).
Phillips, John, *Sade: The Libertine Novels* (London: Pluto Press, 2001).
Pym, Anthony, *On Translator Ethics: Principles for Mediation Between Cultures*, trans. by Heike Walker (Amsterdam: Benjamins, 2012).
Roberts, Deborah H., 'Translation and the "Surreptitious Classic": Obscenity and Translatability', in *Translation and the Classic*, pp. 278–311.
Shattuck, Roger, *Forbidden Knowledge: From Prometheus to Pornography* (San Diego, CA: Harcourt Brace, 1997).
Sontag, Susan, 'The Pornographic Imagination', in *Styles of Radical Will* (London: Secker & Warburg, 1969), pp. 35–73.
—— 'The World as India', in *At The Same Time* (London: Penguin, 2008), pp. 156–79.
Spivak, Gayatri Chakvravorty, 'Translation as Culture', *Parallax* 6.1 (2000), 13–24.
Steiner, George, *Language & Silence: Essays on Language, Literature, and the Inhuman* (London: Faber and Faber, 1967).
Tymoczko, Maria, 'Translation: Ethics, Ideology, Action', *The Massachusetts Review*, 47 (2006), 442–61.
United Kingdom, Act of Parliament, 'Obscene Publications Act 1959' (1959 CHAPTER 66 7 and 8 Eliz 2), http://www.legislation.gov.uk/ukpga/Eliz2/7-8/66/section/1 [accessed 8.10.2016].
Venuti, Lawrence, *The Scandals of Translation: Towards an Ethics of Difference* (London: Routledge, 1998).
Wyngaard, Amy S., 'Translating Sade: The Grove Press Editions, 1953–1968', *Romanic Review*, 104 (2013), 313–31.
Wynn, Thomas, 'Violence, Vulnerability and Subjectivity in Sade', in *Representing Violence in France*, pp. 139–60.

## Notes to Chapter 1

1. *Nation, Language, and the Ethics of Translation*, ed. by Sandra Bermann and Michael Wood (Princeton, NJ: Princeton University Press, 2005); Anthony Pym, *On Translator Ethics: Principles for Mediation between Cultures*, trans. by Heike Walker (Amsterdam: Benjamins, 2012); Emily Apter, *Against World Literature: On the Politics of Untranslatability* (London: Verso, 2013).
2. Donatien Alphonse François de Sade, *The 120 Days of Sodom or the School of Libertinage*, trans. by Will McMorran and Thomas Wynn (London: Penguin, 2016). Unless noted otherwise, all references to the novel will be to this edition.
3. John Phillips, *Sade: the Libertine Novels* (London: Pluto Press, 2001), p. 56.
4. Peter France, 'Translation: The *Serva Padrona*', *Art in Translation*, 2.2 (2010), 119–30 (p. 120). Emphasis in original.
5. Maria Tymoczko, 'Translation: Ethics, Ideology, Action', *The Massachusetts Review*, 47 (2006), 442–61 (p. 443).
6. Tymoczko, 'Translation: Ethics, Ideology, Action', p. 444.
7. Tymoczko, 'Translation: Ethics, Ideology, Action', p. 446.
8. Lawrence Venuti, *The Scandals of Translation: Towards an Ethics of Difference* (London: Routledge, 1998).
9. Pym, *On Translator Ethics*, p. 60.
10. Pym, *On Translator Ethics*, p. 4.
11. Susan Sontag, 'The World as India', in *At The Same Time* (London: Penguin, 2008), pp. 156–79 (p. 157).

12. Sontag, 'The World as India', p. 158.
13. Sontag, 'The World as India', p. 177. Emphasis mine.
14. Frank Furedi, *Power of Reading from Socrates to Twitter* (London: Bloomsbury, 2015), p. 209.
15. On the positioning of Sade's reader, see Eliane Robert Moraes, 'The Reader in the *Boudoir*', in *Sade's Sensibilities*, ed. by Kate Parker and Norbert Sclippa (Lewisburg, PA: Bucknell University Press, 2015), pp. 41–63.
16. James Hulbert, 'The Problem of Canon Formation and the Example of Sade: Orthodox Exclusion and Orthodox Inclusion', *Modern Languages Studies*, 18 (1988), 120–33; Michel Delon, 'Sade dans la Bibliothèque de la Pléiade', in *La Fin de l'ancien régime: Sade, Rétif, Beaumarchais, Laclos*, ed. by Béatrice Didier and Jacques Neefs (Saint Denis: Presses Universitaires de Vincennes, 1991), pp. 95–102; Éric Marty, *Pourquoi le XXe siècle a-t-il pris Sade au sérieux?* (Paris: Seuil, 2011); Will McMorran, 'Introducing the Marquis de Sade', *Forum for Modern Language Studies*, 52 (2015), 133–51.
17. Michel Onfray, *La Passion de la méchanceté: sur un prétendu divin marquis* (Paris: Editions Autrement, 2014).
18. Roger Shattuck, *Forbidden Knowledge: From Prometheus to Pornography* (San Diego; CA: Harcourt Brace, 1997), p. 269.
19. Recent English translations of Sade include: *The Crimes of Love*, trans. by David Coward (Oxford: Oxford University Press, 2005); *Philosophy in the Boudoir, or The Immoral Mentors*, trans. by Joachim Neugroschel (New York: Penguin, 2006); *Justine, or the Misfortunes of Virtue*, trans. by John Phillips (Oxford: Oxford University Press, 2012); and *Rape, Incest, Murder! The Marquis de Sade on Stage*, trans. by John Franceschina, 3 vols (Albany, GA: BearManor Media, 2013).
20. Richard Seaver and Austryn Wainhouse, *Justine, Philosophy in the Bedroom, and Other Writings* (New York, NY: Grove Press, 1965), p. xii. See also Amy S. Wyngaard, 'Translating Sade: the Grove Press Editions, 1953–1968', *Romanic Review*, 104 (2013), 313–31. On the early English translation of Sade, see Will Mc Morran, 'The Marquis de Sade in English, 1800–1850', *The Modern Language Review*, 112 (2017), 549–66.
21. Roland Barthes, *Sade, Fourier, Loyola* (Paris: Seuil, 1971).
22. Geoffrey Bennington, 'Sade: Laying Down the Law', *Oxford Literary Review*, 6 (1984), 54.
23. Will McMorran, 'The Sound of Violence: Listening to Rape in Sade', in *Representing Violence in France, 1760–1820*, ed. by Thomas Wynn, Studies on Voltaire and the Eighteenth Century 2013:10 (Oxford: Voltaire Foundation, 2013), pp. 229–49.
24. Andrea Dworkin, *Pornography: Men Possessing Women* (London: Women's Press, 1981), p. 71. See also Pamela Hansford Johnson, *On Iniquity: Some Personal Reflections Arising out of the Moors Murder Trial* (London: Macmillan, 1967).
25. Richard Pevear and Larissa Volokhonsky, 'The Art of Translation No. 4. Interview with Susannah Hunnewell', *The Paris Review*, 213 (2015) < http://www.theparisreview.org/interviews/6385/the-art-of-translation-no-4-richard-pevear-and-larissa-volokhonsky> [accessed 1 June 2016]. Emphasis mine.
26. Pym, *On Translator Ethics*, p. 68.
27. Pym, *On Translator Ethics*, p. 67. That a translator may distinguish himself from the text's content is exemplified in Peter Cole's discussion of his translation of politically inflected Hebrew poetry: 'Within five minutes of first meeting Aharon Shabtai, he sat me and Harold Schimmel down on the stairs in front of his house in Jerusalem and read us half of the book-length midrashic paean to former right-wing prime minister and Jewish terrorist-underground leader Menachem Begin. He'd finished the poem the night before we showed up at his door, on our way back from the market to Schimmel's apartment for lunch. It's a powerful tribute and an implicit critique of the Israeli Left, which in the mid-eighties Shabtai felt lacked a certain "Jewish" warmth. Granted, Shabtai moved on to write ferociously "left-wing" poetry that I do identify with, but *Begin* remains an inspired and sui generis poem, and one I stand by as a translator.' See Peter Cole, 'The Art of Translation No. 5. Interview with Joshua Cohen', *The Paris Review*, 213 (2015) <http://www.theparisreview.org/interviews/6386/the-art-of-translation-no-5-peter-cole> [accessed 1 June 2016].
28. Pym, *On Translator Ethics*, p. 56.

29. Pym, *On Translator Ethics*, p. 166.
30. Donatien Alphonse François de Sade, *Les 120 Journées de Sodome, ou l'École du libertinage*, éd. Eugène Duhren (Paris: Club des Bibliophiles, 1904), p. 36.
31. Sade, *Les 120 Journées*, p. 91.
32. Nancy Huston, *Mosaïque de la pornographie* (Paris: Éditions Payot & Rivages, 2007), p. 31.
33. See Lynn Hunt (ed.), *The Invention of Pornography: Obscenity and the Origins of Modernity, 1500–1800* (New York, NY: Zone, 1993); Robert Darnton, *The Forbidden Best-Sellers of Pre-Revolutionary France* (New York, NY: HarperCollins, 1995); and Jean-Marie Goulemot, 'Toward a definition of libertine fiction and pornographic novels', *Yale French Studies*, 94 (1998), 133–45.
34. Susan Sontag, 'The Pornographic Imagination', in *Styles of Radical Will* (London: Secker & Warburg, 1969), pp. 35–73 (p. 66).
35. Rita Felski, *The Limits of Critique* (Chicago, IL: University of Chicago, 2015), p. 177.
36. Rita Felski, *Uses of Literature* (Oxford: Blackwell, 2008), p. 26.
37. Rita Felski, 'After Suspicion', *Profession*, 8 (2009), 28–35 (p. 31).
38. Felski, 'After Suspicion', p. 33.
39. George Steiner, *Language & Silence: Essays on Language, Literature, and the Inhuman* (London: Faber and Faber, 1967), p. 29. Michel Delon has similarly suggested that 'Le lecteur [de Sade] est provoqué, pris à parti par un texte qui met en cause, en question, ses catégories fondamentales', 'Notice', Sade, *Œuvres*, 3 vols (Paris: Gallimard, 1990), I, 1129.
40. Webb Keane, *Ethical Life: Its Natural and Social Histories* (Princeton; NJ: Princeton University Press, 2016), p. 99.
41. Keane, *Ethical Life*, p. 100.
42. Keane, *Ethical Life*, p. 244.
43. On food, incorporation and the construction of the omnivore's identity, see Claude Fischler, 'Food, Self and Identity', *Social Science Information*, 27 (1988), 275–93.
44. Gayatri Chakvravorty Spivak, 'Translation as Culture', *Parallax* 6.1 (2000), 13–24 (p. 14). On violence and subjection in Sade's correspondence, see Thomas Wynn, 'Violence, Vulnerability and Subjectivity in Sade', in *Representing Violence in France*, pp. 139–60.
45. Sade, *Les 120 Journées*, p. 442.
46. Sade, *Les 120 Journées*, p. 434.
47. Sade, *Les 120 Journées*, p. 225.
48. Sade, *Les 120 Journées*, p. 355.
49. Sade, *Les 120 Journées*, p. 292.
50. Sade, *Les 120 Journées*, p. 292.
51. Keane, *Ethical Life*, p. 51.
52. Sade, *Les 120 Journées*, p. 81.
53. Alexandra Lianeri and Vanda Zajko, 'Still Being Read after so Many Years: Rethinking the Classic Through Translation', in *Translation and the Classic: Identity as Change in the History of Culture*, ed. by Alexandra Lianeri and Vanda Zajko (Oxford: Oxford University Press, 2008), pp. 1–23 (p. 1). Emphasis in original.
54. Lianeri and Zajko, 'Still Being Read After So Many Years', p. 4.
55. Wayne C. Booth, *The Company We Keep: An Ethics of Fiction* (Berkeley, CA: University of California Press, 1988), p. 294.
56. Deborah H. Roberts, 'Translation and the 'Surreptitious Classic': Obscenity and Translatability', in *Translation and the Classic: Identity as Change in the History of Culture*, ed. by Alexandra Lianeri and Vanda Zajko (Oxford: Oxford University Press, 2008), pp. 278–311.
57. Sade, *Les 120 Journées*, p. 76.
58. Sade, *Virtue*, trans. by David Carter (London: Hesperus Classics, 2011), p. xiii. The translator of another eighteenth-century libertine text similarly remarks that for expressions relating to prostitution, he has 'tried to use English equivalents with a period feel: whore, naturally, but also bawd, harlot, strumpet, kept woman, courtesan, fancy lady or even streetwalker, depending on the context[.]' Fougeret de Monbron, *Margot la ravaudeuse*, ed. and trans. by Édouard Langille (Cambridge: MHRA, 2015), p. 13.
59. Sade, *Les 120 Journées*, p. 447.

60. Sade, *The 120 Days of Sodom*, trans. by Austryn Wainhouse and Richard Seaver (London: Arrow Books, 1990), p. 580.
61. Sade, *Les 120 Journées*, 431.
62. Sade, *The 120 Days of Sodom*, trans. by Wainhouse and Seaver, p. 574.
63. Sade, *Les 120 Journées*, p. 460
64. Sade, *The 120 Days of Sodom*, trans. by Wainhouse and Seaver, p. 593.
65. Sade, *Les 120 Journées*, p. 50.
66. Sade, *The 120 Days of Sodom*, trans. by Wainhouse and Seaver, p. 229.
67. Sade, *Les 120 Journées*, p. 523.
68. Sade, *Les 120 Journées*, p. 440.
69. Sade, *Les 120 Journées*, p. 87.
70. Other scholars treat the *The 120 Days of Sodom* as a finished piece of work: see, for instance, Mladen Kozul, 'L'inachèvement des *Cent Vingt Journées de Sodome* de Sade', *Cahiers d'histoire des Littératures / Romanes Romanistische Zeischrift für Literaturgeschichte*, 1–2 (1995), 60–71.
71. Sade, *Les 120 Journées*, p. 440
72. Sade, *Les 120 Journées*, p. 69.
73. Sade, *Les 120 Journées*, p. 316.
74. Sade, *Les 120 Journées*, p. 354.
75. Presenting the author's original, idiosyncratic text is not, of course, of relevance only to Sade; see, for example, John O'Brien, 'Are We Reading what Montaigne Wrote?', *French Studies* 58 (2004), 527–32.
76. Sade, *Les 120 Journées*, p. 78.
77. Sade, *Les 120 Journées*, p. 495.
78. Sade, *Les 120 Journées*, p. 78.
79. See Peter Cryle, 'Taking Sade Serially: *Les Cent Vingt Journées de Sodome*', in *Geometry in the Boudoir: Configurations of French Erotic Narrative* (Ithaca, NY: Cornell University Press, 1994), pp. 120–46.
80. Sade, *Les 120 Journées*, p. 377.
81. Sade, *Les 120 Journées*, p. 99.
82. Sade, *Les 120 Journées*, p. 494.
83. Sade, *Les 120 Journées*, p. 498.
84. Sade, *Les 120 Journées*, p. 497.
85. Spivak, 'Translation as culture', p. 14.
86. Keane, *Ethical Life*, p. 100.
87. Sade, *Les 120 Journées*, p. 165.
88. Sade, *Les 120 Journées*, p. 124.

CHAPTER 2

# The European Market for Pornography: Some French Texts in German Translation Around 1900

*Johannes Frimmel*

In 1921, an anonymous author complained about the wave of confiscations of privately printed erotic classics in contemporary Germany. The author of the brochure was presumably the Austrian critic Franz Blei, himself one of the most prolific editors of erotic private printings and a connoisseur of the market. He reproached the police's focus on erotica of artistic value, as produced by reputable publishing houses, while clandestine mass pornography was not subjected to any form of persecution: 'The production and distribution of such sorry products takes place in the underground, which the policeman's thick soled shoe never reaches. Currently, in Germany there exist about a hundred of such smutty brochures. They are printed cheaply on blotting paper and trafficked secretly. None of these books has been confiscated because no one knows the trade channels through which they operate'[1] ['Herstellung und Vertrieb dieser Machwerke vollziehen sich in so unterirdischen Gängen, daß keines Polizisten doppelt besohlter Fuß da hindringt. Es werden derzeit in Deutschland ungefähr hundert als schweinisch zu bezeichnende, auf Löschpapier ordinär gedruckte Bücheln heimlich gehandelt. Keines davon ist der Konfiskation verfallen. Weil man die Wege dieses Handels nicht kennt'].[2]

What do we know about these 'smutty brochures'? They visibly differ from the famous erotic French *romans philosophiques* of the Age of Enlightenment, including the Marquis de Sade's infamous novels (see Thomas Wynn's contribution in this volume).[3] These cheaply produced hard-core books circulated in such obscurity that not only the police overlooked them; these hidden books are also rarely preserved in libraries and, as a result, barely examined by researchers. Until now, the pornography traders who worked around 1900 remain largely in the shadows. In this paper, I hope to shed some light on the publication and distribution of these pornographic products and offer a glimpse into their contents.

## Distribution

The *Austrian National Library* holds four anonymous catalogues that most likely go back to a single collector. The catalogues appeared within a larger series published between 1899 and 1900.[4] The catalogues promise 'extremely juicy rarities' ['hochpikante Seltenheiten'] and offer pornographic books, photographs, and rubber toys. As a supplement for some novels, the publisher also offers photographic series.[5]

According to the anonymous publisher of the catalogue, the books were partly original and partly reprints and stock purchased from other publishers. These 32 to 64 page-long brochures are in octavo format and were hastily printed on cheap paper. The title page often represents a vignette of two lightly clad female breasts. Decorative elements of this kind were typical for the production of pornographic books of the time. Sometimes they make it possible to assign the prints to a certain publishing house; but sometimes they are used to obfuscate the publisher's identity. It is safe to assume that the identical decoration of the books points towards an identical origin or, at least, towards one particular printer who cooperated with different publishers.[6]

The customers could place their orders by mail only, this being the preferred means of acquiring prohibited pornographic literature. Publishers and booksellers strictly sought to cover the tracks of any connection between producer and consumer. Preliminary advertisements were either left in mail boxes or placed in journals, offering books of 'scientific interest', 'risqué novels' or 'studies of the nude' in an innocuous way. Only after contacting the publisher directly, prospective clients could access actual catalogues with pornographic contents. This procedure served to guarantee absolute discretion to the customer. Furthermore, buyers were asked only to refer to the order number only and not the actual title. When the books and photographs were finally sent out, they came in secretive wrappers. The clients could also collect their mail at the post office as anonymous *poste restante*. The customer's letter, the only remaining piece of evidence, was destroyed or returned by request.

In order to make police investigation difficult, the books and photographs were often produced in one country and sold in another. Various middlemen in different countries helped with the delivery, making it almost impossible to trace the publisher's origin. Obviously, there always remained the risk that the books were seized at customs. The publisher of the catalogues mentioned initially also procured his books from abroad.

As a matter of course, the catalogues do not disclose the publisher's identity. Many of the books listed, however, refer to the biggest name in the international pornography market between 1880 and 1895: to the Belgian Auguste Brancart.[7] When he immigrated from Brussels to Amsterdam in 1885, the police seized 3,000 volumes from his pornographic stock. At that time, the port city became a haven for several booksellers and publishers from Belgium and quickly superseded Brussels as the centre of the international pornography trade. From the end of 1886 onwards, Brancart started to publish a multitude of clandestine works and reprints of pornographic literature first in English and later also in French and German.

Distribution worked in the same fashion as described above, with advertisements placed in Parisian journals. Among Brancart's authors we find a novelist known by the acronym 'E. D.', arguably the most prolific author of pornographic books at the turn of the century. Brancart is also reputed to be the publisher of the notorious erotic memoirs *My Secret Life,* written by an anonymous Victorian gentleman 'Walter'. However, by the time of the Vienna catalogues' publication (1899/1900), Brancart had, following his expulsion from the Netherlands in 1895, already sunk into obscurity.

The story of the catalogues becomes even more complicated if one takes into account the identical descriptions of the books, which can also be found in another series of catalogues, published from 1903 on. Some of these catalogues have the imprinted address of the Parisian bookseller 'Robert' (S. Robert 25 Bould Ornano, 25 Paris-18), Paris being the undisputed centre of the international pornography trade at the beginning of the twentieth century. The production of pornographic books was often a collective enterprise, defying the usual distinction between creation and distribution. Publishers and printers of pornographic books and photographs often cooperated with one another, once again to better obscure the origins of their products. Brancart himself cooperated with others major figures of the trade, such as Edouard Maheu and François van Crombrugge, and he also employed different printers directly.

Today, the uncertain legal status of pornographic texts in the past often makes it impossible to assign them to a certain publisher. Such anonymous texts were often forbidden upon publication, so that nobody was legally entitled to their possession. While the end of the nineteenth century saw the advent of international copyright laws, pornography remained a freely circulating commodity, which could be shared by everyone.

## The consumers

The traders offered their customers pornographic entertainment and forthrightly promised their clients sexual arousal. Similar to conventional catalogue companies, they promoted the quality of their products and offered maximum choice, promising something for every taste: for example, a catalogue of pornographic photos from 1905 promised more than 10,000 different subjects, including pederasty, sodomy and male and female homosexuality. Explicit and stimulating ekphrasis and brief overviews of the books' plots were supposed to arouse their clients' curiosity. One erotic novel, for example, is described with the following words: 'Extremely piquant and erotic work which even the most spoiled reader will put down highly satisfied. Every line shivers with an innermost thrill of lust' ['Hochpikantes u. hocherotisches Werk welches auch der verwöhnteste Leser hochbefriedigt aus der Hand legen wird. Jede Zeile ist durchhaucht von innerstem Wollustschauer'].[8]

Contrary to the warnings of numerous moral societies, the target customers of pornographic commodities were neither young people nor from the lower classes, but from the intellectual middle class. As a consequence, the catalogue features erotic books from the eighteenth century and modern texts stacked with allusions to bourgeois *Bildung*. Among these parodies of classical literature are translations of the satiric poem *L'Examen de Flora* in Alexandrines and of *Histoire d'un Godemiché*, which was originally English (*The Story of a Dildoe*) and contains many parodistic poems and references to canonical figures like Lord Byron. Members of the working class could hardly afford to order the books: the minimum order cost was ten marks. In 1900, the annual salary of a worker did not go beyond 800 marks.[9]

## The books

Many of the books in the catalogues are translations from French. Some of them are erotic classics such as *Mademoiselle de Brion*, *General Confession of Sir Wilfort* (*Confession générale du chevalier de Wilfort*), Mirabeau's *Hic and Hec or the Erotic Art of Variation* (*Hic et Hec ou l'art de varier les plaisirs de l'amour*) and the famous novel attributed to Alfred de Musset, *Gamiani or Two Nights of Debauchery* (*Gamiani ou deux nuits d'excès*). The vast majority of translations, however, are contemporary books which often existed in different French versions, usually published or reprinted by the notorious Brancart. What were the characteristics of these clandestine texts, which gained such an ardent following among the German bourgeoisie? Did the German translators try to adapt the texts to a different cultural context?

Throughout the eighteenth and nineteenth centuries, Germany relied on erotic and pornographic imports. An asserted French origin served as a seal of quality and the publishers were eager to offer their German clients literal translations. In view of the novel *Lesbia Maitresse d'École*, the publisher promised his clients: 'Word-for-word translation of the famous French original now completely out of print' ['Wortgetreue Übersetzung nach der berühmten französischen Originalausgabe die jetzt vollständig vergriffen ist'].[10]

The books of the German underground trade around 1900 contain motifs typical of the pornographic novel. Eberhard and Phyllis Kronhausen list a series of motifs in novels since the seventeenth century: seduction, defloration, incest, tolerant-seducing parental figures, profanation of the sacred, dirty talk in dirty books, gigantism, nymphomania, black and Asian people as sex symbols, homosexuality, and flagellation.[11]

One of the rare contemporary items with a clearly political context was the anonymous *A Queen's Love Madness* (*Les Folies amoureuses d'une Imperatrice*) which appeared for the first time around 1865 and was subsequently reedited many times, of course also by Brancart. The book describes the events during the wedding night of Eugénie de Montijo, when the servant Jonas prepares the debauched and impotent bridegroom, Emperor Napoleon III, for their first encounter: 'The Emperor had already a paunch, grey eyes and a thick and already hanging bottom lip. He had a moustache which turned already grey; a bulky and pointed chin-beard covered his chin' ['[L'Empereur] était déjà bedonnant, à l'œil gris, à la lèvre inférieure épaisse et déjà pendante. Il portait une forte moustache commençant à grisonner; une barbiche en pointe assez volumineuse, recouvrait son menton'].[12] On the previous day, Jonas had devised a number of erotic stimulants to condition the Emperor to the fulfilment of his conjugal duties. But spying on the commoners' sexual potency only brings his own weakness to mind: 'Alas, he murmured, contemplating the insensibility of his virile member. How lucky the men are who get excited only when they see a woman! This soldier on the photograph with his phallus stiff like an iron rod raising its head with the pride of a king makes me envious' ["Hélas, murmura-t-il, considérant l'insensibilité de son membre viril. — Ah! qu'ils sont heureux ces males, que la vue seule d'une femme met en érection! Ce grenadier de la photographie, avec son phallus, raide comme une barre de fer, redressant la tête avec la fierté d'un roi me rend envieux...'].[13]

Only after many efforts and with the help of a potency remedy and a maybug (!) the much longed for erection ensues. But the rehearsals fail, as the excited Emperor cannot abstain from sleeping with the servant's girlfriend, who had the task of replacing the Empress in the marital bed. As a result, on the next day he is totally exhausted and falls asleep near his young wife. So it becomes the servant's job to satisfy the excited Empress who had earlier amused herself with her maid. At the end the cheated servant gets his revenge over the Emperor:

> When Jonas left the sleeping room of the Empress, it was already in broad daylight. The Emperor was still sleeping... The anti-erotic tablet they had given to the Emperor in place of aphrodisiac tablet had made an impact. Thus Jonas had taken revenge and procured a delicious night for the beautiful Empress... who about five hours in the morning, pronounced that single word, which since that time nobody had heard from her again: enough!
>
> [Quand Jonas quitta la chambre de l'Impératrice, il faisait grand jour. L' Empereur dormait toujours... Les dragées anti-érotiques données à l' Empereur à la place des dragées aphrodisiaques avaient produit leur effet. Et c'est ainsi que Jonas avait pu procurer, tout en se vengeant, une nuit de délices à la belle Impératrice... qui, vers les cinq heures du matin, prononça ce seul mot, que jamais homme ne lui fit répéter depuis: Assez!][14]

The book was translated into German with disregard for the different French context. This indicates that political criticism does not play a central role even in a book that portrays the sexual decadence of Emperors, similar to eighteenth century libertine pamphlets. In fact, many of these books seem to undermine the political order in a more general way, subverting conventions of nineteenth century class society by presenting a pornographic utopia. For Steven Marcus, the historical function of pornography can be seen in the context of the development of industrial society:

> Among the principal tendencies in this process was a steadily increasing pressure to split sexuality off from the rest of life. By a variety of social means which correspond to the psychological processes of isolation, distancing, denial, and even repression, a separate and insulated sphere in which sexuality was to be confined was brought into existence.[15]

Pornography responds to this isolation by presenting a utopian fantasy where space and time are suspended. The underground pornographic books represent a 'Pornotopia' which undermined the values of a pre-Freudian society: women who take pleasure in sex and reject reproduction; old people having sex with the young;

promiscuity rather than marriage; women dominating men; masters sleeping with servants. If Michael Titzmann defines the pornographic novel of the eighteenth century as a negation of social norms (*normnegierend*), the pornographic novel of the nineteenth century can be described as ignoring social norms (*normignorierend*).[16] This is in line with Nadine Stroessen, who argues that 'all social constraints are overwhelmed by a flood of sexual energy. [...] Class, age, custom — all are deliciously sacrificed, dissolved by sex.'[17]

In *A Woman's 36 Pleasures* (*Les 36 jouissances d'une femme*), a mature lady retrospectively describes her sexual initiation and erotic development. During her life, she increasingly savours sexual pleasures, concluding with her credo on erotic enjoyment:

> I became more and more passionate. Anything which could be done on earth, we did it, always looking for new pleasures. [...] I was happy. I had joy. I enjoyed all my life. I gave enjoyment to others. I have emptied the glass until the last drop. [...] Ah! If I could start again, I would invent even other pleasures. Enjoy! Enjoy again! Enjoy always! That's the true existence.
>
> [Je devins toujours plus passionnée. Tout ce qui peut se faire sur la terre, nous le faisions; allant toujours à la recherche de nouvelles jouissances. [...] J'ai épuisé toutes les jouissances. J'ai été heureuse. J'ai eu du Bonheur. J'ai joui toute ma vie. J'ai fait jouir les autres. J'ai vidé la coupe jusqu'à la dernière goutte. [...] Ah! si je pouvais recommencer, j'en inventerais bien d'autres! Jouir! jouir encore! Toujours jouir! voilà la vraie existence!][18]

But this vision of a libidinous utopia also has its dark side. Instead of focusing on consensual sexual practices, the licentious plots turn into a quest for sexual arousal removed from ethical concerns: scenes of child pornography and sadism are omnipresent.

## Toys

Pornography tends to the unconscious where everything coexists in total simultaneity. While concrete relations with the real world are eliminated, many texts are marked by their self-reference: by listing other pornographic novels, intertextual references allow the text to inscribe itself into the pornographic canon. At the same time, intertextuality and self-reference have a performative function: they demonstrate to the reader how to use books and other objects for stimulation. In *A Queen's Love Madness*, the Emperor has a secret box with all the items designated for his sexual arousal. Besides pornographic photographs and playing cards, the servant curates a whole library of canonized pornographic books and a workshop of sex toys to arouse his master.[19]

In *The Story of a Dildoe*, the benefits of the eponymous device are portrayed in great detail. Descriptions not only explain the correct use of such a device, they also discuss the superior quality of Indian rubber and its enhancement by means of an injected liquid. Furthermore, the book informs the reader about the advantage of a dildo over an actual penis: 'It will cure the virgin of the green sickness without the risk of impregnation. It will comfort the widow until she can make a suitable match. And it will be found a never failing source of consolation to those married ladies whose husbands are impotent through age or debauchery.'[20]

In this spirit, three young women also share their first sexual experience by means of a sex toy — enjoying the company of one another. In the text, the seasoned Madame Marcelle initiates the young Flora in the use of books for erotic stimulation:

> I will send you "strictly privately" some charming books which I am sure will delight and excite you. Besides, [M]iss, such reading and the feelings they will produce will develope [!] your frame and make you more fitted for sexual enjoyment when your time comes to have it. [...] I often read and think of the pleasures I once enjoyed until I quite thirst for a return of them.[21]

After Flora receives the books, she is made to look at the illustrations and to read out frivolous poems to her friends:

> As she unpacked them and as she turned over the leaves and displayed the pictures various were the exclamations that followed; and amidst blushes and laughs and exclamations of delight and wonder the books were read. "Oh my!" "Oh how nice!" "Oh! do they do it like that?" "Oh, good gracious! can a woman ever be so shameless to suffer that?" "Oh look! he's getting into the very place!" or, "No; he's doing it from the back!" "Oh look, how they seem to enjoy it!" "Oh my! do read about it" and such like observations fell in rapid utterance from their lips.[22]

In *Lesbia as Schoolteacher* (*Lesbia maitresse d'École*), the head teacher shows her young assistant a Spanish book with a picture of two women making love. The girl is aroused and in the ensuing amorous play the book, having done its duty, falls to the ground. Like many other contemporary pornographic books, *Lesbia as Schoolteacher* focuses on the sexual pleasures of women. Obviously, this stimulates the male voyeuristic gaze, but given the extensive and anatomically detailed descriptions of lesbian and heterosexual practices, one can also regard such books as sex manuals. In *The Honeymoon of Horned Louise* (*La Lune du Miel de Louise de Cornue*), the female protagonist makes her innocent friend the confidant of her experiences since the wedding night:

> According to my promise to you when we were at the convent, my very dear Jeanne, I should like to write to you immediately after my marriage. [...] Undoubtedly, this will be a difficult task for me, telling you all those things to you, dear Jeanne, still so naively living under the veil of candour and virginity. My dear friend, promise me the utmost discretion and, most of all, that you won't blush when reading my letter. You asked for the description of the events, and here you are, under the veil.
>
> [Selon la promesse que je t'ai faite, ma bien chère Jeanne, lorsque nous étions encore au couvent, je tiens á t'écrire aussitôt après mon mariage. [...] Ce sera, sans aucun doute, une rude tâche pour moi de te dire toutes ces choses à toi chère Jeanne, si naïve encore, et sous les voiles de la candeur et de la virginité. Aussi, chère amie, promets-moi la plus grande discrétion, et surtout, de ne pas rougir en lisant ma lettre. Tu as voulu la description dont il s'agit, la voici.][23]

Night per night, she explains her newly acquired sexual expertise to her curious friend who, eventually, will share the bed with her friend and her husband.

Within the pornographic narrative, time and space follow no realistic logics, as time is measured by the imaginary sex act. In place of development, the basic principle of the pornographic novel is repetition and minute variation. Similarly, there exists no consistent idea of space, as these stories lack references to political events or a realistic setting. The time- and placelessness of pornographic fiction of the nineteenth century made it a perfect transnational commodity. In this context, Marcus speaks of the 'lingua franca of sex', as he observes:

> In the century of national literatures, pornography produced a body of writing that was truly international in character. It is often impossible to tell whether a pornographic work of fiction is a translation or an original — one need only change the names, or the spelling of the names, of characters in order to conceal such a novel's origin.[24]

This is also the case with the French books in the catalogue. They were translated into German without sparing any thought about the different context of the target culture. The only external references are other texts, which encourage the reader to participate in the canon of pornography. The appeal for German customers was the promise of sexual explicitness, rendered literally and unabridged from the original. This stands in contrast to numerous eighteenth century translations of French pornographic texts characterized by their tendency to depoliticize and moralize the French original.[25] Nineteenth-century translations eschew such attempts at nativization. Around 1900, pornography stands as an emblem of an already standardized product in a rising entertainment industry.

## Conclusion

The best erotic books of the eighteenth century, the so called *livres philosophiques*, conflated pornography with philosophical and political reflections. Their subversive attitude, however, was not preserved in the pornographic publishing output towards the end of the nineteenth century. As the Age of Industrialization coincided with the large-scale production of reading material, pornography became a highly profitable genre.

Professional underground pornography traders like Brancart, whose business model included middlemen and anonymized mail, soon operated across national borders. The official book market complemented this trend through the sale of bibliophile limited editions, and of illustrated popular science works on sex education. This trend towards diversification coincided with an increasingly militant discourse on — or rather: against — pornography. The government and the religious social purity movements regarded it as a fundamental threat to nation and morality. Three social groups were singled out as particularly threatened by the corrupting force of pornography: the working class, women, and young consumers. This line of argument would remain unchanged until the sexual liberation of the 1960s and 70s, a time when the producers of 'smutty brochures' stepped out of the black market. Rather than seeking anonymity, they became celebrities themselves, like the examples of Hugh Hefner (*Playboy*), Larry Flint (*Hustler*) and Bob Guccione (*Penthouse*) demonstrate.

## Bibliography

BLEI, FRANZ, *Unsittliche Literatur und deutsche Republik: § 184* (Hanover: Steegemann, 1921).
DARNTON, ROBERT, *The Corpus of Clandestine Literature in France 1769–1789* (New York, NY: Norton, 1995).
—— *The Forbidden Best-Sellers of Prerevolutionary France* (New York, NY: Norton, 1995).
*Deutsche Geschichte in Dokumenten und Bildern*, Entry to 'Die durchschnittlichen Jahresverdienste von Arbeitsnehmern in Industrie, Handel und Verkehr (1871–1913)', <http://germanhistorydocs.ghi-dc.org/sub_document.cfm?document_id=1746&language=german> [accessed on 30.12.2015].
DUTEL, JEAN-PIERRE, *Bibliographie des Ouvrages érotiques publiés clandestinement en Français entre 1880 et 1920* (Paris: Chez l'Auteur, 2002).
*Erlebnisse eines Wollustspenders [Godmiché]* (Berlin: [unknown publisher], 1900).
*L'Érotisme second Empire*, ed. by Jean-Jacques Pauvert (Paris: Carrere, 1985).
*Hochpikante und Hocherotische Seltenheiten für Lüsterne und Feinschmecker*, Bücher in deutscher Sprache, Neuester Catalog (1903); Vienna, Österreichische Nationalbibliothek (Austrian National Library) (=ÖNB).
HAYN, HUGO and ALFRED N. GOTENDORF, *Bibliotheca Germanorum Erotica & Curiosa*, 9 vols (Munich: Georg Müller, 1912).
KRONHAUSEN, EBERHARD and PHYLLIS, *Pornography and the Law: The Psychology of Erotic Realism and Pornography* (New York, NY: Ballantine, 1959).
*Lesbia die Schulvorsteherin. Nach der französischen Ausgabe übersetzt von X.Y.* (Amsterdam: [unknown publisher], 1898).
MARCUS, STEVEN, *The Other Victorians: A Study of Sexuality and Pornography in Mid-Nineteenth Century England* (New York, NY: Basic Books, 1966).
*Neuester Catalog hochpikanter Seltenheiten*, Bücher in deutscher Sprache Neueste Auswahl, ÖNB, N° 50.
*Neuester Catalog hochpikanter Seltenheiten*, Bücher in deutscher Sprache Neueste Auswahl (1899), ÖNB, N° 110.
*Neuester Catalog hochpikanter Seltenheiten*, Bücher in deutscher Sprache Neueste Auswahl (1900–01), ÖNB, N° 150.
*Neuester Catalog: Original-Photographien nur erste Qualität keine Reproduction* (1900), ÖNB.
QUESTER, YONG-MI, *Frivoler Import: Die Rezeption freizügiger Romane in Deutschland (1730 bis 1800)* (Tübingen: Niemeyer, 2006), pp. 243–45.
REIRRET, NOËL, *La lune de miel de Louise de Cornue* (Paris: [publisher unknown], 1886).
*The Story of a Dildoe: A Tale in Five Tableaux* (London: [unknown publisher], 1891).
STROSSEN, NADINE, *Defending Pornography* (New York, NY: New York University Press, 2000).

## Notes to Chapter 2

1. The translations are my own, unless noted otherwise, J.F.
2. Franz Blei, *Unsittliche Literatur und deutsche Republik: § 184* (Hanover: Steegemann, 1921), p. 19.
3. See Robert Darnton, *The Forbidden Best-Sellers of Prerevolutionary France* (New York, NY: Norton, 1995) and Robert Darnton, *The Corpus of Clandestine Literature in France 1769–1789* (New York, NY: Norton, 1995).
4. See *Neuester Catalog hochpikanter Seltenheiten*, Bücher in deutscher Sprache Neueste Auswahl. Vienna, Österreichische Nationalbibliothek (Austrian National Library) (=ÖNB), N° 50;

*Neuester Catalog hochpikanter Seltenheiten*, Bücher in deutscher Sprache Neueste Auswahl (1899), ÖNB, N° 110; *Neuester Catalog: Original-Photographien nur erste Qualität keine Reproduction* (1900), ÖNB; *Neuester Catalog hochpikanter Seltenheiten*, Bücher in deutscher Sprache Neueste Auswahl (1900–01), ÖNB, N° 150.

5. This is exemplified by the texts where titles are juxtaposed with precise information about the material content: 'Struggle for Love in the Bridal Chamber, or: The Triumph of a Rascal Over Female Coyness. In addition to the novel, 20 photographs are available. (à MK. 1.-)' ['Liebeskämpfe im Brautgemach Oder der Sieg des Wüstlings über die weibliche Schamhaftigkeit. Hiezu erschienen auch 20 Cab.-Photpgr. (à MK. 1.-)']. Hugo Hayn and Alfred N. Gotendorf, *Bibliotheca Germanorum Erotica & Curiosa*, 9 vols (Munich: Georg Müller, 1912), IV, 190.
6. See Jean-Pierre Dutel, *Bibliographie des Ouvrages érotiques publiés clandestinement en Français entre 1880 et 1920* (Paris: Chez l'Auteur, 2002), p. 22.
7. See Dutel, *Bibliographie*, p. 16.
8. *Hochpikante und Hocherotische Seltenheiten für Lüsterne und Feinschmecker*, Bücher in deutscher Sprache, Neuester Catalog (1903), ÖNB, p. 4.
9. *Deutsche Geschichte in Dokumenten und Bildern*, Entry to 'Die durchschnittlichen Jahresverdienste von Arbeitsnehmern in Industrie, Handel und Verkehr (1871–1913)', <http://germanhistorydocs.ghi-dc.org/sub_document.cfm?document_id=1746&language=german> [accessed on 30.12.2015].
10. *Lesbia die Schulvorsteherin. Nach der französischen Ausgabe übersetzt von X.Y.* (Amsterdam: [unknown publisher], 1898), p. 4.
11. See Eberhard and Phyllis Kronhausen, *Pornography and the Law: The Psychology of Erotic Realism and Pornography* (New York, NY: Ballantine, 1959), p. i.
12. *L'Érotisme second Empire*, ed. by Jean-Jacques Pauvert (Paris: Carrere, 1985), p. 23.
13. *L'Érotisme*, p. 25.
14. *L'Érotisme*, p. 44.
15. Steven Marcus, *The Other Victorians: A Study of Sexuality and Pornography in Mid-Nineteenth Century England* (New York, NY: Basic Books, 1966), p. 283.
16. See Michael Titzmann, 'Sexualität und Anthropologie in der französischen Aufklärung: Der philosophisch-pornographische Roman', in *Anthropologie der Goethezeit: Studien zur Literatur und Wissensgeschichte*, ed. by Wolfgang Lukas and Claus-Michael Ort (Tübingen: Niemeyer, 2012), pp. 433–83 (p. 447).
17. Nadine Strossen, *Defending Pornography* (New York, NY: New York University Press, 2000), p. 270.
18. *Les 36 jouissances d'une femme* (Brussels: Èdition BiblioCuriosa, 2014), p. 11.
19. See *L'Érotisme*, p. 24–25.
20. See *The Story of a Dildoe: A Tale in Five Tableaux* (London: [unknown publisher], 1891), pp. 15–16. The book was originally published in England in 1880 and became popular in Europe after Brancart's French version, titled *L'histoire d' un Godemiché* (1892), which in turn was translated into German as *Erlebnisse eines Wollustspenders* [*Godmiche*] (Berlin: [unknown publisher], 1900).
21. *The Story of a Dildoe*, p. 27–28.
22. *The Story of a Dildoe*, pp. 32–33.
23. Noël Reirret, *La lune de miel de Louise de Cornue* (Paris: [publisher unknown], 1886), Prologue.
24. Marcus, *The Other Victorians*, p. 269.
25. See Yong-Mi Quester, *Frivoler Import: Die Rezeption freizügiger Romane in Deutschland (1730 bis 1800)* (Tübingen: Niemeyer, 2006), pp. 243–45.

CHAPTER 3

# Eroticized Materiality and Postcolonial Agency in Pierre Guyotat's Algerian Works

*Dean A. Brink*

The fractured pansexual and postcolonial ecologies of human and nonhuman actants in Pierre Guyotat's early experimental works are known for their graphic sex and hyperbolic Dantesque fictionalizations of abuses during the Algerian war of independence. Guyotat draws on his own experience of being detained for disrupting morale and inciting desertion as well as his observations of colonial violence and then later, in France, translates the war and complicated agential postcolonial experience into an innovative literary form. Rendered in English, the intensity of objectively presented things and actions, often separated by semicolons within long sentences, sustain a powerful engagement commensurate with the French, but diverging in musicality and tone of presentation, as will be explored. These works delineate what may be understood as a postcolonial will in giving form to a means of overcoming the coloniality of a colonial divide. The French settlers and army and the colonized Algerian Arabs are presented as embroiled in zones of deterritorialization. More specifically, both *Tomb for 500,000 Soldiers* (*Tombeau pour cinq cent mille soldats*, 1967) and *Éden Éden Éden* (1970), unique in the history of postcolonial literature, fuse authorial reportage and compellingly surreal yet plausible erotic visions of a sexual suturing of the colonial wounds of play-acted yet exaggerated (almost burlesque) deadly hierarchies that suggest a *translated* reportage: a re-envisioning of the war as something far more soul-shattering than any intervention of the shrapnel of armaments and explosives could resolve.

The *source text* is first-hand experience and hearsay 'in the street' — a definition of reportage — and yet the poem-novels are translated into a post-surrealist *readerly* experience through long-form intense encounters with a plethora of details presenting a raw, filmic, condensed materiality. The works document an overblown landscape of fictionalized, sexualized hyperbole that translates colonial effects of rage and disgust into fields of erotically-charged matter, including living and non-living, human and nonhuman. The writing thus forms a counter-hegemonic over-determination of French Algerian coloniality and its overcoming. The fiction consumes the fusion of discrete preserves of immunized, numb opposing forces in the Algerian War; while French assumed Algeria to be an eternal, almost natural extension of the French homeland, Algerians maintained a determination to liberate their land, reflecting a movement sweeping colonies worldwide after WWII. Building on Alain Badiou's reading thereof, I will show that Guyotat's work cannot be separated from both its obvious postcolonial mappings onto Algeria and its prototypical post-human levelling of human and nonhuman within its erotic continuum. Here, the erotic is a means to a material realization of force (politics) in flux and the *jouissance* of daily life unravelled to the point of presenting new beginnings. The postcolonial is given body not as competing national identities but rather as a material disembowelment coinciding with its life gropingly re-stitched together on a mythical island in the midst of being liberated from slavery.

## Poetics of incomprehensibility

By Guyotat's own assessment, and as any contemporary reader may surmise, his working antagonisms do not center around erotic arousal in the images of vaginas inundated with secretions or throbbing penises casting their dibs on all matter of people, places, and things. It is not pornographic, at least not in any recognizable sense. Rather, in *Tombeau*, and even more so in *Éden*, a rebirth of society on the Edenic model prevails, concomitant with Algerian liberation from the colonizer and French liberation from the illusion of the colonial relationship. Both sides remain subject to a postcolonial fusion of ironies and the afterlife of coloniality and its transformation, for instance, of both sides into murderers, and, in the wake of coercive uses of French values not only to warp, as intended by the colonizer, but to bring out in exaggerated reaffirmation Arab and Muslim cultural practices.[1]

While French literature provides some intertextual precedents for Guyotat's intense eroticism and pansexual orientation, he pushes the envelope to the point of confronting antagonisms evident, for instance, in the sexual dimension of religion, the colonial relationship (or illusion of it, as Albert Memmi would have it),[2] how animals are treated, and one's relationship to oneself (body, *jouissance*) and the materiality of communities. It is here among the variety of literary texts that one might take note of translations of French erotic writings with pansexual and libertine overtones — from de Sade to Genet — and then note the difficulty in processing — translating, publishing, and reading — Guyotat's early works into English, where not only are his depictions of sexual practices extreme by French standards but the density of the writing itself approaches incomprehensibility. Comparing the English rendition to the source, one does find a more materialist (even dry and empirical) rhetoric in the English, while an enmeshing of the voice in musical turns of phrase characterizes the French:

> RIMA squad pushing into den hollowed out under platform of camp in onyx vein ; faces heated, arms, legs swinging, bottles thrown against walls : glass splinters falling back into darkened circle pricking, sticking to hardened members shaken out of dungarees ; beer, wine — cut with bromide —

splashing over shoulders, bare breasts of waiter ; RIMA squad rolling, vomiting in corners; waiter, greasy shorts slipping down loins, barefoot, tattooed, on ankle, with woman's breast, trampling on floor-cloth ; edging around counter, pushing cloth alongside lips of vomiting soldiers ; / two males tying up animals behind tents[.][3]

[ceux du RIMA s'engouffrent dans le foyer creusé sous la plate-forme du camp dans un gisement d'onyx ; tête échauffée, membres divaguant, ils jettent les bouteilles contre les murs : les éclats de verre retombés dans la rotonde obscurcie criblent, paillettent leurs sexes extraits durcis ballottés hors de la braguette ; la bière, la vin bromuré éclaboussent les épaules, les seins nus du serveur ; ceux du RIMA roulent, vomissent aux angles ; le serveur, son short enduit de graisse glissant sur ses reins, foule, de son pied nu, tatoué, sur la cheville, d'un sein de femme, une serpillière ; contournant le comptoir, il la pousse jusqu'au bord des lèvres des soldats vomissants ; / deux males attachent les bêtes derrière les tentes[.][4]

The translation opts for a cold, dispassionate and muted style of describing events without attempting to capture local musical effects of phonetic repetition (such as 'braguette ; la bière, la vin bromuré' and 'contournant le comptoir'), which might have the effect of further tying together the unified plane of the postcolonial and post-human materiality characterizing the work. Graham Fox's translation of *Éden* works, depending on dry undeniability of reportage from the shadows of the third person, and a roughening of the eloquence that Badiou so prizes in Guyotat. Note how different the opening, 'ceux du RIMA s'engouffrent dans le foyer creusé sous la plate-forme du camp dans un gisement d'onyx,' would be if 'RIMA squad pushing into den hollowed out under platform of camp in onyx vein' were recast as 'those of the RIMA squad rushed into the home hollowed out of an onyx deposit under the camp platform.' In a sense, the translation reads like a parody of bad translations of Chinese poetry (or any poem by Gary Snyder) in its dropping of articles. Thus one finds a marketing of the transgressive image of Guyotat's *Éden*, an exaggeration of the defamiliarizing effects at the expense of basic elegance (in the way the Beat poets rendered Tang poetry). Although similar in terms of its grotesque imagination, this work contrasts visibly with the grammatical clarity of the Marquis de Sade's writings (see Thomas Wynn's contribution in this volume).

Craig Dworkin compares *Tombeau* and Guyotat's subsequent novel, *Éden*, writing: 'At their most horrific, the two works share equally repellent scenes of abject abuse. Stylistically, however, the scenes of corporeal indiscretions and intersections in *Éden, Éden, Éden* [...] find a parallel in the text's linguistic promiscuity. [...] *Éden* dispenses with the romantic rhetoric, linear narrative, and familiar novelistic structure in which *Tombeau* couches its hallucinatory depictions of violent copulations.'[5] In other words, though fractured in its form and shifting point of view, *Tombeau*, for Dworkin, maintains a semblance of novelistic narrative despite the unconventional and transgressive depictions of violence and various sexual obsessions situated in the colonial context. Indeed, entire chants — including the final one conveying closure — situate the novel around questions of asymmetric colonial power relations and the reduction of the children of Inamenas (Algeria) to captive prostitutes — *homo sacer* in

Giorgio Agamben's sense of being rendered inferior, slave-like and expendable.[6] As such, unlike *Éden*, *Tombeau* contains elements of traditional plot, including a sense of actions and counteractions motivated by victimization presented in the novel. Not only does the final chant suggest the redemption of romantic love between two of the surviving abused children, but assessments of narrative continuity throughout the novel must take into account the rather conventional backstory information included to justify character motivations, scopes for choices, and actions taken in the novel.

However, Guyotat himself suggests in a 2010 interview that *Éden* is the novel, by comparison, with a clearer plotline:

> I wanted to get away from the lyricism and the epic nature of *Tombeau* and to work with a clear story line. It was a departure from idealism. [...] There are three parts to the book: first, the war and the rape; then the bordello; and finally the desert. [...] It spoke clearly about my preoccupations at that time: my rejection of idealism and *my quest for absolute materialism*, which would lead to an intense material poetry, beyond simply using poetic words. [...] The objective was clear: to get as close as possible to a nearly scientific reality.[7]

It is precisely this 'nearly scientific reality' that makes *Éden* less potent politically, though more radical in its language use. By writing 'my quest for absolute materialism, which would lead to an intense material poetry, beyond simply using poetic words', Guyotat suggests that he was moving away from the lyrical fragmentation of the epic *Tombeau* to engage the material so as to efface the difference not only from the literary but from the holistic imaginaries of capitalism, the colonizer bourgeoisie, and the ideological fictions of a monadic nature. One recent monograph seems to have given up on treating Guyotat's *Éden* simply because it does not seem to 'represent a turning point in the evolution of modern French erotic literature' and is 'largely unreadable for all but the most conscientious of readers'.[8] Yet, based on the above passage, translation is not only comprehensible but also conveys (and demonstrates) that the density of the original is *naturally* situated in a descriptive dispassionate distance from a matter-of-factness presenting erotically charged interactions as part of a postcolonial leveling as well as a human-nonhuman leveling of presumed norms of control.

Certainly the erotic is essential to his Algerian works as for all his writings. Guyotat's Catholic upbringing, coming of age in 1950s France, somehow gave rise to an intimate interplay of acts of self-pleasuring and the imaginative labour of composition that culminated in the habit of masturbatory writing.[9] As Stephen Barber notes, *Tombeau* 'is utterly semen-drenched by innumerable sex acts — their forms and participants infinitely permutating between slaves, masters, soldiers, generals, dogs and prostitutes' so that it is precisely 'the delirious intervention of sex [that] can explode power' in what Guyotat 'calls "the revolt against abstraction"' in a 'permanent struggle' with the capabilities of repetition that through 'corporeal insistence' transforms 'history, and the fabric of language itself'.[10] Is this not precisely the sort of active response to inexplicable events through the presentation of eventual traces for which Alain Badiou argues?

Indeed, Badiou himself, as a reader of Guyotat, reduces his poem-novels to a series of methods, arguing that he operates under a principle of an uninterrupted *law of equality* among objects and actions presented *in a present* isolated from concerns for the past or future so as to foreground relations of minutiae and obviate any psychological concerns whatsoever. Thus he effects a delinking of conventional assumptions concerning the world and its relations.[11] Badiou demonstrates how Guyotat presents commensurateness among things and actions, a sort of equivalence of interest or interchangeability among all things, human, animal, or even dust. This creates dramatic possibilities beyond simply gay liberation. Not only because Guyotat is personally attracted to a spectrum of genders, but as he puts it in an interview, 'what I've depicted, from *Tomb* to *Progeny* seems incompatible with any kind of categorical assertion' and 'many readers of *Tomb* or *Éden* only saw what I call the "male-to-male". Yet *Tomb*, which is already full of women and girls, ends with an "Adamic" scene of "heterosexual" renewal. *Éden* also begins and ends in the same way.'[12] I read this as an affirmation of a pansexual interest in the world for its erotic possibilities in any object whatsoever. It is in this sense that the literary, ecological, and erotic tensions in his early work set in Algeria follow a sensuous yet non-mental object- and action-oriented presentist method of delinking the doxa of what was, what should be found, and what will be.[13]

Thus the level of transgression is all encompassing and may be somewhat alien to readers of English accustomed to more formulaic translations of mildly erotic popular Japanese novels and manga or the non-literary soft porn of the *Fifty Shades of Gray* variety of dilatant sadomasochism. Guyotat's dense, florid neo-realist clarity combines with lean linguistic compression to form a contextual continuum that transforms expectations. It may indeed seem unreadable for some, but for those up for the challenge one hopes it also to be inspiring in its sheer sense of determination to present an alternative to daily matrices of the colonial attitude: the acceptance of the idea that some humans or cultures are more valuable than others and deserve inferior or superior privileges.[14] In our age, Guyotat's style should remain a shock to Anglophone and Francophone audiences shored up by long-lived colonial illusions of racialized constructs (hierarchies) as well as gendered ones — both targets of his vision as borne in witnessing the Algerian War.

The clarity of his neorealist style of engaging erotic scenes by no means entails an eroticized romantic love–based vision, though the novel closes on such ground. Rather, it exhibits a sort of x-ray revelation of a purely libidinal performativity if the world would be cast to reflect Guyotat's masturbatory fantasy life (to put it crudely). Moreover, it extrapolates to absurd lengths colonial sexualized cultural capital and *at the same time* levels Algerian and French as well as animalia and inanimate objects. The erotic capital enters a Deleuzean immanence of de-/re-territorializations at the cusp of a *post*colonial turn (and the end of a French occupation and presence). Guyotat depicts the turning of tables and how erotic energy builds as the colonial assemblage is transformed. His clarity in depicting erotic material entanglements serves a higher non-ironic performativity — the writing undoes all the hopes of modern trajectories (teleologies), inclusive of faith in technology and its capacity to enable one group to exact the submission of another group by way of sheer, brute force. It gives body to a continuum of colonial army and rebel guerrillas, and sustains the impossible vision by way of libidinal performativity. It also *looks back*, through his re-contextualizing sensorium, on what colonialism *was*. However, it is presentist in form.

Badiou distinguishes an 'expressive dialectics' of 'a classical revolutionary politics' of the twentieth century and a current horizon of change that for him should not be divided from its moment in all its 'social contradictions'.[15] Badiou goes so far as to demand that a given situation, as presented, be recognized as embodying a present's social and ecological contradictions ethically; Guyotat achieves this in *Tombeau*. A Badiouian approach to ethical questions that appear at the nexus of postcolonial ambivalence and violence helps to clarify how Guyotat's dramatic staging of the physicality of living flesh — animal and human — interrelate not randomly in a chaotic hell or even a moral Dantean vision of punishment, but rather present a constant groping for understanding of subjects acting beside themselves, subject to fetishistic obsessions fostered under colonial rule, ones which usually involve acts of violence and appear as animalizations — reductions to material embodiments of actions shorn of the appearance of human sentience.

Writing, for Badiou, cuts both ways. It may merely divert attention from ethical gaps, allowing excuses for degrees of unconscionable behaviour or conditions to persist, or it may, within a given form of art or political action, present a corrective situation that asserts shifts in power configurations. The capitalist imperialist apparatus of colonialism is thus depicted in language to have transformed bodies into functions, which in Guyotat for Algerians bear the marks of broken social ties. '*Là, vivent des familles décimées par la conscription et la trahison, pressées par la faim, le désir et la peur*'[16] is rendered 'There, live families decimated by conscription and betrayal, pressed by hunger, desire and fear.'[17] *Pressées*, translated simply as 'pressed by' might more poignantly be changed to 'driven by' to capture the sense of objectively presented subject-production at the material level of dependencies on food (*faim*), companionship (*désir*) and safety (*peur*): driven by hunger, desire and fear. For the colonizers, family units only functioned in protected communities, and required 'soldiers of the army occupying the island' of Inamenas (Algeria), which in colonial Algeria numbered 500,000 (reflected in the subtitle of *Tombeau*).[18]

It follows that *Tombeau* may be recognized as presenting an alternative material-agential version of a Badiouian ontology that defies glib naming or categorization, remaining queer and ethically non-identitarian, open to transformation based on unincorporated events (such as the liberation of slaves and victims of abuse). On the one hand, the poem-novel exhibits fidelity to a non-identarian open fracturing of the language and culture of colonial empowerment. On the other hand, it seems to queer the postcolonial materially so as to present a world simultaneously horrible (as a product of colonial occupation) and exposed for all to see the ugly 'entrails' of wars of aggression, but also bursting with hope in the form of inarticulate erotic energy. As such, it shows how human desire is contained by the global material of nonhumanity of imperialist-capitalist orders of exchange, which reduce all in

Guyotat's vision to a reactive subject of the sort one associates with animal instincts rather than affective and shrewd engagement.

But his vision also forms a fantastic cauldron for postcolonial transformation. If imperialism is the highest form of capitalism, as Lenin argued, Algerian independence passed through the nightmare of the machinery of capital in a war of liberation that left a nameless postcolonial horizon of ambiguous hope. Ecologically speaking, as Badiou muses in a recent lecture, 'we must refuse the complete separation between history and nature', as 'ecology proposes a new peace between [them]'[19] but requires a rethinking of their relationship, as 'nature' is no longer a backdrop against which modern humans act, but rather are intra-related. Thus we turn to quantum physicist Karen Barad's thesis, regarding the material-agential, how materiality binds us, rather than alienates us (in dialectics of inside and outside). Life and materiality touch in continuums.

## Queer postcolonial ecologies, critical ontologies, and material relations

By way of reading *Tombeau*, this section fills in more details regarding the various interdisciplinary approaches touched upon above. Subsections introduce the importance of the queer dimension, the ontology of active ethical engagement proposed by Badiou, the post-phenomenological intra-relational entanglement conceptualized by Barad, and various postcolonial issues binding ecological and historical conflicts in both local and international dimensions. Thus this introductory frame provides a means of appreciating and situating *Tombeau* as a queer ecologically postcolonial text that, following Badiou, radically alters how we engage the relationships of words, materiality, and capitalism in the waning days of colonialism.

I first introduce the queer dimension of the shifting points of view and subject-production in *Tombeau*, typically focused on some variety of libidinal investment and exchanges between organisms and matter. Using *queer* underscores a non-judgmental openness to what may seem extreme sexual practices or implicit object-fixations suggesting transitory fetishes. *Queer* encompasses an interactive relationality that is visceral, borne of a breakdown of the body of society and ecosystems so that the erotic engenders its own couplings and social bodies. The normal routinized inputs and outputs of bodily organisms are rearranged. The autopoeitic systems of humans and animals are tested. The sexual orientations found in *Tombeau* suggest no semblance of an assumed heteronormativity or homonormativity; it is pansexual and beyond, including bestiality and even sex with the soil of the earth. These relations may be framed in part in light of what Leo Bersani calls a queer 'non-identarian' ethos of a determinedly 'failed subject', one that refuses the norm of an 'inviolable subject'[20] that spills over into material relations. In a colonial context, it is a multicultural failure that erupts as systemic absence.

Bersani writes of 'a solidarity not of identities but of positionings and configurations in space, one that even ignores the apparently most intractable identity-difference: between the human and the nonhuman.'[21] I extend such a queer openness to others — human and nonhuman — in light of a second disciplinary engagement, namely with New Materialist approaches to understanding nonhuman actants in *Tombeau*. Here I turn to what Karen Barad calls agential realism, or 'agency [as] a matter of intra-acting; it is an enactment, not something that someone or something has. It cannot be designated as an attribute of subjects or object (as they do not preexist as such).'[22] Guyotat's *Tombeau* and *Éden* provide excellent examples of how atomistic refiguring of what is accepted as the world has the potential to recast colonial misery for all sides during a guerrilla war to drive away the colonizer. The known cannot stand, and the minutiae of things reassert themselves. Thus some sort of agential-realism engages readers in a process of correcting the old-school materialist extreme of witnessing capital extraction and its national-imperialist subject-formation (French nationalism and chauvinism) required to sustain the colonial impossibility (in Albert Memmi's sense).[23] As Stuart Kendall writes, Guyotat's work 'responds by proposing a radical materialism, an unforeseen encounter with and return to the world of things, where all things — and people — are equal.'[24]

## Material postcolonial entanglements in *Tombeau*

Guyotat's material engagements in *Tombeau* more specifically present paradoxes of a colonial war of independence, both reflecting global cultures associated with such wars and the postwar advent of firm resistance to colonial rule around the world. In addition to the emerging reconfigurations of power, trans-corporeal local engagements in their very materiality radically alter how the Algerian War may be configured and understood. On the relation of Guyotat's writing to real events, Michel Surya writes, 'nothing in what Guyotat writes or shows [...] is not faithfully real and that forces us to compare reality with what he writes and shows', so that 'what justifies the fear' in reading his work is that 'one does not wish to acknowledge [...] the real to which we are contemporaries. And, by extension, we are responsible.'[25] It is as if the dictum of reportage, in its English sense of reporting based on eyewitness or secondhand experience — which as such is undeniable (assuming a reliable witness) — were rendered to the level of the choreographed stage of actants: animals (prominently rats and flies), plants, chemical and material interactions in descriptions of human hunger and lust, implied hormonal flows, various bacterial infections and the weather.

In *Tombeau*, colonial difference is marked by the constant reference to the colonial homeland, Ecbatane (analogous to France) while the action takes place on an island called Inamenas (analogous to Algeria). As Martin Evans, a prominent historian of the Algerian War, writes, 'In 1954, French Algeria was a society rigidly polarized along racial lines, economically, politically and culturally. On the one side there were one million French settlers; on the other nine million Algerians. So from the outset the relationship between Algeria and France, French and Algerians, was a racist, colonial one, based on violence.'[26] In *Tombeau*, we read 'most of them were former slaves or sons of slaves, the present government of Ecbatane [France] had not wished to abolish slavery'[27] ['*la plupart étaient d'anciens esclaves ou fils d'esclaves, l'actuel gouvernement d'Ecbatane n'avait point voulu abolir l'esclavage*'].[28] Throughout the novel the term *esclavage* is used to refer to servants who are entirely at the disposal of another (whether occupier or rebel). Guyotat himself claims that not only the Algerian War, which he witnessed first-hand, but his family experience of WWII and the Resistance are reflected in *Tombeau*, adding to its lyrical, all-inclusive subjective sensibility.[29]

## Agential realism and the question of material actants

As a work of experimental fiction, *Tombeau* may also be understood as a precursor to recent discourse on the convergence of experiential subject and phenomenal object, while refusing the privileging of referential language per se. In addition to Badiou's work making possible a conceptualization of writing as an objective presentation, Barad's argument for the *agential-realistic* helps ground our appreciation of the poem-novel in more explicitly material and ecological terms. As Barad writes, 'matter is not a support, location, referent, or source of sustainability for discourse', but rather 'matter is always already an ongoing historicity'.[30]

 *Tombeau* is a work of fiction that in effect embodies such a *posthuman realism*, one that relieves coloniality of its modernist pathos for meaning as well as points to inherent questions of hybridity, ironic displacements, ambivalence, and other characteristics associated with the postcolonial socio-economic and cultural situations. In precisely the most mundane terms of physical becoming (though not reduced to the subatomic level, where Barad's argument begins) Guyotat foregrounds what Barad calls 'the dynamics of intra-activity [which] entails matter as an *active* "agent" in its ongoing materialization' [emphasis in the original]. For Barad, intra-activity includes 'boundary-making practices, that is, discursive practices [that] are fully implicated in the dynamics of intra-activity through which phenomena come to matter. In other words, materiality is discursive.'[31] Thus, she argues that relationships of 'mutual entailment' should be recognized as the new norm, so as to reflect a truly post-human and thoroughly materialized linguistic use. Although this may sound like yet another version of Hegelian phenomenology (a dialectic of subject-observer and object-world), in light of Barad's active agential ambiguity, the once-privileged human cultural apparatus is demoted; material itself becomes bound up in point of view and subject-reference. Understanding materiality as this process helps one frame scenes and language in terms of the material orientation found in *Tombeau*. In this sense, the posthuman becomes inherently postcolonial in *Tombeau*.[32]

## Postcolonial ecocriticism

In addition to openness to imagining often violent and problematic queering of intimacy with material others and Barad's intra-active entanglement in a material phenomenology, a third field — requisite, given the historical dimension forming the background for this novel — appears: postcolonial ecocriticism. Herein one may appreciate how colonial ecologies, wrought by the violence of long-standing French territorial claims, affect material and biological relations and ecosystems, forming a virtual overlay ultimately borne of imperialist capitalist cultures. French claims on Algeria were naturalized by once-universal economically exploitative practices that justified other practices (inequality in sanitation, housing, educational opportunities, and prostitution) within the colony. As Guyotat writes: 'After five years of war, the large forests of Inamenas are three quarters burnt, the lands waste [lit. left uncultivated], the families decimated. In the harbours, dockers unload now only arms; in the warehouses instead of bags of wheat, bags of ammunition'[33] ['*Après cinq années de guerre, les grandes forêts d'Inaménas sont aux trois quarts brûlées, les terres incultes, les familles dècimées. Dans les ports, les dockers ne déchargent plus que des armes; dans les entrepôts au lieu de sacs de blé, des sacs de munitions*'].[34] Postcolonial Algeria begins with the declaration of independence, a refusal to submit to this system of hierarchies (often justified by differences in perceived race, language, and religion).[35]

In this respect, ecocriticism provides a focus on biological relations and interdependencies, while postcolonial ecocriticism analyzes the mechanisms of the destructiveness of exploitative wars and occupations. To measure the impact of this poem-novel, Alain Badiou's work is introduced to help clarify how *Tombeau* is important in its realization of events that are difficult to comprehend, even to name. *Tombeau* is unique in its anti-war and anticolonial presentation, which explores both the material and somatic engagement with the world without capitulating to a sense of an *a priori* Being of the world; the way one measures and presents the world is itself transformed by decades of colonial occupation and the more recent war. Badiou provides a fresh means of situating poetic production in light of events and recognizing changes in postcolonial situations. Thus this chapter explores relations between colonial rule and war, destruction of the environment, and the animalization of humans, as well as the fine lines between obsessive desire and aggression, empathy and abuse. Guyotat begs us to consider the materialities of dirt, bodies, wind, breathing, and parasites.

## *Tombeau* as poem-novel

In terms of textuality, *Tombeau* is an experimental, critically engaged work containing nonconventional elements of both epic poetry and fiction. Stephen Barber, who has met Guyotat many times, emphasizes Guyotat's cinematic orientation both in terms of being influenced by films and in actually filming landscapes and people so as to stimulate and sustain the writing process. Barber writes:

> At the time when he was writing *Tomb for 500,000 Soldiers*, Guyotat [...] watched [...] austere and mysterious films, in order to refine a transparent form of language within which to insert a dark content, often transected with delirium, and articulated through repetition. That form of language would be one intimately close to film, and capable of containing contrary and irreconcilable elements, to project them towards his reader.[36]

Guyotat has claimed that 'The idea for the book came to me after watching Luis Buñuel's *The Young and the Damned* (*Los Olvidados*, 1950) again.'[37] It is a film, as the title suggests, featuring ritualistic hierarchical interactions between forgotten and impoverished youths in Mexico. It focuses on a crime committed out of hunger — stealing to eat — and the drives for friendship, respect, intimacy and violence as they seem forced by circumstances of hardship, suffering and general institutionalized poverty and social hierarchies in a Mexican urban slum.

Reading Guyotat's letters from 1965, his first biographer, Catherine Brun, shows precisely how *Tombeau* (written between 1963 and 1965) was for him a new direction. Having seen 'the "dull" and "flat" writing'[38] of journalism while working as editor of the culture pages of a newspaper after the war, he, in conceiving *Tombeau*, 'projected the composition of a text sombre and cruel, evoking "war and the crumbling of a country"', claiming 'his book "extends in space and in time, [becoming] epic, comic, lyrical [;] more a saga or a novelistic gesture."'[39] Moreover, Brun writes that for Guyotat 'writing and sexuality are linked very early on' so that his writings reflect a 'complex relation of inclusion-exclusion-collusion-entanglement'.[40] Brun's work helps us understand the stylistic ambitions he held and how they shaped his language along with his intensely sexual engagement with others. Given his experiences in Algeria and his sympathy with the victims of the colonial apparatus of which he played a part, the entanglements in *Tombeau* may even be expected from a writer of his talents.

Turning to specific material presentations in *Tombeau*, one of many examples of extreme fetishes is the princess's obsession with human blood in the First Chant. After she is overcome by the sight of 'a young slave, arms filled with bottles and flasks of hydromel [mead]' ['*un jeune esclave, les bras chargés de bouteilles et de flacons d'hydromel*']. With knees already bleeding, she 'catches his leg, [and] he loses balance' ['*lui saisit la jambe, il perd l'équilibre*']. Then 'the flying glass wounds the naked legs of the small children' ['*les éclats blessent les jambs nues des petits enfants*'], suggesting a proliferation of effects surrounding the sexual excitement over the slave's bloody knee and a link to class hierarchies within the postcolonial context of the devalued lives of Algerian children. The princess maintains her focus: 'the slave standing, hands open on his hips, bends his head, the princess pulls at the leg from behind the knee, the slave advances further, the princess throws her mouth on the wound, nibbles the bone, licks the blood on the leg' ['*l'esclave debout, les mains ouvertes sur les hanches, baisse la tête, la princesse tire la jambe parderrière le genou, l'esclave avance encore, la princesse jette sa bouche sur la blessure, mordille l'os, lèche le sang sur la jambe*'].[41] Note the cinematic visualization in moving from a medium shot to close-ups to extreme close shot in the line 'the princess turns [...] her bloody face, half opens her mouth weltering in blood, a pink saliva foams upon her gums' ['*la princesse tourne vers Iérissos son visage ensanglanté, ouvre à demi sa bouche baignée de sang, une salive rose mousse sur les genvives*'] which grounds her visceral love of blood in matter-of-fact yet somewhat dramatic description. The passage introduces the princess's short monologue, beginning, 'As you see, blood, even the vilest, stifles my melancholy' ['*Tu le vois, le sang même le plus vil, étouffe ma mélancolie*'].[42] All of these images materially and cinematically release words into a dry lyricism, one dispassionately observing actions so as to give a minimal role to the obfuscation of points of view. Rather, the points of view are clear while the physical interactions of embodiments in the environment are recorded. *Éden* can be said to extend this method into both a more atomistic presentation at the level of sentences and a defined narrative structure on the level of the novel.

After another somewhat satirical scene with the bloodthirsty princess pursuing a horse butcher's apprentice, an 'old woman' with an obsession for eating rats and children is shown using the latter as bait for capturing more rats: 'squatting, she eats the grilled rats ; falls asleep until noon, her back against the wall ; when she awakens, again the rats are covering the dead body ; the old woman strangles and clubs them, ... When the body is all torn and can't be used as a bait any more, she drags it into the blaze and roasts it over a slow heat'[43] [*'accroupie, Elle mange les rats grillés ; s'endort jusqu'à midi, le dos au mur ; réveillée, les rats de nouveau couvrent le cadavre ; la vieille femme les étrangle et les assomme, . . . Quand le cadavre est déchiré et ne peut plus servir d'appât, elle le traîne dans le brasier et le fait rôtir à petit feu'*].[44] Then the next day, the cycle begins again with an obsession: 'when she has seen, thrown over the rubbish or coiled up underneath, a little corpse with bare lips, her heart throbs within her bosom'[45] [*'quand elle a vu, jeté sur les ordures ou replié dessous, un petit cadavre aux lèvres nues, son cœur bat sous sa poitrine'*][46] and she soon assaults a child with a pen in the mouth, drawing the interest of the princess. Nothing in this presentation of a caricature of obsessions reduces it to psychoanalytic symptoms. Instead, one finds only ostensible master-slave, adult-child, colonizer-colonized, Ecbatane-Inamenas hierarchical relations embodied not absolutely, but intra-relationally, and reflected as in a naturalistic cinema that is surreal in content not in form. The stream of writing is not of an unconscious breaching into consciousness, but rather a presentation of a material postcolonial setting that is twisted not by abstract ideologies *per se* but by various embodiments of material conditions that reproduce as ecosystems of abuse and that through colonization have distorted natural settings and precolonial communities for the sake of colonial settlements and uses.

In *Explications*, Guyotat says that 'In *Progenitures* [a later work] there is a hierarchy between human beings, animal beings, and non-beings called "whores" [*putains*].' The farce is in the relation between these three states, but in *Tombeau* there was 'already a clear evacuation of the universe known as "bourgeois", with its romantic, criminal, and political psychology, and the bodies within this psychology and its culture.'[47] His placement of humans and nonhumans on the same plane both drives his anti-war and anticolonial deconstruction of violent cultures and exploitative economic relations, but also stems from his stated visceral, radical abhorrence of 'discourse that consists in conceiving man as the most perfect creature in the universe, its king. [...] It is, I believe, a monstrosity to conceive of animals as servants, as food of these superior beings; it is an extremely common ideology, global and totalitarian.'[48] This conviction, expressed in terms befitting the greenest of eco-radicals, can be seen as a foundation for his deconstruction of postcolonial ambivalence by asserting an exaggerated colonial materiality in his Algerian works.

Note how this material embodiment is reflected in the revenge fantasy of a child prostitute. The reader regularly encounters passages suggesting various types of colonial victimization — especially if the brothels are recognized as a colonial institution — and desperation, as when a child prostitute is asked

— Why do you want to die?
— Because I'm a bastard child. I don't exist. ... The world, it's a brothel : all the children are for sale.[49]

[ — Pourquoi veux-tu mourir?
— Parce que je suis un bâtard. J'existe pas. . . . Le monde, c'est un bordel : tous les enfants sont à venture.][50]

But in the ellipsis an interesting material detail appears: 'when I'll kick the bucket, a little spurt of urine will splash [the nurse, the instructress's] hand, revenge, [my] captain'[51] ['*quand je claquerai, un petit jet d'urine éclaboussera sa main, vengeance, mon capitaine*'].[52] The author imagines a boy so twisted by the colonial situation that he envisions a minor revenge in a physical 'spurt of urine' that implies the impossibility of resisting his captors in life. Only when his body is lifeless will such an act be possible.

Here the line between the normalization of a colonial culture of child prostitution and the moment in the novel where it is recognized as depraved can indeed be traced in coordination with its materiality — a sense of claustrophobia sewn into life itself; however, careful attention is required to recognize it amid the overwhelming emphasis on the abuse and exploitation. It is most obvious in contrast with presentations of the norms for the 'French' children, who are depicted as innocents. For instance, after the passing description of the spatial division between the higher ground, where the colonists carefully check on their children sleeping in their own rooms, and the slums below are shown burning after Madam Lulu's brothel was set on fire by rebelling children there.[53] There is also the material eruption of the naïve French radio operator who vomits upon witnessing the depravity of a boy.[54] Among the more enigmatic is the boy Crazy Horse who discovers that when he beats another, he simultaneously ejaculates, which can be read as a sort of instrumentalized reflection of both the abuses and resistance under colonialism: the acting out of violence triggers a *jouissance* that has its own frame in the boy Crazy Horse's relation to others and the thingness of himself and others, to his own despair: 'Crazy Horse again, strikes Novarina's nape : again, sperm splashes his thighs, tears stream down as far as his shirt's collar. He throws the broom in the latrines' ['*Crazy Horse de nouveau, frappe la nuque de Novarina : de nouveau, le sperme éclabousse ses cuisses, les larmes ruissellent jusque sur le col de sa chemise. Il jette le balai dans les latrines*'].[55]

More specifically cross-referencing the realms of material and colonial manifestations, the following passage reflects a sensuous manifestation of cultures of abuse associated with smell:

> Kment breathes the smell of soap and sweat, the smell of soldiers, the smell of rapes, the smell of contempt. The peasants, the wretched, the children, the women fear that smell ; it swoops down on them, by day, by night, especially : it invades the houses, the streets, it blends with the perfumes of night, of trees, of water, it seizes the women by the throat, sometimes it can move them.
>
> Inamena, colonized for a hundred years by Ecbatane, wants to free itself. Half of its buildings, its houses, its places of worship are used as prisons. The whole population is suspect.[56]

[Kment respire l'odeur de savon et de sueur, l'odeur des soldats, l'odeur des viols, l'odeur du mépris. Les paysans, les misérables, les enfants, les femmes redoutent cette odeur ; elle fond sur eux, le jour, la nuit, surtout : elle envahit les maisons, les rues, elle se mêle aux parfums de la nuit, des arbres, de l'eau, elle prend les femmes à la gorge, elle peut les attendrir.

Inaménas, colonisée depuis cent ans par Ecbatane, veut se libérer. La moitié de ses bâtiments, de ses maisons, de ses lieux de culte servent de prisons. Toute la population est suspecte.][57]

This passage demonstrates (in less violent language) how materially and somatically perception itself is transformed during colonial occupation and war, leaving various responses ranging from revenge to the adoption of a slave mentality, eventually leading to liberation, hope, and renewal — which made the novel popular in late 1960s France.

It is in the depiction of the poor and exploited victims of colonial rule that Guyotat presents in raw detail not simply a symbolic representation of harsh treatment and denial of shared wealth in colonial Algeria, but a material deconstruction of the physical embodiments of exclusions and class divisions crossing human and animal lines:

> At night, groups of children ragged and tattered, hair stuck to the skull by an unknown blood, run along the muddy alleys, fall in the rubbish, ride on each other in the soiled grass, knees plunged into the layer of human and animal shit. The women, hair glued to the mouth by the lipstick, in the light of half-opened doors, call while pulling up their stockings under the dress. Screams then shoot out of the piles of wood, the street angles, the bushes, the deserted latrines. Men smoke in front of houses, sitting in circles over the mud. A gunshot tears the night, a sob springs up from a shack. The children, jostling the women busy fastening their garters, throw themselves on the soup, the cats claw the roof's metal sheets.
>
> In the distance, out of the ruts of night, leap starving beasts, they slash the injured storks and the stray children. Human and animal cries then rise from the earth and men watch with indifference the mutilated night. The beasts, heavy, run away, their claws drawn in, towards the top of the hills, jump over ravines, carrying, between their fangs, throbbing prey. Springs gush out, newly born, in the darkness.[58]
>
> [La nuit, des groupes d'enfants haillonneux, les cheveux collés au crâne par un sang inconnu, se poursuivent dans les ruelles boueuses, tombent dans les immondices, se chevauchent dans l'herbe souillée, les genoux enfoncés dans la couche d'excréments humains et animaux. Les femmes, cheveux collés aux lèvres par le rouge, dans la lumière des portes entrouvertes, appellent en remontant leurs bas sous la robe. Des cris jaillissent alors des tas de bois, des angles des rues, des buissons, des latrines abandonnées. Des hommes fument devant les maisons, assis en rond sur la boue. Un coup de feu déchire la nuit, un sanglot sourd d'une baraque. Les enfants, bousculant les femmes occupées à agrafer leurs jarretelles, se jettent sur la soupe, les chats griffent les tôles du toit.
>
> Au loin, des ornières de la nuit, bondissent des bêtes affamées, elle déchirent les cigognes blessées et les enfants égarés. Des cris humains et animaux s'élèvent alors de la terre et les hommes regardent avec indifférence la nuit mutilée. Les

bêtes, lourdes, s'enfuient, leurs griffes repliées, vers le sommet des collines, sautent pardessus les ravins, avec, entre leurs crocs, des proies battantes. Des sources naissent dans l'obscurité.][59]

In this important passage, note how in the first paragraph the subject shifts, reinforcing a sense of posthuman materiality. The first sentence focuses on groups of children who have 'hair stuck to the skull by an unknown blood', while the second focuses on women who have 'hair glued to the mouth by lipstick'. The parallel suggests confusion of blood in war and violence engendered by colonial conditions of substandard living by the colonized, segregated from the best areas reserved for French settlers. 'Screams' is the subject of the third sentence, followed by men smoking in the next, and then a gunshot and a sob. Children are again the focus of the closing sentence, and remain the focus in the second paragraph, which suggests how colonial abuses include the abandonment of minimal care for the children and wildlife outside settlements. Though 'injured storks and stray children' are the clear focus throughout the passage, note how the second, compound sentence has 'human and animal cries' as the subject of the first half and 'men watch with indifference the mutilated night' in the second. This indifference is significant in that it complements the fetishistic object-fixes that run wild in Inamena. Here it leads, in the concluding two sentences, to the 'throbbing prey' of storks and children turned into gushing springs 'in the darkness'. Thus, this passage underscores the intimate link between animal and human in the sense of them both going wild, first in the sense of losing rational control and civilization in the lost children (the future), and second in the sense of moving toward a bio-centric post-human world.

## Experimentalism and material transformation

In terms of experimentalism, Stuart Kendall writes that 'like Sade, Guyotat's vision is enormous, endless in its unfolding, but also insistent, obsessive, intricate' to the extent that one may say he 'does not write novels: he writes epic poems that must masquerade, however ineffectually, as novels in today's marketplace.'[60] He also conveys the sense of materiality embodied in the novel, writing, '*Tombeau* is a baroque panorama of the horrors and delights of its century; perhaps no other piece of literature is as attentive to the minute stirrings of sensual gratification, none so honest in its tracking of desire; but none again so unflinching in its willingness to follow desire to its disastrous results; to place love and war so intricately on the same ground. [...] To read Guyotat is to stare at a mass of entrails.'[61] Indeed, the repetition of certain nouns (vomit, buttocks, brothel, etc.) may indicate a new genre of literary prose that avoids both lapsing into self-parody by building towards an ultimate abject self-loathing subject helplessly obsessed with sado-masochistic entanglements or simply traumatized by the situation as witnessed and relived, recast in literary formation. Rather, one may avoid psychoanalyzing Guyotat and treat the materiality itself as presenting aberrations of human and nonhuman actants within complex scenes that for readers today naturally include discourses on postcoloniality as well as agential realism.

Experimentalism in this work can be thus understood as taking the form of a presentation of a material continuum, which on the surface seems a stream of consciousness, but one that eludes psychoanalytic frames associated with Surrealism. One finds no sense of trauma in the ordinary sense of temporal progression — from event to all-absorbing cathexis of symptoms for a particular subject. In fact, Guyotat's *Tombeau* can be read as a deconstruction of traumatic temporality, revealing trauma to be a lyrical melding of disparate temporal frames. On the contrary, Guyotat thinks through the Algerian aftermath *materially* in a Brechtian or Marxian sense of decoding the colonial illusion as well as an eco-materialist sense of recognizing entangled equivalencies. Political concerns become transformed (metamorphosed) into material presentation rather than a metaphorical safe distance from the brutality described.

While *Tombeau* appears to be an exaggerated burlesque of the aftermath of the war for independence before the exit of French soldiers and exodus of settlers, from an ecological perspective of material actants, it presents a complicated postcolonial situation as infected ecosystems, which include objectively manifest sexual obsessions often of extreme and exaggerated violence. Thus it presents not merely a 'mass of entrails', but the redemption and revenge of the land and people against an abusive invader without telling the story so much as presenting it cinematically frame-by-frame, as if materially self-explanatory. More specifically, it sometimes presents a de-familiarized panorama of inflated fixations and interactive co-dependent depravity that itself reduces human and nonhuman to blind actants so that the virtual colonial apparatus of humanist empire and rebellion in the name of decolonization falls away as so much excess language (very much in the sense of Badiou's famous axiom: 'There are only bodies and languages, except that there are truths').[62] Instead, what is foregrounded is present in material flora, fauna, land and people, all within the novel's depiction of a levelling of hierarchies in the pursuit of base desires constitutive of the scene of war and its aftermath, a grotesque discarded hell of communities overcoming their coloniality and concomitant mutual debasement.

The final scene, beginning near the close of the 'Sixth Chant' and continuing through the final and shortest 'Seventh Chant', suggests Edenic redemption as two of the abused children, Kment and Giauhare, start a new life. It is the sort of overcoming of war and return to innocence that has led commentators to suggest it was a perfect reflection of the age of war resistance and the international 'flower power' movement, published as it was in 1967. Unlike *Éden* and later works, traditional novelistic and dramatic conventions remain, albeit selectively. Most significant is the framing of the novel in the opening and closing pages as a postcolonial intervention. Kment exacts a rescue that recapitulates a will to live (beyond being abject *homo sacer*) out of the automatism of bodies reaching to abuse the young:

> Kment, in the cathedral, is looking for Giauhare ; prostrate women cling to his knees ; pull at his penis ; a blue beam of light bathes his forehead, a woman tears off from him the shreds of a loincloth girding his thighs, he steps over the bodies at the sacristy door ; a rebel is hugging Giauhare against the dresser ;

she screams ; he, the rebel, girded with liturgical pieces of cloth, the muscles of his leg quivering, his left hand leaning on the tapestry soiled with melted wax, growls, his right hand holding his cock and tucking up Giauhare's wet dress ; Kment strikes him in the back with his fist, the naked rebel collapses at his feet, the gilded stole covering his cock ; he has no more lips ; Kment looks at Giauhare, a rat comes out of her mouth :

— Do not kiss me, the rat has just come out. O Kment, the water is rising in the city.[63]

[Kment, dans la cathédrale, cherche Giauhare ; des femmes étendues s'agrippent à ses genoux ; lui tirent le sexe ; un rayon bleu baigne son front, une femme lui arrache le pagne en lambeaux qui lui ceint les cuisses, il enjambe les corps à la porte de la sacristie ; un rebelle étreint Giauhare contre le buffet ; elle crie ; lui, le rebelle, ceint de linges liturgiques, les muscles de la jambe frémissant, la main gauche appuyée à la tapisserie souillée de cire fondue, grogne, la main droite tenant son sexe et retroussant la robe mouillée de Giauhare ; Kment le frappe dans le dos avec son poing, le rebelle nu s'écroule à ses pieds, l'étole d'or lui couvrant le sexe ; il n'a plus de lèvres ; Kment lève ses yeux vers Giauhare, un rat sort de sa bouche :

— Ne m'embrasse pas, le rat vient de sortir. Ô Kment, l'eau monte dans la ville.][64]

Note the surreal Dantesque and Fellini-like imagery rendered in materializing detail. It includes a rat (which Giauhare later claims impregnated her), a beam of light, a flood and snakes (all biblical imagery).[65] Kment and Giauhare are in the process of overcoming the lecherous world of colonialism which is not depicted as such, but rather is presented as a colonial context of behavior reflected in the rebels not the colonial soldiers here, and more precisely *actions* manifest (as in agential realism) in the pathetic autonomous 'quivering' leg muscles, 'growls', presence of 'melted wax' on the tapestry, and Giauhare's scream as well as the rat emerging from her mouth in a surreal regaining of autopoietic integrity of her body in preparation for the romantic bonding with Kment, in a postcolonial redemptive return to a nonviolent materiality of a liberated Inamena (Algeria). Rats are among the most material and burlesque actants in *Tombeau*, both the historical residue of colonial disaster and embodiments of defilement.

Earlier in this Sixth Chant, a sense of revenge (directed against the invading soldiers) and redemption in the slave city of Titov Veles is succinctly depicted with a similar automatism: 'soldiers from the garrison, who had raped one of those females, were thrown in the swimming pools and died under the slaves' cold gaze'[66] ['*Des soldats de la garnison, qui avaient violé une de ces femelles, furent jetés dans les piscines et moururent sous le regard froid des esclaves*'].[67] Similarly, in the final battle several passages foreground both material actants embroiled in a sense of automatic human/nonhuman intra-actions and surreally depicted processes of death and decay appear, as in the sentence, 'The soldiers come out of the building site ... throw out their charred arms towards the open air ; [Captain] Xaintrailles comes close, he touches one of those hands, it crumbles, ash runs on the soldier's bloody foot'[68] ['*Les soldats sortent du chantier, . . . jettent leurs bras carbonisés vers l'air libre ; Xaintrailles s'approche il touche une de ces mains, elle s'effondre, la cendre coule sur le pied ensanglanté du soldat*'].[69]

This Dantean materiality of colonial sinners turned to ashes in hell is not the climax of this epic poem-novel.

The closing Chant cannot be reduced to such images of revenge, ecological and postcolonial correction, or redemption alone. Indeed, Kment 'mates with the dark and mute earth' ['*saille la terre obscure et muette*'] after 'the breathing of the sea, similar to that of love, gives him back speech and his cry finishes in a moan formed with ancient, mutilated, softened words' ['*la respiration de la mer, semblable à celle de l'amour, lui rend la parole et son cri s'achève en plainte formée de mots anciens, mutilés, adoucis*'].[70] This suggests a victory for the locals after the decisive defeat of the invaders during previous night and a re-joining with the earth in a visceral embodiment within its ecosystems, even sexually, as well as familially, and politically, so that 'all mix together and, from that heap of furs, of feathers, of claws, of talons, of little horns and little fangs come out a noise of tongue and of muscles, some cheepings, moans, pantings'[71] ['*tous s'entremêlent et, de ce tas de pelages, de plumages, de griffes, de serres, de petites cornes et de petits crocs sortent un bruit de langue et de muscles, des piaulements, des plaintes, des halètements*'].[72] Guiahare and Kment gradually engage each other's bodies in various combinations of touch[73] so that closure is indeed suggested, but it is not focused only on empathy with a protagonist, but also, in a Brechtian sense, on the social and ecological milieu as raped, exploited, war-ravaged divided and transgressed spaces that have been transformed and wounded by colonization, leaving only staggering populations still full of youthful energy and a restlessness approaching hope.

In effect, Guyotat translates postcolonial discourse into erotic manifestations of sexual excess that only could become manifest under conditions (and conditioning) of colonial differentiation of the colonized and the colonizer. Postcolonial discourse itself tends to analyze stereotypes and images as means of maintaining colonial hierarchies and how they may become reified in postcolonial cultural and political situations. By focusing on an imaginary commons of libidinal investment that reduces all subjects to materially embodied non-symbolic and non-metaphorical actants in a choreographed burlesque, Guyotat in effect *bridges* or translates the gap between cultures *without* simply re-hierarchizing them. Instead, he offers in French rather than Arabic a textual basis for occluding the cultural and linguistic gaps *created* by the colonial (vertical) hierarchies. He enacts a haptic visuality of a sensuous dynamic that forms an often inexplicable erotic opacity that shatters the binary fiction that *is* coloniality itself by way of a translation of foundational colonial difference into this extravagant eroticism. His refusal to uphold colonial discourse, while not attempting to represent in any satisfactory detail native Algerian practices as the colonized, takes the form of a translation of the metaphoricity of colonial language of master and slave into fields of metonymically and horizontally co-present and interpenetrating flesh of the most mundane, descriptive language. This haptic visuality — a term borrowed from film studies (aptly, given Guyotat's debt to Buñuel) — as Laura Marks argues presents an immediacy approaching a 'mutually constitutive exchange [...] the germ of an inter-subjective eroticism'.[74] As such, Guyotat can be said to draw readers into the world of colonial divisions and severances, processes of capture, breaking free, and healing.

## Conclusion

This study attempts to appreciate experimental works that may at first seem erotically perplexing and exotic exercises in anticolonial counter-hegemonic discursive production. As I hope has been shown, Guyotat has translated attention from the big picture of colonialism to the minute libidinal shifts that occur as hierarchies imposed by occupying forces of another culture turn sour with the advent of independence movements and resistance. In doing so, he has also created a template for a politicization of an ecological studies reoriented to a levelled materiality of human-nonhuman that links them with discourse not only in New Materialist post-humanism and material dialectics — in the sense of Barad's intra-relationality — but queer and postcolonial critiques of capital. By way of cinematic inspiration, the poem-novel translates audio-visual medium into a language with a material orientation and frame-by-frame development. In theorizing this framing, Badiou's work distinguishing eventual ontological realization, based on political and aesthetic procedures, thus provides a means for modeling change — which is precisely Guyotat's focus in the Algerian works.

In this journey out of the colonial disfiguration of two peoples, Guyotat forces us to see the material world as shorn of the pomp of civilizing and 'othering' colonial rhetoric. Though he declines to foreground Arab cultures in detail that would lend itself to essentializing pre-colonial cultures and identity politics, he instead presents a colonial animalization of all partaking in the colonial relationship: lives broken at the libidinal level, the very will to live destroyed in some, and of course, the colonizer vanquished from the land. Human and nonhuman alike rebel in this world, turn ugly in the breaking of the colonial stalemate, yet are shown emerging through violent common material interaction of urban guerrilla warfare undoing the relationship predicated on imperialist capitalism. As the island of Inamena liberates itself from Ecbatane, the poem-novel traces the rough, epic shifts as power based on blind obsession and fixations with the earth and all creatures participate in a caricatured farce-like movement of return through the founding violence of the colonial relationship (that like the sexual relationship does not exist) to new emplacement: a meeting of broken flesh in high spirits as two young people in love, albeit waiting for the wounds and trauma of abuses to their bodies to clear, but with erotic and social hope of new forms of life.

## Bibliography

AGAMBEN, GIORGIO, *Homo Sacer: Sovereign Power and Bare Life* (Stanford: Stanford University Press, 1998).

ALAIMO, STACY, *Bodily Natures: Science, Environment, and the Material Self* (Bloomington, IN: Indiana University Press, 2010).

BADIOU, ALAIN, *The Age of the Poets: And Other Writings on Twentieth-Century Poetry and Prose*, ed. and trans. by Bruno Bosteels (London: Verso, 2014).

—— *Logics of Worlds: Being and Event 2*, trans. by Alberto Toscano (London: Continuum, 2009).

—— *Philosophy for Militants* (London: Verso, 2012).

BADIOU, ALAIN, and JACQUES HENRIC, 'The Strange Illness of Poetry: A conversation with Jacques Henric in Art Press, March 2010', trans. by Ariana Reines, in *Animal Shelter* 3, ed. by Hedi Kholti (Los Angeles, CA: Semiotext(e), 2013), pp. 98–113.

BADIOU, ALAIN, and DUANE ROUSSELLE, *The Subject of Change: Lessons from the European Graduate School* (New York, NY: Atropos Press, 2013).

BARAD, KAREN, *Meeting the Universe Halfway: Quantum Physics and the Entanglement of Matter and Meaning* (Durham, NC: Duke University Press, 2007).

BARAD, KAREN, 'Posthumanist Performativity: Toward an Understanding of How Matter Comes to Matter', *Signs: Journal of Women in Culture and Society*, 28.3 (2003), 801–31.

BARBER, STEPHEN, 'Into the Zone: Guyotat and Film', *3:AM Magazine* (2012) <http://www.3ammagazine.com/3am/into-the-zone-guyotat-film/> [last accessed 2 Aug. 2015].

BARBER, STEPHEN, 'Introduction', in Guyotat, Pierre, *Tomb for 500,000 Soldiers* (London: Creation, 2003).

BARBER, STEPHEN, *Pierre Guyotat: Révolutions & Aberrations* (London: Vauxhall & Company, 2016).

BERSANI, LEO, *Is the Rectum a Grave? and Other Essays* (Chicago, IL: University of Chicago Press, 2010).

BRINK, DEAN, 'Epistemological Opacity and a Queer Relational *Jouissance*', *Journal of Bisexuality*, 16.4 (2016), 468–83.

——*Japanese Poetry and Its Publics: From Colonial Taiwan to Fukushima* (London: Routledge, 2018).

BRUN, CATHERINE, *Pierre Guyotat. Essai biographique* (Paris: Editions Léo Scheer, 2005).

DWORKIN, CRAIG, 'The Stutter of Form', in *The Sound of Poetry, the Poetry of Sound*, ed. by Marjorie Perloff, and Craig D. Dworkin (Chicago, IL: University of Chicago Press, 2009), pp. 166–83.

EVANS, MARTIN, *Algeria: France's Undeclared War* (Oxford: Oxford University Press, 2012).

FANON, FRANTZ, *A Dying Colonialism* (New York, NY: Grove Press, 1967).

GUYOTAT, PIERRE, *Eden, Eden, Eden*, trans. by Graham Fox (London: Creation Books, 2003).

——*Éden, Éden, Éden* (Paris: Gallimard, 1970).

——*In the Deep*, trans. by Noura Wedell (South Pasadena, CA: Semiotext(e), 2014).

——*Tomb for 500,000 Soldiers*, trans. by Romain Slocombe (London: Creation, 2003).

——*Tombeau pour cinq cent mille soldats: Sept chants* (Paris: Gallimard, 1980).

——and MARIANNE ALPHANT, *Explications* (Paris: Scheer, 2000).

——and DONATIEN GRAU, 'Interview with Pierre Guyotat', *Purple Magazine*, 14 (Fall/Winter 2010) <http://purple.fr/magazine/fw-2010-issue-14/pierre-guyotat/> [last accessed 2 Aug. 2015].

——and TATIANA KONDRATOVITCH, 'Art Is What Remains of History', *art press*, 292 (July 2003), 388–401.

KENDALL, STUART, 'Eden and Atrocity: Pierre Guyotat's Algeria', *Comparative Studies of South Asia, Africa and the Middle East*, 28.1 (2008), 11–19.

——Rev. of *Pierre Guyotat: Essai Biographique*, by Catherine Brun. *SubStance*, 34.3, 108 (2005), 136–39.

MARKS, LAURA U., *Touch: Sensuous Theory and Multisensory Media* (Minneapolis, MN: University of Minnesota Press, 2002).

MEMMI, ALBERT, *The Colonizer and the Colonized*, trans. by Howard Greenfeld (London: Souvenir Press, 1974).

PHILLIPS, JOHN, *Forbidden Fictions: Pornography and Censorship in Twentieth-century French Literature* (London: Pluto Press, 1999).

SURYA, MICHEL, *Matériologies* (Paris: Farrago, ScheerLignes, 1999).

## Notes to Chapter 3

1. See Frantz Fanon, *A Dying Colonialism* (New York, NY: Grove Press, 1967), especially Chapter. 1.
2. See 'The colonial does not exist, because it is not up to the European in the colonies to remain a colonial, even if he [*sic*] had so intended.' Albert Memmi, *The Colonizer and the Colonized*, trans. by Howard Greenfeld (London: Souvenir Press, 1974), p. 17.
3. Pierre Guyotat, *Eden, Eden, Eden*, trans. by Graham Fox (London: Creation Books, 2003), p. 2.
4. Pierre Guyotat, *Éden, Éden, Éden* (Paris: Gallimard, 1970), pp. 17–18. If not marked otherwise, all italics in the original.
5. Craig Dworkin, 'The Stutter of Form', in *The Sound of Poetry, the Poetry of Sound*, ed. by Marjorie Perloff, and Craig D. Dworkin (Chicago, IL: University of Chicago Press, 2009), pp. 166–83 (p. 173).
6. Giorgio Agamben, *Homo Sacer: Sovereign Power and Bare Life* (Stanford, CA: Stanford University Press, 1998), p. 48.
7. Pierre Guyotat and Donatien Gruau, 'Interview with Pierre Guyotat', *Purple Magazine*, 14 (Fall/Winter 2010) <http://purple.fr/magazine/fw-2010-issue-14/pierre-guyotat/> [last accessed 2 Aug. 2015]. Emphasis added.
8. John Phillips, *Forbidden Fictions: Pornography and Censorship in Twentieth-century French Literature* (London: Pluto Press, 1999), p. 3.
9. He remarks in an interview, 'once I'd reached the age of thirteen or fourteen, the sexual act was necessarily accompanied by a textual act'. Alain Badiou and Jacques Henric, 'The Strange Illness of Poetry: A conversation with Jacques Henric in Art Press, March 2010', trans. by Ariana Reines, in *Animal Shelter* 3, ed. by Hedi Kholti (Los Angeles: Semiotext(e), 2013), pp. 98–113 (p. 103). Many of his autobiographical writings focus in part on how he becomes this way and how it influences his life and writing. See, for instance, Pierre Guyotat and Marianne Alphant, *Explications* (Paris: Scheer, 2000); and Pierre Guyotat, *In the Deep*, trans. by Noura Wedell (South Pasadena, CA: Semiotext(e), 2014).
10. Stephen Barber, *Pierre Guyotat: Révolutions & Aberrations* (London: Vauxhall & Company, 2016), pp. 24–25 (pp. 6, 15).
11. Alain Badiou, *The Age of the Poets: And Other Writings on Twentieth-Century Poetry and Prose*, ed. and trans. by Bruno Bosteels (London: Verso, 2014), p. 195.
12. Badiou and Henric, 'The Strange Illness of Poetry', pp. 102, 104.
13. See my recent argument elsewhere that this pan-queer openness to others is an identity that is non-identitarian and both more radical and cosmopolitan — an attitude more than a binary category of sexual orientation mapped onto gender combinations. Dean Brink, 'Epistemological Opacity and a Queer Relational *Jouissance*', *Journal of Bisexuality*, 16:4 (2016), 468–83.
14. On how matrices of association may operate in colonial contexts, see Dean Brink, *Japanese Poetry and Its Publics: From Colonial Taiwan to Fukushima* (London: Routledge, 2018), esp. Chapters 1 to 2.
15. Alain Badiou, *Philosophy for Militants* (London: Verso, 2012), p. 61.
16. Pierre Guyotat, *Tombeau pour cinq cent mille soldats: Sept chants* (Paris: Gallimard, 1980), p. 73.
17. Pierre Guyotat, *Tomb for 500,000 Soldiers*, trans. by Romain Slocombe (London: Creation, 2003), p. 47.
18. Martin Evans, *Algeria: France's Undeclared War* (Oxford: Oxford University Press, 2012), p. 273.
19. Alain Badiou and Duane Rousselle, *The Subject of Change: Lessons from the European Graduate School* (New York, NY: Atropos Press, 2013), p. 7.
20. Leo Bersani, *Is the Rectum a Grave? and Other Essays* (Chicago, IL: University of Chicago Press, 2010), p. 183.
21. See Bersani, *Is the Rectum a Grave?*, p. 184. This material and postcolonial dimension goes beyond Guyotat's own expressed thoughts on such matters, as when he writes that he 'always felt [he] more or less lived both sexual "orientations" at the same time.' See Pierre Guyotat and Tatiana Kondratovitch, 'Art Is What Remains of History', *art press*, 292 (July 2003), 388–401 (p. 393).

22. Karen Barad, *Meeting the Universe Halfway: Quantum Physics and the Entanglement of Matter and Meaning* (Durham, NC: Duke University Press, 2007), p. 178.
23. Albert Memmi, *The Colonizer and the Colonized*, trans. by Howard Greenfeld (London: Souvenir Press, 1974), p. 17.
24. Stuart Kendall, 'Eden and Atrocity: Pierre Guyotat's Algeria', *Comparative Studies of South Asia, Africa and the Middle East*, 28.1 (2008), 11–19 (p. 11).
25. Michel Surya, *Matériologies* (Paris: Farrago, ScheerLignes, 1999), p. 14. My translation.
26. Martin Evans, *Algeria: France's Undeclared War* (Oxford: Oxford University Press, 2012), p. 43.
27. *Tomb*, p. 22.
28. *Tombeau*, p. 32.
29. Pierre Guyotat and Donatien Gruau, 'Interview with Pierre Guyotat', *Purple Magazine* 14 (Fall/Winter 2010) <http://purple.fr/magazine/fw-2010-issue-14/pierre-guyotat/> [last accessed 2 Aug. 2015].
30. Karen Barad, 'Posthumanist Performativity: Toward an Understanding of How Matter Comes to Matter', *Signs: Journal of Women in Culture and Society*, 28.3 (2003), 801–31 (p. 821).
31. Barad, 'Posthumanist', p. 822.
32. This approach echoes and builds on recent ecologically-oriented cultural criticism that has begun to explore nonhuman modes of agency so as to shift the forces of subjection from human to a dialectic among material potentialities of any variety. As Stacy Alaimo writes: 'Although trans-corporeality as the transit between body and environment is exceedingly local, tracing a toxic substance from production to consumption often reveals global networks of social injustice, lax regulations, and environmental degradation'; moreover, trans-corporeality 'denies the human subject the sovereign, central position. Instead, ethical considerations and practices must emerge from a more uncomfortable and perplexing place where the "human" is always already part of an active, often unpredictable, material world.' Stacy Alaimo, *Bodily Natures: Science, Environment, and the Material Self* (Bloomington, IN: Indiana University Press, 2010), pp. 15–17.
33. *Tomb*, p. 58.
34. *Tombeau*, p. 91.
35. The religious element in *Tomb* at first seems gratuitous and out of place in such a wildly erotic poem-novel; however, when approached in terms of the (post-)colonial dimension, it is fundamental. It justifies *both* French and Algerian hubris by grounding monotheistic cultural assumptions as givens (god-granted). But, more than the either-or of the colonial relationship, it is the justification of a French distinction of the *us* 'with god behind us' and the Algerian *them* living in low lands, hemmed in by colonial design, trapped. See Frantz Fanon, *A Dying Colonialism* (New York, NY: Grove Press, 1967), pp. 51–52.
36. Stephen Barber, 'Into the Zone: Guyotat and Film', *3:AM Magazine* (2012) <http://www.3ammagazine.com/3am/into-the-zone-guyotat-film/> [last accessed 2 Aug. 2015].
37. Stephen Barber, 'Introduction', in *Tomb*, p. 6.
38. Catherine Brun, *Pierre Guyotat. Essai biographique* (Paris: Editions Léo Scheer, 2005), p. 130. My translation.
39. Brun, *Pierre Guyotat*, p. 131.
40. Brun, *Pierre Guyotat*, p. 47.
41. *Tombeau*, p. 49, *Tomb*, p. 32.
42. *Tombeau*, p. 49, *Tomb*, p. 33.
43. *Tomb*, p. 37.
44. *Tombeau*, p. 56.
45. *Tomb*, p. 37.
46. *Tombeau*, p. 56.
47. Pierre Guyotat and Marianne Alphant, *Explications* (Paris: Scheer, 2000), p. 11. My translation.
48. Guyotat and Alphant, *Explications*, p. 73. My translation.
49. *Tomb*, p. 238.
50. *Tombeau*, pp. 380–81.
51. *Tomb*, p. 238.

52. *Tombeau*, pp. 380–81.
53. See *Tombeau*, pp. 422–23, *Tomb*, p. 264.
54. See *Tombeau*, p. 135, *Tomb*, p. 85.
55. *Tombeau*, p. 122, *Tomb*, p. 77.
56. *Tomb*, p. 57.
57. *Tombeau*, p. 90.
58. *Tomb*, p. 47.
59. *Tombeau*, pp. 73–74.
60. Stuart Kendall, Rev. of *Pierre Guyotat: Essai Biographique*, by Catherine Brun, *SubStance*, 34.3, issue 108 (2005), 136–39 (p. 137).
61. Kendall, Rev. of *Pierre Guyotat*, p. 138.
62. Alain Badiou, *Logics of Worlds: Being and Event 2*, trans. by Alberto Toscano (London: Continuum, 2009), p. 4.
63. *Tomb*, p. 371.
64. *Tombeau*, pp. 595–96,
65. Although Guyotat penned *Tomb* not long after the English publication of William Burroughs's *Naked Lunch*, he seems solely indebted to French literary models. As Stephen Barber suggests in his introduction to *Tomb*, writing 'Guyotat himself is universally seen as the sole living writer to rank with such crucial figures as Artaud, Bataille, Genet and de Sade' (Barber, 'Introduction', p. 5), confirmed in personal correspondence. Moreover, at the risk of sounding reductive, it would seem that these French writers are less oriented toward drug-induced visions than toward more other-oriented matrices of socio-subjective interplay of bodies, class, state functionaries, and so on.
66. *Tomb*, p. 346.
67. *Tombeau*, p. 556.
68. *Tomb*, p. 351.
69. *Tombeau*, p. 564.
70. *Tombeau*, pp. 605–06, *Tomb*, p. 376.
71. *Tomb*, p. 374.
72. *Tombeau*, p. 603.
73. See *Tombeau*, pp. 604–09, *Tomb*, pp. 375–78.
74. Laura U. Marks, *Touch: Sensuous Theory and Multisensory Media* (Minneapolis, MN: University of Minnesota Press, 2002), p. 13.

CHAPTER 4

# Let's Talk about Sex: How to Find Words for what You Cannot Speak of

*Stephanie Heimgartner*

Le texte de plaisir, c'est Babel heureuse.
ROLAND BARTHES[1]

There is not much that one cannot speak of these days. In general, we do not ask ourselves if it is socially admissible or advisable to speak about a certain topic — instead, we doubt that words help at all. Arguably, erotic and pornographic texts help readers to regulate their emotional life, as have books of other genres. In contrast to the wider public, however, literary scholars and critics struggle to make sense of pornography. The key question of twentieth century criticism remains: can erotic literature be of any aesthetic worth, can it form a legitimate part of the canon?

I would like to discuss two prose texts that try to answer this question positively, using experimental rhetorical and poetic strategies of eccentricity, exuberance, hyperbole, which are also characteristics of visual pornography. The strategies in both texts differ radically in their use of language: A. L. Kennedy's *Original Bliss* (1997) recounts an impossible love story, and Nicholson Baker's *House of Holes* (2011) ironizes style conventions of pornographic literature. Both novels develop a self-reflexive language in order to challenge and integrate the literary canon. Kennedy's as well as Baker's texts have been widely translated. I will analyze the translation of Kennedy's novella into German to demonstrate how linguistic shifts affect its subtexts and meta-poetical strategies. For Baker's novel, the translation is relatively inconspicuous; here it seems more rewarding to analyze its critical reception, which differs considerably between English and German reviews.

## A. L. Kennedy: Original Bliss

While sex talk has turned out to be a versatile instrument of public self-staging, the topic is still difficult to address in close relationships and, when addressed, tends to complicate communication immensely. Often enough, talking sex disturbs rather than helps,[2] after all it tries to establish the delicate balance between the partners' conflicting interests.[3]

This also applies to characters in fictional narratives. Ever since literature started to address inward developments and emotions rather than adventures, modern literature has taken great interest in the failure of communication and in rendering unfulfillable and differing expectations of intimacy.[4] In the case of communication about sexual matters, language shows a remarkable tendency to lack its usual capacity for problem-solving. This difficulty is beautifully exemplified by a passage in Kennedy's *Original Bliss* where the two protagonists, Edward and Helen, avoid straight-forward communication:

> "Well?"
> "I don't know. Would it be enough, Edward?"
> "For me? It would be perfectly enough for me. What about you? That's what I'm asking. If it's going to be ... I don't want to do something wrong and I might because I don't know my way... around. You know I don't."
> "It'll be, it'll be fine."[5]

Edward and Helen obviously feel awkward about the topic of their conversation. Their elliptic sentences revolve around a centre both refuse to hit: like many other characters in Kennedy's prose, they won't dare speak about deep-set wishes for fear of rejection and shame. As the reader already knows at this point, their sexual past is equally troubled: Helen has just fled from an abusive husband, and Edward is caught between his soaring intellectualism and a shameful addiction to hard-core pornography.[6]

Shame is perhaps the most persistent theme in A. L. Kennedy's work. Her protagonists feel ashamed because they drink too much, because they hate to speak, because they suffer under the burden of real or imaginary guilt. It keeps them from developing close relationships with other people, despite their desperate wish for more interpersonal contact. This intimacy can be achieved through conversation or sexual intercourse, so they hope, as both forms of encounter link shame and closeness to one another.

Often, Kennedy's characters are at a loss for words. They exhaust themselves in incomplete sentences that end in three dots. The important is left unsaid. Their language tends towards simplicity,[7] it becomes monotonous and repetitive.[8] Sometimes, *apiosiopesis* is used to create pathos, for example during love-making:

> "Oh, God ...
> "That's nice ...
> "I think ...
> "If we ...
> "Make it slow ...
> "This will ...
> "Turn out ...
> "Fine.[9]

When talking, Kennedy's characters are either very careful or completely ruthless

— choosing the latter whenever they want to hide their vulnerability. Whoever weighs his words too carefully instead of being specific can succeed in sparing the partner's feelings, but risks being misunderstood. This risk extends to the reader. Very often, Kennedy's scenes start in medias res, and it takes an attentive (or imaginative) reader to comprehend the situation. As readers we share the characters' experience: there remains the risk to misunderstand what is going on between people. A feeling of insufficiency and shame may ensue and eventually shatter the hopes for mutual understanding. This applies not only to *Original Bliss*, but also to many other of A. L. Kennedy's plots and protagonists.

During the initial stage of their relationship, Edward and Helen avoid sexual and most physical contact, despite being well aware of their mutual desire. In order to avoid any trace of the violence Helen has experienced in her marriage, Edward must keep his own preferences as a consumer of pornography in check.[10] In a complicated conversational dance, they try to elaborate a non-violent, non-coercive language for their sexual wishes and physical stimulations that address their special needs. In the course of this attempt, a lot is left unsaid and delegated to the reader's imagination.

During the above dialogue, the couple is preparing Horlicks, a drink made from malted milk powder. This innocent activity initiates their first touch, an infantile touch that instantly arouses Helen who is not used to such tenderness.[11] In addition to its sexual connotations, the name of this traditional British instant drink also connotes untidiness or confusion.[12] Eventually, the situation changes into a more openly sexual encounter. Consequently, the sexual connotations are not only present in what the protagonists say, but are conveyed through a sexual subtext within the narration. Kennedy drops hints to her readers' awareness, thus integrating simple concepts like Horlicks into the realm of the erotic: they become witness of the subtle pacts not only between the lovers, but also between author and reader.

Helen laughs because she is increasingly becoming aware of this subtext, and Edward, seemingly not understanding what is going on, asks:

> "What? Am I a bad stirrer?" He looked worried happily, "What?" then just worried, "What?"
> "I think ... I'm not sure ... what I think."[13]

Helen knows exactly what she thinks, namely that she is 'stirred' by his activity, but seeing that he hasn't caught up yet, she replaces ephemeral words with physical touch to make him understand: 'She stood by him and squeezed his free hand around her wrist, her pulse.'[14] The way she tries to describe her feelings to him has to be free of obvious sexual allusions, so she chooses a word that connotes pregnancy ('expecting') and a quenched sexual desire. During her elaborations, she abstains from the use of a predicative phrase with clear subject and conjugated verb, and thus from a direct confession of her desire. Eventually, she wants Edward to check her pulse.

Subsequently, they change roles in this medical request: what is more, Helen gets to feel his voice. Exposing the neck during an erotic encounter signals acquiescence, normally a female gesture. By adopting it, Edward pledges to non-violence and surrender. The awkward search for words has reached its utmost frontier, from here on desire has to be ultimately authenticated by the body. But maybe this seemingly realistic scene is programmatic and stages precarious intimacy in itself. Here, the matching chemistry of the characters has to be taken into account. Kennedy's choice for the most implausible candidates for a romantic relationship — a religious and abused housewife and a scientist runner-up to the Nobel prize who also happens to be a porn addict — speaks for an experimental setup. Kennedy wants to prove a point: she hyperbolizes the genre of improbable romance. She wants to show what a narrative can do by making the reader believe that this love works out against all odds. And at the same time, its artifice illustrates the absurdity of romantic love, as it might remain unattainable forever.[15] If human communication is precarious and constantly haunted by the risk of misunderstanding, translation becomes an even more risky affair. Translating is in itself is a movement towards the other, who it tries to embody and to incarnate,[16] and it can only succeed by taking chances.

In Ingo Herzke's German version, Edward and Helen get through to each other a little easier. First of all, the Horlicks-scene becomes more of a foreplay and less of a struggle, allowing for a retardation prior to the sexual encounter. The hidden eroticism of their playfully innocent behaviour remains on plot level and does not extend to the narration itself: instead of Horlicks, they prepare hot chocolate — for the simple reason that Horlicks does not exist in German-speaking countries. Not to speak of the connotations that comes with it. In contrast to 'stirring', the German verb 'umrühren' carries no sexual connotation whatsoever. Additionally, the translator or editor replaced unconventional descriptions of physical processes with fairly conventional ones.[17]

The speech acts and thoughts of the protagonists are translated into semantically less ambiguous constructions, which cannot be related to typological differences between the languages. For example 'That's the same speed, but not the same thing' (Kennedy 1998, 273) is rendered 'Derselbe Pulsschlag, aber nicht derselbe Grund', with the mentioning of the pulse and translation of the non-specific 'thing' into the quite specific 'Grund' (reason) (2002a, 147); the same tendency to concretise can be observed in the translation of the idiomatic phrase in this sentence: 'I watch men shoving Perrier bottles where the sun will never shine [...]' (1998, 243) as 'Ich schau Männern zu, wie sie sich Perrierflaschen in den Arsch schieben [...]' (re-translated: '[...] how they shove Perrier bottles into their asses' (2002a, 113). Additionally, there are general idiomatic differences in the way that speakers of English and German address sexuality. Today, much of the vocabulary (especially of deviant) sexual practices has been influenced by English jargon, but remains outside of common usage. When Edward describes some pornographic content to Helen, he speaks of "the guy who loves to fist them"[18]. In German, this is rendered as: "der Typ, der am liebsten die Faust benutzt"[19] — 'the guy who prefers to use his fist'. While a specific practice is named in the source text, the translation relies on the next sentence to explain. The most striking difference is the German preference for swearwords taken from the lexicon of defecation; in English, as in most other

Western European languages, they are taken from the lexicon of sex and genitalia. In German, swearwords lose the touch of violent sexuality inherent to English. Once the sexuality of a text is expressed through words and deeds, this translational difficulty becomes endemic. For example, this is evident in the title story of the volume 'Indelible Acts' where a lover comments on a woman's vibrator:

> I fetched it through for him, still in the box, so that he could unveil it.
> "Fuck."
> My implement was longer, fatter — unmistakably larger than his. [...]
> He turned it in his hands like a condensed adultery.
> "Fuck."[20]

In both instants, the translation into German is — correctly, according to use — 'Scheiße'. But the intricate mechanism of sexualized conversation is lost with this choice. Translating A. L. Kennedy's stories risks missing the intimate connection between deeds and words, between the sexual acts described and the words that mould these descriptions. Her prose insists on a variant of speech act theory in at least two scenes of *Original Bliss*, as verbal sexual advances between the characters are authenticated by touching the Adam's apple and the voice chords: speaking is shown to be a touchable and therefore verifiable event, not dependent on the volatility of words alone, but recognizable as a physical act. Here, making love and making words literally converge.[21]

## Nicholson Baker: House of Holes

In contrast to A. L. Kennedy's careful dialogues and descriptions of sexual encounters on the verge of failure, Nicholson Baker's novels offer a concept of ingenuous, ironic and self-confident explicitness, as exemplified by the following passage:

> Lila's got us all doing the fucky-fuck and the sucky-suck and the humpy and the squirty and the juicy-Lucy and the ooh, ah, ooh. Everything we do they keep track of, and they know what we want most, and they want to milk us till our money's all gone and our balls ache, if we have balls [...]. Because it's the House of Holes, and is there anything worth paying court to more than a woman with a pretty face and two good titties and one hot switchy ass she wants to shove in your face? Hmm?[22]

In its coincidence of sexual lust and nonsensical, hyperbolic speech, the novel imitates and deconstructs the conventional language of pornography — language not of literature, but of video clips. They share explicitness and a focus on genital zones while simultaneously cultivating an intricate linguistic style. In the above quote, the combination of simplistic wordplay and onomatopoetic elements alludes to nursery rhymes or advertisement jingles, creating the grotesque effects.[23]

The 'House of Holes' is a place to which people are transported via a variety of circular openings. Here, they enjoy the realization of their wildest, most comical and absurd sexual phantasies. In short, it is *Alice's Adventures in Wonderland* for adults, not only in view of its fantastic plot, but also in terms of linguistics, as it explores the expression of complex and hitherto non-explored sensual experiences. While the sentences are often simple, the translator must find a way to render the puns, its idiomatic expressions, cultural allusions, onomatopoeia, unconventional metaphors for sexual organs. Baker calls this form of communication "dildo talk"[24], a form of speech that designates sexual arousal or attempts to create such. In addition, fantastic "masturboats" and "pornsucker ships" and other bizarre items populate Baker's "dildungsroman".[25]

Baker's most notorious novels, including *Vox* (1992) and *The Fermata* (1994), all benefit from the forceful combination of humour and sex, of intellectual and corporeal fun. They seem a programmatic format for the elements considered immoral in most literary histories: sex and laughter.[26] In his other novels, for example *The Mezzanine* 1988), *A Box of Matches* or *Travelling Sprinkler* (2013), Baker develops a narrative technique in which the most trivial details and practices of daily life are described in great detail and dominate the narration — protagonists describe the filling of a coffee filter or how they go about using a travelling sprinkler.[27] The two topics — sex and day-to-day living — appear different, but equally raise the question of canon, a main concern for Baker.[28] In writing about the uncanonised and the non-canonizable, he uses a diverse set of stylistic and rhetoric instruments, which conventionally designate high literature: sensibility to form, a high degree of *ornatus,* a wide range of stylistic parameters and allusions to canonic works of art.[29]

While Baker suggested in an interview that the comical-grotesque pornographic episodes in *House of Holes* stem from his own imagination,[30] many scenes highlight the text's intertextuality. The idea of a 'penis wash', as it exists in the 'House of Holes' probably goes back to Theodor W. Adorno, who mentions a similar construction. After giving an account of his phantasy in his *Dream Notes*, Adorno resumes: 'Woke up laughing.'[31] That Adorno, whose rejection of pornography is notorious, combines an erotic narration with humour, might have caused Baker's ironic motion to choose this phantasy. Other examples of intertextual references include the motif of a temporarily amputated arm: separated from its owner, this arm administers pleasure to the other sex. It refers to Yasunari Kawabata's story *One Arm* (片腕 *Kataude*), for it relates the story of a woman who lends her right arm to a man overnight.[32] This intertextual strategy highlights the secondary nature of sexual phantasy. It is not pure, original invention, but stems from one text and points to another. Similar to Baker's other works *Vox* and *The Fermata*, sexual acts are not merely recounted, but intimately interwoven with narrative techniques. Their mediated nature is always present.

The novel *Vox* tells of two people on the phone who tell each other of their sexual phantasies and experiences. Once again, mediality plays an important role for the narration insofar as the partners describe in detail what they cannot see. In *The Fermata*, protagonist Arno Strine has the extraordinary power to freezing time, just by pushing his glasses up. He uses such leaps in time for sexual experiments that he extends and refines over time. In several chapters, he writes or records porn stories and deposits them for some previously chosen woman to find as soon as the current of time resumes. He then watches the woman's reaction, always hoping that she will be stirred rather than irritated or appalled. In both novels, sexual activity is narrated and filtered through different media, be it a telephone, a film, the manuscript of a story or an audio-tape. This creates an ironic distance to the described acts which conventional pornography lacks. In *House of Holes*, Baker invents a parallel world only linked to reality through people's sexual phantasies. But it also inverts the real world: what is purely fantastic here becomes the only relevant truth over there, and vice versa.

## Critical reception

Eike Schönfeld's translation successfully transports this 'Book of Raunch' (the English subtitle) into German. While source and target texts cannot be said to exhibit considerable ruptures, the different reception of the book by literary critics deserves our critical attention. While American and English reviewers were irritated and repulsed — Matt Thorne writes in *The Independent:* 'The purpose of this smutty gibberish isn't clear'[33] — , German critique is at worst a little bored[34] and mostly enthusiastic.[35] The reaction is so unanimous on both sides that one cannot help but suppose that explicit literature has a different literary status in the Anglo-Saxon world, an assumption already expressed in Susan Sontag's essay *The Pornographic Imagination*.[36] Sontag, using examples from modern French literature like Pauline Réage's *Story of O* (*Histoire d'O*, 1954), argues that American literature has not integrated the stimuli of the European avant-gardes. However, Sontag's essay dates from 1966. One could suspect that literary criticism adheres to a traditional canon and is even more reluctant in its acceptance of literary innovations than authors themselves. This would have to be observed in a greater number of examples, though.

What can be said with respect to the authors discussed here is that A. L. Kennedy's and Nicholson Baker's erotic narratives differ radically from each other and inform different notions of sex. In Kennedy's work, sexual scenes are manifestations of the characters' urge to develop a working form of communication, be it verbal or corporeal. Therefore, it addresses one of the central topics of modern literature. The reader encounters uncertain allusions, *aposiopeses* and word repetitions to illustrate the characters' existential fragility and their awkwardness in their interpersonal contacts. Dialogue is as important as it is precarious, sexuality a form of communication equally important and endangered. Sexual scenes weave together descriptive, if sketchy plot elements, fragmented and faltering dialogue and suggestive vocabulary, thus extending the sexual situation into the narrative structure. In German, the fragmentary impression is not always rendered successfully and endangers the sexual subtext. In fact, German reviewers do not consider the novella (which was published separately, rather than with several other stories as it was in English) an example of erotic writing at all.[37] English and American reviews are much more aware of the topic,[38] but this might be so because they are able to view the whole story collection, in which other stories are also concerned with erotic love.

The case for Nicholson Baker's books is different. Here, language is not viewed as a fragile means of communication, but as creative matter. The observation of linguistic and realistic detail is central. As shown above, the author draws ideas from a wide range of intertextual references. His prose wants to escape the boring pornographic routine of naming the always identical parts by creating a whole dictionary of new names for them. He hyperbolizes and ironizes the narration of the sexual encounter by introducing fantastic elements, ranging from the standstill of time to the exchange of genitals. For the translator, wordplay is certainly a challenge, but Baker's typographic playfulness and the mediality of his language seem to be easier to handle than Kennedy's fragmentary, authentic expressions of love. Baker's obsession is not with sex, but with writing, respectively the interaction of both: the combination of words becomes a matter of arousal. The pleasure that lies in the production of words is also a central concept in Roland Barthes's essay *The Pleasure of the Text* (*Le plaisir du texte*, 1973), where he argues:

> If I read this sentence, this story, or this word with pleasure, it is because they were written in pleasure [...]. But the opposite? Does writing in pleasure guarantee — guarantee me, the writer — my reader's pleasure? Not at all. I must seek out this reader [...] *without knowing where he is*. A site of bliss is then created.[39]

Baker transforms Barthes's 'site of bliss' between the writer and the reader into a fictional place, where pleasure is granted and relished. To Barthes, writing and reading are bodily as well as creative activities and can thereby generate lust. His theory of writing and pleasure consciously includes erotic pleasure into a theory of text production. Baker's explicit texts put this into practice on a stylistically advanced level, by means of intertextual allusions and by amputations, transplantations and organ exchanges that reflect the human body as a machine. This humorous dimension defies the seriousness of much pornographic literature. Its mediality highlights the wilful and conscious production of pornography and exploits it as a playground for creativity.

## Works Cited

*Primary Sources*

ADORNO, THEODOR W., *Dream notes*, trans. by Rodney Livingstone, ed. by Christoph Gödde and Henri Lonitz (Cambridge: Polity, 2007).
BAKER, NICHOLSON, *Rolltreppe oder Die Herkunft der Dinge*, trans. by Eike Schönfeld (Reinbek b. Hamburg: Rowohlt, 1991).
—— *Vox* (New York, NY: Random House, 1992).
—— *The Fermata* (London: Vintage, 1994).
—— *Double Fold: Libraries and the Assault on Paper* (New York, NY: Random House, 2001).
—— *Eine Schachtel Streichhölzer*, trans. by Eike Schönfeld (Reinbek b. Hamburg: Rowohlt, 2004).
—— *The Anthologist* (New York, NY: Simon & Schuster, 2009).
—— *House of Holes: A Book of Raunch* (New York, NY: Simon & Schuster, 2011).
—— *Travelling Sprinkler* (London: Serpent's Tail, 2014).
KAWABATA, YASUNARI, *Träume im Kristall*, trans. by Siegfried Schaarschmidt (Frankfurt a.M.: Suhrkamp, 1974).

KENNEDY, A. L., *Original Bliss* (London: Vintage, 1998).
—— *Everything You Need* (London: Vintage, 2000).
—— *Gleissendes Glück*, trans. by Ingo Herzke (Frankfurt a.M.: Fischer, 2002).
—— *Alles was du brauchst*, trans. by Ingo Herzke (Berlin: Wagenbach, 2002).
—— *Indelible Acts* (London: Vintage, 2002).
—— *Hat nichts zu tun mit Liebe*, trans. by Ingo Herzke (Berlin: Wagenbach, 2003).
PLATO, *The Republic*, ed. by C. J. Emlyn-Jones (Oxford: Oxbow Books, 2007).

*Secondary Sources*

BARTHES, ROLAND, *Le plaisir du texte* (Paris: Éditions du Seuil, 1973).
—— *The Pleasure of the Text*, trans. by Richard Miller (New York, NY: Hill and Wang, 1975).
CURTIUS, ERNST ROBERT, *Lateinische Literatur und europäisches Mittelalter* (Tübingen: Francke, 1948; repr. 1993).
ILLOUZ, EVA, *Warum Liebe weh tut: Eine soziologische Erklärung*, trans. by Michael Adrian (Berlin: Suhrkamp, 2011).
KELLMAN, STEVEN, 'Promiscuous Tongues: Erotics of Translingualism and Translation', *Neohelicon*, 40 (2013), 35–45.
LUHMANN, NIKLAS, *Love as Passion: The Codification of Intimacy*, trans. by Jeremy Gaines and Doris L. Jones (Stanford CA: Stanford University Press, 1998).
SONTAG, SUSAN, *Styles of Radical Will* (London: Secker & Warburg, 1969).

*Reviews*

[ANON.], 'Original Bliss', *Publisher's Weekly*, 1 April 1999 <http://www.publishersweekly.com/978-0-375-40272-2> [accessed 2 August 2016].
CONRAD, PETER, 'Nicholson Baker: "Writing this book was the most fun I ever had": The American Author Discusses the Bizarre Sexual Fantasy World of His New Novel, House of Holes', *The Guardian*, 14 August 2011 <http://www.theguardian.com/books/2011/aug/14/nicholson-baker-house-holes-interview> [accessed 2 August 2016].
DIEZ, GEORG, 'Der Gott der geilen Dinge' [review on Baker, *Das Haus der Löcher*], *Der Spiegel*, 16 January 2012, pp. 130–31.
HARTWIG, INA, 'Alice in Pornoland' [review on Baker, *Das Haus der Löcher*], *Süddeutsche Zeitung*, 18 January 2012, p. 14.
HÜFNER, AGNES, 'Als Mrs. Brindle Fleischwürfel wendete' [review on Kennedy, *Gleissendes Glück*], *Süddeutsche Zeitung*, 9 December 2000, p. IV.
LASDUN, JAMES, 'Nicholson Baker's New Novel Reads Like a Ridiculous Porn-Fest' [review on Baker, *House of Holes*], The Guardian, 11 August 2011 <https://www.theguardian.com/books/2011/aug/11/house-holes-nicholson-baker-review> [accessed 2 August 2016].
LAURENCE, ALEXANDER, and DAVID STRAUSS, 'An Interview with Nicholson Baker' <http://www.altx.com/interviews/nicholson.baker.html> [accessed 2 August 2016].
LUEKEN, VERENA, 'Es ist genug Lust für alle da. Nicholson Baker hat seinen dritten pornographischen Roman geschrieben: "Das Haus der Löcher" ist eine Phantasie aus dem Schlaraffenland der Sexualität', *Frankfurter Allgemeine Zeitung*, 13 January 2012, p. 33.
LYNCH, THOMAS, 'Passion play. An abused wife and a self-help pornographer find redemption', *New York Times*, 14 February 1999 [accessed 2 August 2016].
MASLIN, JANET, 'One Man's Gluddle-Luddle Is Another's Squoosh Squoosh' [review

on Baker, *House of Holes*], *New York Times*, 7 August 2011 <http://www.nytimes.com/2011/08/08/books/house-of-holes-nicholson-bakers-book-of-raunch-review.html?_r=0> [accessed 2 August 2016].

MEIER, SIMONE: 'Der Wahnsinn wahrer Liebe' [rev. on Kennedy, *Gleissendes Glück*], *Der Spiegel*, 4 December 2000, p. 304.

RADISCH, IRIS, 'Belletristik' [contains a review on Kennedy, *Gleissendes Glück*], *Die Zeit*, 4 January 2001 <http://www.zeit.de/2001/02/BELLETRISTIK> [accessed 2 August 2016].

RADISCH, IRIS, 'Die Sex-jetzt-Taste drücken. Der amerikanische Autor Nicholson Baker wollte einen richtig supernetten, schönen Porno schreiben' [review on Baker, Haus der Löcher], *Die Zeit*, 26 January 2012 <http://www.zeit.de/2012/05/L-B-Baker> [accessed 2 August 2016].

STEIN, HANNES, 'Lüstern, ungeliebt, verloren. Voller unanständiger Miniaturen: Nicholson Bakers "Haus der Löcher"', *Die Welt*, 14 January 2012 <http://www.welt.de/print/die_welt/vermischtes/article13814771/Luestern-ungeliebt-verloren.html> [accessed 2 August 2016].

THORNE, MATT, '*House of Holes* by Nicholson Baker', *The Independent*, 2 September 2011 <http://www.independent.co.uk/arts-entertainment/books/reviews/house-of-holes-by-nicholson-baker-2347494.html> [accessed 2 August 2016].

## Notes to Chapter 4

1. Roland Barthes, *Le plaisir du texte* (Paris: Éditions du Seuil, 1973), p. 10.
2. See Niklas Luhmann, *Love as Passion: The Codification of Intimacy,* trans. by Jeremy Gaines and Doris L. Jones (Stanford, CA: Stanford University Press, 1998), pp. 121–22. According to Luhmann, from the 18th century on, literary love stories are less concerned with moral concerns and more with conflicts in communication about intimate matters: 'Incommunicability no longer just meant that passion set rhetoric off stuttering, upset the most eloquent speech and thus betrayed itself. It no longer involves psychic and situationally determined disturbances that were themselves suitable for passionate communication. Rather, categorical barriers to communication now began to emerge. It was not the failure of skillfulness that is the problem, but the lack of a capacity for sincerity' (p. 122).
3. See Eva Illouz, *Warum Liebe weh tut: Eine soziologische Erklärung,* trans. by Michael Adrian (Berlin: Suhrkamp, 2011), p. 300.
4. See Luhmann, *Love as Passion*, p. 153.
5. A. L. Kennedy, *Original Bliss* (London: Vintage, 1998), p. 273.
6. At one point, Edward describes himself as 'terminally inarticulate when it comes to people' (p. 260) and mentions his father's abuse of his mother (p. 266).
7. "I think ... I'm not sure ... what I think" (p. 273).
8. E.g. the use of sexually connoted swearwords in A. L. Kennedy, *Everything You Need* (London: Vintage, 2000), pp. 528–32.
9. Kennedy, *Original Bliss*, p. 310.
10. Helen draws the connection between the two when saying: "If I'd been a video, you'd have watched" (Kennedy, *Original Bliss*, p. 266).
11. "He ran the curl of one finger down the slope of her cheek until the muscles in her back began to shudder" (Kennedy, *Original Bliss*, p. 273).
12. As an informal expression, 'to make Horlicks of' signifies 'to make a mess of'. See Oxford English Dictionary, Entry to *Horlick*, <http://www.oed.com/view/Entry/88467?redirectedFrom=Horlick&> [last retrieved on 2 August 2016].
13. Kennedy, *Original Bliss*, p. 273.
14. Ibid.
15. In her book, Illouz shows how our picture of what erotic love should be is permeated by deep-

set contradictions at its very core: emotionally and economically stable long-term relationships do not normally coincide with the continuing experience of intense romantic passion — yet in our society, people tend to want both. See Illouz, *Warum Liebe weh tut*, p. 31.
16. For a detailed account of translation metaphors, see Steven Kellman, 'Promiscuous Tongues: Erotics of Translingualism and Translation', *Neohelicon*, 40 (2013), 35–45.
17. The "broad need, drumming" is rendered as "ein großes Verlangen, das pulsiert" (a great desire, pulsing), "the kind of time his blood was keeping" as "der Rhythmus seines Blutes" (the rhythm of his blood); Kennedy, *Original Bliss*, pp. 273–74 and A. L. Kennedy, *Gleissendes Glück*, trans. by Ingo Herzke (Frankfurt a.M.: Fischer, 2002), p. 147.
18. Kennedy, *Original Bliss*, p. 243.
19. Kennedy, *Gleissendes Glück*, p. 113.
20. A. L. Kennedy, *Indelible Acts* (London: Vintage, 2002), p. 105 and A. L. Kennedy, *Hat nichts zu tun mit Liebe*, trans. by Ingo Herzke (Berlin: Wagenbach, 2003), p. 24. See also A. L. Kennedy, *Everything You Need* (London: Vintage, 2000), pp. 528–32 and A. L. Kennedy, *Alles was du brauchst*, trans. by Ingo Herzke (Berlin: Wagenbach, 2002), pp. 536–39.
21. See Kennedy, *Original Bliss*, pp. 273 and 309.
22. Nicholson Baker, *House of Holes: A Book of Raunch* (New York, NY: Simon & Schuster, 2011), p. 229.
23. The translation gets the syntax wrong, turning the rhetorical question ("What could be more worth the effort?") into a direct one by misreading the comparative 'more': "Denn es ist ja das Haus der Löcher, und hat es wirklich Wert, mehr als eine Frau mit einem hübschen Gesicht und zwei guten Tittis und einem heißen Tausch-Arsch zu hofieren, den sie einem ins Gesicht rammen will?" (re-translated: 'Could it be worth to court more than one woman [...]?') (Nicholson Baker, *Haus der Löcher* (Reinbek: Rowohlt, 2011), p. 278).
24. Nicholson Baker, *The Fermata* (London: Vintage, 1994), p. 212.
25. See Baker, *House of Holes*, pp. 164, 72 and 208.
26. For the exclusion of laughter from the canon, see Ernst Robert Curtius, *Lateinische Literatur und europäisches Mittelalter* (Tübingen: Francke, 1948; repr. 1993), pp. 421–23. Furthermore, Plato pleads for the banishment of intensive laughter and its representation from social intercourse among educated people and from the arts. See Plato, *The Republic*, ed. by C. J. Emlyn-Jones (Oxford: Oxbow Books, 2007), p. 389.
27. "I wrote a book that ignored all the grand themes that the novel is supposed to take up. That was in *The Mezzanine*" (Alexander Laurence and David Strauss, 'An Interview with Nicholson Baker', <http://www.altx.com/interviews/nicholson.baker.html> [accessed 2 August 2016]).
28. His novel *The Anthologist* reflects on the canon of English poetry and metrics. Similarly, his long essay *Double Fold,* where he argues for a preservation of historical newspapers and library card catalogues.
29. Often enough, Baker chooses strange pretexts or extraordinary techniques to integrate them. E.g. "There's so many bad meta-novels that are out there. *The Fermata* is, I hope, making fun of that." (in an interview with Laurence/Strauss, 1994). Peter Conrad names some of the canonic works of art that *House of Holes* alludes to, see Peter Conrad, 'Nicholson Baker: "Writing this book was the most fun I ever had": The American Author Discusses the Bizarre Sexual Fantasy World of His New Novel, House of Holes', *The Guardian*, 14 August 2011, <http://www.theguardian.com/books/2011/aug/14/nicholson-baker-house-holes-interview> [accessed 2 August 2016].
30. 'It's my personal funhouse[.]" (Ibid.)
31. In his dream protocols, published posthumously in 2005, the German philosopher notes under the date of Dec 17th, 1967: "I had an indescribably beautiful and elegant mistress; she reminded me of A., but had something of the grand dame about her. I was extremely proud of her. She told me that I absolutely had to acquire a prick-washing machine. I pointed out that I took a bath every day and that I kept myself scrupulously clean. She replied that only such a machine could guarantee that one would be free of every objectionable odour in the relevant place. Only if I were to buy one would she make love to me with her mouth. I was uncertain whether she might not be a saleswoman for the firm that manufactured the machine. Woke up laughing"

(Theodor W. Adorno, *Dream Notes*, trans. by Rodney Livingstone, ed. by Christoph Gödde and Henri Lonitz (Cambridge: Polity, 2007), p. 75). In *House of Holes*, Shandee, the woman who arrives with Dave's bodiless arm, is instantly delegated to a feature called 'the Penis Wash' (Baker, *House of Holes*, pp. 36–37). An allusion to Adorno would also ironically refer to his assumption that pornography lacks the Aristotelic criterion for all literary narration, namely that it has beginning, middle, and end. See Susan Sontag, *Styles of Radical Will* (London: Secker & Warburg, 1969), p. 39).

32. *Ein Arm* (片腕, *kata-ude*, 1963/1964), in: Yasunari Kawabata, *Träume im Kristall*, trans. by Siegfried Schaarschmidt (Frankfurt a.M.: Suhrkamp, 1974), pp. 76–110.
33. Matt Thorne, '*House of Holes* by Nicholson Baker', *The Independent*, 2 September 2011, <http://www.independent.co.uk/arts-entertainment/books/reviews/house-of-holes-by-nicholson-baker-2347494.html> [accessed 2 August 2016].
34. Iris Radisch, 'Die Sex-jetzt-Taste drücken. Der amerikanische Autor Nicholson Baker wollte einen richtig supernetten, schönen Porno schreiben' [review of Baker, *Haus der Löcher*], in *Die Zeit*, 26 January 2012 <http://www.zeit.de/2012/05/L-B-Baker> [accessed 2 August 2016]. Other German reviews include Verena Lueken, 'Es ist genug Lust für alle da. Nicholson Baker hat seinen dritten pornographischen Roman geschrieben: "Das Haus der Löcher" ist eine Phantasie aus dem Schlaraffenland der Sexualität', *Frankfurter Allgemeine Zeitung*, 13 January 2012, p. 33; Ina Hartwig, 'Alice in Pornoland' [review of Baker, *Das Haus der Löcher*], *Süddeutsche Zeitung*, 18 January 2012, p. 14; and Georg Diez, 'Der Gott der geilen Dinge' [review of Baker, *Das Haus der Löcher*], *Der Spiegel*, 16 January 2012, pp. 130–31.
35. The same applies to English and American reviews of *The Fermata*. For *House of Holes* see James Lasdun, 'Nicholson Baker's New Novel Reads Like a Ridiculous Porn-Fest' [review on Baker, *House of Holes*], *The Guardian*, 11 August 2011 <https://www.theguardian.com/books/2011/aug/11/house-holes-nicholson-baker-review> [accessed 2 August 2016]; Janet Maslin, 'One Man's Gluddle-Luddle Is Another's Squoosh Squoosh' [review on Baker, *House of Holes*], *New York Times*, 7 August 2011 < http://www.nytimes.com/2011/08/08/books/house-of-holes-nicholson-bakers-book-of-raunch-review.html?_r=0> [accessed 2 August 2016].
36. See Sontag, *Styles of Radical Will*, pp. 40–41.
37. E.g. Radisch, 'Die Sex-jetzt-Taste drücken'; Simone Meier, 'Der Wahnsinn wahrer Liebe' [review of Kennedy, *Gleissendes Glück*], *Der Spiegel*, 4 December 2000, p. 304; and Agnes Hüfner, 'Als Mrs. Brindle Fleischwürfel wendete' [review of Kennedy, *Gleissendes Glück*], *Süddeutsche Zeitung*, 9 December 2000, p. IV.
38. E.g. [anon.], 'Original Bliss', *Publisher's Weekly*, 1 April 1999 <http://www.publishersweekly.com/978-0-375-40272-2> [accessed 2 August 2016]; Thomas Lynch, 'Passion play. An abused wife and a self-help pornographer find redemption', *New York Times*, 14 February 1999 [accessed 2 August 2016].
39. Roland Barthes, *The Pleasure of the Text*, trans. by Richard Miller (New York: Hill and Wang, 1975), p. 4.

CHAPTER 5

# Seduced by Preconditions: The Eroticism of Power, Money and Love in Goethe, Sacher-Masoch and E. L. James

*Carina Gröner*

Romances sell well; erotic romances can sell and spread even faster: E. L. James' *Fifty Shades* trilogy (2011–2012), said to be 'the fastest-selling adult series of all time',[1] had sold more than 100 million copies worldwide by 2014. The three novels, published between 2011 and 2012, have been translated into 51 languages, including Arabic and Hindi.[2] How did this stylistically rather plain 'Billionaire Romance'[3] achieve such success throughout the world? According to Eva Illouz best-sellers like *Fifty Shades* series reflect the cultural values and key experiences of their historical period and cultural background.[4] But these values and experiences do not need to be communicated openly in order to resonate with the readers:

> [A] book can also resonate when it formulates something that many people *want* to say but are unable to say, either because they do not dare to say it [...] or because they do not have the language to say it [...].[5]

These experiences can also be communicated between the lines. Taboos often hamper direct communication; this is particularly true in the field of eroticism. Niklas Luhmann's sociological concept of 'symbolically generalized communication media'[6] is helpful in this regard, as it introduces non-verbal entities as codes of communication in addition to language and scripture. His theory points out that 'society is an *operationally closed social system based on communication*'.[7] Besides language, there are also other communication media in society, which work like codes in certain fields and replace verbal communication.

For Luhmann, these 'success media',[8] such as power, money, love and art, endow individual actions with information about expectable motivations in complex modern societies without using language as a direct communication tool.[9] Functioning like codes, they raise the likelihood of successful communication. Luhmann argues:

> Symbolically generalized communication media establish a novel kind of link between conditioning and motivation. They gear communication in a given media area, for example, in the money economy or the exercise of power in political office, to certain conditions that enhance the chances of acceptance even in the case of "uncomfortable" communication. For example, goods are supplied or services rendered if (and only if) they are paid for.[10]

These 'success media'[11] work beyond the boundaries of national languages and translation because they also serve as preconditions for social behaviour within the societies in which they appear. Arguably, erotic situations can be seen as an area that produces scenes of 'uncomfortable communication'[12] in need of codes to replace direct communication in order to achieve understanding. Therefore, the narratives of erotic situations do not only amuse or arouse the reader, but also reverberate with precise ideas about social status and indicate possibilities of social mobility.

Apart from language, what we consider erotic is always largely informed by its social preconditions. According to Eva Illoz's *Cold Intimacies* (2007), the invention of romance accompanied the raise of capitalism.[13] In a globalized and mainly capitalist world, preconditions like love, power and money play an important role in the depiction of erotic situations in literature. In prose, gift-giving often acts as a narrative device that translates symbolically generalized communication media into plot.

In this paper, I examine how such social preconditions are depicted in erotic literary texts from different centuries — by Johann Wolfgang Goethe, Leopold von Sacher-Masoch, and E. L. James. In all three texts, it is the action of gift-giving that serves as a medium of communication in erotic matters. In Goethe's *Sorrows of Young Werther* (*Die Leiden des jungen Werthers* (1774/1787), the protagonist gives his female friend a translation of Ossian texts, moves her with this gesture and wrongly interprets that emotional movement as a sign of mutual erotic attraction. In Sacher-Masoch's *Catherine II: Tales from the Russian Court* (*Katharina II: Russische Hofgeschichten*, 1891), a princess gives away military promotions to her favourite lovers and sometimes a death penalty to those who do something wrong. In James's *Fifty Shades* (2011–12), gift-giving becomes a non-verbal form of communication that, on the one hand, relieves the capitalist and materialist Christian Grey from speaking about his feelings and, on the other hand, counterbalances the strong hierarchical structure of the couple's sexual practices.

## Goethe: Love

The German poet Johann Wolfgang von Goethe (1749–1832) lived and wrote during a historical period that saw great changes in the depiction and practice of marriage and coupling. One of the most important changes at this time was the nascent idea of romantic love. Niklas Luhmann's study *Love as Passion: The Codification of Intimacy* sees this historical change not in the emotions themselves, but in the symbolic code of communication about them.[14] 'Love semantics' coincide with certain speech patterns that enable individuals to put feelings into words and participate in the social practice of coupling and marriage.[15] In the early 17th century, the semantic love code aimed at idealisation; it saw the loved object itself as the very reason for love. Around 1800, the idea of romantic love became self-referential: the reason for love inhered in the existence of the feeling itself. Through the emergence of the bourgeoisie, this love code spread widely and made the idea of romantic love a precondition for marriage in general.

The idea of romantic love as a basis for marriage, however, is fairly recent and extends over the last two hundred years only. Within this code, love is seen as a passion that arises passively. It comes suddenly and unites opposing feelings like pleasure and pain. This paradoxical love code serves as a precondition for communication about intimacy in Goethe's most commercially successful novel, *The Sorrows of Young Werther*. It was one of the first novels to use love as a code of communication and has been translated into 55 languages.[16] It presents the tragic life story of a young dilettante, Werther, who describes himself as an artist, but does not produce anything resembling a work of art. He falls in love with Lotte, a woman who is engaged to a more successful man and thus out of his reach. Throughout the novel, Werther fails to find an appropriate social position for himself and eventually kills himself.

The novel consists largely of Werther's letters and gives detailed evidence of the paradoxical love code in use. In the letter dated 16 June, he describes the moment he fell in love with Lotte:

> To tell you in orderly fashion how it happened that I have met one of the most charming creatures will be difficult. I am cheerful and happy, and thus no good at writing chronicles.[17]

> [Dir in Ordnung zu erzählen, wie's zugegangen ist, daß ich eins der liebenswürdigsten Geschöpfe habe kennen lernen, wird schwer halten, ich bin vergnügt und glücklich, und so kein guter Historienschreiber.][18]

Despite this admission, 'writing chronicles' is exactly what he continues to do at length. The couple's first moment of physical contact occurs when they are dancing at a ball. As everyone is dancing, a thunderstorm suddenly strikes and scares the young people. Lotte proposes a game:

> We'll play Counting, she said. Pay attention! I'll go round the circle from right to left, and you will count as I go around, each one the number that's his, it has to go like bushfire, and whoever stumbles or makes a mistake gets a box on the ear, and so up to a thousand. [...] I myself received two slaps, and with inward pleasure thought I noticed that they were stronger than those meted out to the others.[19]

> [Wir spielen Zählens, sagte sie, nun gebt Acht! Ich gehe im Kreise herum von der Rechten zur Linken, und so zählt ihr auch rings herum jeder die Zahl die an ihn kommt, und das muß gehn wie ein Lauffeuer, und wer stockt, oder sich irrt, kriegt eine Ohrfeige, und so bis tausend. [...] Ich selbst kriegte zwei Maulschellen und glaubte mit innigem Vergnügen zu bemerken, daß sie stärker seien, als sie den übrigen beizumessen pflegte.][20]

In this situation of implicit communication, Werther begins to interpret the slap in a simple children's game as a sign of intimacy. Under normal circumstances this form of touch would be considered undesirable, but here the sensation becomes readjusted to the paradoxical nature of the love code. Immediately afterwards, when the two young people are alone, Werther interprets his encounter with Lotte as highly 'erotic'. It is a very sentimental situation: Werther describes his feelings for Lotte by using several liquid metaphors that match the tears in her eyes. The whole situation reaches its climax not in erotic action but in the reference to a sentimental poet:[21]

> She was standing, resting on her elbows, her glance penetrated the scene, she looked up at the sky and at me, I saw her eyes fill with tears, she placed her hand on mine and said — Klopstock — I immediately remembered the magnificent ode that was in her thoughts, and sank in the stream of feelings she poured over me with this one word.[22]

> [Sie stand auf ihrem Ellenbogen gestützt und ihr Blick durchdrang die Gegend, sie sah gen Himmel und auf mich, ich sah ihr Auge tränenvoll, sie legte ihre Hand auf die meinige und sagte — Klopstock! Ich versank in dem Strome von Empfindungen, den sie in dieser Losung über mich ausgoß.][23]

This scene illustrates and exposes the self-referential nature of the love code. Werther's description of the situation highlights the paradox: here, eroticism derives from the mutual understanding of the reference to a sentimental poet and not from physical contact. The feelings are second-hand and only mirror their artistic representation. After this first encounter, Werther increasingly derives self-esteem from his interpretation of Lotte's feelings towards him and sees her love more and more as a general precondition for his existence, like in the letter from 13 July.[24]

In the last erotic scene, when Werther visits Lotte against her orders and reads out passages from his own Ossian translation,[25] different layers of translation lead to erotic action. Infused with literary feelings that Werther had partially evoked through his own choice of words in the translation, he intends to steal a kiss and so 'translates' the love code into action:

> The whole weight of these words fell on the unfortunate man. Frantic with despair, he threw himself down before Lotte, seized her hands, pressed them to his eyes, against his forehead, and an intimidation of his terrible purpose seemed to fly though her soul. Her senses became confused, she pressed his hands, pressed them against her breast, bent down to him with a melancholy gesture, and their burning cheeks touched. The world was blotted out for them. He threw his arms around her, pressed her to his breast, and covered her trembling stammering lips with raging kisses. — [...] She tore herself away, and in fearful confusion, trembling between love and anger she said: This is the last time! Werther! You shall not see me again![26]

> [Die ganze Gewalt dieser Worte fiel über den Unglücklichen, er warf sich vor Lotten nieder in der vollen Verzweiflung, faßte ihre Hände, druckte sie in seine Augen, wider seine Stirn, und ihr schien eine Ahndung seines schröcklichen Vorhabens durch die Seele zu fliegen. Ihre Sinnen verwirrten sich, sie druckte seine Hände, druckte sie wider ihre Brust, neigte sich mit einer wehmütigen Bewegung zu ihm, und ihre glühenden Wangen berührten sich. Die Welt verging ihnen, er schlang seine Arme um sie her, preßte sie an seine Brust, und

deckte ihre zitternde stammelnde Lippen mit wütenden Küssen. [...] Sie riß sich auf, und in ängstlicher Verwirrung, bebend zwischen Liebe und Zorn sagte sie: Das ist das letztemal! Werther! Sie sehen mich nicht wieder.]²⁷

Here, love clearly serves as Luhmann's symbolically generalized communication medium and as a precondition for the erotic experience: the depiction of the paradoxical love code not only morally legitimises Werther's kissing a married woman but also creates understanding in the reader for his eventual suicide. In the light of the code, we can draw conclusions about motivations. The two protagonists follow different value systems regarding marriage: Werther radically follows the idea of love marriage and becomes more and more involved in his own translations of non-verbal signs from Lotte that he sees as support for his interpretation. However, Lotte prefers her new husband's status and social position to mere affection.

Therefore, Goethe's *Werther* demonstrates the moral function of the love code, which provides the reader with a morally acceptable motivation for intimate actions. Since Goethe's time, love and the love code have served as a precondition for marriage and intimacy and as a means to establish ethical behaviour and economic stability for the rising bourgeoisie.

### Sacher-Masoch: Power

Another symbolically generalized communication medium, that often plays a pivotal role in erotic relations, is power. According to Eva Illouz '[h]aving sex is a way of performing and reproducing social and cultural structures because sexuality contains responses to such questions as who has power [...]'.[28] Luhmann divides power into two different phenomena: first, as the straight-forward force of coercion, and second, as an abstract system and communication medium of a political system. In the first case, power helps to solve the problem of choosing between many possibilities. In the case of a threat, that means people choose the less unpleasant option and surrender. Threats, however, are not enough to make power the communication medium of a political system. As a consequence, power must be generalized and legitimized, for example through the monopoly of force executed by the police or the armed forces.[29]

The combination of power and eroticism is an important topic for the Austrian author Leopold von Sacher-Masoch (1836–1895). The term *masochism* was coined after this theme became popular in his works, most notably in *Venus in Furs* (*Venus im Pelz*, 1870) and *Catherine II* (1891). In the latter, power is the ultimate precondition for eroticism. Yet, unlike *Venus in Furs*,[30] the *Catherine II* stories depict power not only in a limited and theatrical erotic setting, but also as institutionalized power in combination with love as a precondition for eroticism. Therefore, these stories are much better at showing how power works as a communication medium in this context. These short stories revolve around Catherine the Great, Empress of Russia (1729–1796). In many of the *Catherine* stories, women appear in powerful military positions and use this power to fulfil their erotic desires.[31] Already, their institutionalized powerful position thus communicates a possible threat in the case of a legal offence. A very good example is the story 'Amor with a Corporal's Cane'

['Amor mit dem Korporalstock'].³² When the story begins, Princess Mellin and Empress Catherine the Great of Russia are chatting about erotic adventures, and the princess complains about the infidelity of her ex-lover, a colonel, and men in general:

> [I am going to take revenge on him and his whole mendacious and unfaithful sex; I hate men more than ever, I despise them so much that I cannot understand how it was possible that such weak and feckless creatures governed us for so long.³³
>
> [I]ch werde Rache an ihm nehmen, an dem ganzen lügnerischen, treulosen Geschlechte; ich hasse die Männer mehr als je, ich verachte sie so sehr, daß ich nicht begreifen kann, wie es möglich war, daß diese schwachen willenlosen Geschöpfe so lange über uns geherrscht haben.]³⁴

The story stages the meltdown of gender roles in an aristocratic setting and presents dominant females as the agents of this change. Women are characterised as powerful and seem equitable throughout the text: the princess is described as a 'terrifying beauty' ['Furcht einflößende[...] Schönheit'],³⁵ Catherine's face is said to display the 'beautifully strict traits of a Nero' ['schön strengen Züge eines Nero'].³⁶ The empress soon decides to grant her friend's request the for revenge by giving her command over one of her regiments, just because, as she says, 'indeed it would amuse me' ['Es würde mich in der Tat unterhalten']³⁷ — a statement that reveals her pleasure in exercising power. However, the empress does not put the princess's former lover under her command before checking on his motivations, which of course soon prove to be misogynistic, as is clear from the colonel's complaint:

> It was quite convenient, as long as women raised their children, as long as they cooked, spun or sewed, but nowadays they preside over the scholars and command regiments.
>
> [I]ndes war es doch auszuhalten, solange die Frauenzimmer ihre Kinder aufzogen, kochten, spannen und nähten, jetzt aber präsidieren sie die Gelehrten und kommandieren Regimenter.]³⁸

On the one hand, this deed shows Catherine's imperial vision as a fair ruler, as she does not arbitrarily punish people but rationally makes decisions about her legal actions. On the other hand, she acts as a woman, who champions emancipatory ideas and fulfils the erotic wishes of her revenge-seeking friend. When the princess delivers a speech to her soldiers she points out that she wants to respect the soldiers' honour, even if they have to be punished. Simultaneously, she announces the abolition of the cane.³⁹ This statement reveals the irony of the story's title: since the corporal's cane is a sign of male military despotism, a female Amor's cane can only be metaphorical and show how much better women are in this position.

However, the story does not lack erotic connotations: on the one hand, the narrator keeps calling the princess a 'beautiful female commander' ['schönen weiblichen Obersten']⁴⁰ and uses half a page to depict the details of her figure and uniform.⁴¹ On the other hand, he repeatedly describes her delight in exercising power: 'the dreaded female despot made the soldiers play run the gauntlet until the wrinkles had disappeared from her forehead' ['die gefürchtete Soldatendespotin [...] [ließ sie] so lange Knute und Spießruten spielen [...], bis die Falten von ihrer Stirne verschwunden waren'].[42] Apart from that, the princess uses her military power not only for her personal pleasure but also to establish more enlightened behaviour on the part of her subjects. She tests her former lover by having him train new recruits in front of her eyes. One extremely beautiful but incapable recruit poses problems. But while the colonel wants to beat him, the princess insists on patiently showing him how to load a gun, which naturally results in a highly erotic scene.[43] She even decides to educate him so that he becomes 'a man of education und fine manners' ['ein Mann von Bildung und feinen Sitten'].[44] Soon, the chauvinistic colonel is downgraded, and the young soldier is put in his position. After an attack on his new superior, however, the jealous lover is sentenced to death, only to be given amnesty by the princess. Eventually, they confess their love to each other and get married.

In this short story, the princess's use of power combines eroticism with educational and emancipatory ideas. In this vein, power serves as a symbolically generalized communication medium, because used in its institutionalized form it constantly communicates the superiority of the women bearing rank. Furthermore, power is also used as a precondition for erotic situations, not only because the plot features dominant women in military costumes and positions, but also because they use their power of control to enforce an emancipatory agenda. In contrast to tragic Werther, the love code here serves as an underlying principle to morally legitimize a surprisingly happy ending that would otherwise appear implausible.

### E. L. James: Money

In addition to love and power, material wealth is often thought to be a common driving force in erotic relationships. The reason for this lies in the historical development of marriage, which, until the 18th century, was openly motivated by social structure and economic reasoning.[45] Since the 18th century, however, love has come to complement economic reasoning in order to add moral value. Eva Illouz coined the term 'Emotional Capitalism'[46] in that context:

> Emotional Capitalism is a culture in which emotional and economic discourses and practices mutually shape each other [...] in which emotional life — especially that of the middle classes — follows the logic of economic relations and exchange.[47]

In a modern, functionally differentiated society, money serves as a generally accepted code in most economic exchange situations:

> Materially, money functions as a measure of value and as a basis for comparing different goods. [...] Socially, money functions as a universally applicable means of exchange [...] money opens up possibilities for comparison.[48]

This possibility of comparison applies to all relationships: the value of one's presents indicates one's value in the eyes of the giver. While there are openly communicated economic exchange operations in the erotic context, like prostitution or strip-tease, this money-based evaluation also underpins more deliberate erotic relationships.

A very good example is E. L. James's *Fifty Shades of Grey* trilogy (2011–12), where money and material wealth serve as symbolically generalized communication media. Critics have described the books as a Cinderella story:[49] Anastasia Steele, a rather ordinary literature student, starts an erotic relationship with Christian Grey, a rich, successful, handsome, and sexually kinky businessman. In the third and final volume, their relationship even leads to marriage and the birth of a child. Except for the graphic descriptions of specialized sexual practices, it adjusts the traditional fairytale narrative slightly and seems rather out-dated, especially when held up against Sacher-Masoch's emancipatory ideas from more than a century earlier. But if we understand *Venus in Furs* and the *Catherine II* stories as the beginning of a historical period of emancipation, then *Fifty Shades of Grey* coincides with its consolidation. According to Eva Illouz, popular texts like *Fifty Shades of Grey* 'encode and address social contradictions'[50] and 'offer (symbolic) resolutions':[51] clearly it is the different social statuses of Ana and Cristian Grey, as well as the difference in their sexual experiences that serve as social contradictions. The resolution can be found in a relationship that finally leads to a morally acceptable marriage motivated by love and 'it is the sex that is the pink paper in which the love story is wrapped.'[52]

The sexual practices depicted in *Fifty Shades* can be described as BDSM, an acronym derived from *bondage*, *discipline*, and *submission* (or *sadism* and *masochism*). It usually includes a contract between the dominant and the submissive, and according to some critics, such formal agreements about role allocations can be interpreted as compensations for the psychological insecurities in real life.[53] Eva Illouz argued in *Hard-Core Romance* that the depiction of BDSM in *Fifty Shades* can be seen as a liberating act for women.[54] Such psychological insecurity marks the very beginning of *Fifty Shades of Grey*: since the narration is told from the autodiegetic perspective of Anastasia, her sensations of inner life are related in great detail. The first book opens with a portrait of her low self-esteem: 'I scowl with frustration at myself in the mirror'.[55] These symptoms remain unchanged prior to the first meeting with the male protagonist: 'The uncertainty is galling, and my nerves resurface, making me fidget.'[56] In contrast to her, Christian Grey is defined by ample descriptions of his material wealth from the start, as Ana relates:

> My destination is the headquarters of Mr. Grey's global enterprise. It's a huge twenty-story office building, all curved glass and steel, an architect's utilitarian fantasy, with GREY HOUSE written discreetly in steel over the glass front.[57]

Anastasia, coming from what appears to be a lower-middle-class family, is intimidated. In the course of the novels, however, her value gradually increases along with her self-esteem and her erotic courage — a development that is indicated not so much by words as by the monetary value of the presents she receives from Grey. Here, money clearly serves as a symbolically generalized communication medium, as it communicates the growing emotional value that Christian Grey assigns to Ana without using verbal communication.

Whereas in Werther, the present of the Ossian translation serves the purpose of paraphrasing feelings that were verbally expressed before, the presents in *Fifty Shades* are reduced to their plainly spoken monetary function and replace communication about emotional value. The first present Ana receives from Grey is a first edition of Thomas Hardy's *Tess of the D'Urbervilles* from 1891, 'for fourteen thousand dollars',[58] along with a card featuring a quotation from the book:

> Why didn't you tell me there was danger? Why didn't you warn me? Ladies know what to guard against, because they read novels that tell them of these tricks...[59]

In picking a quotation that renders Anastasia's possible reaction to him, Christian Grey's intertextual reference puts the novel on par with classics dealing with sexually taboo topics. Furthermore, it brings forward a self-reflexive comment on the reader's own interest in learning more about unspoken social preconditions and mechanisms. Soon after receiving this expensive present, Ana and Christin Grey start their affair.[60] More impressive demonstrations of wealth ensue: after losing her virginity to him and agreeing to sign a BDSM contract, she is presented with a 'red hatchback car, a two-door compact Audi'.[61] Anna accepts these expensive presents only 'on loan',[62] after all, she is subconsciously aware of the reciprocal structure of the gifts, which socially degrade the person who does not return the favour.[63]

In the second volume of the trilogy, *Fifty Shades Darker*, the economic struggle within the relationship becomes even more obvious: the exchange logic becomes more mutual. Ana gives her lover a model aeroplane kit and, in return, receives an iPad with full access to the British Library.[64] Shortly afterwards, Grey buys the company Ana is working for and thus disturbs the fragile economic and moral balance of their relationship, as Ana puts it angrily: 'And, technically, it's gross moral turpitude — the fact that I am fucking my boss's boss's boss.'[65] Arguing out these difficulties about the balance of economic and moral values leads to a tension between the two that unloads in sexual interaction.

The climax of this economic layer of meaning is the auction scene in the second volume, where Christian pays '[o]ne-hundred thousand dollars for the lovely Ana'[66] during a charity event just to have the first dance with her. With this action, he uses money again as a communication medium: Ana's value is now openly compared with the value of other girls, and finally ascertained to be extremely high. In this scene, the amount of money replaces elaborate explanations about the value of a person. More than that, the message of this monetary action is easily understood without translation in different cultural settings as long as capitalistic values are in force. Here, the connection between the monetary and the erotic realm becomes most evident: Christian's goal is a sexually functional and efficiency-based relationship, as also evidenced by his anxious care for Ana's physical health.[67] Christian intends to maintain the value of his expensive 'product'. Nevertheless, especially in the third volume of the trilogy, *Fifty Shades Freed*, love again strongly complements money as a second symbolically generalized communication medium and a necessary moral legitimisation of the relationship. The couple gets married, and an engraving on 'the platinum Omega watch' confirms the link between money and love: 'Anastasia | You are my more | My love | My life | Christian'.[68] Eventually, Ana is given the publishing company she used to work for as a belated wedding present,[69] a step that consequently elevates her to a position that is socially and financially comparable to that of her husband.

## Conclusion

As we observe in the three literary examples, implicit communication about the preconditions of social structures is an important part of what is considered erotic. Sex and intimacy are social interactions. An analysis of symbolically generalized communication media, which often control the 'uncomfortable communication' in erotic matters without the necessity of using words, as Luhmann argues,[70] helps to unpack motivations and implicit structures of social life. There is a specific erotic-*cum*-economic argument in the narratives of taboo subjects, as brought forward by E. L. James's, Leopold von Sacher-Masoch's and Goethe's texts.

In E. L. James's and Sacher-Masoch's works, social advancement and female emancipation are the main driving forces, while power and money form an implicit second layer of social communication that works beyond words. Sacher-Masoch's *Catherine* stories about powerful women could not match the time's cultural values and experiences. They did not translate. By contrast, the *Fifty Shades* romances could depict an almost globally common female fantasy of gaining a high social status by offering erotic favours and simultaneously staying morally upright and securing their status by marriage. The love code, as featured in Goethe's *Werther*, connects these different driving forces and provides them with a moral legitimisation of intimacy. This proves that 'success media' provide the necessary non-verbal codes for social communication about erotic matters and determine their preconditions.

## Bibliography

### I. Primary texts

GOETHE, JOHANN WOLFGANG, 'Die Leiden des jungen Werthers', in *Johann Wolfgang Goethe, Sämtliche Werke* 1.2, ed. by Gerhard Sauder (Munich: Hanser, 1987).
JAMES, E. L., *Fifty Shades Darker* (London: Arrow Books, 2012).
—— *Fifty Shades Freed* (London: Arrow Books, 2012).
—— *Fifty Shades of Grey* (London: Arrow Books, 2011).
NEUGROSCHEL, JOACHIM (trans.), *Venus in Furs* (New York, NY: Penguin Classics 2010).
PIKE, BURTON (trans.), *The Sorrows of Young Werther* (New York, NY: The Modern Library, 2004).
SACHER-MASOCH, LEOPOLD VON, *Katharina II: Russische Hofgeschichten* (Berlin: Schreitersche Verlagsbuchhandlung, ca. 1890).

### II. Critical literature

DEAHL, RACHEL, 'E. L. James: Person of the Year', *Publishers Weekly* (December 3rd 2012), 21–22.
FLOOD, ALLISON, 'Fifty Shades of Grey Trilogy has sold 100m copies worldwide', *The Guardian*, (27 February 2014).
GRATZKE, MICHAEL, *Liebesschmerz und Textlust: Figuren der Liebe und des Masochismus in der Literatur* (Würzburg: Königshausen und Neumann, 2000).
ILLOUZ, EVA, *Cold Intimacies: The Making of Emotional Capitalism* (Cambridge: Polity, 2007).
—— *Hard Core Romance* (Chicago, IL: The University of Chicago Press, 2014).
KLYMENKO, IRYNA (et al.), 'Begriffe', in *Luhmann Handbuch, Leben — Werk — Wirkung*, ed. by Oliver Jahrhaus and Armin Nassehi (Stuttgart: Metzler, 2012), pp. 69–128.

LEHNERT-RAABE, KATHARINA, ...mein Werther — dein Werther — unser Werther... „Die Leiden des jungen Werthers" von J. W. Goethe. Ein Roman überwindet Grenzen, (exhibition at Frankfurter Goethe-Haus, February, 6–24 March 2013).

LUHMANN, NIKLAS, *The Differentiation of Society* (New York, NY: Columbia University Press, 1982).

—— *Love as Passion* (*Liebe als Passion*), trans. by Jeremy Gaines and Doris L. Jones (Cambridge, MA: Harvard University Press, 1986 [1969]).

—— *Theory of Society*, 2 vols (Stanford, CA: Stanford University Press, 2012).

MAUSS, MARCEL, *Essai sur le don: Forme et raison de l'échange dans les societés archaïques* [*An Essay on the Gift: The Form and Reason of Exchange in Archaic Societies*] (Paris: Presses Universitäires de France, 2007 [1925]).

REESE-SCHÄFER, WALTER, *Luhmann zur Einführung* (Hamburg: Junius, 1992).

ROUNDING, VIRGINIA, *Catherine the Great: Love, Sex and Power* (London: Hutchinson, 2006).

SAAKE, IRMHILD (et al.), 'Theoriestränge', in *Luhmann Handbuch, Leben — Werk — Wirkung*, ed. by Oliver Jahrhaus and Armin Nassehi (Stuttgart: Metzler, 2012), pp. 41–67.

WHITEHALL, HALEY, *Romance tropes for Novelists and Screenwriters* (E-Book: Pronoun, 2017).

## Notes to Chapter 5

1. Rachel Deahl, 'E. L. James. Person of the year', *Publishers Weekly* (December 3rd 2012), 21–22.
2. See Allison Flood, 'Fifty Shades of Grey Trilogy has sold 100m copies worldwide', *The Guardian* (27 February 2014) <https://www.theguardian.com/books/2014/feb/27/fifty-shades-of-grey-book-100m-sales> (last retrieved 10 December 2017).
3. Haley Whitehall, *Romance tropes for Novelists and Screenwriters* (E-Book: Pronoun, 2017).
4. Eva Illouz, *Hard Core Romance* (Chicago: The University of Chicago Press, 2014), p. 22.
5. Ibid.
6. Niklas Luhmann, *Theory of Society*, 2 vols (Stanford, CA: Stanford University Press, 2012), 1, p. 121.
7. Ibid., p. 122. [*Emphasis in the original.*]
8. Luhmann, *Theory of Society*, 1, 121.
9. See Irmhild Saake (et al.), 'Theoriestränge', in *Luhmann Handbuch, Leben — Werk — Wirkung*, ed. by Oliver Jahrhaus and Armin Nassehi (Stuttgart: Metzler, 2012) p. 59.
10. Luhmann, *Theory of Society*, 1, pp. 121–22.
11. Ibid., p. 121.
12. Ibid., p. 122.
13. Eva Illouz, *Cold Intimacies: The Making of Emotional Capitalism* (Cambridge: Polity, 2007), pp. 5–7.
14. See Niklas Luhmann: *Love as Passion*, trans. by Jeremy Gaines and Doris L. Jones (Cambridge, MA: Harvard University Press, 1986).
15. See Walter Reese-Schäfer, *Luhmann zur Einführung* (Hamburg: Junius, 1992), p. 58.
16. See Katharina Lehnert-Raabe, ...mein Werther — dein Werther — unser Werther... „Die Leiden des jungen Werthers" von J. W. Goethe. Ein Roman überwindet Grenzen, (exhibition at Frankfurter Goethe-Haus, February, 6–24 March 2013), p. 34.
17. Burton Pike (trans.), *The Sorrows of Young Werther* (New York, NY: The Modern Library, 2004), p. 21.
18. Johann Wolfgang Goethe, *Sämtliche Werke* 1.2, ed. by Gerhard Sauder (Munich: Hanser, 1987), p. 207.
19. Pike, *The Sorrows of Young Werther*, p. 29.
20. Goethe, *Sämtliche Werke* 1.2, p. 215.
21. At the time, Friedrich Gottlieb Klopstock (1724–1803) was well known for his overly emotional poems.
22. Pike, *The Sorrows of Young Werther*, pp. 29–30.
23. Goethe, *Sämtliche Werke* 1.2, p. 215.

24. See Goethe, *Sämtliche Werke* 1.2, p. 226; Pike, *The Sorrows of Young Werther*, p. 42.
25. James McPherson's *Poems of Ossian* (1760) was popular among the educated readership of Goethe's time. Mistaken for authentic translations from ancient Gaelic, these poems were regarded as important testimonials of Norse mythology. In *Werther*, the *Ossian* passages are Goethe's own translations into German (see Goethe, *Sämtliche Werke* 1.2, pp. 284–90).
26. Pike, *The Sorrows of Young Werther*, pp. 137–38.
27. Goethe, *Sämtliche Werke* 1.2, pp. 290–91.
28. Illouz, *Hard Core Romance*, p. 36.
29. See Iryna Klymenko (et al.), 'Begriffe', in *Luhmann Handbuch*, pp. 69–128, (p. 97–98).
30. Joachim Neugroschel (trans.), *Venus in Furs,* (New York: Penguin Classics, 2010).
31. Under Catherine the Great, a noble woman could hold a military rank because she would share her husband's rank. See Virginia Rounding, *Catherine the Great: Love, Sex and Power* (London: Hutchinson 2006), p. 82. However, the active and official use of military power executed by women, as described by Sacher-Masoch, remains largely fictional.
32. Leopold von Sacher-Masoch, *Katharina II: Russische Hofgeschichten* (Berlin: Schreitersche Verlagsbuchhandlung, ca. 1890), pp. 52–86.
33. As there are no official English translations of the *Catherina* novellas, all English translations of the original German were made by the author, C. G.
34. Ibid., p. 52.
35. Ibid., p. 51.
36. Ibid., p. 50.
37. Ibid., p. 53.
38. Ibid., p. 56.
39. See ibid., p. 59.
40. Ibid., p. 57.
41. See ibid., p. 58.
42. Ibid., p. 71.
43. See ibid., pp. 63–65.
44. Ibid., p. 67.
45. See Luhmann, *Love as Passion*, p. 145.
46. Illouz, *Cold Intimacies*, p.5.
47. Ibid.
48. Niklas Luhmann, *The Differentiation of Society* (New York, NY: Columbia University Press, 1982), p. 207.
49. See Deahl, 'E. L. James. Person of the year', p. 21.
50. Illouz, *Hard Core Romance*, p. 25.
51. Ibid.
52. Ibid., p.35.
53. See Michael Gratzke, Liebesschmerz und Textlust: Figuren der Liebe und des Masochismus in der Literatur (Würzburg: Königshausen und Neumann, 2000), p. 68.
54. See Illouz, *Hard Core Romance*, p. 79–81.
55. E. L. James, *Fifty Shades of Grey* (London: Arrow Books, 2011), p. 3.
56. Ibid., p. 6.
57. Ibid., p. 4.
58. Ibid., p. 55.
59. Ibid., p. 54.
60. See ibid., pp. 57–58.
61. Ibid., p. 261.
62. Ibid., p. 262.
63. See Marcel Mauss, *Essai sur le don: Forme et raison de l'échange dans les societés archaïques* [An Essay on the Gift: The Form and Reason of Exchange in Archaic Societies] (Paris: Presses Universitäires de France 2007 [1925]), p. 219.
64. See E. L. James, *Fifty Shades Darker* (London: Arrow Books, 2012), p. 40.
65. Ibid., p. 58.

66. Ibid., p. 149.
67. See James, *Fifty Shades of Grey*, p. 411.
68. E. L. James, *Fifty Shades Freed* (London: Arrow Books, 2012), p. 56.
69. See ibid. p. 147.
70. Luhmann, *Theory of Society*, I, 121–22.

CHAPTER 6

# Audio-Erotics

*Johannes D. Kaminski*

In our contemporary pornographic imagination, it appears that visual stimuli prevail. A recent internet phenomenon, however, serves as a reminder of the auditory dimension of human sensuality. *Autonomous sensory meridian response* (ASMR) videos feature softly articulated noises that viewers — or much rather listeners — report as triggering 'a tingling, static-like sensation across the scalp, back of the neck and at times further areas in response to specific triggering audio and visual stimuli.'[1] In contrast to visual erotica, however, it is difficult to pinpoint what is so erotic about these whispering and hissing voices — or if they are erotic at all. The indeterminate nature of a stimulus, it appears, is the natural ally of the erotic, which Roland Barthes identified as 'appearance-as-disappearance':[2] rather than representing an identifiable moment of presence, it is marked by flashes of perception. The erotic emerges in the gap between two articles of clothing or through the brief presence of a noise that gives away more than intended.

    The present article discusses representations of sound in erotic literature. The corpus is comprised of an idiosyncratic selection of texts from discrete cultural contexts. Johann Wolfgang Goethe's classic novel *Wilhelm Meister's Years of Apprenticeship* (*Wilhelm Meisters Lehrjahre*, 1795/96) serves as a starting point. As a comparably tame text, it was widely translated and illustrates some of the challenges involved in the translation of audio-erotics. Furthermore, it also gives a first taste of the epistemological issue addressed in the following sections: the disjunction between sound and its source. Although Li Yu's novel[3] *Carnal Prayer Mat* (肉蒲團 *Rou Pu Tuan*, 1693) and Goethe's cycle of poems *Roman Elegies* (*Römische Elegien*, 1795) have little in common otherwise, they share a strong predilection for sonic representations of sex. They also share a similarly uncertain position within their respective literary canons. Despite praise for its aesthetic merits, Goethe's cycle of poems was dismissed as pornography,[4] and on a similar account, Li Yu's work, which faced censorship during the reign of the Qing dynasty, only belatedly entered the literary canon.[5] While comparative analysis of the two texts cannot draw on any form of shared intellectual background, they bring forward an analogous struggle between sound and text, between subjective reflexivity and physical action.

    In order to do justice to the gradual escalation of audio-erotic experiences, this article abandons chronological order in favour of a systematic approach. At the beginning stand innocent representations of the trope *sound as a by-product of sexual activity*. Gradually, we turn our attention to the trope *sound as a replacement for sexual activity*.

### Theory: sound as a double-edged sword

Owing to physiological preconditions, our eyes can deflect external stimuli, but not our ears. Eyes have lids, ears do not. Such distinctions matter, as they are accompanied by a whole set of judgements regarding their reliability. We regard certain sensory organs as particularly prone to delusion. The realm of auditory stimuli is often seen as particularly dangerous, as they inhibit or undermine rational thought. Surprisingly, such reservations are not limited to European Enlightenment philosophy, where the light metaphor articulates a clear preference for visual observation. As Jie Guo's contribution in this volume demonstrates, the Chinese tradition conceives of the sexual act primarily as a visual phenomenon (see the subchapter *Voyeurism*). The effect of sound on the human psyche, in contrast, is met with an ambivalent assessment.

The history of philosophy has a poor record of engaging with sound. As Salomé Voegelin argues, '[c]ritical discourse does badly in dealing with sound as it assumes and insists on the gap between that which it describes and its description — it is the very opposite of sound, which is always the heard, immersive and present.'[6] Instead, music — that is, sounds put together in melodic, harmonic or rhythmical combination — prompted philosophers to articulate judgements, warnings and recommendations. In Chinese philosophy, the idea that rational control should be exercised over the selection of inflowing auditory stimuli is featured in such early texts as the *Book of Rites* (禮記 *Li Ji*), a core compendium of Confucian thought.[7] Emphasizing the interconnectedness between mind and sound, the text draws on the importance of music: 'All modulations of sound take their rise from the mind of man; and music is the intercommunication of them in their relations and differences' [凡音者,生於人心者也;樂者,通倫理者也][8]. Every type of sound, it is assumed, produces one type of emotional reaction.[9] Ex negativo, this attention to sounds implies that their wrong use sets the wrong emotions in motion. Consequently, the Xunzi, an important Confucian text, not only reminds virtuous men to abstain from listening to licentious sounds and/or music (淫聲), but warns rulers of its dangers. In a somewhat overblown suggestion, the text urges rulers to put those involved in the performance of such illicit sounds to death.[10]

Ancient Greek philosophy places equal importance on music. Plato considers musical training 'a more potent instrument than any other, because rhythm and harmony find their way into the inward places of the soul, on which they mightily fasten, imparting grace, and making the soul of him who is rightly educated graceful, or of him who is ill-educated ungraceful'.[11] While this judgement shares Confucianism's positive assessment of music, it does not subscribe to the same condemnation of 'wrong' sounds, as brought forward by Xunzi. Poets are banned in Plato's Ideal State, not musicians who play odd tunes. This blasé attitude changes with the Enlightenment, when sensory perception was growingly considered a danger to the rational faculties.

In contrast with his contemporaries Immanuel Kant and the Marquis de Sade,[12] the encyclopaedist Denis Diderot displays a more nuanced appreciation of the fragility of human rationality. In his dialogue with Jean le Rond d'Alembert, he compares the human soul to vibrating strings: once plucked, they not only vibrate for an extended period of time, but also make adjacent strings vibrate. According to this metaphor, reason is threatened by the noise of empirical stimuli and the interlinked associations it produces.[13] This metaphoric description of human rationality is directly opposed to classical light metaphors, where 'the mind mimetically represents the outside world while at the same time remaining separate from it.'[14] Diderot's chain of reaction among the strings points towards the unruly aspects of our consciousness. Light follows a strict, foreseeable course, but sound travels and takes detours.

Johann Gottfried Herder goes a step further and views sound as an intruder into a largely passive human psyche. While he regards vision as the most loyal ally of rational thought, hearing proves a double-edged sword: on the one hand, it potentially exposes the individual to unwelcome stimuli; on the other hand, it allows for an authentic experience of the world. In *Kritische Wälder*, he argues:

> The sense of hearing alone is the most heartfelt, the deepest sense. While not as plain as the eye, it lacks its coldness; while not as thorough as our feelings, it lacks its crudeness. But it corresponds just as closely with our sensations as the eye with our ideas and our feeling with our imagination. Nature itself proves this closeness: the key to our soul is through our ears and through language itself.[15]
>
> [Das Gehör allein ist der innigste, der tiefste der Sinne. Nicht so deutlich wie das Auge, ist es auch nicht so kalt; nicht so gründlich wie das Gefühl, ist es auch nicht so grob; aber es ist so der Empfindung am nächsten wie das Auge den Ideen und das Gefühl der Einbildungskraft. Die Natur selbst hat diese Nahheit bestätigt, da sie keinen Weg zur Seele besser wußte als durch Ohr und — Sprache.][16]

Arguably, the European Enlightenment only belatedly discovers the dangers involved in auditory perception. While Xunzi already proposes harsh punishment for the dissemination of lecherous music, Enlightenment thinkers discover that rationality is easily affected by the auditory sense. As the following section demonstrates, the threshold between sound and music is a particularly interesting field of audio-erotics.

### The semantics of clicking heels

In *Wilhelm Meister*, the protagonist's exposure to external stimuli forms an important part of the narrative. As one of the first novels that leave behind the determinism of the realist genre, the narration focusses on how Wilhelm Meister makes sense of the exterior events that guide his life journey.[17] Although sensual experiences inevitably form part of his subjective journey, the narrator is reluctant to share them directly with the reader. While his first sexual experiences are related in quasi-religious terminology and another one-night-stand is shrouded in mystery, Philina's clicking shoes enrich the novel with a complex erotic motif.

In company of Wilhelm and Serlo, a theatrical director, Philina, an attractive dancer, places her mules on the table, only to have Serlo become strangely excited. After a while, he holds a short lecture on the sound of clicking heels:

> It's night, we are in bed, and hear a rustling. We are startled, the door opens, and we hear a sweet little piping voice, something creeps in, the curtains swish, *click! clack!* the mules fall to the ground, and whoosh! we're no longer alone. Oh that sweet, unique sound of mules falling on the floor. The smaller they are, the finer they sound. You may talk about nightingales, murmuring brooks, rustling winds, organs and pipes, I'll stick with my *click! clack!* — that is the best tune to dance to, over and over again.[18]

> [Es ist Nacht, man liegt im Bette, es raschelt, man schaudert, die Türe tut sich auf, man erkennt ein liebes pisperndes Stimmchen, es schleicht was herbei, die Vorhänge rauschen, klipp! klapp! die Pantoffeln fallen, und husch! man ist nicht mehr allein. Ach der liebe, der einzige Klang, wenn die Absätzchen auf den Boden aufschlagen! Je zierlicher sie sind, je feiner klingt's. Man spreche mir von Philomelen, von rauschenden Bächen, vom Säuseln der Winde und von allem, was je georgelt und gepfiffen worden ist, ich halte mich an das *Klipp! Klapp!* — *Klipp! Klapp!* ist das schönste Thema zu einem Rondeau, das man immer wieder von vorne zu hören wünscht.][19]

Serlo's conditioning by the sound 'Klipp! Klapp!' occurs in three steps: first, the narrator finds himself in a state of child-like abandonment. This phase of confusion and anxiety is then interrupted by the sudden entrance of his lover, who announces her arrival through a set of noises that culminate in the sound of dropping heels. Subsequently, a blissful state is induced by her physical proximity. In what seems like excessive praise for the sound, Serlo invokes cliché motifs of romantic poetry only to underscore his shoe fetish.[20] Strikingly, Serlo's speech glosses over the lover herself, who, after all, is the source of the sound. One learns nothing about her feet or her physique, not to mention her personality. It seems as if the sound has taken on a life of its own. Eventually, Philina interrupts his reverie:

> "Click! Clack!" she said, giving him such a sharp blow with the heel that he withdrew his hand with a yelp. "I'll teach you to think otherwise about my mules," said Philine with a laugh.[21]

> ["Klipp! Klapp!" rief sie, indem sie ihm einen derben Schlag mit dem Absatz versetzte, daß er schreiend die Hand zurückzog. "Ich will euch lehren bei meinen Pantoffeln was anders denken!" sagte Philine lachend.][22]

Since she is using the cherished object itself to hit him, it remains unclear whether she means to reward or to punish his passion.

In eighteenth century German, the onomatopoeia used by Sero and Philina to refer to her mules is a common indicator for a broad variety of sounds, ranging from the sound of heels, as featured in the above passage, to the rattling of a mill wheel to the monotonous sound of alexandrines.[23] In his English rendition (1835),

Thomas Carlyle reproduces the onomatopoeia almost identically as 'Clip! clap!'[24] In French, Aloïse Christine de Carlowitz's 1843–translation established 'clic, clac', a wording which Blaise Briod reproduces in his post-war rendering.[25] More recent translations render the original 'Klipp! Klapp!' in English slightly different as 'click-clack!'[26] and 'Click! Clack!'[27], in Italian as 'clip clap!'[28], in Spanish as '¡clip!, ¡clap!'[29] and in Brazilian Portuguese as 'clap! clap!'[30]. Only the Chinese rendering breaks with this auditory consistency, as Feng Zhi's first full translation reads: 的橐!的橐!'[31] In romanisation, the acoustic difference becomes evident: di-tuo! di-tuo! While the first syllable is a filler, the second (tuo) is an established onomatopoeia designating footsteps.[32] Yang Wuneng's translation opts for 劈！啪!'[33] (pi! pa!), endowing the heels with bellicosity, as these characters indicate hitting sounds.[34]

As Peter Fenves argues, onomatopoeia indicate the '"primitive" stratum of historical languages', an observation that led early scholarship to identify them with the beginning of human language.[35] Nonetheless, heels that emit sounds belong to a semantic complex difficult to balance. In the case of *Wilhelm Meister*, the sexual symbolism of Philina's shoe forces the translator to make a decision regarding the appropriate level of physicality. While Serlo's shoe-speech can be interpreted as idiosyncratic and bizarre, Philina's reaction is comparably difficult to shrug off as trivial. As she takes her mules back, she deliberately admits her promiscuity: 'Just look how I have bent them! They're much too wide for me now'[36] ['Wie ich sie krumm getreten habe! Sie sind mir viel zu weit.'][37] In literature, the identification of shoes with female genitalia is an established trope: modern fairy-tales like Giambattista Basile's *Cinderella* (1634) and Charles Perrault's *Cendrillon* (1697) feature lost shoes that evoke the male desire to slip it back on the owner's foot, a metaphor for other forms of penetration.[38] From a psychoanalytical perspective, there is hardly another motif that so elegantly sublimates the most fundamental sexual experiences: according to the child psychologist Bruno Bettelheim, heels covered in blood denote period blood and, when worn out, lost virginity.[39]

Consequently, early translators took offense and looked for ways to rephrase or even omit this passage. Dillon Boylan's 1855-translation, for example, was not mentioned above, as it omits Serlo's erotic shoe-eulogy. Holding Philina's slippers, he confines his speech to pointing out their 'first-rate workmanship'. Likewise, Boylan avoids her admission of promiscuity, as he changes her words for: 'You have squeezed them [i.e. her slippers] till they are quite spoiled; you have made them too large.'[40] Thomas Carlyle's translation, aimed at introducing Goethe to an English audience,[41] also takes offense at this sexually charged passage and tiptoes around it. Again, by attributing the worn-out condition of the heels to Serlo, Philina's sexual agency is neutralised, as she cries: 'You have squeezed them all! They are far too wide for me!'[42] Given the established tradition of erotic writing in French, it is not surprising that Aloïse Christine de Carlowitz's translation of 1843 follows a different procedure. Herself a writer of sentimental novels that openly engage with adultery,[43] she renders Philina's self-aware comment as 'Comme je les ai gauchis'.[44] Unfortunately, there is no contemporary translation in Chinese. Feng Zhi's and Yang Wuneng's translations were published during a period in which high heels were widely worn by Chinese women. In 1795 A.D., however, when *Wilhelm Meister* was first published, their shoes would have certainly not produced a hearty 'Klipp! Klapp!', but rather a faint dragging sound; after all, women, especially performers like Philina, were expected to have bound feet.[45]

Philina's clicking heels trigger a complex semantic process that reaches far beyond the translator's dilemma of how to render this highly charged passage. Serlo's idiosyncratic digression, notably his disregard for the love act itself, indeed addresses some of the most pertinent issues at stake with audio-erotics. In the next section, we move on to Goethe's erotic poetry, which demonstrates that Serlo's eulogy touches upon a dangerous implication of auditory erotics.

### Goethe's alleged celebration of the bodily

A recent study by Veit Erlmann shows how German Romantics, most notably Wilhelm Heinse, built on the primacy of the ear and dropped Herder's precaution against its potential threat to rationality. What is more, by emphasizing sensual passivity over cognitive activity, Heinse celebrated the erotic dimension of hearing by 'linking, in a mystical, almost Dionysian hypertrope, hearing with sex'.[46] In his polar conception of the world, the ear also stands in for 'female' receptivity; the voice, for 'male' penetration. More so than Heinse, Goethe chooses sound as a pivotal marker of erotic situations within the *Roman Elegies*.

Owing to its obscenity, the originally second elegy did not make it into the final publication. Its doggerel verse describes the process leading up to a sexual act. The lover first peels off the girl's cotton dress, then carries her onto a shaky bed and portrays a strong image of rough sex by means of a sound reference:

> Uns ergötzen die Freuden des echten, nacketen Amors
> Und des geschaukelten Betts *lieblicher knarrender Ton*.[47]

The creaking sound leaves little to the imagination and challenges the reader's sense of propriety. In David Luke's much reprinted translation, however, this unabashed description is toned down. Rather than merely creaking noisily, these sounds culminate in music:

> Ours is the true, the authentic, the naked Love; and beneath us,
> Rocking in rhythm, the bed creaks the dear song of our joy.[48]

The emphasis on the physical strain on the bed frame recalls Michail Bakhtin's notion of carnival, which overcomes excessive rationality through its celebration of the bodily.[49] In relating this erotic encounter to the grotesque and physical, the *Elegien* defy the Romantic transfiguration of the beloved. Strikingly, the subjective experience of the couple plays a subordinate role, as two bodies meet. Free of moral qualms, Goethe's apocryphal poem is best equipped to challenge eighteenth-century aesthetic and cultural norms, as Eleanor ter Horst argues.[50]

The fifth *Elegie* brings forward a more complex encounter that, as I will demonstrate, contradicts the cliché notion that the *Elegien* celebrate sexual jouissance. Here, the narrator and his lover, Faustine, are taking a post-coital nap, allowing the wide-awake poet to recall the synchronicity of sexual act and poetic inception:

> Oftmals hab ich auch schon in ihren Armen gedichtet
> Und des Hexameters Maß, leise, *mit fingernder Hand*,
> Ihr auf den Rücken gezählt.⁵¹

It is left unsaid how this 'fingernde Hand' counts the hexameter: maybe his fingertips softly beat her skin, maybe the meter is only reproduced via increased pressure on the girl's skin. Luke's translation, however, opts for a more prominent strike:

> Often I even compose my poetry in her embraces,
> Counting hexameter beats, *tapping them out on her back*
> Softly, *with one hand's fingers*.⁵²

The juxtaposition of poetic production and love-making leaves what the narrator considers his priority unclear. It is difficult to conceive of both actions as mutually complimentary, as erotic encounters do not follow strict rhythmical regimes (excluding contemporary hard core pornography). Uwe Japp infers that the poet is caught in a dilemma from this discrepancy: while intending to advance his poetic production, he finds himself caught in a life of debauchery.⁵³ If one is not inclined to take the poet for a complete greenhorn and, instead, takes his search for Antiquity's lost glory seriously, then his 'erratic' behaviour becomes apparent. In this context, 'erratic' indicates the loss of a previously fixed trajectory, as the narrator's love-making slowly fades into the background. Representing far more than an incidental gesture, his concern for metric accuracy sets the semantic hierarchy right: the poet does not intend to please, but strives to live up to the main purpose of his Roman sojourn: to advance his studies. His primary aim is to produce poetry according to Latin models set by Catullus, Tibullus and Ovid; only in a second step does he find himself in a lover's arms, one who enables him to reimagine pleasures enjoyed by his Roman predecessors. To put it pointedly, in the eyes of the German lover, Faustine is a metronome to advance poetic creativity. Although dactyls are derived from Ancient Greek δάκτυλος (dáktylos, 'finger'),⁵⁴ the poem exemplifies how far this form of speech is removed from the instrument of touch; after all, poetic speech is only ever conceived *post factum*, when the object of touch has already disappeared.

If the erotic can be described as 'appearance-as-disappearance', then both poems are located at different ends of the spectrum. While in the first text the bed's creaks result in an excess of 'appearance', the second show how these hexameter lines removes the narrator from his sexual encounter — until the erotic 'gap' almost disappears. In lieu of the lover, the heroes of a bygone era of Antiquity appear as the poet's true addressee. By means of an allegory, the poem's final lines introduce his actual object of desire: 'Eros recalls, as he tends our lamp, how he did the same service / For his Triumvirs, the three poets of Love, long ago'⁵⁵ ['Amor schüret die Lamp' indes und denket der Zeiten, / Da er den nämlichen Dienst seinen Triumvirn getan'].⁵⁶ Only the attendance of representatives of the lost glory of Antiquity can satisfy the poet's desire. As Amor and the Triumvirs are invoked as voyeurs to ennoble the physical act, the erotic encounter itself becomes a mere extension of the poet's work in the archive of a past that has disappeared.

Akin to Serlo's odd digression on clicking heels, the poet engages with sound in a manner that allows it to develop a libidinal life of its own. By almost detaching it from the lover's body, such passages force the sexual act itself into the background and, instead, address 'erratic' sources of pleasure.

### Eavesdropping and onomatopoeia

The best way to experience sound, however, is not tapping rhythmic patterns on one's partner, but to follow Amor's example and eavesdrop on two people making love. Such scenes are fairly common in Chinese vernacular literature. Li Yu's prose text *Carnal Prayer Mat* is especially significant with respect to audio-erotics, as it contrasts prominently with the nostalgic sexuality in Goethe's elegies. Here, scenes involving sounds feature onomatopoeia that exceed the obscenity of a bed's creaking. Furthermore, they facilitate narrative digressions that are not cut short like Serlo's sermon, but elaborate on the disturbing nature of audio-erotics in great detail.

At one point, the protagonist Vesperus finds himself interested in a beautiful married woman, Yanfang. Since she intends to avoid a possibly disappointing affair with a stranger, she asks her ugly neighbour to step in for her. Amid darkness, Vesperus mistakes her for Yanfang. Meanwhile, the latter eavesdrops on the couple and takes note if this potential lover is worth the trouble. Taking Yanfang's perspective, the narrative emphasizes the acoustic dimension of their love-making. The perspective shifts between the factual description of the hero's physical moves and the acoustic output of the woman, whose passionate cries not only serve as an indicator for her state of arousal, but also for Vesperus's sexual prowess:

> 笑了一笑,就運動起來,起初幾下就還當不起,每送一次,就叫一聲「啊嗄」,送到半百之數就不見到聲了。及至送到半百之後,有重新起來「啊嗄」,起初是疼痛的「啊嗄」,如今是快樂的「啊嗄」,抽到數百之後,那夫人就有無限的淫聲交出來[。]⁵⁷

After a while, Yanfang dismisses her neighbour and, much to the lover's surprise, takes her place.

In Patrick Hanan's English translation, however, this straight-forward sequence of actions is complicated by the translator's inserted comments on her passionate cries:

> Laughing, he began to move again. She could not bear the first few thrusts and let out an *aiya*! with each one. But then, after fifty or more thrusts, nothing more was heard from her-until, after a hundred, she began crying *aiya*! once more, but in delight now, rather than pain. (*Aiya* has a range of meanings.) After several hundred strokes she began making numerous wanton moves and uttering countless cries of passion, enough to make it impossible for a man to restrain himself.⁵⁸

There is little consistency in this translation. First, Hanan renders the woman's scream 啊嗄 not according to the correct transliteration, which would read 'a-a' (or alternatively 'a-sha'), but replaces her cry with a far more conventional Chinese exclamation: 'aiya' (啊呀). While 'a-a' is rare, vernacular texts frequently feature Hanan's exclamation. Nonetheless, it is not common in the English language, thus hardly conducive to the reading flow. Secondly, he inserts a comment in parenthesis pointing out that the imprecise utterance *aiya* has 'a range of meanings', which are not further specified. Albeit in a clumsy manner, Hanan's translation points to the important observations that the original is part of a linguistic system which is largely incompatible with the target language, English. While Indo-European languages can merely transcribe sounds into a sequence of phonemes, the Chinese language drags whole body parts into the text: the original characters representing Yanfang's screams (啊嗄) feature the 'mouth' radical (口) on the left.

Furthermore, in contrast to the European literary canon, onomatopoeia are legitimate forms of expression in the Chinese classics. After all, the opening line of the *Book of Songs* (詩經), perhaps the oldest and most influential collection of Chinese poetry, reads: '*Kuan, kuan*, cry the ospreys' [關關雎鳩].[59] Therefore, it is appropriate that Franz Kuhn, the author of the novel's first translation into a European language (German), invests more thought in his rendering. He opts for bold onomatopoetics:

> [F]röhlich lachend [...] begann [er] nach Kräften zu werken und zu walken. Anfangs löste sein Walken bei ihr jedesmal, wenn es nach unten ging, ein Aufstöhnen, ein 'hach ... bh ...!' aus. Nach einem halben Hundert Tiefstößen verstummte sie. Nachdem das Hundert überschritten war, war es von neuem aus ihrem Munde zu vernehmen, das stöhnende 'hach ... bh ...!' Anfangs hatte ihr Stöhnen Schmerz bedeutet, jetzt bedeutete es Wonne.[60]

By resorting to his own onomatopoeia, Kuhn but allows the text to exhibit its own idiosyncratic sound, as there are no references for 'hach ... bh ...!' in German. Strikingly, a re-translation of Kuhn's text into English keeps this peculiar expression.[61]

Kuhn's decision pays homage to Li Yu's systematic approach to audio-erotics. In a comparably unsentimental manner, the author does not stop short of classifying the sounds women make during sex. Acting as a mouthpiece for the savvy author, Sai Kunlun lectures Vesperus about his exclusive knowledge. Having often climbed into wealthy households at night-time, Sai Kunlun knows the ins and outs of female sexuality just by silently spying on the sexual activity of its residents. First and foremost, he shares his insight into the 'three unrestrained ways' [三種浪法] of how women articulate their state of arousal. Their 'first way' is fake, he argues, and only intends to trigger male desire: 'although they cry out, they don't move at all and their words are distinct rather than garbled' [口裏叫喊,身子不動,交出來字眼清清楚楚,不混亂的]; the 'second' indicates beginning arousal: 'the cries are audible, but the words come out incoherent and disjointed' [這種聲音也聽得出,叫出來的字眼是模模糊糊]; and the 'third way' indicates the approaching climax: 'the sound comes from their throats rather than their mouths and is barely audible'[62] [原在喉嚨裏面聽得,在口舌之間,就有些聽不出了].[63]

According to Sai Kunlun, the third sound is powerful enough to excite him, the hard-boiled thief. He relates a bizarre episode:

> I cocked an ear and drew closer. All I could hear was a wheezing and gasping from her throat that sounded like something between speech and a sigh, and I knew she had reached her climax. A wave of excitement swept over me, I began to tingle all over, and my semen came of its own accord without resort to the handgun.[64] That is how I know women are capable of this sort of cry as well.[65]
>
> [我又側著耳朵走近前去,只聽見喉嚨裡面咿咿呀呀,竟似說話非說話,似嘆氣非嘆氣,我聽了這種光景,知道她快活極了,不覺淫興大動,全身酸養,又不曾打秋蟲,那精液自流出來,所以曉得婦人口裏又有這一種浪法。][66]

As someone who is repeatedly characterized as asexual, Sai Kunlun's tale gives evidence of a miracle: not only is he aroused by her sounds, he even climaxes without touching himself. In Henan's rendering, these magical moans are described as 'wheezing and gasping'. The Chinese original once again attempts to imitate these sounds and uses characters that feature the mouth radical: *yi-yi-ya-ya* (咿咿呀呀). Sai Kunlun's loss of self-control is further intensified by Vesperus's reaction to this anecdote: he imagines those passionate cries, only to find himself climaxing at the thought of them. It turns out that Xunzi's call for the death penalty is not that overblown. If lewd sounds and/or music are powerful enough to cloud the senses of a man like Sai Kunlun, how will ordinary men avoid succumbing to their corrupting influence?

Despite Kuhn's interest in onomatopoeia ('hach ... bh ...!'), he drops Sai Kunlun's confession from his translation. Keeping in mind that he was the master of 'congenial' translation from Chinese into German, the idea of ejaculating from merely listening to the sounds of a woman is unsettling for his trade. If inarticulate expressions, such as cries of passion, can defy language and bypass linguistic enunciation, the tedious search for semantic equivalents loses much of its aura. It is no longer the best way to grasp another person or another culture, but a mere substitute for a different sort of encounter. While sound travels and implants arousal through the mere transmission of waves, literary translation only emphasises the gap that emerges between different linguistic systems. After dedicating the final years of his life to this translation, Kuhn appears reluctant to share Sai Kunlun's triumphant experience of non-verbal communication with his German readership. In Western rational thought, a hierarchical idea is tied to the word types within a language: here, onomatopoeia 'constitute evidence for a "primitive" stratum of historical languages',[67] as Fenves argues. As long as they only have an illustrative function ('hach ... bh ...!') they do not challenge the conventional hierarchy of meaning and sound. But once they take over the narration and replace the act of communication, these primitive speech acts delegitimize the sacrosanct status of language as the primary tool of interpersonal action.

In *Carnal Prayer Mat*, the acoustic threesome calls not only language, but also the requirement of the haptic encounter into question. If Sai Kunlun's sound-induced orgasm is possible, even the sensual frictions involved in hetero- and auto-sexual practices become obsolete. Goethe's poet may subordinate his lovemaking to a nostalgic yearning for Antiquity, yet he cannot dispense with a physical lover. In his experience of pure sonic pleasure, Sai Kunlun moves on from the bodily realm and encounters a supreme libidinal event. The 'erratic' nature of his audio-orgasm eliminates all the other available stimuli, including sight, taste, smell and touch. Vesperus's own climax is triggered by the mere imagination of such a strong auditory stimulus. This cognitive act completes the disjunction of human sensuality and the bodily functions which, at least in terms of biology, form the basis of sexuality.

Just like Goethe's fifth elegy, *Carnal Prayer Mat* exemplifies situations in which 'erratic' auditory stimuli eclipse their own sources. Sai Kunlun's physical distance and his haptic isolation, however, do not represent the greatest disjunction between source and stimulus. Strikingly, it is again Goethe who proves that the act of recalling a sound facilitates the most intense erotic reveries.

## Pavlov's dog, revisited

The mesmerizing effect of non-haptic erotic stimulation features prominently in the seventeenth elegy. The trigger-stimulus is even further removed from the direct experience of the subject, as the narrator links his arousal to the barking of a dog. After expressing his dislike for this sound in general, he mentions the free associations triggered by one dog in particular.

> Only my neighbour's dog is now an exception: so often
> Hearing his bark and his yelp, I am contented and glad.
> For he barked at my darling once, when secretly she was
> Stealing a visit to me, and nearly gave us away.
> Now, if I hear him bark, I always think: she must be coming![68]
>
> [Einen Hund [...] hör ich sehr oft mit frohem Behagen
> Bellend kläffen, den Hund, den sich der Nachbar erzog.
> Denn er bellte mir einst mein Mädchen an, da sie sich heimlich
> Zu mir stahl, und verriet unser Geheimnis beinah.
> Jetzo, hör ich ihn bellen, so denk ich mir immer: sie kommt wohl!][69]

In the past, barking announced the secret arrival of the narrator's lover. Today, as their relationship has ended, the dog's barks no longer announce her arrival, yet the poet submits to a Pavlovian reaction: a neutral stimulus becomes anticipatory of another. As modern psychological discourse relates, 'the latter usually is of biological significance, i.e., a reward',[70] in this case the sexual encounter that follows the lover's arrival.

Contrary to classic conditioning, where the reaction starts to fade once the reward is withdrawn, the seventeenth elegy shows how such mnemo-technical effects do not vanish. Instead, we witness a synecdochic procedure tied to the auditory stimulus: within the libidinal economy of the narrator, the dog's barking has become identical with the sexual encounter itself. Roman Jacobson's attributes to the musical artifice — 'anticipation, retrospection, and integration'[71] — highlight this indelible effect of the auditory stimulus: as the present tone leads the listener from the remembered to the anticipated tone, the barking allows the poet to integrate the memories of a blissful past into a much lonelier present.

Simultaneously, this operation also exhibits the potential for neurosis: just as much as the sound evokes desire without providing the company necessary for its gratification, the narrator's conditioning threatens to interfere with any sexual encounter that is not presaged by barks. What if this sound has already become a precondition of the poet's arousal? Granted that such mnemo-technical effects last, is seems possible that Pavlov's well-conditioned dog refuses to eat in absence of bell-ringing. In analogy, our poet will find himself preferring the sound over the actual appearance of his former lover. The substitution of sexual stimulus with a secondary sound — notably, one that does not even originate in the lover's voice — disturbs naive appreciation of the original source of pleasure.

If one follows Jacques Derrida's reading, Jean-Jacques Rousseau's *Confessions* exemplify this interplay of presence and absence. Taking a scene of Rousseau's remembered childhood as a starting point, when his caretaker, Mademoiselle de Lambercier, gave him sexually arousing spankings, Derrida conceives the notion of the supplement. Only paving the way to mere substitutions of the original event, Rousseau's desire for Lambercier will forever be disappointed, argues Derrida. Just like in the case of (lively) speech and its detours via (dead) writing, the supplement separates the subject from the enjoyment of its passions: eventually, the fantasy of a remembered past outshines the actual sexual encounters. Lambercier is lost forever.[72]

This observation can be extended to Sai Kunlun: after this compelling auditory encounter, he is no longer fit for 'normal' sexual encounters. Indeed, at a very early stage he confesses to Vesperus: 'Gradually a vulva came to resemble some kitchen utensil and aroused about as much feeling in me'[73] [看看陰戶,就是尋常動用的傢伙,一毫不覺得動情].[74] After savouring the pleasure of his erratic auditory ecstasy, he can no longer find pleasure in common sexual encounters. The reader never learns why exactly Sai Kunlun shares his knowledge so generously with Vesperus. Most probably, he follows his friend like a shadow. During the other man's sexual exploits, Sai Kunlun acts as a silent witness waiting to experience the most erratic sexual delights our senses have on offer.

## Conclusion: bodies as sound boxes

In the selected passages, the epistemologically uncertain position of sound facilitates scenes in which auditory perception takes over the narration and challenges quotidian ideas of sexuality. The power of sound decentres the human subject and limits its interpersonal encounters to the passive process of receiving stimuli. Simple conditioning does not explain why Serlo, Goethe's prime foot-fetishist, raves about clicking heels and not about his ex-lover's beautiful legs, feet, or toenails. While the creaks of a bed remain in the background, those clicks, hexameter beats, screams and dog barks are not only represented through speech, but become the prime object of reveries about physical jouissance past. Once the focus is on sound, the lover's body becomes a magical sound box that facilitates more subtle pleasures than simple intercourse.

This disjunction between matter and sound serves different people to different ends: for Goethe's poet (fifth elegy), it facilitates his communication with a bygone era of glory and for Sai Kunlun, a supreme ecstasy that renders all other forms of sexuality superfluous. Finally, Goethe's seventeenth elegy even discards the lover's function as a sound box, as he projects joyous memories at the barking of a dog. Once the deictic connection between trigger and stimulus is broken, the radiant beauty of the 'erratic' trigger eclipses the joys of immediacy. In this light, Xunzi's reminder that virtuous men should abstain from listening to lewd sounds and/or music no longer seems excessive. After all, virtuous men cannot afford to be drawn into strange reveries and to lose their self-control like Sai Kunlun. It turns out that hearing indeed is 'the most heartfelt, the deepest sense', as Herder claimed, as it accesses sensations that defy rational thinking and set in motion 'erratic' feelings of bliss.

Audio-erotics are difficult to incorporate into conventional narratives, which is why Serlo's speech, for example, remains an isolated episode in the novel. Facing a world full of confusing libidos, Wilhelm proceeds to marry 'asexual Natalie'[75] rather than the girl with clicking heels. In a similar vein, Vesperus's years of apprenticeship in the world of sensual pleasure also culminate in its sweeping rejection. Fitting with the crude imagery of the entire text, he proceeds to cutting off his genitals. On the one hand, auditory erotics unsettle the world as we know it and threaten to reduce interpersonal relationships to passive consumption. On the other hand, audio-erotics contribute to a new appreciation of the external world. In this mindset, one no longer communicates with other people who inhabit an analogous mental space, as constructivism has it, but with other organisms that emit odours, fluids, and sounds.

This attention to the exterior world is fitting with recent developments in philosophy, notably object-oriented ontology. Drawing on Edmund Husserl and Martin Heidegger, Graham Harman's work seeks to address our relationship with the world of things in a way that is emotive and rich in associations: 'In any experience, there are countless layers of background perceptions and muffled syllogism that can gradually be unearthed — whether they be unnoticed sounds and colours and memories, or raw categorical structures.'[76] As the present article shows, such attention to the exterior world is full of ecstatic possibilities, yet it may fail to live up to the ethics of interpersonal relationships. One's partner may have second thoughts about serving as a sound box.

## Bibliography

*I. Editions and translations*

ANON., *The Before Midnight Scholar* (London: Arrow, 1985).
ANON., *Li Chi/ Book of Rites: An Encyclopedia of Ancient Ceremonial Usages, Religious Creeds, and Social Institutions* (bilingual ed.), trans. and ed. by James Legge, 2 vols (New York, NY: University Books, 1967).

BELLINGACCI, ISABELLA (trans.), *Gli anni di apprendisato die Wilhelm Meister* (Milan: Mondadori, 2013).
BLACKALL, ERIC A. (trans.), *Wilhelm Meister's Apprenticeship* (Princeton, NJ: Princeton University Press, 1989).
BOYLAN, R. DILLON (trans.), *Wilhelm Meister's Apprenticeship* (London: Henry G. Bohn, 1855).
BRIOD, BLAISE (trans.), *Les années d'apprentissage de Wilhelm Meister* (Paris: Gallimard, 1954).
CARLOWITZ, ALOÏSE CHRISTINE DE (trans.), *Wilhelm Meister: Les années d'apprentissage* (Paris: Charpentier, 1843).
CARLYLE, THOMAS (trans.), *Wilhelm Meister's Apprenticeship and Travels*, 2 vols (New York NY: Charles Scribner's Sons, 1904).
CONFUCIUS, *Confucianism: The Four books and Five Classics — Collected Works of Confucius*, trans. William Jennings (Hastings: Delphi Classics, 2016).
—— *Li Ji: jin zhu jin yi* (禮記今註今譯), ed. by Wang Meng'ou 王夢鷗 (Taipei: Shangwu yinshuguan, 2009).
DIDEROT, DENIS, 'Entretien entre d'Alembert et Diderot', in *Oeuvres complètes de Diderot*, ed. by Assézat Tourneux, 20 vols (Paris: Garnier Frères, 1875).
FENG, ZHI 馮至 (trans.), *Weilian Maisite de xuexi shidai* (威廉·麥斯特的學習時代) (Beijing: Renmin wenxue chubanshe, 1988).
GOETHE, JOHANN WOLFGANG VON, *Poetische Werke*, ed. by Siegfried Seidel, 16 vols (Berlin: Aufbau, 1965–1978).
—— *Werke*, ed. by Erich Trunz, 14 vols (Hamburg: Christian Wegener, 1949–60).
HANAN, PATRICK (trans.), *The Carnal Prayer Mat* (London: Arrow, 1990).
HERDER, JOHANN GOTTFRIED, *Sämtliche Werke*, ed. by Günther Arnold, Martin Bollacher et al., 10 vols (Frankfurt a.M.: Suhrkamp, 1985–1990).
KUHN, FRANZ (trans.), *Jou Pu Tuan* (Braunschweig: Die Waage, 1995).
LI, YU 李漁, *Rou Pu Tuan* (肉蒲團) (Taipei: Guojia chubanshe, 2012).
LUKE, DAVID (trans.), *'Roman Elegies', and 'The Diary'* (London: Libris, 1988).
NETO, NICOLINO SIMONE, *Os anos de aprendizado de Wilhelm Meister* (Sao Paolo: Editora, 2006).
PLATO, *The Republic* (New York, NY: Anchor, 1989).
SADE, DONATIEN ALPHONSE FRANÇOIS DE, *Œuvres complètes*, ed. by Jean-Jacques Pauvert and Annie Le Brun, 4 vols (Paris: Les Petits Papiers, 1986).
SALMERÓN, MIGUEL (trans.), *Los años itinerantes de Wilhelm Meister* (Madrid: Cátedra, 2000).
WAIDSON, H.M. (trans.), *Wilhelm Meister* (London: Alma, 1978).
YANG, WUNENG 楊武能, *Weilian Maisite de xuexi niandai* (威廉·邁斯特的學習時代) (Nanjing: Yilin chubanshe, 2002).

*II. Critical literature*

ALBERTSEN, LEIF LUDWIG, 'Die Anerkennung des Sexuellen vor und bei Goethe: Was war an den Römischen Elegien so aufregend?' *Text & Kontext*, 9 (1981), 331–42.
ANTENHOFER, CHRISTINA, 'Fetisch als heuristische Kategorie', in *Fetisch als heuristische Kategorie: Geschichte-Rezeption-Interpretation*, ed. by C.A. (Bielefeld: transcript, 2011), pp. 9–40.
BARTHES, ROLAND, *The Pleasure of the Text*, trans. by Richard Miller (New York, NY: Hill and Wang, 1975).
BARRATT, E.L. and N.J. DAVIS, 'Autonomous Sensory Meridian Response (ASMR): A Flow-Like Mental State', *PeerJ*, 3:e851 (26 March 2015) <https://peerj.com/articles/851/> [last retrieved 28 August 2016].
BETTELHEIM, BRUNO, *Kinder brauchen Märchen* (Stuttgart: Deutsche Verlagsanstalt, 1977).

CLARK, KATERINA and MICHAEL HOLQUIST: *Mikhail Bakhtin* (Cambridge, MA: Belknap, 1984).
COHEN, MARGARET, *The Sentimental Education of the Novel* (Princeton, NJ: Princeton University Press, 1999).
DERRIDA, JACQUES, *De la grammatologie* (Paris: Minuit, 1967).
ENGEL, MANFRED, *Roman der Goethezeit* (Stuttgart: Metzler, 1993).
ERLMANN, VEIT, *Reason and Resonance: A History of Modern Aurality* (New York, NY: Zone, 2010).
FRIEDRICH, MICHAEL and BERNHARD FÜHRER, 'Bemerkungen zu Überwachung und Unterdrückung literarischer und künstlerischer Erzeugnisse in China', in *Zensur: Text und Autorität in China in Geschichte und Gegenwart*, ed. by Bernhard Führer (Wiesbaden: Harrassowitz, 2003), pp. 1–19.
GRIMM, JAKOB and WILHELM (eds.), *Deutsches Wörterbuch*, <http://woerterbuchnetz.de/DWB/> [last retrieved 25 August 2016].
GREEN, PETER, 'Introduction' in *The Poems of Catullus* (Berkeley, CA: University of California Press, 2007).
FAN, HONG, *Footbinding, Feminism and Freedom: The Liberation of Women's Bodies in Modern China* (London: Frank Cass, 1997).
FENVES, PETER, *Arresting Language: From Leibniz to Benjamin* (Stanford, CA: Stanford University Press, 2001).
HORST, ELEANOR TER, 'Masks and Metamorphoses: The Transformation of Classical Tradition in Goethe's "Römische Elegien"', *The German Quarterly*, 84.5 (Fall 2012), 401–19.
HUSHAHN, HELGA, 'Goethe Translated: Carlyle's "Wilhelm Meister"', in *Victorian Keats and Romantic Carlyle: The Fusions and Confusions of Literary Periods*, ed. by C.C. Barfoot (Amsterdam: Rodopi, 1999), pp. 141–29.
JACOBSON, ROMAN, *Language in Literature* (Cambridge, MA: Belknap 1987).
JAPP, UWE, 'Amor / Roma: Goethes Liebeskonzeption in den Römischen Elegien', in *Goethes Liebeslyrik: Semantiken der Leidenschaft um 1800*, ed. by Carsten Rohde and Thorsten Valk (Berlin: De Gruyter, 2013), pp. 145–63.
KEULEMANS, PAIZE, 'Listening to the Printed Martial Arts Scene: Onomatopoeia and the Qing Dynasty Storyteller's Voice', *Harvard Journal of Asiatic Studies*, 67.1 (2007), 51–87.
KOPKE, WULF, 'Jean Paul's Battles with the Censors and his Freiheits-Büchlein', in *Censorship and Culture: From Weimar Classicism to Weimar Republic and Beyond*, ed. by John A. McCarthy & Werner von der Ohe (Tübingen: Niemeyer, 1995), pp. 99–111.
KIM, KYONG-DONG, *Confucianism & Modernization in East Asia: Critical Reflection* (New York, NY: Palgrave, 2017).
LECERCLE, JEAN-JACQUES and DENISE RILEY, THE FORCE OF LANGUAGE (New York, NY: Palgrave Macmillan, 2004).
LIU, JAMES J. Y., *The Art of Chinese Poetry* (Chicago, IL: University of Chicago Press, 1962).
RICHTER, DIETER, 'Das Volk und die Schuhe: Von nackten und beschuhten Füßen in Märchen und Popularkultur', in *schuhtick: Von kalten Füßen und heißen Sohlen*, ed. by Hartmut Roder (Mainz: Zabern, 2008), pp. 193–200.
RICHTER, SIMON, 'Introduction', in *The Literature of Weimar Classicism* (Rochester, NY: Camden House, 2005), pp. 33–38.
ROPP, PAUL S., *China in World History* (Oxford: Oxford University Press, 2010).
SCHINGS, HANS-JÜRGEN, 'Symbolik des Glücks: Zu Wilhelm Meisters Bildergeschichte', in *Johann Wolfgang von Goethe: One Hundred and Fifty Years of Continuing Vitality*, ed. by Ulrich Goebel et al. (Lubbock, TX: 1984), pp. 157–78.
VOEGELIN, SALOMÉ, *Listening to Noise and Silence: Towards a Philosophy of Sound Art* (London: Continuum, 2010).

TSUCHIYA, KIYOSHI, 'Buddhism', in *Major World Religions: From their Origins to the Present*, ed. by Lloyd Ridgeon (London: RoutledgeCurzon, 2003), pp. 59–115.

WEINBERGER, NORMAN M., 'The Cognitive Auditory Cortex', in *The Oxford Handbook of Auditory Science*, ed. by Adrian Rees and Alan R. Palmer, 2 vols (Oxford: Oxford University Press, 2010), II, 441–78.

## Notes to Chapter 6

1. E. L. Barratt and N. J. Davis, 'Autonomous Sensory Meridian Response (ASMR): A Flow-Like Mental State', *PeerJ*, 3:e851 (26 March 2015) <https://peerj.com/articles/851/> [last retrieved 28 August 2016].
2. See Roland Barthes, *The Pleasure of the Text*, trans. by Richard Miller (New York, NY: Hill and Wang, 1975), p. 10.
3. Although it is problematic to identify the Chinese *xiaoshuo*-genre (or *zhanghui xiaoshuo* 章回小說) with the European novel, their equivalent usage is irrelevant for this article.
4. Wulf Kopke, 'Jean Paul's Battles with the Censors and his Freiheits-Büchlein', in *Censorship and Culture: From Weimar Classicism to Weimar Republic and Beyond*, ed. by John A. McCarthy & Werner von der Ohe (Tübingen: Niemeyer, 1995), pp. 99–111 (p. 104). For more information regarding the scandal that accompanied Goethe's publication: Simon Richter, 'Introduction', in *The Literature of Weimar Classicism* (Rochester, NY: Camden House, 2005), pp. 33–38. For an overview of its publication history and trivia related to its reception at the Weimar court, see Leif Ludwig Albertsen, 'Die Anerkennung des Sexuellen vor und bei Goethe: Was war an den Römischen Elegien so aufregend?', *Text & Kontext*, 9 (1981), 331–42.
5. See Michael Friedrich and Bernhard Führer, 'Bemerkungen zu Überwachung und Unterdrückung literarischer und künstlerischer Erzeugnisse in China', in *Zensur: Text und Autorität in China in Geschichte und Gegenwart*, ed. by Bernhard Führer (Wiesbaden: Harrassowitz, 2003), pp. 1–19 (p. 14).
6. Salomé Voegelin, *Listening to Noise and Silence: Towards a Philosophy of Sound Art* (London: Continuum, 2010), xiv.
7. The *Book of Rites* is a collection of texts written during the late Warring States (5th century to 221 BC) and Former Han periods (206 BCE to 8 AD).
8. *Li Chi/ Book of Rites: An Encyclopedia of Ancient Ceremonial Usages, Religious Creeds, and Social Institutions* (bilingual ed.), trans. and ed. by James Legge, 2 vols (New York, NY: University Books, 1967), I, 95.
9. Accordingly, there are six types of emotion that music can trigger: *sorrow* by sound that is 'sharp and fading away'; *pleasure* when it is 'slow and gentle'; *joy* when 'exclamatory and scattered'; *anger* when 'coarse and fierce'; *reverence* when 'straightforward with an indication of humbleness'; and *love* when 'harmonious and soft'. See Kim Kyong-Dong, *Confucianism & Modernization in East Asia: Critical Reflection* (New York, Palgrave, 2017), p. 221.
10. The *Royal Regulations* (王制) feature the harsh statement: 'Using licentious music; strange garments; wonderful contrivances and extraordinary implements, thus raising doubts among the multitudes: all who used or formed such things were put to death.' *Confucianism: The Four books and Five Classics — Collected Works of Confucius*, trans. William Jennings (Hastings: Delphi Classics, 2016), p. 719. The original Chinese reads: 作淫聲、異服、奇技、奇器以疑眾,殺。 *Li Ji: jin zhu jin yi* (禮記今註今譯), ed. by Wang Meng'ou 王夢鷗 (Taipei: Shangwu yinshuguan, 2009), p. 237.
11. Plato, *The Republic* (New York, NY: Anchor, 1989), p. 90.
12. Kant's *Critique of Pure Reason* (*Kritik der reinen Vernunft*, 1781), in particular the chapter 'Antizipationen der Wahrnehmung', downplays the importance of empirical stimuli as mere data to be processed by our rational faculties. See Immanuel Kant, *Werke*, ed. by Wilhelm Weischedel, 12 vols (Frankfurt a.M.: Suhrkamp, 1977), III, 208. In a similar vein, the Marquis de Sade exhibits a comparably conservative assessment of hearing and rationality. In the *120 journées de Sodome* (*The 120 Days of Sodom*), the narrator explains the protagonists' design to meet

at the end of each day and relate their debauchery to another: 'les sensations communiquées par l'organe de l'ouïe sont celles qui flattent davantage et dont les impressions sont les plus vives.' Donatien Alphonse François de Sade, *Œuvres complètes*, ed. by Jean-Jacques Pauvert and Annie Le Brun, 4 vols (Paris: Les Petits Papiers, 1986), I, 64.

13. See Denis Diderot, 'Entretien entre d'Alembert et Diderot', in *Oeuvres complètes de Diderot*, ed. by Assézat Tourneux, 20 vols (Paris: Garnier Frères, 1875), II, 105–21.
14. Veit Erlmann, *Reason and Resonance: A History of Modern Aurality* (New York, NY: Zone, 2010), p. 9.
15. Translations are my own, unless stated otherwise, J. K.
16. Johann Gottfried Herder, *Sämtliche Werke*, ed. by Günther Arnold, Martin Bollacher et al., 10 vols (Frankfurt a.M.: Suhrkamp, 1985–1990), II, 357.
17. See Manfred Engel, *Roman der Goethezeit* (Stuttgart: Metzler, 1993), p. 280; see also Hans-Jürgen Schings, 'Symbolik des Glücks: Zu Wilhelm Meisters Bildergeschichte', in *Johann Wolfgang von Goethe: One Hundred and Fifty Years of Continuing Vitality*, ed. by Ulrich Goebel et al. (Lubbock, TX: 1984), pp. 157–78 (p. 162).
18. Eric A. Blackall (trans.), *Wilhelm Meister's Apprenticeship* (Princeton, NJ: Princeton University Press, 1989), p. 181. [*My emphasis, J. K.*]
19. Johann Wolfgang von Goethe, *Werke*, ed. by Erich Trunz, 14 vols (Hamburg: Christian Wegener, 1949–60), VII, 300.
20. According to Christina Antenhofer, Philine's mules fulfil all aspects that define a fetish. It is comprised by its materiality (as opposed to its symbolic content), the social communication that it manifests, and the close relationship to an individual which is substitutes. See Christina Antenhofer, 'Fetisch als heuristische Kategorie', in *Fetisch als heuristische Kategorie: Geschichte-Rezeption-Interpretation*, ed. by C. A. (Bielefeld: transcript, 2011), pp. 9–40 (p. 19).
21. Blackall, *Wilhelm Meister's Apprenticeship*, p. 181.
22. Goethe, *Werke*, VII, 300.
23. See 'Klippklapp' in *Deutsches Wörterbuch*, ed. by Jakob and Wilhelm Grimm <http://woerterbuchnetz.de/DWB/> [last retrieved 25 August 2016].
24. Thomas Carlyle (trans.), *Wilhelm Meister's Apprenticeship and Travels*, 2 vols (New York NY: Charles Scribner's Sons, 1904 [1824]), p. 339.
25. Aloïse Christine de Carlowitz (trans.), *Wilhelm Meister: Les années d'apprentissage* (Paris: Charpentier, 1843), p. 276. Blaise Briod (trans.), *Les années d'apprentissage de Wilhelm Meister* (Paris: Gallimard, 1954), p. 47.
26. H.M. Waidson (trans.), *Wilhelm Meister* (London: Alma, 1978), p. 89.
27. Blackall, *Wilhelm Meister's Apprenticeship*, p. 181.
28. Isabella Bellingacci (trans.), *Gli anni di apprendisato die Wilhelm Meister* (Milan: Mondadori, 2013), p. 312.
29. Miguel Salmerón (trans.), *Los años itinerantes de Wilhelm Meister* (Madrid: Cátedra, 2000), p. 420.
30. Nicolino Simone Neto, *Os anos de aprendizado de Wilhelm Meister* (Sao Paolo: Editora, 2006), p. 295.
31. Feng Zhi 馮至, *Weilian Maisite de xuexi shidai* (威廉·麥斯特的學習時代) (Beijing: Renmin wenxue chubanshe, 1988), p. 277.
32. An English-Chinese dictionary renders this character as 'dhak-dhak'.
33. Yang Wuneng 楊武能, *Weilian Maisite de xuexi niandai* (威廉·邁斯特的學習時代) (Nanjing: Yilin chubanshe, 2002), p. 309.
34. See Paize Keulemans, 'Listening to the Printed Martial Arts Scene: Onomatopoeia and the Qing Dynasty Storyteller's Voice', *Harvard Journal of Asiatic Studies*, 67.1 (2007), 51–87.
35. Jean-Jacques Lecercle and Denise Riley, The Force of Language (New York, NY: Palgrave Macmillan, 2004), p. 119.
36. Blackall, *Wilhelm Meister's Apprenticeship*, p. 181.
37. Goethe, *Werke*, VII, 300.
38. See Dieter Richter, 'Das Volk und die Schuhe: Von nackten und beschuhten Füßen in Märchen und Popularkultur', in *schuhtick: Von kalten Füßen und heißen Sohlen*, ed. by Hartmut Roder

(Mainz: Zabern, 2008), pp. 193–200 (p.198).
39. See Bruno Bettelheim, *Kinder brauchen Märchen* (Stuttgart: Deutsche Verlagsanstalt, 1977), p. 255.
40. R. Dillon Boylan (trans.), *Wilhelm Meister's Apprenticeship* (London: Henry G. Bohn, 1855), p. 279.
41. Helga Hushahn, 'Goethe Translated: Carlyle's "Wilhelm Meister"', in *Victorian Keats and Romantic Carlyle: The Fusions and Confusions of Literary Periods*, ed. by C.C. Barfoot (Amsterdam: Rodopi, 1999), pp. 141–29, (pp. 149 and 151). Asked what he made of the novel himself, Carlyle answered: 'For really it is a most mixed performance, and tho' intellectually good, much of it is morally bad.' Quoted in Hushahn, 'Goethe Translated', p. 146.
42. Carlyle, *Wilhelm Meister's Apprenticeship and Travels*, I, 338.
43. See Margaret Cohen, *The Sentimental Education of the Novel* (Princeton, NJ: Princeton University Press, 1999), p. 138.
44. Carlowitz, *Wilhelm Meister: Les années d'apprentissage*, p. 276. [My emphasis, J. K.] Blaise Briod's translation keeps this rendering, see Briod, *Les années d'apprentissage de Wilhelm Meister*, p. 47.
45. The tradition of foot binding was established during the Song dynasty (960–1279) and endowed the crippled female foot with erotic associations: 'The small feet, measured steps and gentle swaying gait were thought to be reminiscent of the willow or poplar in the wind. The slight body looked ready to fall at the slightest touch.' Fan Hong, *Footbinding, Feminism and Freedom: The Liberation of Women's Bodies in Modern China* (London: Frank Cass, 1997), p. 22. See also Paul S. Ropp, *China in World History* (Oxford: Oxford University Press, 2010), p. 74.
46. Erlmann, *Reason and Resonance*, p. 163.
47. Goethe, *Poetische Werke*, II, 82. [My emphasis, J. K.]
48. David Luke (trans.), *'Roman Elegies', and 'The Diary'* (London: Libris, 1988), p. 41 [My emphasis, J. K.].
49. See Katerina Clark and Michael Holquist: *Mikhail Bakhtin* (Cambridge, MA: Belknap, 1984), p. 312
50. Eleanor ter Horst, 'Masks and Metamorphoses: The Transformation of Classical Tradition in Goethe's "Römische Elegien"', *The German Quarterly*, 84.5 (Fall 2012), 401–19 (p. 402).
51. Johann Wolfgang von Goethe, *Poetische Werke*, ed. by Siegfried Seidel, 16 vols (Berlin: Aufbau, 1965–1978), I, 169 [My emphasis, J. K.].
52. Luke, *'Roman Elegies', and 'The Diary'*, p. 49. [My emphasis, J. K.]
53. See Uwe Japp, 'Amor / Roma: Goethes Liebeskonzeption in den Römischen Elegien', in *Goethes Liebeslyrik: Semantiken der Leidenschaft um 1800*, ed. by Carsten Rohde and Thorsten Valk (Berlin: De Gruyter, 2013), pp. 145–63 (p. 153).
54. Dactyls are named from the one long and two short joints of the index finger. See Peter Green, 'Introduction' in *The Poems of Catullus* (Berkeley, CA: University of California Press, 2007), p. 39.
55. Luke, *'Roman Elegies', and 'The Diary'*, p. 49.
56. Goethe, *Poetische Werke*, p. 169.
57. Li Yu 李漁, *Rou Pu Tuan* (肉蒲團) (Taipei: Guojia chubanshe, 2012), p. 88
58. Patrick Hanan (trans.), *The Carnal Prayer Mat* (London: Arrow, 1990), p. 108.
59. James J. Y. Liu, *The Art of Chinese Poetry* (Chicago, IL: University of Chicago Press, 1962), p. 37.
60. Franz Kuhn (trans.), *Jou Pu Tuan* (Braunschweig: Die Waage, 1995), p. 225.
61. Anon., *The Before Midnight Scholar* (London: Arrow, 1985), p. 115.
62. Hanan, *The Carnal Prayer Mat*, p. 50.
63. Li 李漁, *Rou Pu Tuan*, p. 44.
64. Hanan's euphemism for masturbation is derived from the term *da shouqiang* 打手槍, but the present edition of *Carnal Prayer Mat* uses the term *da qiuchong* 打秋蟲, 'beating the coccidia'.
65. Hanan, *The Carnal Prayer Mat*, p. 51.
66. Li 李漁, *Rou Pu Tuan*, p. 45.
67. See Peter Fenves, *Arresting Language: From Leibniz to Benjamin* (Stanford, CA: Stanford University Press, 2001), p. 42.
68. Luke, *'Roman Elegies', and 'The Diary'*, p. 85.

69. Goethe, *Poetische Werke*, I, 178.
70. Norman M. Weinberger, 'The Cognitive Auditory Cortex', in *The Oxford Handbook of Auditory Science*, ed. by Adrian Rees and Alan R. Palmer, 2 vols (Oxford: Oxford University Press, 2010), II, 441–78 (p. 442).
71. Roman Jacobson, *Language in Literature* (Cambridge, MA: Belknap 1987), p. 453.
72. See Jacques Derrida, *De la grammatologie* (Paris: Minuit, 1967), p. 227.
73. Hanan, *The Carnal Prayer Mat*, p. 48.
74. Li 李漁, *Rou Pu Tuan*, p. 42.
75. Giovanna Summerfield, 'Mastery and Apprenticeship(s): Departing from Goethe's Turm', in *New Perspectives on the European Bildungsroman*, ed. by Giovanna Summerfield and Lisa Downward (London: Continuum, 2010), pp. 11–28 (p. 27).
76. Graham Harman, *Tool Being: Heidegger and the Metaphysics of Objects* (Chicago, IL: Open Court, 2002), p. 131.

CHAPTER 7

# Erotica in Erotica: Adaptation and Somatic Translation in Late Imperial Chinese Erotic Culture

*Jie Guo*

This paper examines a convention commonly found in late imperial Chinese erotic literature: the lovemaking couple's use of erotica as a tool of sexual arousal. Ming-Qing erotic novels and stories often feature scenes in which a man and a woman read or view erotic works together and meticulously imitate the positions verbally or visually depicted in them.[1] This convention can be found in some of the best-known erotic novels of the Ming (1368–1644) and Qing dynasties (1644–1911), i.e, *History of a Libertine* (浪史 *Langshi*),[2] *Plum in the Golden Vase* (金瓶梅 *Jin Ping Mei*),[3] and *Lascivious History of Hailing* (海陵佚史 *Hailing Yishi*),[4] *Unofficial History of the Embroidered Couch* (繡榻野史 *Xiuta Yeshi*),[5] and *Carnal Prayer Mat* (肉蒲團 *Rou Pu Tuan*),[6] just to name a few.

Scholars have long noticed this prevalent convention in Ming-Qing erotic literature. However, while many have commented on it, this convention is only mentioned in passing. For instance, both Patrick Hanan and Craig Clunas take notice of the episode in Li Yu's 李漁 *Carnal Prayer Mat*, in which the male protagonist Vesperus[7] uses erotic pictures to help his wife achieve 'sexual awakening'. For both Hanan and Clunas, these erotic images, which 'have the effect of kindling in a woman for the first time desires',[8] are used by the male protagonist as a tool to 'to help in the sexual education of his wife.'[9] Furthermore, for Hanan, the reference to other erotic novels in *Carnal Prayer Mat* provides him a starting point to compare and contrast the features of the *Carnal Prayer Mat* with those of other novels. For Clunas, this episode serves as an example of 'a male fantasy' not uncommon in Chinese erotic literature.[10]

The 'erotica-in-erotica' convention, however, deserves further consideration. In this paper, I examine this convention against the background of the late imperial erotic tradition. I am interested in the uses of erotica in Ming-Qing erotic novels: i.e., as a handy instrument for sexual education, as part of the seduction scheme, and as a tool of erotic stimulation. However, this paper is not merely concerned with how fictional characters use erotica in their sexual escapades. Rather, as this convention is located at the intersection between literature and picture, between word and image, it serves as a window onto the intimate interrelationships between forms, mediums, and genres of Ming-Qing erotica. Furthermore, late imperial Chinese erotica's fascination with this convention also has to do with its belief in the importance of sight in achieving sexual pleasure. Therefore, understanding this convention helps us rethink another commonly found convention in Ming-Qing erotica, i.e., voyeurism, which involves the use of a kind of 'live' erotica for sexual stimulation and enjoyment.

## Uses of erotica: *dongqing* and *dongxing*

As mentioned in the outset, the male protagonist of *Carnal Prayer Mat* uses erotic pictures — conventionally referred to as *chungong* 春宮 ('spring palace') or *chunyi tu* 春意圖 ('pictures of spring feelings') — to help his wife discover the pleasure of sex for the first time. This is a typical case of *dongqing* 動情, which means 'to stir up passion' — usually for the first time. The late Ming novel *Lascivious History of Hailing* features an episode in which a young man named Hamidulu 哈密都盧 successfully seduces the girl Mile 彌勒 by showing her an erotic album titled *Summer Elegantium*[11] (風流絕暢 *Fengliu Juechang*). As Mile is a virgin, this erotic album not only serves as a tool of seduction in the hands of Hamidulu, but also as a 'textbook' for the innocent girl. By having Mile look closely at the naked human figures in the prints, Hamidulu enlightens Mile to the differences between male and female genitalia as well as their functions. Then, by imitating with Hamidulu the positions of intercourse depicted in the pictures, Mile loses her virginity and at the same time discovers the pleasure of sex.[12]

An episode in the Ming novel *History of a Libertine* also features using erotic images in the sexual awakening of an innocent young woman. Set in the Yuan dynasty, the plot revolves around the amorous career of a young scholar nicknamed Langzi 浪子 (literally 'libertine'). In contrast to her uninhibited brother, Langzi's younger sister Junqing 俊卿 is said to be completely ignorant of sexual matters. Lushu 陸姝, a young servant patronized by Langzi, schemes to seduce Junqing with the help of her maid. Equipped with a set of 'pictures of spring feelings and lovemaking' [春意交歡圖],[13] which she pretends to be an album of embroidery patterns, the shrewd maid easily stirs up dormant 'spring feelings' in her young mistress:

> [Junqing] looked at the pictures closely, and found that they were all erotic ones. [...] She was already sixteen or seventeen years old, and was not dumb. The sight of these pictures unconsciously stirred up her desires, and her spring feelings emerged.
>
> [細細一玩,卻都是出像的風月事。[...]他是十六七歲女兒,又兼聰明乖巧,見了這些事體,當時不覺興動於中,春心頓發。][14]

From then on, Junqing sinks into a trance, constantly lamenting her loneliness.[15] Taking advantage of the girl's distress, the maid relates her own sexual relationship with Lushu, describing her encounters in graphic detail. After this conversation further disturbs the girl, she is finally introduced to Lushu. It is worth noting that the maid's oral account of her own sexual experience functions in ways similar to erotic pictures. As the concluding commentary in the novel astutely points out: 'Just by picturing herself, the maid successfully stirs up her mistress's passion. What an experienced matchmaker' [但將自己模寫,便蕩漾了小姐神情。好一個老世事].[16]

It would be wrong, however, to assume that erotica are only used to stir up the 'spring feelings' of innocent young women or virgins. In fact, in late imperial representations, it is common to find sexually experienced women as avid consumers or even connoisseurs of erotica.[17] In the sixteenth-century erotic novel *Plum in the Golden Vase*, the male protagonist Ximen Qing 西門慶 brings an erotic album to his concubine Pan Jinlian 潘金蓮, a scene that Clunas identifies as a 'standard topos'[18] in this text genre. Much in contrast to the pornographic discourse in the West, where such practices are designated to solitary males only, Chinese erotic literature primarily depicts women to be fascinated and influenced by erotica.[19] The female consumer,[20] however, can also include experienced women who voluntarily use erotica for sexual enjoyment. For instance, *Carnal Prayer Mat* features a scene in which Jade Scent 玉香, after her husband leaves home, enjoys erotic albums on her own for pleasure.[21]

Experienced women's use of erotica often has to do with the idea of *dongxing* 動興, a term that exhibits a subtle difference to *dongqing*: 'to stir up desire', as opposed to 'passion'. While *dongqing* is often applied to virgins or inexperienced women, *dongxing* is associated with erotic stimulation in the case of sexually experienced women. These terms speak to two assumptions concerning women in the Chinese erotic novel: first, all women are sexual beings, no matter if she is a virgin or not. Second, provided with proper help, both will find true pleasure in sex.

Still, in Ming-Qing erotic fiction, sexual encounters involving experienced women differ considerably from those involving virgins. This points to another difference between European and Chinese erotica. In the introduction to his English translation of *Carnal Prayer Mat*, Hanan observes, 'It is in the nature of erotic fiction to seek out forbidden territory to explore. In China that was likely to mean adultery, not defloration as in the corresponding European genre. (In Europe adultery was left to the bourgeois novel.)'[22] Indeed, while Chinese erotic fiction sometimes also features scenes of 'defloration' as a device for staging sexual scenes, it is much less used than adultery.

Hanan argues that Chinese erotic fiction's obsession with adultery has to do with ethics: 'adultery violated the husband-wife ethic, one of the key Confucian social obligations. In a family-centered morality, it was a natural choice as the crucial sin [...]. The libertine's adulterous adventures may enthral the reader with their glimpse of forbidden pleasure'.[23] This argument seems to suggest that defloration was not as problematic as adultery in late imperial Chinese society. I argue, however, that Chinese erotic fiction's fascination with adultery should be understood from a different perspective. As the parties involved in an adulterous relationship are usually sexually experienced and even 'hyperactive', adultery is a much more useful device than 'defloration' in bringing into the narrative an assortment of sex acts and positions. Indeed, one of the most salient features of Chinese erotic fiction is its obsession with depicting a variety of sex acts and positions. James Cahill relates them to handbooks of sex: '[e]rotic fiction up to late Ming has the same quasi-taxonomic character: they did it *this* way, and then *that* way, and then *this* way.'[24] The sexually experienced, sometimes insatiable, man and woman involved in an adulterous relationship thus are the ideal actors for putting on view a wide range of sex acts for the reader.

We should understand the *dongxing*-effect of the 'erotica-in-erotica' against this background. As mentioned above, erotica are often used to 'enlighten' innocent young women about sex. In the hands of sexually experienced men and women, erotica play the role of sexual stimulation, or *dongxing*. By consuming erotica through reading, viewing, and imitating, their act, in turn, achieves an extradiegetic effect: the lovers' somatic 'translation' of the texts and images they read and view entice the readers to imitate on their own account.

*Lascivious History of Hailing* and *History of a Libertine* both feature this kind of 'somatic translation'. In the first novel, Shigu 什古, the widow of a general known for his virility, is one of the most sexually experienced women King Hailing intends to seduce. As Ling Xiaoqiao points out, the novel depicts Shigu's relation with Hailing in military terms in order to relate his sexual prowess to his power as a king.[25] As a 'veteran' well trained by her late husband, it is difficult for Shigu to get sexually aroused on the 'battlefield' of sex. To 'conquer' her, Hailing prepares an erotic album featuring twenty-four sex positions, inviting Shigu to try the positions one by one. The narrative offers a detailed account of how 'they did it *this* way, and then *that* way, and then *this* way' — to borrow Cahill's wording. After Shigu finally climaxes, she admits to King Hailing: 'Your Majesty is really good at this' [陛下可謂善戰矣].[26]

Chapter 14 of *History of a Libertine* features a similar scene of 'somatic translation', when Langzi and a married woman named Wenfei 文妃 imitate the positions depicted in an erotic album. Wenfei is not only extremely experienced but is said to be sexually insatiable. Upon seeing the pictures, her '"spring desires" were tremendously aroused' [春興勃發].[27] The narrative then depicts how the two enjoy themselves by changing positions, until Langzi is so exhausted that he is unable to move.[28]

These two examples have several features in common. First, both feature an adulterous relationship, which, as mentioned earlier, is useful for showcasing a wide range of sex acts. Second, in both cases, erotica are primarily used to meet the sexual needs of the woman rather than those of the men, for whom erotic pictures only serve to enhance their sexual prowess in order to please the woman. These examples point to strong male anxiety, as they clearly attach great importance to women's pleasure rather than men's. This is in line with Hanan's observation that the Chinese erotic novel typically puts 'emphasis on the women's orgasm'.[29] It seems that for men, reputation matters more than pleasure, and their pleasure lies in proving to women their sexual prowess. In the episode from *History of a Libertine*, for instance, while Wenfei in the end climaxes, her partner Langzi is totally exhausted;

his 'conquest' is deemed successful, however, for it is he who helped her taste the true pleasure of sex.

### Erotic novels in erotic novels

In the above we examined uses of erotic pictures in literary representations. It should be noted that erotica used for sexual arousal are not limited to pictures. In late Ming author Lü Tiancheng's *Unofficial History of the Embroidered Couch*, which according to Wilt Idema is not only 'a highly original work', but 'may well have the dubious distinction of being the very first vernacular pornographic novel',[30] erotic novels play a role similar to pictures. The second tome of the novel contains a detailed description of the female protagonist Jinshi's 金氏 room, where she secretly meets her lover Dali 大里, a young man her husband patronizes. The objects in the room are meticulously described. In addition to a portrait of a beautiful woman by the sixteenth-century painter Qiu Ying 仇英, to whom many erotic paintings are attributed, there are several well-known erotic novels — i.e., *The Empress and her Gigolo* (如意君傳 *Ruyi Jun Zhuan*), *The Story of Jiaoniang* (嬌紅記 *Jiao Hong Ji*), and *The Story of Sanmiao* (三妙記 *San Miao Zhuan*) — on the table, lying side by side with 'all kinds of erotic pictures' [各樣的春意圖兒].[31] Other objects the narrative describes in detail include a bed, the quilt and the pillow on it, and, importantly, a sex toy. All sex-related, these objects clearly are deemed important in creating the sensuous ambience of the sex scene in this episode.[32]

This form of intertextual *dongqing* extends beyond the realm of erotic fiction. In the eighteenth-century masterpiece *Dream of the Red Chamber* (紅樓夢 *Hong Lou Meng*), Lin Daiyu 林黛玉 also experiences her sexual awakening by means of reading, in this case the play *The Story of the Western Chamber* (西廂記 *Xi Xiang Ji* or 會真記 *Hui Zhen Ji*), which she acquired through her cousin Baoyu 寶玉.[33] As the idealized relationship in the world of this novel is non-sexual, reading erotic fiction only triggers Daiyu's sensuality, while Baoyu's feelings seem to remain platonic. The inherent danger of erotic literature to young women is highlighted in Chapter 54, when Madame Jia, the powerful matriarch of the Jia family, cautions the young girls in the household about the detrimental potential of all 'scholar-beauty romances' (才子佳人 *caizi jiaren*), not to mention explicitly erotic ones.[34]

Li Yu's *Carnal Prayer Mat* treats erotic novels as powerful tools of sexual stimulation. After the protagonist Vesperus uses erotic pictures to 'enlighten' his wife Jade Scent to sexual pleasure, it yields the desired results: 'After looking at the erotic pictures, Jade Scent was converted from puritanism to libertinism'[35] [玉香自看春宮之後,道學變做風流][36]. Then, the narrator explains:

> In order to enhance [her excitement], Vesperus paid a visit to the bookstore and bought a quantity of erotic works, such as *The Unofficial History of the Embroidered Couch*, *The Life of the Lord of Perfect Satisfaction*, and *The Foolish Woman's Story*, a dozen or so titles in a boxed set, which he left on the table for her to peruse.[37]
>
> [未央生要助他淫興,又到書鋪中買了許多風月之書,如繡榻野史、如意君傳、痴婆子傳之類,共有一二十種,裝釘成套,放在案頭任他翻閱。][38]

While there is no description of how exactly the couple uses these erotic novels, Vesperus later encounters Flora 花晨. As a female sex guru, she owns a 'large stock [of erotica], several dozen albums and several hundred novels'.[39] Taking much pride in this collection, she lectures Vesperus on how to use erotic pictures and novels:

> [Erotic pictures should be looked at before sex, while the partners still have their clothes on and are behaving correctly. When looking at a picture and analyzing its subtleties, you should not do anything, even if your feelings happen to be aroused. If the penis stands up and the fluid starts to flow, you must ignore both developments until you've looked at several dozen pictures and can restrain yourselves no longer. That's the way to get the full effect of an erotic album. For erotic novels to be of any practical use, they should be read after you've begun but before you've finished. Place the book in front of you before you begin. Then when you've done it for a while, one or other of you should open the book and read aloud from it. When you come to an exciting passage, start sex again. When you reach a less interesting stage in sex, start reading again. That's the way to get the full effect of an erotic novel.[40]
>
> [看春意要在未曾動手之先,兩個穿了衣服,相對如賓。看一幅講究一幅的妙處,就是偶然興動,也還不要做事。陽物等他自舉,淫水等他自流,只是不要去理他,直等看到數十副之後,萬萬禁止不得,方纔幹起事來。這等一個看法,方纔得那春宮之力。讀淫書,要在已經動手之後,未曾竣事之前,讀來方有用處。將幹的時節先把淫書擺在面前,兩個幹了一會然後揭開。或是他念我聽,或是我念他聽。念到高興之處,又幹起來。幹到興闌之處,又念起來。這等一個讀法,方纔得那淫書之力。][41]

Hanan has noted that *Carnal Prayer Mat* has a 'wealth of discourse',[42] and one of the forms that discourse takes is 'a character's monologue or mental soliloquy.'[43] Given Li Yu's label as a 'comic erotiker',[44] one wonders if Flora's solemn lecture on such a vulgar topic is to be taken seriously at all. Its sound depiction of the nuanced use of different tools of stimulation, however, can be understood as an apology for the genre of erotic fiction at large.

### 'Erotica-in-erotica': nested representations, nested realities

In *Carnal Prayer Mat*, Vesperus's investment in erotic novels and albums proves to be worthwhile. With the help of these powerful tools, the narrator tells us that the couple achieves perfect harmony in the realm of sexuality:

> The lute and the zither are inadequate symbols for the harmony of their bedroom bliss, just as the bell and the drum are incapable of expressing their joy. Even if you were to paint three hundred and sixty erotic pictures, they would not suffice to depict the lovemaking of Vesperus and Jade Scent. In later times a poet composed a lyric on the pleasure this couple took in looking at their album. It ran,
>
>> She's on his lap by the bedroom window,
>> While he on her scented shoulder leans.
>> As they open the book and linger upon its scenes,
>> She finds these joys aren't secrets, after all,
>> But age-old lore.

> Her hair disordered more and more,
> They tumble like a phoenix pair;
> Nine times in ten the lotuses point up.
> Immortal-like, she'd play the scenes forever,
> With joys as rare.[45]
>
> [他夫妻二口的枕席之歡,真是琴瑟不足喻其和,鐘鼓不能鳴其樂,就畫三百六十幅春宮,也還描寫他不盡。後人由詞一首,單說他夫妻二人看春宮的樂處。詞云:
> 疊坐繡窗前,斜倚香肩,揭開冊子共流連,始信合歡非隱事。
> 今古相傳,個個鬢雲偏。鳳倒鸞顛,金蓮十對九朝天。
> 願學畫中人到老,夜夜神仙。][46]

The couple's achievement of perfect harmony derives from its successful 'somatic translation' of the mentioned erotic pictures. Stressing the viewer's willingness to 'play the scenes forever', the lyric affirms the usefulness of erotic pictures in facilitating lovemaking. It also emphasizes the role of 'spring palace' pictures in the transmission of the age-old lore of sexual knowledge. Most importantly, in re-presenting the couple's lovemaking, the poem verbally translates the couple's somatic translation.

The *Xiechunyuan*-edition of the novel (寫春園叢刊肉蒲團) features another type of nested, multimedia translation. There are two illustrations rendering the couple's viewing of erotica in Chapter 3 (see figures 1 and 2).[47] What is particularly interesting about these two pictures is the multiple layers of translation/adaptation involved. In the verbal account of the episode, Vesperus and Jade Scent, as viewers of erotic pictures, 'translate' the content of these pictures into action. This verbal account of their somatic translation then is adapted into two illustrations, capturing not only the erotic pictures as objects lying on the table, but also the process of the couple's bodily translation as they move from the chair to the bed. Furthermore, by depicting the couple's somatic translation, the illustrations replicate the erotic pictures the couple viewed. Indeed, if we understand the illustrations as representation of the intradiegetic erotic pictures, they are endowed with an extradiegetic dimension, implying the identification between the viewer of these illustrations with the couple that makes such good use of erotic stimuli. As a result, the consumer may him- or herself experience *dongxing*.

Here the line between representation and reality, between character and reader, is blurred. Instead of a simple case of 'erotica-in-erotica', we are looking at an infinitely nested structure of representations, each of which constitutes the 'reality layer' of a further layer.

### Voyeurism: live 'erotica-in-erotica'

Located at the intersection between representation and reality, the erotica-in-erotica convention not only shows the fascination of Ming-Qing erotica with shuttling between mediums and between representation and reality, it also offers a window into voyeurism, another important convention in late imperial erotica.

Commenting on *Plum in the Golden Vase*, Martin Huang observes, 'This novel,

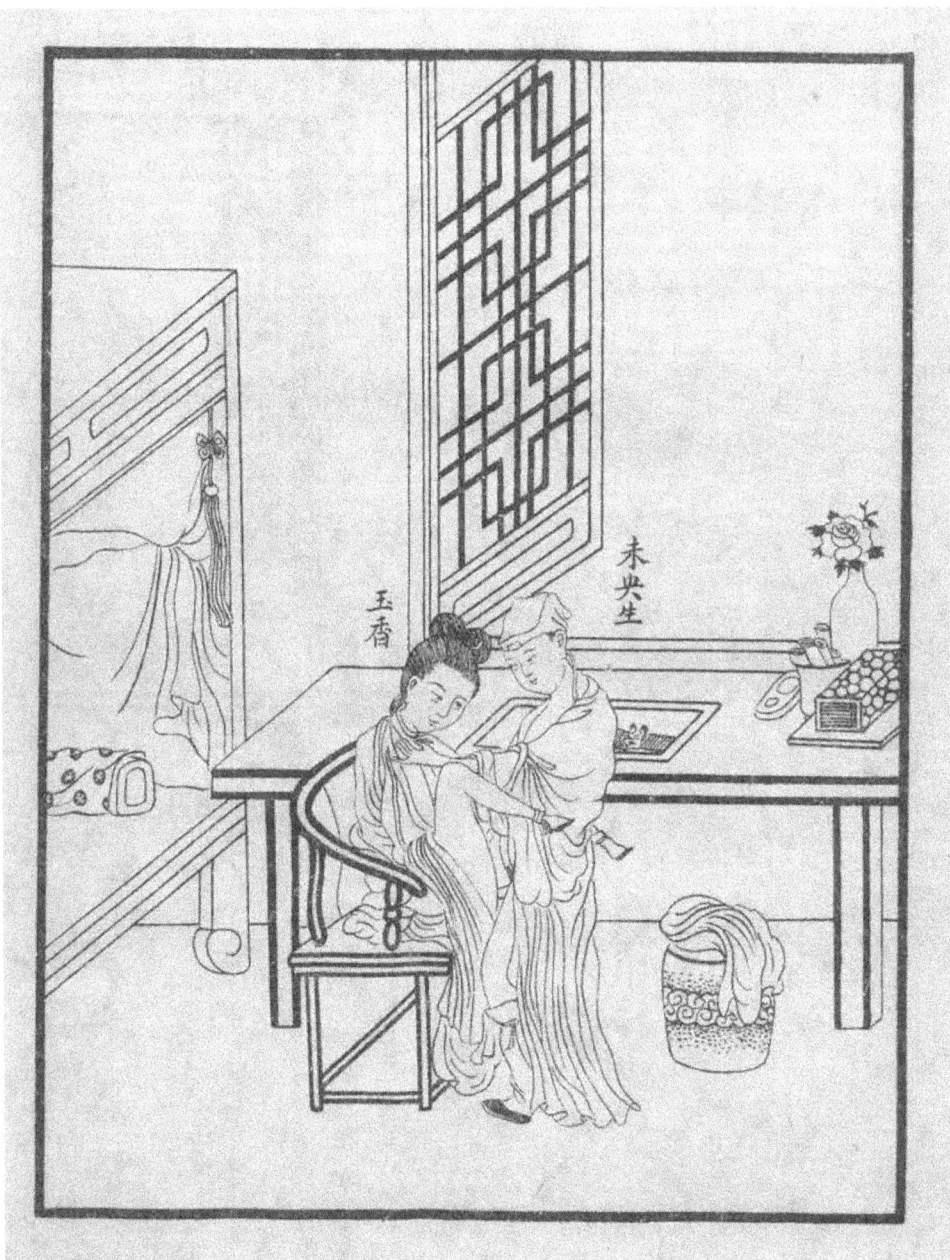

Fig. 7.1. Anonymous. Illustrations from the *Xiechunyuan* edition of the *Rou Pu Tuan*. *Xiechunyuan congkan diyi ji*. 1943. Robert Hans van Gulik Collection, Leiden University Library, SINOL. Gulik E Hsieh CY. Reprinted here with permission from Leiden University Library.

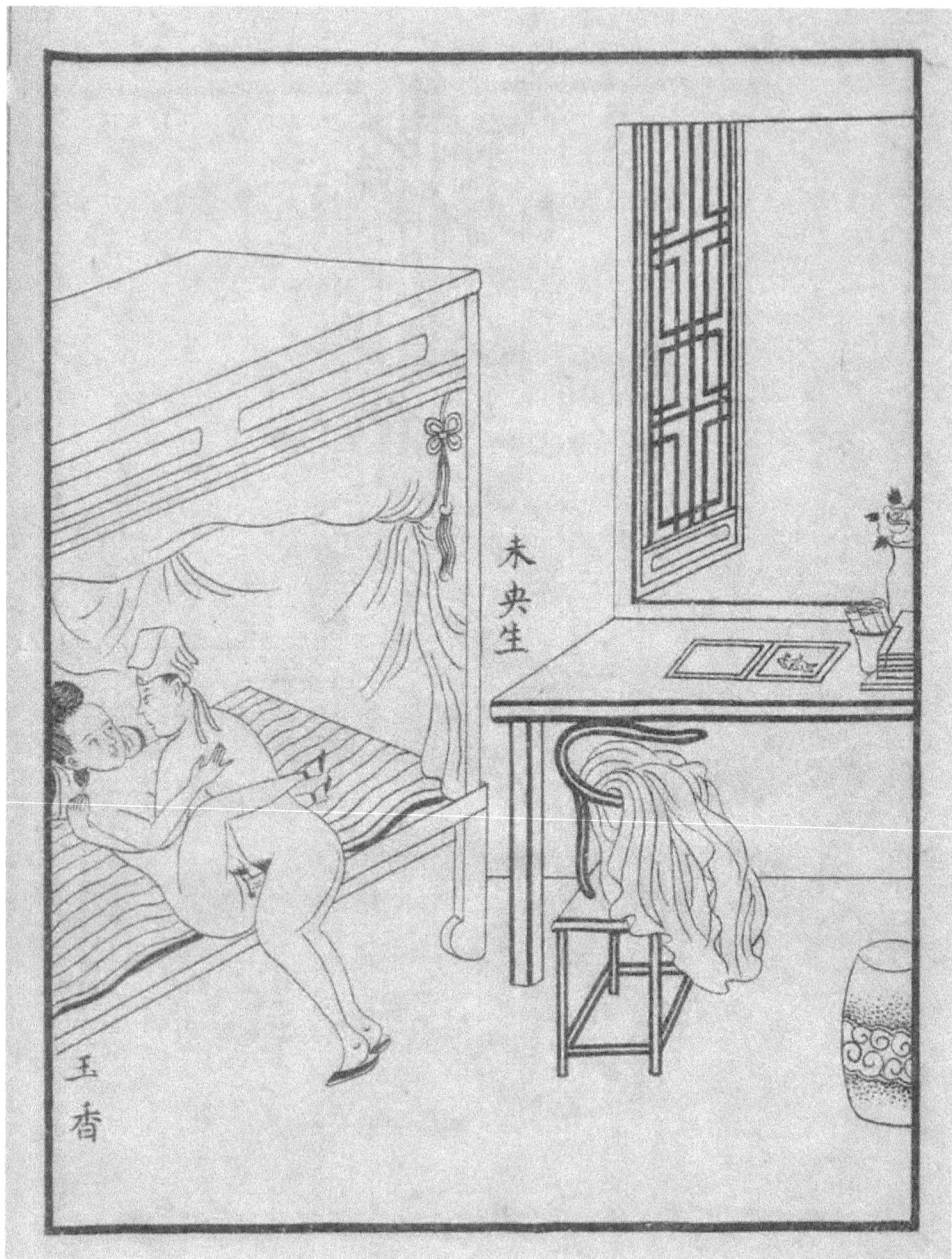

FIG. 7.2. Anonymous. Illustrations from the *Xiechunyuan* edition of the *Rou Pu Tuan*. *Xiechunyuan congkan diyi ji*. 1943. Robert Hans van Gulik Collection, Leiden University Library, SINOL. Gulik E Hsieh CY. Reprinted here with permission from Leiden University Library.

which is dominated by images of screens, shut gates, and closed blinds, is full of incidents of eavesdropping and peeping. Voyeurism, which depends on enclosed spaces, thus becomes one of the most important narrative features.'[48] The privileged position of voyeurism in Chinese erotica partly has to do with the belief in the importance of sight to sex, a point the 'erotica-in-erotica' convention already proves. In erotic novels, scenes of lovemaking are in fact often likened to 'spring palace' pictures. Take, for instance, an episode in *Carnal Prayer Mat*: while Vesperus is having a wild night with three women, Flora walks in on them. Panicking, Vesperus hides in a trunk used for storing paintings and albums.[49] Upon opening the trunk, Flora is immediately mesmerized by the naked Vesperus, whose sight is compared to that of a 'live erotic picture' (活春宮 *huo chungong*).[50] In fact, Flora is so aroused by what she sees that she forcefully takes this 'live erotic picture' away.

In *Carnal Prayer Mat*, voyeurism starts with the participants of the sexual act themselves. Vesperus finds darkness detrimental for *dongxing* and explains to Jade Scent: 'It's ten times more enjoyable in the daytime, and the wonderful thing is that it's precisely when we're looking at each other that we get really excited [*dongxing*]'[51] [日裡行房,比夜間的快活更加十倍。其間妙處,正在我看了你,你看了我,才覺得動興].[52] Since he and Jade Scent are both good-looking, they should 'take [their] pleasure in the daylight and show [their] bodies to one another'[53] [在日間取樂,顯一顯肌膚].[54]

*Chungong* also lack the arousing effect of sound. Flora claims that there are three methods one can use to enhance one's sexual prowess: 'viewing erotic pictures, reading erotic books, listening to lewd sounds'[55] [看春意讀淫書聽騷聲].[56] For her, the last method is even more important than the first two:

> In my opinion, [...] there is nothing to surpass it among all the thrills and pleasures of sex. It means lying beside a pair of lovers and listening to the sounds they make — enough to drive you wild with delight. I've always taken a special pleasure in listening to other people in action. [...] As a method, it's even more fun than erotic pictures and novels.[57]
>
> [男子與婦人幹事,那種歡暢之情,淫佚之趣,自己看來也還不過如此。倒是在旁邊側耳聽聲的人,替他快活不過。我生平極喜聽任幹事。[...] 這個法子,比看春宮讀淫書更覺得有趣。][58]

Similar to erotic pictures, 'live *chungong*' are also often put to two uses: to seduce inexperienced women (*dongqing*) and to stimulate experienced women (*dongxing*). In *Lascivious History of Hailing*, King Hailing deliberately has sex with women in a brightly lit room in order to seduce the young girl Zhongjie 重節. As anticipated, the girl, living next doors, starts peeping at the 'live *chungong*' through a hole, and her desires are stirred up. Soon Hailing successfully seduces the girl.

In *Carnal Prayer Mat*, voyeurism plays a key role in the adulterous relationship between Jade Scent and Honest Quan 權老實. After Quan's wife cheated on him with Vesperus, Quan seeks revenge by seducing Vesperus' wife Jade Scent. Assuming that the lonely Jade Scent will not be able to resist the sight of lovemaking, Quan deliberately has sex with his new bride, a maid at Jade Scent's, in their well-lit room, knowing that Jade Scent will be eavesdropping. As he predicts, Jade Scent is aroused upon peeping at them. In order to 'excite his lust' [動他淫興],⁵⁹ Jade Scent also lures Quan to peep at her while she is taking a bath. Having presented each other 'live erotic pictures', the two soon become lovers.

*By way of conclusion: the self-referentiality of Ming-Qing erotica*

Scholars have long noticed the prominence of intertextuality and intermediality in Ming-Qing erotica. This starts with the lasting influence of *Unofficial History of the Embroidered Couch*, not only on later erotic fiction, but also on the plots and motifs of other text genres, such as Feng Menglong's vernacular short stories and even *Dream of the Red Chamber*.⁶⁰ To an equal extent, its influence reaches beyond the textual realm, as it had a 'great influence on the erotic albums'⁶¹ of the same period. Once popular, erotic novels 'constituted also the "livre de chevet" of all designers of erotic paintings and picture albums.'⁶² *Plum in the Golden Vase* and *Carnal Prayer Mat* became reference points for flirtatious scenes of seduction, the open portrayal of the ensuing sex acts and also, on a more subtle note, for scenes of romantic love.⁶³

The present study holds that, in the light of the 'erotica-in-erotica' convention, Chinese erotica form a semi-enclosed, self-reliant, and self-generating system. We should note that the erotica mentioned in these novels are seldom imaginary, but consists of actual novels, pictures or albums circulated in the Ming-Qing period, not only in China, but also in Japan.⁶⁴ They not only create a sensuous ambience, but pay homage to an established genre tradition.

## Bibliography

### I. Primary texts

CAO, XUEQIN 曹雪芹, *Hong Lou Meng* (紅樓夢 [Dream of the Red Chamber]) (Beijing: Renmin wenxue chuban she, 1993).
CHEN, QINGHAO 陳慶浩 and WANG QIUGUI 王秋桂, *Siwuxie huibao* (思無邪匯寶 [Treasured Collection of Innocent Thoughts]), 31 vols (Taipei: Taiwan daying baike, 1995).
*Hailing Yishi* (海陵佚史 [*The Lost History of Hailing*]), in *Siwuxie huibao*, ed. by Qinghao Chen and Wan Qiugui, 31 vols (Taipei: Taiwan daying baike, 1995), I.
*Jin Ping Mei cihua* (金瓶梅詞話 [*Plum in the Golden Vase*]), ed. by Mei Jie 梅節 (Taipei: Liren shuju, 2007).
*Langshi* (浪史 [*History of a Libertine*]), in *Siwuxie huibao*, ed. by Qinghao Chen and Wan Qiugui, 31 vols (Taipei: Taiwan daying baike, 1995), IV.
LI, YU 李漁, *Rou Pu Tuan* (肉蒲團 [*The Carnal Prayer Mat*]), in *Siwuxie huibao*, ed. by Qinghao Chen and Wan Qiugui, 31 vols (Taipei: Taiwan daying baike, 1995), II.
LÜ, TIANCHENG 呂天成, *Xiuta yeshi* (繡榻野史 [*Unofficial History of the Embroidered Couch*]), in *Siwuxie huibao*, ed. by Qinghao Chen and Wan Qiugui, 31 vols (Taipei: Taiwan daying baike, 1995), II.

### II. Critical literature

CAHILL, JAMES, 'Introduction to R. H. van Gulik, *Erotic Colour Prints of the Late Ming Period*', in *Erotic Colour Prints of the Ming Period: With an Essay on Chinese Sex Life from the Han to the Ch'ing Dynasty, B.C. 206–A.D. 1644*, ed. by Robert Hans van Gulik (Leiden: Brill, 2004), pp. ix–xxv.

CLARK, TIMOTHY, and C. ANDREW GERSTLE, AKI ISHIGAMI, and AKIKO YANO (eds.), *Shunga: Sex and Pleasure in Japanese Art* (Leiden: Hotei Publishing, 2014).
CLUNAS, CRAIG, *Pictures and Visuality in Early Modern China* (Princeton, NJ: Princeton University Press, 1997).
GULIK, ROBERT HANS VAN, *Erotic Colour Prints of the Ming Period: With an Essay on Chinese Sex Life from the Han to the Ch'ing Dynasty, B.C. 206-A.D. 1644* (Leiden: Brill, 2004).
GUO, JIE, 'Robert Hans van Gulik Reading Late Ming Erotica', in *Hanxue yanjiu* (漢學研究) [*Chinese Studies*], 28.2 (June 2010), 225–65.
HANAN, PATRICK (trans.), *The Carnal Prayer Mat*, written by Li Yu (Honolulu, HI: University of Hawai'i Press, 1988).
—— *The Invention of Li Yu* (Cambridge, MA: Harvard University Press, 1988).
HAYAKAWA, MONTA 早川聞多, 'Who Were the Audiences for *Shunga*?', in *Shunga: Sex and Pleasure in Japanese Art*, ed. by Timothy Clark, C. Andrew Gerstle, Aki Ishigami, and Akiko Yano (Leiden: Hotei Publishing, 2014), pp. 34–47.
HUANG, MARTIN W., *Desire and Fictional Narrative in Late Imperial China* (Cambridge, MA: Harvard University Press, 2001).
IDEMA, WILT, '"Blasé Literati": Lü T'ien-ch'eng and the Lifestyle of the Chiang-nan Elite in the Final Decades of the Wan-Li Period', in *Erotic Colour Prints of the Ming Period: With an Essay on Chinese Sex Life from the Han to the Ch'ing Dynasty, B.C. 206–A.D. 1644*, ed. by Robert Hans van Gulik (Leiden: Brill, 2004), pp. xxxi–lix.
ISHIGAMI, AKI 石上阿希, 'Chinese *Chunhua* and Japanese *Shunga*', in *Shunga: Sex and Pleasure in Japanese Art*, ed. by Timothy Clark, C. Andrew Gerstle, Aki Ishigami, and Akiko Yano (Leiden: Hotei Publishing, 2014), pp. 92–103.
JULLIEN, FRANÇOIS, *The Impossible Nude: Chinese Art and Western Aesthetics*, trans. by Maev de la Guardia (Chicago, IL: The University of Chicago Press, 2000).
LING, XIAOQIAO 凌筱嶠, 'Yilu yindu zhi can: jie "Xixiangji" yuedu "Hailing yishi" (夷虜淫毒之慘:借《西廂記》閱讀《海陵佚史》 [Debauchery and Barbarity: Reading *Retrieved History of Hailing* against *The Western Chamber*]), *Qinghua Zhongwen xuebao* 清華中文學報 [*Qinghua Chinese Journal*], 12 (December 2014), 153–200.
TIAN, XIAOFEI, 'A Preliminary Comparison of the Two Recensions of *Jinpingmei*', *Harvard Journal of Asiatic Studies*, 62.2 (December 2002), 347–88.
YANO, AKIKO 矢野明子, '*Shunga* Painting before the "Floating World"', in *Shunga: Sex and Pleasure in Japanese Art*, ed. by Timothy Clark, C. Andrew Gerstle, Aki Ishigami, and Akiko Yano (Leiden: Hotei Publishing, 2014), pp. 62–73.

## Acknowledgements

I wish to thank Johannes Kaminski and Rudolph Ng for inviting me to attend the conference 'Erotic Literature: Adaptation and Translation in Europe and Asia' and my fellow participants and audience for their comments and support. Special thanks go to Johannes Kaminski for his feedback and meticulous editing, to Laura Moretti for her helpful questions and suggestions, and to Wilt Idema, Ling Xiaoqiao and Chen Jianqing for their help and encouragement.

## Notes to Chapter 7

1. There is a sizable body of homoerotic literature from the Ming-Qing period, but I am still to find examples of 'erotica-in-erotica' involving same-sex couples.
2. *History of a Libertine* dates from the mid to late Wanli era (1573–1620) and was published under

the pseudonym Fengyue xuan youxuanzi 風月軒又玄子. See Chen Qinghao 陳慶浩 and Wang Qiugui 王秋桂, 'Publication Notes', in *Siwuye huibao* (思無邪匯寶 [Treasured Collection of Innocent Thoughts]), ed. by C. Q. and W. Q., 39 vols. (Taipei: Taiwan daying baike, 1995), IV, p. 16.

3. The anonymous novel *Plum in the Golden Vase* appeared in the sixteenth-century and circulated as manuscripts among literati. For an introduction to the different versions of the novel, see Xiaofei Tian, 'A Preliminary Comparison of the Two Recensions of *Jinpingmei*', *Harvard Journal of Asiatic Studies*, 62.2 (2002), 347–88.

4. *Lascivious History of Hailing* is attributed to the pseudonym Wuzhe Daoren 無遮道人 and was written between 1616 and 1644. See Chen and Wang, 'Publication Notes', I, pp. 26–28. For a discussion of the work as well as its employment of lines from Wang Shifu's 王實甫 *Western Chamber* (西廂記 *Xi Xiangji*) in its marginal commentary, see Ling Xiaoqiao 淩筱嶠, 'Yilu Yindu Zhi Can: Jie "Xixiangji" Yuedu "Hailing Yishi"' (夷虜淫毒之慘:借《西廂記》閱讀《海陵佚史》[Debauchery and Barbarity: Reading *Retrieved History of Hailing* against *The Western Chamber*]), *Qinghua Zhongwen xuebao* (清華中文學報 [Qinghua Chinese Journal], 12 (December 2014), pp. 153–200.

5. For an overview of Lü Tiancheng's 呂天成 novel and the cultural context of its publication around 1597, see Wilt Idema, ' "Blasé Literati": Lü T'ien-ch'eng and the Lifestyle of the Chiangnan Elite in the Final Decades of the Wan-Li Period', in *Erotic Colour Prints of the Ming Period: With an Essay on Chinese Sex Life from the Han to the Ch'ing Dynasty, B.C. 206-A.D. 1644*, ed. by Robert Hans van Gulik (Leiden: Brill, 2004), pp. xxxi–lix.

6. *Carnal Prayer Mat* was published in 1657. See Patrick Hanan, 'Introduction', in *The Carnal Prayer Mat*, trans. by in P. H. (Honolulu, HI: University of Hawai'i Press, 1988), p. xi.

7. I will use Hanan's name translation throughout this paper. All translations are my own, unless otherwise stated, J. G.

8. Craig Clunas, *Pictures and Visuality in Early Modern China* (Princeton, NJ: Princeton University Press, 1997), p. 157.

9. Patrick Hanan, *The Invention of Li Yu* (Cambridge MA: Harvard University Press, 1988), p. 123.

10. See 'It is a fantasy about how women will behave, but more specially, it is a fantasy about how women will respond to pictorial representation'. Clunas, *Pictures and Visuality in Early Modern China*, p. 58.

11. The translation is found in Robert Hans van Gulik, *Erotic Colour Prints of the Ming Period: With an Essay on Chinese Sex Life from the Han to the Ch'ing Dynasty, B.C. 206–A.D. 1644* (Leiden: Brill, 2004), p. 177.

12. For a discussion of the language style of this episode, see Ling Xiaoqiao, 淩筱嶠, 'Yilu Yindu Zhi Can', pp. 160–63.

13. *Langshi*, in *Siwuye huibao*, IV, p. 96.

14. *Langshi*, p. 96. Note here the term for 'passion stirring' is 興動 *xingdong*, literally 'desired [being] stirred up'. Unless stated otherwise, translations are my own, J.G.

15. This is reminiscent of the lovesickness of the female protagonist Du Liniang 杜麗娘 in the late Ming playwright Tang Xianzu's 湯顯祖 *Peony Pavillion* 牡丹亭.

16. *Langshi*, p. 99.

17. According to Hayakawa Monta, in Edo Japan, many women avidly enjoyed woodblock erotic pictures known as *shunga* ('spring pictures') — indeed, as he puts it, the 'fantasy world of shunga was enjoyed by men and women, young and old'. Hayakawa Monta, 'Who Were the Audiences for *Shunga*?', trans., C. Andrew Gerstle, in *Shunga: Sex and Pleasure in Japanese Art*, ed. by Timothy Clark, Andrew Gerstle, Aki Ishigami, and Akiko Yano (Leiden: Hotei Publishing, 2014), pp. 34–47 (p. 34).

18. Clunas, *Pictures and Visuality in Early Modern China*, p. 157.

19. See ibid., p. 157.

20. Some Ming-Qing fictional works feature men reading or viewing erotica alone. In Chapter 23 of *Dream of the Red Chamber*, Baoyu 寶玉 reads erotic fiction alone. See Cao Xueqin 曹雪芹, *Honglou meng* 紅樓夢 (Beijing: Renmin wenxue chuban she, 1993), p. 233.

21. See Li Yu, *Rou Pu Tuan*, in *Siwuye huibao*, II, p. 187.
22. Hanan, 'Introduction', pp. vii–viii.
23. Ibid., p. viii.
24. James Cahill, 'Introduction', in *Erotic Colour Prints of the Ming Period*, p. xxiii. See below for further discussion on the similarity between sex handbooks and erotic novels.
25. Ling Xiaoqiao, 凌筱嶠, 'Yilu Yindu Zhi Can', pp. 191–92.
26. *Hailing Yishi*, in *Siwuye huibao*, I, p. 128.
27. *Langshi*, pp. 113–14.
28. See *Langshi*, pp. 114–15.
29. Hanan, *The Invention of Li Yu*, p. 124.
30. Idema, '"Blasé Literati", p. lv.
31. Lü Tiancheng 呂天成, *Xiuta yeshi* (繡榻野史), in *Siwuye huibao*, II, p. 157.
32. See Lü, *Xiuta yeshi* (繡榻野史), pp. 157–58. In a later episode, Jinshi uses erotic pictures to help her husband seduce a woman, see ibid., p. 268.
33. Baoyu's copy of the play is provided by his page boy Mingyan 茗煙, who bought it together with numerous other novels and 'biographies' featuring female historical figures such Zhao Feiyan 趙飛燕, Wu Zetian 武則天, and Yang Yuhuan 楊玉環. See Cao, *Honglou meng* 紅樓夢, pp. 233–34.
34. See Cao, *Honglou meng* 紅樓夢, pp. 588–89. In an earlier episode, Baoyu's other cousin Baochai 寶釵, having discovered that Daiyu was reading *The Story of the Western Chamber*, also warns her of the danger such works pose to young women, see ibid., pp. 448–49.
35. Hanan, *The Carnal Prayer Mat*, p. 53.
36. Li Yu, *Rou Pu Tuan*, p. 186.
37. Hanan, *The Carnal Prayer Mat*, p. 54.
38. Li Yu, *Rou Pu Tuan*, p. 187.
39. Ibid., p. 257.
40. Hanan, *The Carnal Prayer Mat*, p. 258.
41. Li Yu, *Rou Pu Tuan*, pp. 433–34. [Emphasis mine.]
42. Hanan, *The Invention of Li Yu*, p. 125.
43. Ibid., p. 128.
44. Ibid., p. 111.
45. Hanan, *The Carnal Prayer Mat*, pp. 54–55.
46. Li Yu, *Rou Pu Tuan*, p. 187.
47. These pictures are third and the fourth illustrations attached to the second volume (*juan* 卷). There are sixty-five illustrations in this edition, first published in 1943. For a brief introduction of the *Xiechunyuan* edition, see Chen and Wang, 'Publication Notes' in *Siwuye huibao*, II, pp. 22–23.
48. Martin W. Huang, *Desire and Fictional Narrative in Late Imperial China* (Cambridge MA: Harvard University Press, 2001), p. 59.
49. See Chapter 16 of the novel.
50. Li Yu, *Rou Pu Tuan*, p. 419. Hanan translates 活春宮 as 'live erotic album', see Hanan, *The Carnal Prayer Mat*, p. 250.
51. Hanan, *The Carnal Prayer Mat*, p. 45.
52. Li Yu, *Rou Pu Tuan*, p. 178.
53. Hanan, *The Carnal Prayer Mat*, p. 46.
54. Li Yu, *Rou Pu Tuan*, p. 179.
55. Hanan, *The Carnal Prayer Mat*, p. 257.
56. Li Yu, *Rou Pu Tuan*, p. 433.
57. Hanan, *The Carnal Prayer Mat*, p. 258.
58. Li Yu, *Rou Pu Tuan*, p. 435.
59. Li Yu, *Rou Pu Tuan*, p. 376.
60. Idema, '"Blasé Literati", p. lvii.
61. Van Gulik, *Erotic Colour Prints of the Ming Period*, p. 128.
62. Ibid., p. 129.

63. See Cahill, 'Introduction', p. xxiii.
64. As shown in Chen Qinghao and Wang Qiugui's publication notes, much of this body of literature can today only be found in Japanese libraries and collections. Ishigami Aki discusses the impact of Chinese erotica on Japanese erotica. See Ishigami Aki 石上阿希, 'Chinese *Chunhua* and Japanese *Shunga*', in *Shunga*, pp. 92–103.

CHAPTER 8

# National Erotics, Gender, and the Representation of Sexuality in Heian Japan (794–1185)

*Joshua S. Mostow*

According to the *Oxford English Dictionary*, the first definition of 'sexuality' in a sense that goes beyond the biological is found in Havelock Ellis's work *Studies in the Psychology of Sex*.[1] In coining the term 'inverted sexuality'[2] Ellis defines the term against an Other, in this case homosexuality. In the first volume of his *History of Sexuality* (*L'Histoire de la sexualité*, 1984), Foucault also invokes an Other in order to portray the origins of modern sexuality in the seventeenth century. Here, he contrasts Western *scientia sexualis* with Eastern *ars erotica*:

> Historically, there have been two great procedures for producing the truth of sex. On the one hand, the societies — and they are numerous: China, Japan, India, Rome, the Arabo-Moslem societies — which endowed themselves with an *ars erotica*. [...] On the face of it at least, our civilization possesses no *ars erotica*. In return, it is undoubtedly the only civilization to practice a *scientia sexualis*.[3]

According to Hinrich Fink-Eitel, Foucault originally 'hoped for evidence from the Orient for an exemplary *ars erotica*.'[4] The following volumes of Foucault's *History*, however, reveal a much greater affinity between the Greco-Roman discourse on sexuality and that of Christianity on the one hand, and on the other hand, an affinity between τα αφροδίσια (*ta afrodisia*) — the ancient Greek term for 'the things that belong to Aphrodite' — with ancient Chinese sexual practices.[5] We would be mistaken to ignore the Orientalist fantasy that originally nurtured Foucault's study.

The OED and Foucault's definition of sexuality respectively rely on an Other. In doing so, they mirror the 'identity politics' of the Heian period (平安時代). Dating from 794 to 1185, this period saw the established writing in Chinese *kanbun* (漢文) extended by vernacular forms. This development also coincided with the development of distinctive visual imagery and the construction of a native Japanese aesthetic discourse of eroticism in opposition to the Chinese Other. In both cases, foreign semantics systems are perceived to challenge existing norms. In order to achieve their reconciliation, the foreign agent needs to be translated and re-contextualised in a new setting.

## Chinese Explicitness

Foucault's description of *ars erotica orientalis* is unreferenced and, in view of ancient Chinese practices, inaccurate. They were not static, rather having undergone significant changes throughout the centuries: from the beginning of Han dynasty (206 BC) until the Tang dynasty (618–907 AD), sexual techniques focused on pleasure and health. In the late Tang, however, sexual yoga became dominant as sex was understood to be a meditative act. The position of women changed accordingly: 'In the early texts, the female partner is called "woman" or "enemy", but by the last she has become "other", "crucible", or "stove".'[6]

The overarching concern of ancient Chinese approaches to sex is health and longevity, not *ars erotica*. Donald Harper argues that 'the ancient Chinese regarded sexual relations as a vital part of the therapeutic arts of physical cultivation. Along with breath cultivation, callisthenic exercises, and dietetics, sexual intercourse was one of the methods for "nurturing life" (*yang sheng* 養生).'[7] There were indeed detailed techniques and secret teachings, but they were not aimed at pleasure as an end in itself. Instead, they were predicated on the necessity for the male to not ejaculate: nourishing himself on the *yin* 陰 set free by the female partner's multiple orgasms, the man aimed at strengthening his *yang* 陽.[8] (See Jie Guo's article in this volume, especially the section *Uses of erotica*.)

Interestingly enough, until the discovery of the manuscripts in Mawangdui, Hunan in the 1970s, most of what was known of ancient Chinese sexual discourse came from a Japanese work, the *The Essentials of Medicine* (醫心法 *Ishimpō*), a compendium of Chinese sources compiled by Tamba Yasuyori 丹波康頼 (912–95),[9] a descendant of immigrants and a medical practitioner himself. With the introduction of Tang governmental structures and accompanying culture, the Japanese adopted the societal and artistic practices of the cosmopolitan Sinitic sphere. In this spirit, the *Essentials* elaborate on 'The Qualities of a Fine Woman' by juxtaposing Chinese texts like *Secrets of the Jade Chamber* (玉房秘決 *Yufang mijue*) and *The Classic of Great Purity* (大清經 *Daqingjing*), and which we can compare with the Japanese reproduction of a Tang-styled beauty (Figure 8.1):

> The signs of noble and respectable females are smooth skin, tenderness in bone structure, a devoted heart, a harmonious disposition, hair glossy like varnish, a beautiful countenance and features, no hair above the Yin, a refined conversational voice and an opening (孔穴 *kongxue*) which faces forward. Intercourse with such a woman, even lasting a whole day, is not tiring. By searching for such a woman, a man can nurture his mind and prolong his years of life.[10]
>
> [凡相貴人尊女之法,欲得滑內弱骨,專心和性,發澤如漆,面目悅美,陰上無毛,言語聲細,孔穴向前,與之交會,終日不勞,務求此女,可以養性延年矣。][11]

This discourse also appears in the *belles lettres* written by Japanese men at the time, such as *Rhyme-prose on the Marriage of Man and Woman* (男女婚姻賦 *Danjo kon'in*

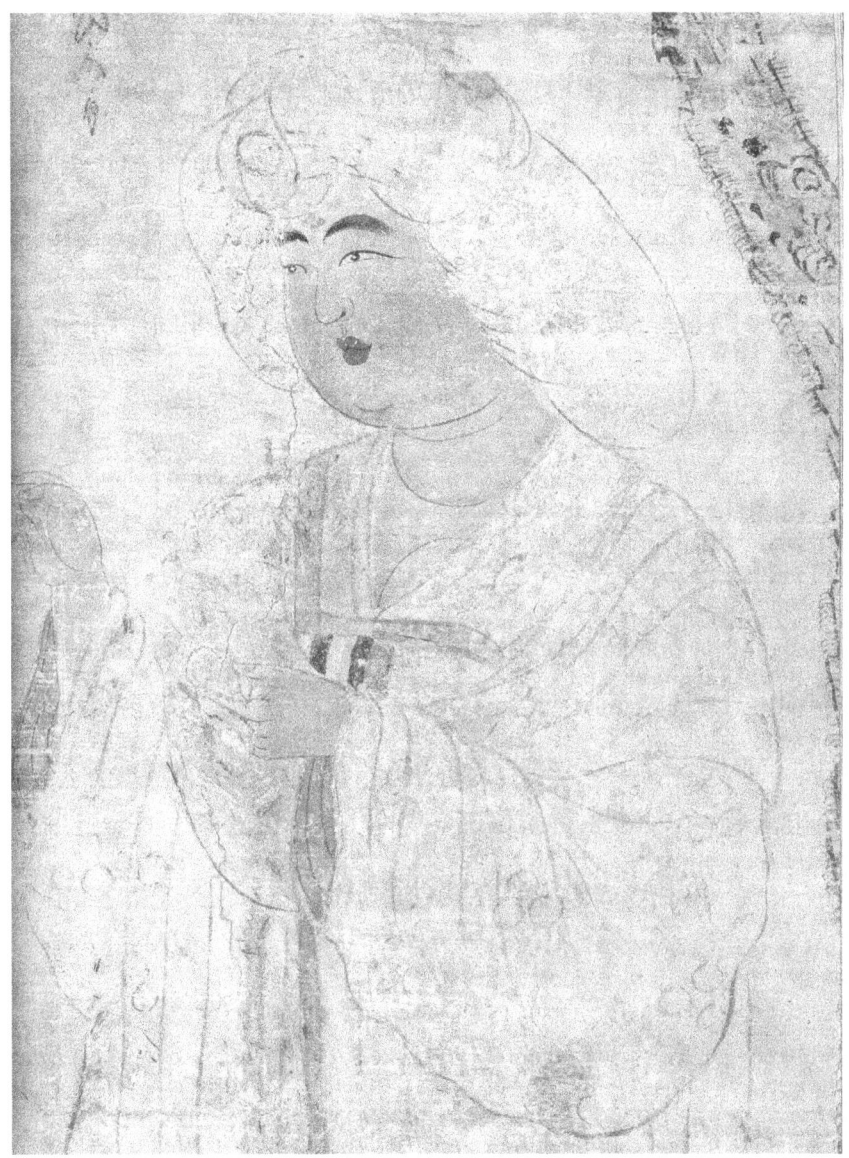

FIG. 8.1. Detail of *Folding screen panel with bird-feathers decorating the painting of a lady under a tree; North Section 44*. Panel of a screen, ink and color on paper, height 49 1/2". First quarter of 8th century. Shōsōin Treasure. Courtesy of the Shōsōin Treasure House, Nara, Japan.

*fu*) by Ōe no Asatsuna 大江朝綱 (886–957), collected in the *Literary Essence of Our Country* (本朝文粹 *Honchō monzui*) dating from the mid-eleventh century. While the work is written in *kanbun* (classical Chinese), it adds decidedly local colour by depicting courtship by means of Japanese *waka* poetry (和歌) and likening the lovers to the famous Heian poets Ono no Komachi 小野小町 and Ariwara no Narihira 在原業平:

> Then [*he*] plies her with Japanese poems, bit by bit tangling the strings of her heart. [...],
> And now bodies grow subtly mild, their wills little by little aroused,
> she dwells in loveliness, in charms a match for Ono no Komachi,
> He speaking with a quiet elegance that would shame Ariwara no Narihira.
>
> [繼以倭歌,彌亂心機之緒。[...] 徒觀夫其體微和,其意漸感。婀娜以居,類野小町之操。閑雅而語,抽在中將之瞻。]

Here, the poet builds on palace-style poetry (宮體詞 *gongti ci*), where the female subject is often reduced to waiting passively in her boudoir for her absent lover. Nonetheless, while Chinese sources emphasize docility and passiveness, the woman here is given a certain degree of agency:

> What at first she only endures later becomes most familiar.
> Unbinding the sash of her single robe, knowing she cannot tie it again,
> baring flesh white as snow, forgetting for once to be ashamed [...]
> He broaches the gate where moisture abounds, and fluids overflow to stain their undergarments;
> They look about, but there's no one at the door: moans grow louder, impossible to still [...]
> The mutual response of yin and yang, this is the Creator's natural way.[12]
>
> [於是,忍其初,親其後,解單袴之紐,更不知結。露白雪之膚,還忘厭醜。[...] 入門有濕,淫水出以污褌。窺戶無人,吟聲高而不禁。[...] 苟陰陽之相感,知造化之自然。][13]

Her sexual responsiveness accords with a passage from *The Essentials of Medicine* where the Yellow Emperor learns of the qualities of a fine woman:

> At the time of intercourse her love fluid oozes and anoints, her body moves and shakes; she can hardly hold herself still. Her perspiration reaches every part of her body as it follows in close response to the man's actions. Such a woman will not harm a man even though he does not follow correct chamber technique.[14]
>
> [交接之時,精液流漾,身體動搖,不能自定,汗流四逋,隨人舉止。男子者,雖不行法,得此人由不為損。][15]

In view of noblewomen's literary activity and their authorship of vernacular literature, however, Heian Japan differs from Tang China.

### Japanese 'national erotics'

Most notably, one can find a rejection of the Sinitic sexological discourse in texts such as *The Tale of the Lady Ochikubo* (落窪物語 *Ochikubo monogatari*). Initially composed during the mid-tenth century, it tells of a Japanese Cinderella. As a dashing officer contrives to meet with her secretly, this endeavour is frustrated by the evil stepmother, who locks her into a storehouse. An old and licentious (戯し *tawashi*) man is dispatched to violate the girl and claim her as his wife. Significantly, this man is introduced as a Ten'yaku no suke 典薬助, that is, Assistant Director of the Bureau of Medicine.[16] Thereby, he represents a trade that advocates the intercourse of old men with young women as a means to foster the man's *yang* and prolong his life. Since this character also appears in other texts,[17] his comic and repellent role hints at what I have in another context called 'national erotics'.[18] Under the stewardship of women, indigenous culture is being constructed in contrast to the Chinese Other.

Indeed, in contrast to the explicitness of the Chinese tradition, Heian vernacular culture is comparably restrained in its representation of sexuality. I would like to illustrate this with an old debate concerning the definition of the term 女絵 *onna-e*, an indigenous Japanese word represented by the juxtaposition of the *kanji* for 'woman' and 'picture'. In *The Pillow Book* (枕草子 *Makura no sōshi*), the author Sei Shōnagon 清少納言 describes *onna-e* with the following words: 'A well-executed picture done in the female style, with lots of beautifully written accompanying text around it'[19] [ようかきたる女絵の、ことばをかしうつけておほかる *you kakitaru onna-we, kotoba wokashiu tsukete ohokaru*].[20]

While an earlier English translation thought this label would indicate explicit imagery,[21] the female-centered part of Heian culture avoids representations of actual sex. The rare examples of Heian sexual imagery that have survived for almost a millennium give evidence of the aesthetic preferences of the aristocratic elite. The most notable set of early erotic illustrations dates from 1154 and is found in *The Lotus Sutra Painted on Fans* (扇面法華経 *Senmen Hokekyō*). Here, the *Lotus Sutra*, is inscribed over fifty-nine fan paintings of secular subjects, including a number of human figures. Next to apparent illustrations of literary romances — or 物語絵 *monogatari-e*[22] — there are three fans showing couples lying down together. The clearest is *Hokekyō* Scroll 8 Fan 10 (Figure 8.2):

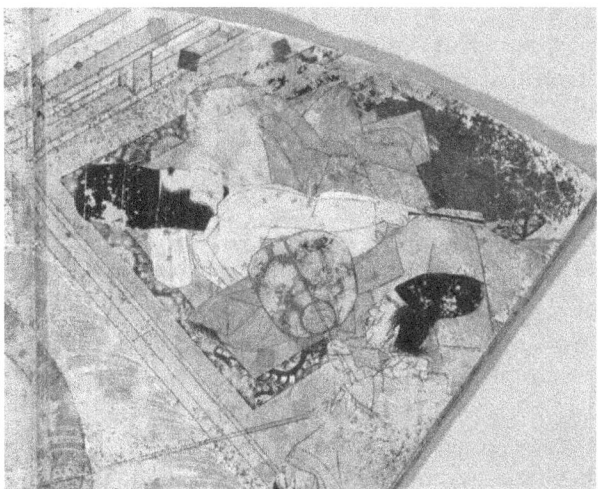

FIG. 8.2. Detail of *Senmen Hokekyō sōshi*: *Hokekyō* Scroll 8, Fan 10. 1254. Colours on paper. Tokyo National Museum.

It has been argued that because this fan had no obscuring sutra text copied over it, it was deemed too explicit by some later owner, who had the figure of the woman erased.²³ The man is wearing a translucent gown and is being fanned by an attendant. In a reconstruction (Figure 8.3) that includes the erased female figure, the role of the attendant becomes somewhat surprising:

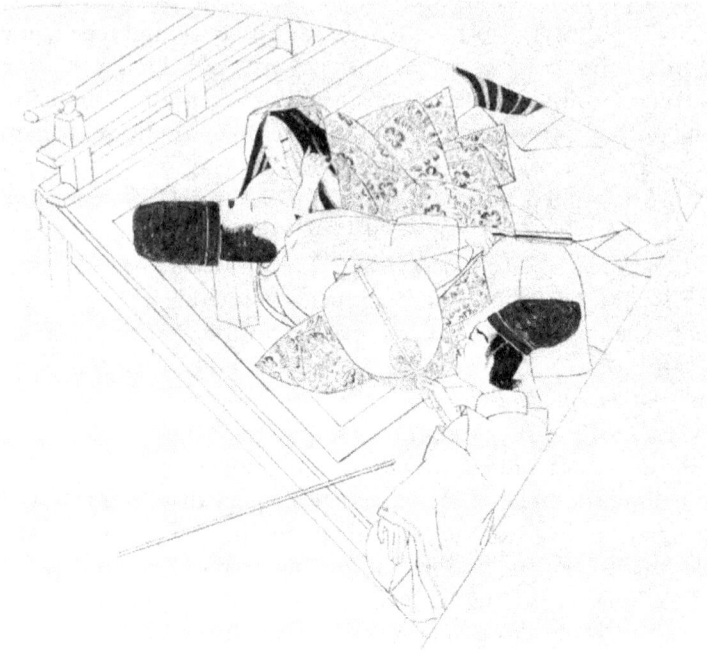

FIG. 8.3. Reconstruction of *Senmen Hokekyō*, *Hokekyō* Scroll 8, Fan 10. Image by Suzuki Keizō, in Akiyama Terukazu, Yanagisawa Taka, and Suzuki Keizō, *Senmen Hokekyō no kenkyū* (Tokyo: Kajima Shuppankai, 1972), p. 219.

Heian aristocrats exhibited an indifference to near-nudity and the lack of privacy in front of social inferiors. Here, the servant is reduced to the subordinate function of alleviating the heat.

In the next image (Figure 8.4), the role of the third is occupied by a young boy who spies on the couple. Both the man and the woman are naked under their singlets (単 *hitoe*) and the man is pulling back the woman's hair — a comparatively erotic gesture. Underneath the man's sword there is a paper and, were this an Edo-period print, one could take it for a wipe for clean-up after sex — it perhaps has the same function here.

Clearly, these are 'lying down pictures'. Yet there are no depictions of oversized sex organs as, for example, described in the *Stories Heard from Writers Old and New* (古今著聞集 *Kokon chomonjū*). Edited by Tachibana no Narisue 橘成季 in 1254, one anecdote mentions the genre おそくづの繪 *osokudzu no we*, a term that can be translated as 'lying-down picture': 'Regard such things as "lying-down pictures" by the skilled ancients! They exceed the actual size of "those parts" (*sono mono*)

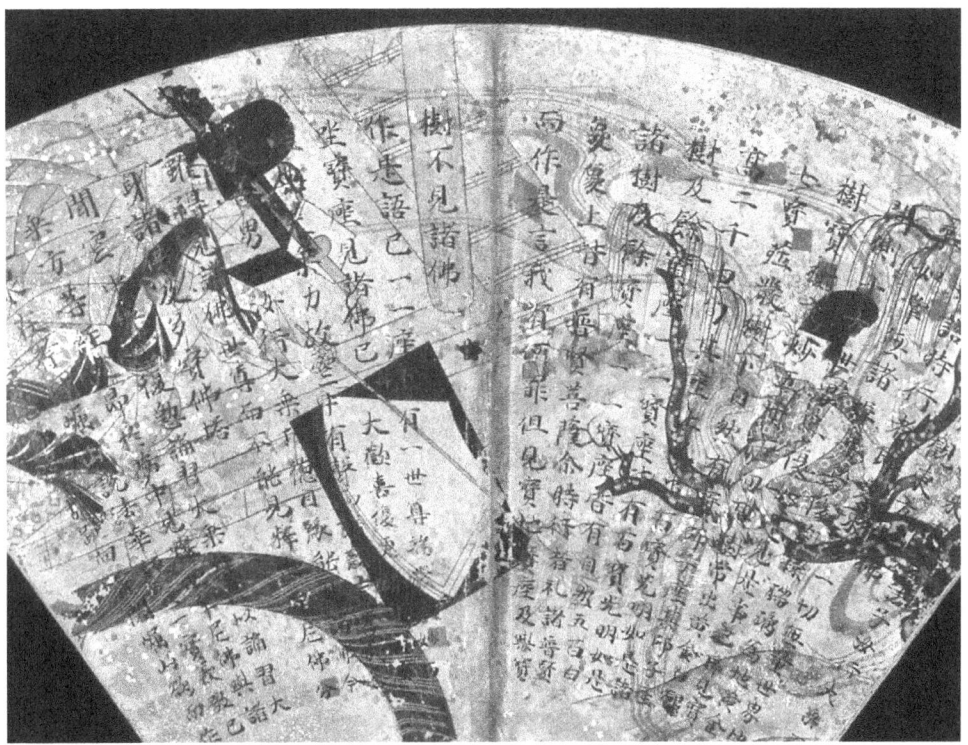

FIG. 8.4. *Senmen Hokekyō sōshi: Kanfugenkyō*, Fan 7. Shitennōji, Osaka.

and draw them large — how can the truth be like that? But if one draws them as they actually are, there is no longer anything remarkable, and it is in that case that one calls them "pictures of falsehoods" (*e-soragoto*)'[24] [ふるき上手どものかきて候おそくづの絵などを御覽も候へ。その物の寸法は分に過て大に書て候事、いかでか実にはさは候べき。ありのまゝの寸法にかきて候はゞ、見所なき物に候故に、絵そらごとゝは申事にて候].[25] The only surviving images featuring enlarged organs from this period, however, are so-called 陽物比べ *Yōbutsu kurabe*, which literally translates into 'Male Member Competition' (Figure 8.5).[26] This genre has traditionally been attributed to the Toba Sōjō 鳥羽僧正 and is usually seen not as an erotic, but as a comical art form.

In literature, there is evidence for negative reactions to fans showing erotic couples, such as an episode in the late-Heian collection *A Treatise of Ten Rules* (十訓抄 *Jikkinshō*). The story tells of Kaya no In 高陽院 (1094–1155), who had originally joined imperial service relatively late in life, and later became a nun. Her unworldly taste is illustrated by the following passage:

> Kaya no In was so removed from men that it is said that she even threw away fans that had pictures of men and women side-by-side drawn on them. Although she was ridiculed as knowing nothing of the ways of the world, surely we must call her a fine example of someone keeping deeply to the ancient ways.[27]

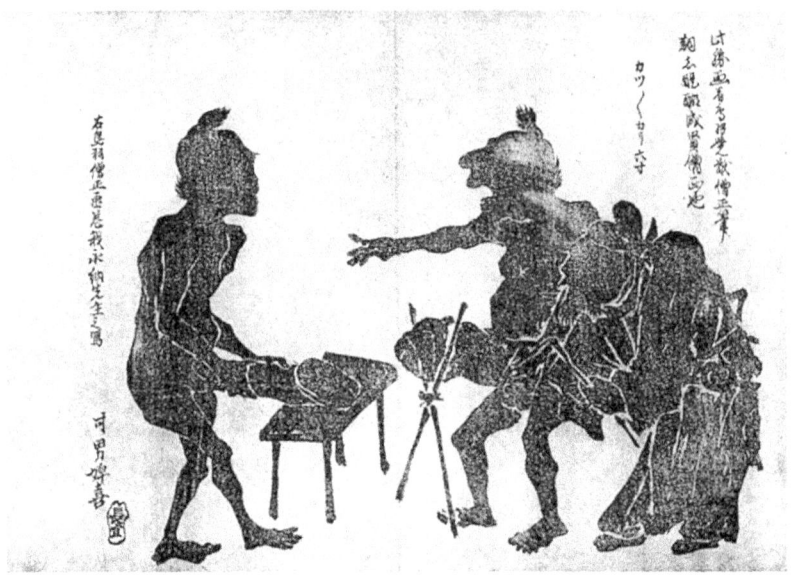

FIG. 8.5. *Yōbutsu kurabe*, from *Kagetsu-chō*. 1836. Private collection. Ritsumeikan ARC database.

[高陽院の御様はあまりに男とをくて、男女ならびゐたる絵かける扇をばすてられけるとかや。かへりてよづかぬさまにあざけれども、ふかく昔びたらん方はいみじきためしと申べし。]²⁸

It follows that pictures of 'men and women side-by-side' were understood to be erotic — despite their lack of explicitness — and were rejected by Kaya no In for this precise reason.

Now what exactly happens on *The Lotus Sutra Painted on Fans,* and what makes these images erotic? First and foremost, in classical Japanese paintings (大和絵 *yamato-e*), the proximity of adult noblemen and noblewomen is rare and is in itself already regarded as suggestive. In all that remains of the twelfth-century *Tale of Genji* scrolls (源氏物語絵巻 *Genji monogatari emaki*), only six of the extant twenty scenes fall into this category — three being clearly tragic or comical.²⁹ This leaves only three quasi-erotic scenes: one painting shows a couple with a crying infant,³⁰ then there is a couple with the female sitting behind a translucent curtain (几帳 *kichō*), and the scene of Yūgiri 夕霧 and Roku no Kimi 六君 on the morning after their wedding night (Figure 8.6). The composition of this image is closely related to figures 8.2, 8.3 and 8.4:

When it comes to early classical Japanese paintings (*yamato-e*), viewers easily succumb to the 'modern oblivion' that Leo Steinberg addressed in his book on the sexuality of Christ in Renaissance art. Steinberg argues that when confronted with an image such as Hans Baldung Grien's St. Anne playing with the genitals of the Christ Child, it makes no sense to suggest that 'this is just what grandmothers do with their grandsons' or to refer to regional folk beliefs. Rather, we moderns have become oblivious to the deep theological import of the sexuality of God made flesh.³¹ In other words, we see a representation of reality when in fact we should be

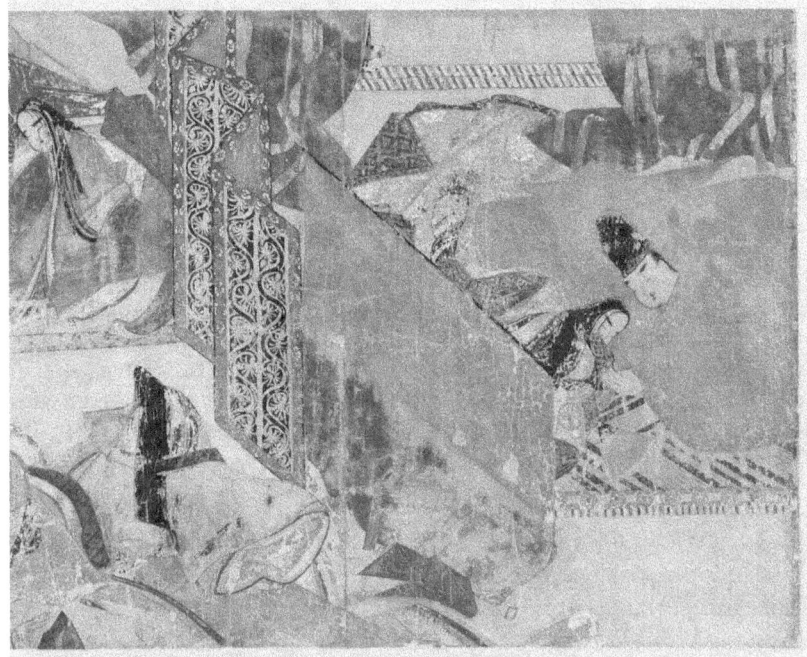

Fig. 8.6. Detail of *The Picture Scroll of The Tale of Genji* (Genji monogatari emaki): Yadorigi ('The Ivy') II. Twelfth century. Tokugawa Art Museum, Nagoya.

seeing symbols and code. In a similar way, one easily becomes oblivious to the rarity of the coexistence of a male and female side-by-side in *yamato-e* and its profound semiotic, indeed erotic, content. In contrast to 'romantic' *onna-e*, where an isolated figure longs for the absent lover,[32] the depiction of the lover's proximity no longer addresses pure longing, but 'desire' and 'passion', that is, *iro* 色.

This presupposes different expectations towards the explicitness of erotic works. While Heian aristocrats had an indifference to near-nudity in front of social inferiors (see figure 3), aristocratic women were not supposed to be seen by any same-class men other than their fathers, husbands, or sons. As a consequence, paired depictions of men and women of the same social rank do not have to depict a physiological union in order to suggest such a sexual encounter.

Arguably, male aristocrats may well have also enjoyed 'stronger stuff'. In such a case, they would have turned to *kanbun*, such as *Literary Essence of Our Country* or *A Dalliance in the Immortals' Den* (遊仙窟 *Youxianku/ Yūsenkutsu*). But there would have been the scent of the exotic and the foreign in their appreciation that stood in opposition to the native style. This is, then, one more example of the double binary structure of Japanese culture that Chino Kaori discussed. In Figure 8.7, large 'A' is China, and large 'B' Japan. But within large 'B', small 'a' refers to the Japanese male participation in the erotic discourses of China, while small 'b' represents the feminine-oriented vernacular of Japanese 'national erotics':

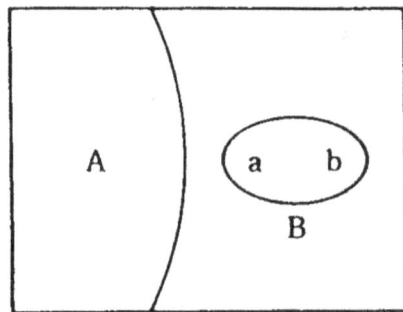

Fig. 8.7. Chino Kaori. Graph of the dual binary structure. Chino Kaori, 'Gender in Japanese Art', in *Gender and Power in the Japanese Visual Field*, ed. by Joshua Mostow, Norman Bryson, and Maribeth Graybill (Honolulu, HI: University of Hawai'i Press, 2003), pp. 17–54 (p.25).

This model of transculturality avoids the essentialism of Foucault's formulation where Western sexuality is imagined in a polar opposition to Eastern *ars erotica*. In spite of Heian Japan's increasing self-awareness, it constructed a sexual discourse in which the internalized foreign Other remained part of the national identity.

## Conclusion

In view of the low survival rates of the visual evidence, our findings cannot go beyond providing informed speculations. Most of the twelfth-century illustrated scrolls of *The Tale of Genji* have been lost, and much of *The Lotus Sutra Painted on Fans* is lost or disfigured. Unfortunately, it is precisely the visual material that could provide the evidence we need. As John R. Clarke pointed out, many classical cultures like ancient Rome were more restrictive towards written material.[33] Unlike modern society, classical cultures treated the visual as ephemeral, especially in the secular realm. Michitsuna no Haha only describes scenes of isolated figures, and Sei Shōnagon refrains from describing her 'women's pictures' at all. Even if there once existed a substantial corpus of explicit Heian-period visual erotica, written evidence of it would not necessarily follow.

More importantly, what our investigation tells us about sexuality and its representation in the Heian period is, first, that it is entirely class-based. In *osokuzu* the only figures that embody sexuality are noblewomen and noblemen. And they are free to be amorously engaged even if observed by those of the lower orders — lower-class servants and children simply do not count, do not have subjectivity. In this sense, then, it would make no sense to speak of 'male' or 'female' sexuality. Here, sexuality — as a discourse — is limited to the aristocracy.

Yet, on the other hand, there is a clear gender axis: Heian noblemen participated in a dual culture that was comprised of both the cosmopolitan, that is, sinitic culture, and the vernacular. Yet whereas the cosmopolitan culture largely marginalized noblewomen, the vernacular culture was designed in some sense specifically to include them. *This* sexuality and its representation were the construction of a kind of 'national', or vernacular, identity — what I have been calling a national erotics.

And it is here that we might, at the end, return to Foucault. Because what Foucault ended up exploring in the last two volumes of *The History of Sexuality* was the notion of problematization, especially in view of the 'structure of subjectification' involving 'the acts that concern sexual behaviour'.[34] As Gary Gutting points out, '[p]roblematizations formulate the fundamental issues and choices through which individuals confront their existence'.[35] While in ancient Greece women and slaves were 'marginalized', freeborn males were 'problematized'. In the Greek context, this culminates in the 'problem of the boy': 'the boy, who is sought as the passive partner of a dominating male, is nonetheless being groomed as a future leader of the *polis*. How could such a person be a sexual object on the same level as women and slaves?'[36] What, then, was problematized by the nobility of Heian Japan? Research by Doris Croissant, Catherine Vance Yeh, and others such as myself has shown that, in the modern period in Japan and China, this problematization often revolves around a 'third sex', or some kind of androgynous or sexually interstitial figure.[37] Is this true for Japan's premodern period as well? What are we to make of the fact that all the surviving images of the *Senmen Hokekyō* depict heterosexuality? Or is some kind of problematization in any way indicated by the seemingly incongruous pairing of erotic imagery with religious text as seen in the *Senmen Hokekyō*? The 1150s were during the reign of emperor Go-Shirakawa, who was well-known for his love of *imayō* (今様, 'contemporary') songs as performed by cross-dressing *shirabyōshi* (白拍子), female entertainers. Surviving *imayō* include such bawdy lyrics as the listing of names for women's genitals, but the overwhelming majority of texts are on deeply religious Buddhist themes.[38] Does, then, the figure of the *shirabyōshi* serve as the focus of some sort of problematization? Chino's 'dual binary structure' restricts gender distinctions to two levels: masculine Chinese 'A' versus feminine Japanese 'B', and within 'B,' masculine 'a' and feminine 'b'. But the vernacular 'b' contains its own representations of masculine and feminine — might this not precisely interpellate problematizing figures such as the cross-dressing *shirabyōshi*? With, hopefully, a clearer idea of what Heian sexuality was and how it was represented, these are the kinds of questions that I hope can be explored in the future.

# Bibliography

## I. Primary texts and translations

*The Essentials of Medicine in Ancient China and Japan: Yasuyori Tamba's Ishimpō*, trans. and annotated by Emil C. H. Hsia, Ilza Veith, and Robert H. Geertsma, 2 vols (Leiden: Brill, 1986).

MICHITSUNA, NO HAHA 藤原道綱母, *Tosa nikki, Kagerō nikki* (土佐日記、蜻蛉日記), ed. by Matsumura Sei'ichi 松村誠一, Kimura Masanori 木村正中, and Imuta Tsunehisa 伊牟田経久 (Tokyo: Shōgakukan 1973).

—— *The Kagerō Diary*, trans. by Sonja Arntzen (Ann Arbor, MI: University of Michigan/Center for Japanese Studies, 1997).

TACHIBANA, NO NARISUE 橘成季, *Kokon chōmonjū* 古今著聞集, ed. Nagazumi Yasuaki 永積安明and Shimada Isao 島田勇雄 (Tokyo: Iwanami Shoten 岩波書店, 1966).

*Ochikubo monogatari, Tsutsumi Chūnagon monogatari* (落窪物語、堤中納言物語), ed. by Mitani Ei'ichi 三谷栄一, Mitani Kuniaki 三谷邦明, and Inaga Keiji 稲賀敬二 (Tokyo: Shogakukan, 1972).

ŌSORA, SHÔSUKE 大曽根章介, *Honchō monzui* 本朝文粋 (Tokyo: Iwanami Shoten, 1992).

SEI, SHŌNAGON 清少納言, *Makura no sōshi* (枕草子), ed. by Matsuo Satoshi 松尾聡 and Nagai Kazuko 永井和子 (Tokyo: Shōgakukan 小学館, 1984).

—— *The Pillow Book*, trans. by Meredith McKinney (New York, NY: Penguin, 2006).

TAMBA, YASUYORI 丹波康賴, *Ishinpō* (醫心房), in *Great Anthology of Ancient Chinese Medical Records* (中醫典籍大全集) <http://fi-n.net/detial.php?id=21561&catid=429&catname=%E4%B8%AD%E9%86%AB%E6%99%BA%E6%85%A7> [accessed 29 Sept 2016].

WATSON, BURTON (trans.), *Japanese Literature in Chinese: Poetry and Prose in Chinese by Japanese Writers of the Early Period*, 2 vols (New York, NY: Columbia University Press, 1975).

*II. Critical literature*

AKIYAMA, TERUKAZU 秋山光和, 平安時代世俗画の研究 *Heian jidai sezokuga no kenkyū* (Tokyo: Yoshikawa Kōbunkan, 1964).

AKIYAMA, TERUKAZU, YANAGISAWA TAKA, and SUZUKI KEIZŌ, *Senmen Hokekyō no kenkyū* (Tokyo: Kajima Shuppankai, 1972).

CLARKE, JOHN R., *Looking at Lovemaking: Constructions of Sexuality in Roman Art 100 B.C. — A.D. 250* (Berkeley, CA: University of California Press, 1998).

CROISSANT, DORIS, YEH, CATHERINE VANCE, and MOSTOW, JOSHUA S., *Performing 'Nation'* (Leiden: Brill, 2008).

ELLIS, HAVELOCK, *Studies in the Psychology of Sex*, 2 vols (Philadelphia, PA: F.A. Davis, 1905).

FINK-EITEL, HINRICH, *Foucault: An Introduction*, trans. Edward Dixon (Philadelphia: Pennbridge Books, 1992).

FOUCAULT, MICHEL, *The History of Sexuality*, trans. Robert Hurley, 3 vols (New York, NY: Vintage, 1990).

GUTTING, GARY, *Foucault: A Very Short Introduction* (Oxford: Oxford University Press, 2005).

HARPER, DONALD, 'The Sexual Arts of Ancient China as Described in a Manuscript of The Second Century B.C.', *Harvard Journal of Asiatic Studies*, 47 (1987), 539–93.

LANE, RICHARD リチャード・レイン, *(Higa emaki) Koshibagaki-zōshi* (秘画) 小柴垣草紙 (Tokyo: Kawade Shobō Shinsha, 1997).

LIPPIT, YUKIO, 'Figure and Facture in the Genji Scrolls: Text, Calligraphy, Paper, and Painting', in Haruo Shirane, ed., *Envisioning* The Tale of Genji: *Media, Gender, and Cultural Production* (New York: Columbia University Pres, 2008), pp. 54–56.

MCDONALD READ, LOUISA, *The Masculine and Feminine Modes of Heian Secular Painting and Their Relationship to Chinese Painting: A Redefinition of Yamato-E* (unpublished Ph.D. dissertation, Stanford University, 1976).

MORRIS, IVAN, *The Pillow Book of Sei Shōnagon*, 2 vols (New York, NY: Columbia University Press, 1967).

MOSTOW, JOSHUA S., 'Utagawa *Shunga*, Kuki's "Chic", and the Construction of a National Erotics in Japan', in *Performing "Nation": Gender Politics in Literature, Theater, and the Visual Arts of China and Japan, 1880–1940*, ed. by Doris Croissant, Catherine Vance Yeh, and Joshua S. Mostow (Leiden: Brill, 2008), pp. 383–424.

OED ONLINE (Oxford University Press), <http://www.oed.com> [accessed 4.10.2016].

STEINBERG, LEO, *The Sexuality of Christ in Renaissance Art and in Modern Oblivion* (Chicago, IL: University of Chicago Press, 1996 [1983]).

Umekawa, Sumiyo, '*Tiandi Yinyang Jiaohuang Dalefu* and the Art of the Bedchamber', in *Medieval Chinese Medicine: The Dunhuang medical manuscripts*, ed. by Vivienne Lo and Christopher Cullen (London: Routledge, 2005), pp. 252–77.

Wile, Douglas, *Art of the Bedchamber: The Chinese Sexual Yoga Classics, including Women's Solo Meditation Texts* (Albany, NY: State University of New York Press, 1992).

Yano, Akiko, 'Historiography of the "Phallic Contest" Handscroll in Japanese Art', *Japan Review, Journal of the International Research Center for Japanese Studies*, 26 (2013), 59–82.

## Notes to Chapter 8

1. One of the OED's multiple definitions reads: 'A person's sexual identity in relation to the gender to which he or she is typically attracted; the fact of being heterosexual, homosexual, or bisexual; sexual orientation'. Entry *sexuality*, OED Online (Oxford University Press), <http://www.oed.com/view/Entry/177087#> [accessed 4.10.2016].
2. See Havelock Ellis, *Studies in the Psychology of Sex*, 2 vols (Philadelphia, PA: F. A. Davis, 1905), I, 258–86.
3. Michel Foucault, *The History of Sexuality*, trans. Robert Hurley, 3 vols (New York, NY: Vintage, 1990), I, 57–58.
4. Hinrich Fink-Eitel, *Foucault: An Introduction*, trans. Edward Dixon (Philadelphia: Pennbridge Books, 1992), p. 18.
5. Gary Gutting argues that volumes 2 and 3 of *The History of Sexuality* are unrelated to the *Introduction* and to his genealogy of 'bio-power'. See Gary Gutting, *Foucault: A Very Short Introduction* (Oxford: Oxford University Press, 2005), p. 100.
6. Douglas Wile, *Art of the Bedchamber: The Chinese Sexual Yoga Classics, including Women's Solo Meditation Texts* (Albany, NY: State University of New York Press, 1992), p. 45.
7. Donald Harper, 'The Sexual Arts of Ancient China as Described in a Manuscript of The Second Century B. C.', *Harvard Journal of Asiatic Studies*, 47 (1987), 539–93 (p. 539).
8. Again, this last statement should be somewhat amended: Sumiyo Umekawa, in her discussion of *The Heaven and Earth, Yin and Yang Songs of Great Satisfaction in Sexual Pleasure* (天地陰陽交歡大樂賦), attributed to Xingjian 行簡 (776?–826), notes that '[i]t is important to emphasize that methods of conception and childbirth had been recognized as an intrinsic part of the sexual arts from a very early stage.' Sumiyo Umekawa, '*Tiandi Yinyang Jiaohuang Dalefu* and the Art of the Bedchamber', in *Medieval Chinese Medicine: The Dunhuang medical manuscripts*, ed. by Vivienne Lo and Christopher Cullen (London: Routledge, 2005), pp. 252–77 (p. 253). Umekawa defines the 'arts of the bedchamber' as techniques which value the harmony between *yin* and *yang*, and the control of *qi* 氣 by means of sexual activity. The techniques aim at: 1. nourishing life, 2. achieving longevity or immortality, 3. becoming an immortal, 4. establishing lineage continuation or conception and childbirth, 5. healing and preventing diseases, and 6. celebrating Taoist religious ceremonies (pp. 254–55). Nonetheless, she ultimately rejects the notion of this work as a manual of the sexual arts: '*The Songs* is concerned more with the pleasures of sexual intercourse, the joy of harmonious relationships and the excellence of life' (p. 273). These pleasures also include the pederastic, which would appear to be contrary to contemporaneous sexology.
9. Japanese names are given in the Japanese order, with the surname first, unless it is an author writing in English.
10. *The Essentials of Medicine in Ancient China and Japan: Yasuyori Tamba's Ishimpō*, trans. and annotated by Emil C. H. Hsia, Ilza Veith, and Robert H. Geertsma, 2 vols (Leiden: Brill, 1986), II, 208.
11. Tamba Yasuyori 丹波康賴, *Ishinpō* (醫心房), in *Great Anthology of Ancient Chinese Medical Records* (中醫典籍大全集) <http://fi-n.net/detial.php?id=21561&catid=429&catname=%E4%B8%AD%E9%86%AB%E6%99%BA%E6%85%A7> [accessed 29 Sept 2016].
12. Burton Watson (trans.), *Japanese Literature in Chinese: Poetry and Prose in Chinese by Japanese Writers of the Early Period*, 2 vols (New York, NY: Columbia University Press, 1975), I, 53–56.
13. Ōsora Shōsuke 大曽根章介, *Honchō monzui* 本朝文粋 (Tokyo: Iwanami Shoten 岩波書店, 1992), pp. 130–31.

14. *The Essentials*, II, 207.
15. Tamba Yasuyori, *Ishinpō* (醫心房).
16. See 落窪物語、堤中納言物語 *Ochikubo monogatari, Tsutsumi Chūnagon monogatari*, ed. by Mitani Ei'ichi 三谷栄一, Mitani Kuniaki 三谷邦明, and Inaga Keiji 稲賀敬二 (Tokyo: Shogakukan 小学館, 1972), p. 157.
17. He also appears several times in 今昔物語集 (*Tales of Times Now Past/ Konjaku monogatari shū*], a twelfth century collection of didactic tales.
18. See Joshua S. Mostow, 'Utagawa *Shunga*, Kuki's "Chic", and the Construction of a National Erotics in Japan', in *Performing "Nation": Gender Politics in Literature, Theater, and the Visual Arts of China and Japan, 1880–1940*, ed. by Doris Croissant, Catherine Vance Yeh, and Joshua S. Mostow (Leiden: Brill, 2008), pp. 383–424.
19. Sei Shōnagon, *The Pillow Book*, trans. by Meredith McKinney (New York, NY: Penguin, 2006), p. 30.
20. Sei Shōnagon 清少納言, 枕草子 *Makura no sōshi*, ed. by Matsuo Satoshi 松尾聡 and Nagai Kazuko 永井和子 (Tokyo: Shōgakukan 小学館, 1984), p. 108.
21. Ivan Morris, *The Pillow Book of Sei Shōnagon*, 2 vols (New York, NY: Columbia University Press, 1967), II, 307.
22. See *Kanfugekyō* 6 and *Hokekyō* Scroll 7 Fan 5.
23. See Akiyama Terukazu, Yanagisawa Taka, and Suzuki Keizō, *Senmen Hokekyō no kenkyū* (Tokyo: Kajima Shuppankai, 1972), p. 219.
24. Given the anecdote's reference to the monk Kakuyū 覚猷[24], who lived from 1053–1140, this passage documents pornographic art going back to the late Heian period or early Kamakura period — that is, 1140 at the earliest or 1254 at the latest.
25. Tachibana no Narisue 橘成季, *Kokon chōmonjū* 古今著聞集, ed. Nagazumi Yasuaki 永積安明 and Shimada Isao 島田勇雄 (Tokyo: Iwanami Shoten 岩波書店, 1966), p. 317.
26. The original of the *Yōbutsu kurabe* has been lost and the work is known only through late Edo-period copies such as the 'shadow-pictures' (陰絵 *kage-e*) printed in the 花月帖 (*Kagetsu-chō*), published in 1836, which claims to be based on a copy by Kano Eishin 狩野永真 (Yasunobu, 安信) of a copy by Kano Einō 永納 (1631–97). As late Richard Lane pointed out such pictures are hardly erotic, but solely humorous. See Richard Lane リチャード・レイン, *(Higa emaki) Koshibagaki-zōshi* (秘画) 小柴垣草紙 (Tokyo: Kawade Shobō Shinsha, 1997), p. 8. See Akiko Yano, 'Historiography of the "Phallic Contest" Handscroll in Japanese Art', *Japan Review, Journal of the International Research Center for Japanese Studies*, 26 (2013), 59–82.
27. All translations are mine, unless otherwise indicated, J.M.
28. Akiyama *Senmen Hokekyō*, pp. 27–28.
29. The tragic scenes are Genji's principal wife becoming a nun and the death of his first wife; the comic one Kumoinokari 雲井雁 snatching a letter from her husband.
30. This scene has an erotic innuendo. See Yukio Lippit, 'Figure and Facture in the Genji Scrolls: Text, Calligraphy, Paper, and Painting', in Haruo Shirane, ed., *Envisioning* The Tale of Genji*: Media, Gender, and Cultural Production* (New York: Columbia University Pres, 2008), pp. 54–56.
31. See Leo Steinberg, *The Sexuality of Christ in Renaissance Art and in Modern Oblivion* (Chicago, IL: University of Chicago Press, 1996 [1983]), p. 388.
32. E.g. the two *onna-e* that Michitsuna no Haha 道綱の母 describes in the *Kagerō Diary* (蜻蛉日記 *Kagerō nikki*): 'a woman leaning on the balustrade of a building called a fishing pavilion, gazing at the pines on the little islands in the middle of the pond' (Michitsuna no Haha, *The Kagerō Diary*, trans. by Sonja Arntzen (Ann Arbor, MI: Center for Japanese Studies/ The University of Michigan, 1997), p. 349) [釣殿とおぼしき高欄におしかかりて、中島の松をまぼりたる女; Michitsuna no Haha 藤原道綱母, *Tosa nikki, Kagerō nikki* 土佐日記、蜻蛉日記, ed. by Matsumura Sei'ichi 松村誠一, Kimura Masanori 木村正中, and Imuta Tsunehisa 伊牟田経久 (Tokyo: Shōgakukan 1973), pp. 370–71].
33. John R. Clarke, *Looking at Lovemaking: Constructions of Sexuality in Roman Art 100 B.C. — A.D. 250* (Berkeley, CA: University of California Press, 1998).
34. Gutting, *Foucault: A Very Short Introduction*, p. 102.
35. Ibid., p. 103.

36. Ibid.
37. For an overview see Doris Croissant, Catherine Vance Yeh and Joshua S. Mostow, 'Introduction', in Croissant et al., *Performing 'Nation'* (Leiden:Brill, 2008), pp. 1–16.
38. For English translations of *imayō*, see Yung-Hee Kim, *Songs to Make the Dust Dance: The Ryōjin hishō of Twelfth-Century Japan* (Berkeley: University of California Press, 1994), p. 3. For a general discussion of *yūjo* and *shirabyōshi*, see Janet R. Goodwin, *Selling Songs and Smiles: The Sex Trade in Heian and Kamakura Japan* (Honolulu: University of Hawai'i Press, 2007), esp. pp. 35–40.

CHAPTER 9

# Tragic Eroticism: or, the Silent Awakening of Meta-Pornography

*Julia Boog-Kaminski and Kathrin Emeis*

In academia, studies on erotic literature are still rare and isolated. What is more, there are few scholars who focus on literary eroticism itself rather than approaching it from a sociological or psychological angle.[1] Contributions by Michel Foucault, Roland Barthes, and Susan Sontag, however, are notable exceptions and engage with the artistic articulations of sexual encounters. They are not interested in the act itself, but in its representation by tropes, motifs, and rhetorical strategies. This contribution will focus on one of the most dazzling features of erotic literature: its metafictional dimension. According to Sontag, it makes 'the reader think of [...] other pornographic books, rather than sex unmediated'.[2]

Sophisticated examples of erotic literature play with intertextuality, polyphony, and complex narrative means. There is a uniquely postmodern quality to this genre, as it exhibits a high degree of self-consciousness with regard to the effects on its readership. Showing and telling is not enough here; erotic literature strives to trigger the reader's desire. As Sontag puts it, 'only in the absence of directly stated emotions can the reader of pornography find room for his own responses.'[3] It arouses the reader and inspires his or her 'pornographic imagination'. Such examples of 'meta-pornography'[4] involve the reader in an elaborate game revolving around the said and the unsaid. As the prefix 'meta' implies, meta-pornography does not fashion the narration in a mimetic sense, but triggers the reader 'to reflect on the textuality and fictionality of narrative in terms of its artifactuality'.[5] This also includes the use of self-reflexive comments that break the authenticity of the content and intensify the relationship between narrator and reader.[6] Monika Fludernik describes this type of narration as 'a deliberate meta-narrative celebration of the act of narration.'[7] Adapted to the context of erotic literature, one could rephrase this definition as a 'deliberate celebration of an erotic act in the reader's mind'. It turns the text into a pleasurable object in its own right.

In this manner, pornography aims 'to "excite" in the same way that books which render an extreme form of religious experience aim to "convert"',[8] as Sontag outlines. In her argument, she harks back to the first radical theorist of eroticism:

Georges Bataille, who 'renders a darker sense of the erotic [...] than anyone else'.[9] The present article builds on this observation and inquires into the intricate narrative techniques that make this effect possible. We focus on a number of examples in Bataille's oeuvre that are concerned with 'tragic eroticism', most notably: the short story *Madame Edwarda* (1941) and the essayistic texts *Eroticism* (*L'Érotisme*, 1957) and *Tears of Eros* (*Larmes d'Éros*, 1961). This article discusses the tension between narrated desire and the desire of the reader, and addresses the difficulties of expressing the erotic within scholarly discourse. For Bataille, our instrumental language is unfit to express the excess of eroticism, as it belongs to the realm of the 'unsaid' rather than the 'said'. Here, it is placed in direct proximity to the divine and death, the other two tropes which defy language. Lacking other agents of reference, Bataille employs these referents in order to translate elusive Eros into words.

## Bataille's 'tragic eroticism'

'Eroticism, it may be said, is assenting to life up to the point of death'[10] ['De l'érotisme, il est possible de dire qu'il est l'approbation de la vie jusque dans la mort'],[11] reads the beginning of Bataille's study *Eroticism*. He argues that Eros and Thanatos, attraction and horror, and lust and agony are inseparable dichotomies. In the erotic act, the human individual is bound to sacrifice itself in order to discover 'a feeling of profound continuity'[12] ['un instant fondamental de continuité'][13] akin to religious ecstasy. Bataille's 'tragic eroticism' is a transgressive force that touches the psychological and physiological limits of what it means to be human. As Sontag argues, it 'pushes to dangerous desires, which range from the impulse to commit sudden arbitrary violence upon another person to the voluptuous yearning for the extinction of one's consciousness, for death itself.'[14] Eroticism triggers 'a breaking down [...] of the regulated social order basic to our discontinuous mode of existence as defined and separate individuals'[15] ['une dissolution [...] de ces formes de vie sociale, régulière, qui fondent l'ordre discontinu des individualités définies que nous sommes'].[16]

This anarchist thrust also informs Bataille's singular way of communicating his idea of eroticism. In the eponymous book, the author intends to go beyond established forms of knowledge, after all 'eroticism has a significance for mankind that the scientific attitude cannot reach'[17] ['l'érotisme a pour les homes un sens que la démarche scientifique ne peut atteindre'].[18] In contrast to the discursive style of conventional scholarly writing, Bataille uses a plurality of text genres in order to broach the problem of eroticism. His own writing includes philosophical monographs, novels, short prose, and poetry, and as a journal editor, he brings together discrete discursive areas, bridging statistical studies, myth, dialectics, genealogy, biology, and poetry.[19] Influenced by the Surrealists' predilection for collage and fragmentary forms of writing,[20] his texts often oscillate between scholarly, fictional, and autobiographical writing, a juxtaposition that in turn creates metanarrative effects.

*Eroticism*, for example, starts out with a frank confession: 'nothing has intrigued me more than the idea of once more coming across the image that haunted my adolescence, the image of God'[21] ['rien ne m'a plus attaché que la possibilité de retrouver dans uns perspective générale l'image dont mon adolescence fut obsédée, celle de Dieu'].[22] Although Bataille is here referring to the image of God, the further argument of his philosophical study shows that this 'image' also includes his syphilitic father and his suicidal mother. Both lay the foundation of a deeply traumatic childhood, and some biographers take this as the starting point of his notion of 'tragic eroticism'.[23]

Both *Eroticism* and his biography include scenes of extreme profanity and of religiousness.[24] The chapters 'Le christianisme', 'La transgression', and 'L'objet du désir: la prostitution' refer to such turning points. In this context, the narrative self appears in the dual role of a confessant and a preacher, addressing himself as well as the reader and hinting at the extreme pain and extreme pleasure he experienced in life: 'I shall never forget the wonder and violence of the determination to open my eyes, to look straight at what is happening, at what *is*'[25] ['Je n'oublierai jamais ce qui se lie de violent et de merveilleux à la volonté d'ouvrir les yeux, de voir en face *ce qui arrive, ce qui est*'].[26] Here, the author emerges from behind the façade of his work, if only as a construct.[27] Sontag points out: 'The underlying theme is Bataille's own consciousness, a consciousness in an acute, unrelenting state of agony'[28] that wants the reader to think and suffer with him. The first-person narrator addresses the contradiction that one becomes human at the same time as one loses one's humanity in the transgressive act. This 'tragic' understanding designates a complete reversal of the ordinary situation of both living and writing, and both demand new ways of representation.

Bataille's self-reflexive autobiographical notes intensify the dialogue with the reader. In light of the narrator's repeated apostrophes to the reader, Fludernik calls this technique 'a deliberate meta-narrative celebration of the act of narration'.[29] What is more, Bataille makes ample use of unconventional metaphors that recall the mystical writings of Francis de Sales, Jeanne Guyon, François Fénelon, and Blaise Pascal. The connection between Eros and Thanatos, for example, is illustrated as follows: 'The whole business of eroticism is to strike to the inmost core of the living being, so that the heart stands still'[30] ['Toute la mise en œuvre de l'érotisme a pour fin d'atteindre l'être au plus intime, au point où le cœur manque'].[31] Bataille explicitly speaks of the erotic as 'mystical experience'[32] ['l'expérience mystique'][33] and of its comprehension as 'silent awakening'[34] ['l'éveil silencieux'].[35] Self-conscious of his unconventional style, he apologizes for the occasional repetition and gives a running commentary on how to read this book: 'One way of looking at this book is to regard it as a general view of human life seen from constantly changing standpoints'[36] ['En un sens, ce livre se réduit à la vue d'ensemble de la vie humaine, sans cesse reprise à partir d'un point de vue différent'].[37]

This confusing and nonlinear style exhibits Bataille's awareness of the difficulties involved in the attempt to communicate radical alterity. Language, once intended to help the individual describe and explain the world, fails in the face of tragic eroticism. After all, 'common language will not express violence'[38] ['[l]e langage commun se refuse à l'expression de la violence'].[39] Akin to the metaphoric sexual imagery in Pierre Guyotat's work (see Dean Brink's contribution in the present article), Bataille identifies the erotic act as a set of nonverbal fantasies which reach directly into 'the inmost core of the living being.' There must exist another way of relating it. In this context, Bataille even criticizes Marquis de Sade. Otherwise admired for his literary representation of every thinkable sexual cruelty, he is reproached for excessively relying on rational language (see Thomas Wynn's article in this volume). In de Sade's intellectual narratives, narrator and reader keep a safe distance from another. The narrator tries to enlighten his reader rather than making him feel the scope of transgressions.[40] In contrast, Bataille's confusing and 'irrational' narration annuls the distance between them in order to open up an inner experience of the erotic beyond reason and language.

This becomes most visible in a striking auctorial passage, where Bataille includes the reader in a chiastic apostrophe, addressing the limits of language and communication:

> This gulf exits, for instance, between *you*, listening to *me*, and *me*, speaking to *you*. We are attempting to communicate, but no communication between us can abolish our fundamental difference.[41]
>
> [Cet abîme se situe, par exemple, entre *vous* qui m'écoutez et *moi* qui *vous* parle. Nous essayons de communiquer, mais nulle communication entre nous ne pourra supprimer une différence première.][42]

At this point, eroticism gives way to a fundamental criticism of language itself that also casts doubts on Bataille's own writing. But the author also offers an alternative and mentions poetry as a means to understand the paradox of the erotic: 'We all feel what poetry is. Poetry is one of our foundation stones, but we cannot talk about it'[43] ['nous sentons tous ce qu'est la poésie. Elle nous fonde, mais nous ne savons pas en parler'].[44] Bataille stops here and draws on Arthur Rimbaud:

> I found it again.
> What? Eternity:
> the sea's run off
> with the blazing sun.[45]
>
> [Elle est retrouvée.
> Quoi? L'eternité.
> C'est la mer allée
> Avec le soleil.][46]

With its highly symbolical imagery — eternity, the sea, and the sun — this poem places eroticism in the realm of the eternal, a realm that cannot be translated into common language. This mediated way of telling includes the reader in the narrative process, facilitating premonition rather than knowledge. In order to 'strike the inmost core' of the reader, he increasingly uses symbols, images, and even the lack of language.

## The limits of writing

The preface of the short story *Madame Edwarda* explicitly addresses its form:

> I invite the reader [...] to turn his thoughts for a moment to the attitude traditionally observed towards pleasure (which, in sexual play attains a wild intensity, an insanity) and towards pain (finally assuaged by death, of course, but which, before that, dying winds to the highest pitch).[47]

> [[J]e demande au lecteur de ma préface de réfléchir un court instant sur l'attitude traditionnelle à l'égard du plaisir (qui, dans le jeu des sexes, atteint la folle intensité) et de la douleur (que la mort apaise, il est vrai, mais que d'abord elle porte au pire).][48]

Characterized by a complex metanarrative structure and an almost compulsive use of ellipsis, Bataille engages the reader in an intense game that defies language. In brackets, first doubts about the limits of speech are expressed: '(I too speak, but as I speak I do not forget that not only will speech escape me, but that it is escaping me now)'[49] ['(je parle aussi, mais en parlant je n'oublie pas que la parole, non seulement m'échappera, mai qu'elle m'échappe)'].[50]

The story itself starts out with the narrator's drunken and rapturous thoughts:

> There — I had to come to a street corner — there a foul dizzying anguish got its nails into me (perhaps because I'd been staring at a pair of furtive whores sneaking down the stair of an urinal).[51]

> [Au coin d'une rue, l'angoisse, une angoisse sale et grisante, me décomposa (peut-être d'avoir vu deux filles furtives dans l'escalier d'un lavabo).][52]

Abrupt breaks and the loss of a linear structure make up the syntax of the narrator's incoherent desires. They are not voiced directly, but hide behind dashes and brackets, hinting at the dark erotic force that drives the narrator. He continues his search for a whore that will give him relief: 'I wanted to be laid as bare as was the night there in those empty streets'[53] ['La nuit était nue dans des rues désertes et je voulus me dénuder comme elle'].[54] This lyrical tone is interrupted, however, as the drunkard slips off his pants and grasps his 'straight-risen sex'[55] ['sexe droit'].[56] Now a commentary is inserted in brackets, reproducing the sober tone of the preface:

> (The beginning is tough. My way of telling about these things is raw. I could avoid that and still made it sound plausible [...] But this is how it has to be. I continue .... And it gets tougher.)[57]

> [(Mon entrée en matière est dure. J'aurais pu l'éviter et rester "vraisemblable". J'avais intérêt aux détours. Mais il en est ainsi, le commencement est sans détour. Je continue... plus dur...)][58]

The abrupt change between obscene image and abstraction engages the reader in the dialectics of transgression. Instead of de Sade's moral aloofness, Bataille's narrator grants the reader relief from the sudden sequence of events and, in addition, gives a note of warning. The nudity and the anguish of the narrator are motifs that bring forward the central idea of losing oneself in a sexual act and its narration. Here, obscene nakedness is shown as a break in the (narrative) convention that can be only covered by brackets.

Eventually, the narrator enters the brothel and meets Madame Edwarda, a prostitute that calls herself 'GOD' ['DIEU']. After having confronted the narrator with her genital, they sleep with each other. Later, she decides to roam the streets alongside the narrator, where she suddenly enters a state of trance. Dressed by nothing but a black domino cloak, which occasionally exposes her bare flesh, her monk-like figure increases the narrator's desire. Simultaneously, the sight of Edwarda's silent convulsions triggers a season of agony in him: 'I consented to suffer, I desired to suffer, to go farther, as far as the "emptiness" itself, even were I to be stricken, destroyed, no matter'[59] ['J'acceptais, je désirais de souffrir, d'aller plus loin, d'aller, dussé-je être abattu, jusqu'au "vide" même'].[60] The prostitute's genital spiritually and physiologically designates the void where Eros and Tanatos, sex-wish and death-wish, coincide. The narrator's wish to lose himself, however, is not fulfilled until the last scene of the novel: in a taxi, Edwarda copulates with the driver, while the narrator supports her. Absorbed by the movements of the mating couple, the latter looks straight into the whites of her eyes. In this climax, the closeness of self-dissolution and self-assertion becomes visible. The name of the whore, 'DIEU', connects her with the deceived hopes of a post-metaphysical age and addresses the tragedy of eroticism. Just as Bataille points out in the preface, the formula 'God' implies the dialectical surpassing of its meaning: 'God is nothing if He is not, in every sense, the surpassing of God: in the sense of common everyday being, in the sense of dread, horror and impurity, and, finally, in the sense of nothing'[61] ['Dieu n'est rien s'il n'est pas dépassement de Dieu dans tous les sens; dans le sens de l'être vulgaire, dans celui de l'horreur et de l'impureté'].[62]

In the end, the male narrator is exposed to the loss of himself and the loss of meaning. He does not really understand what happened and wonders if anyone is able to make sense of his bizarre adventure with Edwarda. Inspired by the prostitute's name, 'DIEU', he goes as far as actually invoking divine help:

> But as for GOD? And you, Monsieur Godfearer? — God, would He at least know? GOD, if He "knew", would be a swine.\* O Thou my Lord [in my distress I call out unto "my heart"], O deliver me, make them blind! The story — how shall I go on with it?[63]

> [Mais DIEU? qu'en dire, messieurs Disert, messieurs Croyant? — Dieu, du moins, saurait-il? DIEU, s'il "savait", serait un porc\*. Seigneur [j'en appelle, dans ma détresse, à "mon cœur"] délivrez-moi, aveuglez-les! Le récit, le continuerai-je?[64]]

The reference to the divine itself is a climax, an excess in itself. Brought into the context of the prostitute Edwarda, making sense of it all becomes an obscene act in itself: 'GOD, if He "knew", would be a swine' — a blasphemy that Bataille's text accompanies with a footnote:

> He [...] would entirely grasp the idea ... but what would there be of the human about him? Beyond, beyond everything ... HIMSELF, in an ecstasy, above an emptiness ... and now? I TREMBLE.[65]

> [Celui qui [...] saisirait l'idée jusqu'au bout, mais qu'aurait-il d'humain? au-delà, et de tout... plus loin, et plus loin... LUI-MÊME, en extase au-dessus d'un vide... Et maintenant? JE TREMBLE.][66]

As the narrator pushes himself to imagine the unimaginable, Bataille's meta-narrative comment jumps from the main text to the bottom of the page, where the font size is altered and interrupts the linear trajectory of the text. For Bataille, trembling indicates the fundamental paradox of eroticism: to feel attraction and horror, lust and agony at the same time. On a plot level, this passage addresses the mixed feelings of the narrator toward Madame Edwarda. On a narrative level, it produces the similar feelings in the reader who is irritated and intrigued: first, by the asterisk that promises an explanation in footnotes, and second, by the capitalized words he encounters. Nonetheless, there follows no discursive elaboration; instead, the footnote resumes the emphatic speech and fragmented language of the main text body, it even engages with blasphemy.

The bizarre juxtaposition of blasphemy and a disordered narration also accompanies the only sexual encounter of Madame Edwarda and the protagonist. As her ecstasy increases, a grid of dots substitutes the narration, possibly in order to visually recreate the mirror panels that reflect the sexual encounter:

> . . . . . . . . . . . . . . . . . . . . . . . . . . . . . . . . . . . . . . . . . . . . . . . . . . . . . . . . . . . . . . .
> . . . . . . . . . . . . . . . . . . . . . . . . . . . . . . . . . . . . . . . . . . . . . . . . . . . . . . . . . . . . . . .
> . . . . . . . . . . . . . . . . . . . . . . . . . . . . . . . . . . . . . . . . . . . . . . . . . . . . . . . . . . . . . . .
> . . . . . . . . . . . . . . . . . . . . . . . . . . . . . . . . . . . . . . . . . . . . . . . . . . . . . . . . . . . . . . .
> . . . . . . . . . . . . . . . . . . . . . . . . . . . . . . . . . . . . . . . . . . . . les glaces qui tapissaient les murs, et dont le plafond lui même était fait, multipliaient l'image animale d'un accouplement: au plus léger mouvement, nos cœurs rompus s'ouvraient au vide où nous perdait l'infinité de nos reflets.[67]

Austryn Wainehouse's English translation skips the geometrical effect of this passage and substitutes it with the dotted lines of ellipsis.

> [.........................................................................................
> ...........................................................................
> ...................the mirrors where-with the room's walls were everywhere sheathed and the ceiling too, cast multiple reflections of an animal coupling, but, each least movement, our bursting hearts would strain wide-open to welcome "the emptiness of heaven".][68]

Aside from the different formatting of Bataille's formal representation of the sexual encounter, Wainehouse skips the moment in which Bataille's 'meta-pornography' finds its scenic materialisation: the mirrors facilitate auctorial self-reference through 'the infinity of our reflections' ('l'infinité de nos reflets'), a wording which Wainehouse substitutes with a reference to the absent God ('the emptiness of heaven'). Yet the translator has a point. Mere reflections in the mirrors insinuate the happening of the unspeakable, a moment of extreme desire and anguish. This passage takes the euphemistic notion of orgasm as the 'little death' seriously: after having discarded language, the heavens are emptied out to make room for the self-liberating power of eroticism.

Once more, Bataille differs from de Sade. By eliminating the usual order of narration and by stringing together meta- and object-language, the narrator cannot revert to conventional modes of understanding, but comes close to experiencing the story of *Madame Edwarda*. First, one is provoked by the text's obscenity, and then, one must confront the disappearance of language itself. As a consequence, the book turns into an object of desire in itself. As Yukio Mishima, a Japanese post-war author with similarly macabre tastes as Bataille, argues, 'the narrator represents the reader's own naïve investigative desire, his desire to intellectually analyse, his self-consciousness'.[69] Bataille further refined this approach in his last philosophical work, where his preference for heterogeneity of stylistic devices is taken a step further.

## The dialectics of text and image

*Tears of Eros* was compiled during Bataille's final illness and was published posthumously in 1961. According to Michel Surya and Paul Hegarty, the author's rheumatic and asthmatic condition is visible in the confusing arrangement of the work. Alternating 'between absence, pain and lucid awareness [...], he seems to be leaving words behind, leaving them to their failure.'[70] Arguably, this failure radicalizes his play with meta-narrative effects. In a letter to his editor, he emphasizes: 'I think the book should be one of the best I have written, and at the same time one of the most accessible.'[71] This accessibility, however, depends heavily on the reader's readiness to accept formal experimentation.

A history of art rather than a philosophical treatise, *Tears of Eros* allows the reader to witness the process of conceiving the connection between the erotic and death. Aside from its main text body, the volume is cluttered with photographic reproductions that range from cave paintings to canonical works of the European tradition (Lukas Cranach the Elder, El Greco, Francisco Goya, Pablo Picasso, and Balthus). In addition, there are pictures of Christian sacrifices, African rituals and, famously, Chinese torture. The history of images, according to Bataille, points towards one common obsession: Eros and Thanatos.

The text, however, does not directly answer to the images. The reader's wish to see these pictures from different epochs and cultures related to one another is frustrated by the sheer absence of commentary. Bataille does not embed them into an argument in the conventional sense, but regards them as 'illustrations': they are intended to 'shed light' — or even replace — the scholarly discourse.

The text begins with a biologically and archaeologically informed study of the development of human sexuality. While cave paintings, sculptures, and vases act as photographic evidence, the text discusses the progress of human beings from *homo faber* to *Neanderthal man*. Only one hermetic phrase mentions the erotic imagery of the Lascaux cave paintings that accompany the text: 'A man with a bird's face, who asserts his being with an erect penis, but who is falling down'[72] ['l'image [...] d'un homme au visage d'oiseau, qu'affirme un sexe droit, mais qui s'effondre'].[73] Here, Bataille sees the unity of Eros and Thanatos represented for the first time in human history. But again, instead of elaborating on his object and the implicated connection of joy (erection) and death (falling down), the narrator explains the function of work as the foundation of human existence. This is followed by prehistoric objects like phalli, Venuses and sculpted puns that actually defy notions of hard labour. In the absence of commentary, the reader becomes growingly aware that dialectics are at play: work (thesis) and joy (antithesis).

The narrator makes ample use of rhetorical questions, apostrophes and exclamations marks, giving voice to an emphatic, almost prophetical sermon that recalls certain passages in *Eroticism*.[74] The reader is urged to search for meaning beyond a mere acknowledgement of scholarly hypotheses about the evolution of humankind. He must engage with the subjective meaning of Bataille's inquiry into the interrelation between Eros and Thanatos. To this end, Bataille uses rhetorical strategies known from his short stories, most evident in the use of cursive writing, exclamatory speech and, again, dots. After an initial admonition that there is something laughable about eroticism,[75] he breaks out in an ejaculation: '*Sacred!*'[76] ['*Sacré!...*'[77]], invoking the indebtedness of the *sacred* to the *sacrifice*. After this opening, he makes another self-reflexive comment, then interrupts himself with the geometric dot squares known from 'Madame Edwarda':

> But, in me, definitive death has the sense of a strange victory. It bathes me with its glow, it opens in me an infinitively joyous laughter: that of disappearance!
>
> ............................................................................................................................
> ............................................................................................................................
>
> ...................If I had not, in these few phrases, enclosed myself in that moment when death destroys being, how could I speak about this "little death" in which, without actually dying, I collapse in a feeling of triumph!
>
> [Mais, en moi, la mort définitive a le sens d'une étrange victoire. Elle me baigne de sa lueur, elle ouvre en moi le rire infiniment joyeux: celui de la disparition!
>
> . . . . . . . . . . . . . . . . . . . . . . . . . . . . . . . . . . . . . . . . . . . . . . . . . . . .
> . . . . . . . . . . . . . . . . . . . . . . . . . . . . . . . . . . . . . . . . . . . . . . . . . . . .
>
> Si je ne m'étais, en ces quelques phrases, enfermé dans l'instant oú la mort détruit l'être, pourrais-je parler de cette "petite mort", où sans craiment mourir, je m'affaisserais dans le sentiment d'un triomphe![78]][79]

Again, Bataille stages the failure of language and the incommensurability of speech. Eroticism cannot be cast in language at all. The reader can just follow the dots, follow Bataille's enthusiasm, his 'spasm' — or simply skip such passages. This failure relates to the radical nature of Eros and makes its connection to death and violence tangible. *Larmes d'Éros* eventually climaxes in a photo taken in 1905, which exhibits *lingchi*[80] — a Chinese form of torture. It depicts a convict dismembered by a thousand cuts. In a close-up, the large wound carved into the victim's chest becomes impossible to ignore. Next to the image of *lingchi*, the iconic martyrdom of Jesus Christ, the subject of thousands of altar pieces, appears a mannered genre convention. Next to this image, Francis Bacon's paintings of sliced and deformed bodies lose their goriness. In Bataille's oeuvre, the notion of *lingchi* is said to represent nothing less than 'the basis of "his" need to write'.[81]

The macabre allure of this photo lies in the expression of the victim's face rather than the gory traces of systematic violence. The victim's eyes are turned to heaven, showing only their whites and recalling the mystic charge of the taxi-driver scene in 'Madame Edwarda'.[82] This image become a key witness for 'tragic eroticism', as

Bataille confesses: 'I have never stopped being obsessed by this image of pain, at once ecstatic(?) and intolerable'[83] ['Je n'ai pas cessé d'être obsédé par cette image de la douleur, à la fois extatique (?) et intolérable'].[84] It is said to point at a mystical link between religious ecstasy, eroticism, and sadism. And yet Bataille inserts a question mark in brackets, worrying that his conclusion is too extreme. A dark and anti-humanist anthropology lurks behind the acknowledgement of this ecstatic bliss where language and rationality must inevitably fail. The author's struggle to address this problem tallies with the reader's struggle to make sense of the gaps between image and text.

Bataille productively uses this moment of shock and does not intend the reader to dwell excessively in this state of mind. Provided with a meta-language for this dark anthropology, the reader casts off his horror and can allow him- or herself the pleasure of measured fascination. According to Barthes, joyful reading consists not in continuous, but interrupted reading: 'I read on, I skip, I look up, I dip in again'[85] ['je cours, je saute, je lève la tête, je replonge'].[86] With its multiple breaks and shifts, *Larmes d'Éros* establishes a reading rhythm which can be summed up as the 'silent awakening' of scholarly discourse to eroticism.

## Bataille's poststructural revival

Bataille died before *Larmes d'Éros* went into print and was spared from seeing it indexed. While his oeuvre's unorthodox style prevented its canonization by mainstream criticism, it became a key reference for French post-structural thought. In influencing Barthes and Foucault's opposition against naive notions of representation, his afterlife nevertheless altered the intellectual landscape of the twentieth century. Bataille's oeuvre remains a precondition of post-individualist literary aesthetics and the exploration of meta-narrative forms of writing.[87]

In the essay 'A Preface of Transgression' ('Préface à la transgression'), Foucault praises Bataille for breaking the categories of sexuality and religion as well as those between discursive language and poetry. Accordingly, Bataille's broken language inaugurates 'the end of the philosopher as the sovereign and primary form of philosophical language'[88] ['la fin du philosophe comme forme souveraine et première du langage philosophique'][89] and paves the way for other modes of writing and thinking. While Foucault already makes ample use of rhetorical questions, Barthes' fragmentary style is most visibly indebted to Bataille. In using abrupt brakes, multiple dashes and brackets, he calls upon the reader to acknowledge the great struggle inherent to erotic literature:

> the texts, like those by Bataille [...] which are written against neurosis from the center of madness, contain within themselves, *if they want to be read*, that bit of neurosis necessary to the seduction of their readers: these terrible texts are *all the same* flirtatious texts.[90]

> [les textes, comme ceux de Bataille [...] qui sont écrits contre la névrose, du sein de la folie, ont en eux, s'ils veulent être lus, ce peu de névrose nécessaire à la séduction de leurs lecteurs: ces textes terribles sont tout de même des textes coquets.[91]]

Barthes calls such texts 'flirtatious' ('coquets') because they free language from the boundaries of established syntax and stylistic convention. Bataille's transgressions range from rhetoric extravaganzas to ellipsis to the substitution of language with pictures. The advancing thrust of the scholarly *logos* is replaced by the rhythm of reading, avoiding, and browsing through a text.

Bataille's oeuvre, in its content and form, is a decisive rejection of the conventional tropes of scholarly work. When addressing such existential notions of Eros and Thanatos, such tropes inevitably fail to touch the truth of human experience: '*Eroticism is an experience that cannot be assessed from outside in the way an object can*'[92] ['*L'érotisme est une expérience que nous ne pouvons apprécier du dehors comme une chose*'].[93] Lyrical and associative elements provide the inner perspective necessary to trigger the 'silent awakening' of descriptive writing. When successful, this awakening unfolds in the reader's mind, allowing him or her to make sense of Bataille's contradictory and wayward narration. Confronted with ellipsis instead of denotative speech acts and images of horror instead of intact bodies, the reader will stumble upon a dark anthropology. Here, eroticism eventually culminates in its ultimate goal: sensing rather than making sense.

## Bibliography

BARTHES, ROLAND, *Oeuvres completes*, 3 vols. (Paris: Seuil, 1994).

—— *Le Plaisir du texte* (Paris: Seuil, 2002, repr. 1973).

—— *The Pleasure of the Text*, trans. by Richard Miller (New York, NY: Hill and Wang, 1975).

BATAILLE, GEORGES, *Œuvres complètes*, 13 vols. (Paris: Gallimard, 1970–88).

—— *Eroticism*, trans. by Mary Dalwood (London: Marion Boyars Modern Classic, 2006).

—— 'Madame Edwarda', in *My Mother, Madame Edwarda, The Dead Man*, trans. by Austryn Wainehouse (New York, NY: Penguin Books, 2000).

BERG, STEPHEN (trans.), *Rimbaus Versions and Inventions* (Rhinebeck, NY: Sheep Meadow Press, 2005).

FLUDERNIK, MONIKA, *Towards a 'Natural' Narratology* (London: Routledge, 1996).

FOUCAULT, MICHEL, 'Préface à la transgression', *Critique*, 19 (August-September 1963), 751–69.

—— 'Que'est-que c'est un Auteur?', *Bulletin de la Société Française de Philosophie*, 63 (1969), 73–104.

HEGARTY, PAUL, *George Bataille: Core Cultural Theorist* (London: Sage, 2000).

ILLOUZ, EVA, 'How Bondage Solves the Problem of Modern Love', *Spiegel Online*, 13 July 2013 <http://www.spiegel.de/international/zeitgeist/eva-illouz-explains-how-fifty-shades-of-grey-solves-problems-of-love-a-843644.html> [accessed 6 September 2016].

NEUMANN, BIRGIT and ANSGAR NÜNNING, ENTRY TO 'Metanarration and Metafiction', in *the living handbook of narratology*, ed by Peter Hühn et al. <http://www.lhn.uni-hamburg.de> [accessed 6 September 2016]

SONTAG, SUSAN, *Styles of Radical Will* (London: Penguin, 1969).

SURYA, MICHEL, *Georges Bataille: An Intellectual Biography*, trans. by Krzysztof Fijalkowski and Michael Richardson (London: Verso, 2002).

## Notes to Chapter 9

1. See Carina Gröner's contribution in this volume and Eva Illouz's elaborations on E. L. James's *Fifty Shades* trilogy. In an essay for *Spiegel Online*, Illouz argues that this book describes an 'antidote to modern relationships' by means of BDSM-techniques. The contract between Christian Grey and Anastasia Steele solves the problem of our 'complicated and elusive' lives. See Eva Illouz, 'How Bondage Solves the Problem of Modern Love', *Spiegel Online*, 13 July 2013 <http://www.spiegel.de/international/zeitgeist/eva-illouz-explains-how-fifty-shades-of-grey-solves-problems-of-love-a-843644.html> [accessed 6 September 2016].
2. Susan Sontag, 'The Pornographic Imagination', in *Styles of Radical Will* (London: Penguin, 1969), pp. 35–73 (p. 49).
3. See Sontag, 'The Pornographic Imagination', p. 54.
4. Ibid., p. 51.
5. Birgit Neumann and Ansgar Nünning, Entry to 'Metanarration and Metafiction', in *the living handbook of narratology*, ed. by Peter Hühn et al. <http://www.lhn.uni-hamburg.de> [accessed 6 September 2016].
6. Ibid.
7. Monika Fludernik, *Towards a 'Natural' Narratology* (London: Routledge, 1996), p. 278.
8. Sontag, 'The Pornographic Imagination', p. 48.
9. Ibid., p. 59.
10. Georges Bataille, *Eroticism*, trans. by Mary Dalwood (London: Marion Boyars Modern Classic, 2006), p. 11.
11. Georges Bataille, *Œuvres complètes*, 13 vols. (Paris: Gallimard, 1970–88), x, 17.
12. Bataille, *Eroticism*, p. 15.
13. Bataille, *Œuvres*, x, 20.
14. Sontag, 'The Pornographic Imagination', p. 57.
15. Bataille, *Eroticism*, p. 18.
16. Bataille, *Œuvres*, x, 24.
17. Bataille, *Eroticism*, p. 8.
18. Bataille, *Œuvres*, x, 12.
19. Bataille edited the journals *Acéphale*, *Contre-Attaque*, and *Documents*. While *Acéphale* primarily concerned itself with commenting on Nietzsche, *Contre-Attaque* provided a forum for communist and leftists. *Documents* discussed anthropological and archaeological material. See Michel Surya, *Georges Bataille: An Intellectual Biography*, trans. by Krzysztof Fijalkowski and Michael Richardson (London: Verso, 2002), pp. 125–27.
20. *Contre-Attaque* was directed against fascism, capitalism, and French communism; *Acéphale* was a secret society named after 'the headless one', a symbolical figure for the 'unrational, sacrificial man'. Walter Benjamin and Jacques Lacan also joined the group. See Paul Hegarty, *George Bataille: Core Cultural Theorist* (London: Sage, 2000), pp. 6–7.
21. Bataille, *Eroticism*, p. 8.
22. Bataille, *Œuvres*, x, 12.
23. Especially Surya's biography places Bataille's work in this context, an argument that the author himself hinted at in interviews. See Surya, *Georges Bataille*, pp. 3–14.
24. Distancing himself from his unreligious father, Bataille converted to Catholicism and even considered to become a priest. See Surya, *Georges Bataille*, pp. 3–14.
25. Bataille, *Eroticism*, p. 266. [Emphasis in the original.]
26. Bataille, *Œuvres*, x, 260. [Emphasis in the original.]
27. Surya shows that even Bataille's 'authentic' childhood-memories 'are organised in such a way that we could unreservedly say they are fictional' (Surya, *Georges Bataille*, p. 11).
28. Sontag, 'The Pornographic Imagination', p. 60–61.
29. Fludernik, *Towards a 'Natural' Narratology*, p. 278.
30. Bataille, *Eroticism*, p. 17.
31. Bataille, *Œuvres*, x, 23.
32. Bataille, *Eroticism*, p. 23.

33. Bataille, *Œuvres*, x, 29.
34. Bataille, *Eroticism*, p. 161.
35. Bataille, *Œuvres*, x, 161.
36. Bataille, *Eroticism*, p. 8.
37. Bataille, *Œuvres*, x, 12.
38. Bataille, *Eroticism*, p. 186.
39. Bataille, *Œuvres*, x, 185.
40. Sontag also points out that in Sade's writings death 'always seem unreal' and that 'his fictional alter egos regularly interrupted a bout of rape and buggery to deliver to their victims his latest reworkings of lengthy sermons on what real "Enlightment" means — the nasty truth about God, society, nature, individuality, virtue' (Sontag, 'The Pornographic Imagination', p. 62).
41. Bataille, *Eroticism*, p. 12. [*Emphasis by J. B. & K. E.*]
42. Bataille, *Œuvres*, x, 18–19. [*Emphasis by J. B. & K. E.*]
43. Bataille, *Eroticism*, p. 24.
44. Bataille, *Œuvres*, x, 30.
45. Stephen Berg (trans.), *Rimbaus Versions and Inventions* (Rhinebeck, NY: Sheep Meadow Press, 2005), p. 20.
46. Bataille, *Œuvres*, x, 30.
47. Georges Bataille, 'Madame Edwarda', in *My Mother, Madame Edwarda, The Dead Man*, trans. by Austryn Wainehouse (New York: Penguin Books, 2000), pp. 123–43 (p. 123). The novel was first published in 1937 under the pseudonym of 'Pierre Angelique'. Bataille used a number of pseudonyms, such as 'Lord Auch' and 'Louis Trente', not only to protect himself and his livelihood, but also to fictionalize autobiographical references. See Surya, *Georges Bataille*, pp. 88–92.
48. Bataille, *Œuvres*, III, 9.
49. Bataille, 'Madame Edwarda', p. 130.
50. Bataille, *Œuvres*, III, 12.
51. Bataille, 'Madame Edwarda', p. 133.
52. Bataille, *Œuvres*, III, 19.
53. Bataille, 'Madame Edwarda', p. 133.
54. Bataille, *Œuvres*, III, 19.
55. Bataille, 'Madame Edwarda', p. 133.
56. Bataille, *Œuvres*, III, 19.
57. Bataille, 'Madame Edwarda', p. 135.
58. Bataille, *Œuvres*, III, 19.
59. Bataille, 'Madame Edwarda', p. 137.
60. Bataille, *Œuvres*, III, 25.
61. Bataille, 'Madame Edwarda', p. 127.
62. Bataille, *Œuvres*, III, 12.
63. Bataille, 'Madame Edwarda', p. 143. [*Original translation amended by J. B. & K. E.*]
64. Bataille, *Œuvres*, III, 30. [*Capitalisations and square brackets in the original.*]
65. Bataille, 'Madame Edwarda', p. 143.
66. Bataille, *Œuvres*, III, 31.
67. Bataille, *Œuvres*, III, 22.
68. Bataille, 'Madame Edwarda', p. 136.
69. Yukio Mishima, 'Georges Bataille and Divinus Deus', in Bataille, *My Mother*, pp. 1–12 (p. 10).
70. See Hegarty, *George Bataille*, p. 11. Joseph-Marie Lo Duca also highlights the long and difficult genesis of the book. See Joseph-Marie Lo Duca, 'Introduction', in George Bataille, *The Tears of Eros* (San Francisco: City Light Books, 1989), pp. 1–7.
71. Bataille, *Tears of Eros*, p. 15.
72. Bataille, *The Tears of Eros*, p. 35.
73. Bataille, *Œuvres*, x, 587.
74. See Bataille, *The Tears of Eros*, p. 34.
75. See Bataille, *The Tears of Eros*, p. 66.

76. Bataille, *The Tears of Eros*, p. 68.
77. Bataille, *Œuvres*, x, 607.
78. Bataille, *Œuvres*, x, 607–08.
79. Bataille, *The Tears of Eros*, p. 68.
80. *Lingchi chusi* 凌遲處死, 'slow execution', is the vulgar term for *qiandao wangua* 千刀萬剮, literally 'thousand knives, ten thousand cuts'. The photograph is 'Massacre in China (*lingchi* torture in Beijing around 1910): [press photograph] / [Agence Rol]', Wikimedia Commons, <https://commons.wikimedia.org/wiki/File%3ALingchi_(cropped).jpg> [last accessed 6.01.2018].
81. See Hegarty, *George Bataille*, p. 11. Bataille relates his personal history with the image in detail (see Bataille, *Tears of Eros*, p. 204–05) and also refers to this pictures in his short stories 'L'expérience intérieure' (1943) and 'Le coupable' (1944).
82. The archetype of this motif is his blind father. See Surya, *Georges Bataille*, p. 7.
83. Bataille, *Tears of Eros*, p. 206.
84. Bataille, *Œuvres*, x, 627
85. Roland Barthes, *The Pleasure of the Text*, trans. by Richard Miller (New York, NY: Hill and Wang, 1975), p. 12.
86. Roland Barthes, *Le Plaisir du texte* (Paris: Seuil, 2002, repr. 1973), p. 11.
87. See Michel Foucault's study 'Que'est-que c'est un Auteur?' (*Bulletin de la Société Française de Philosophie*, 63 (1969), 73–104) and Roland Barthes 'La morte de l'auteur' (*Oeuvres completes*, 3 vols. (Paris: Seuil, 1994), II, 191–95).
88. Ibid., p. 42.
89. Michel Foucault, 'Préface à la transgression', in *Critique*, 19 (August-September 1963), 751–69 (p.759).
90. Barthes, *Pleasure*, pp. 5–6.
91. Barthes, *Plaisir*, pp. 6–7.
92. Bataille, *Eroticism*, p. 149. [*Emphasis in the original.*]
93. Bataille, *Œuvres*, x, 149. [*Emphasis in the original.*]

CHAPTER 10

# Sensational Pain: Filming the Eroticized Trauma Narrative

*Katie Jones*

In *The Erotic* (*Die Erotik*, 1910), Lou Andreas-Salomé writes of the one-sidedness of attempts to define or theorise eroticism, noting the way that the outer and physical aspects of this phenomenon become the focal point of theoreticians at the expense of subjective experience, with the result that it appears almost distinct from our everyday lives. While first published in 1910, her observation that 'the erotic seems to resist immediate definition, suspended as it is between the physical and the spiritual'[1] still holds true. For instance, despite the employment of a series of common erotic tropes and images (relationships defined by power imbalances, the revelation of secret and illicit desires, and explicit descriptions of sex acts and sexualised bodies), D. M. Thomas's *The White Hotel* (1981) and Elfriede Jelinek's *The Piano Player* (*Die Klavierspielerin*, 1983) do not comfortably belong to the 'erotic genre'. By weaving together representations of National Socialism, sadomasochism, pornographic imagery, and central female characters deemed 'hysterical', these texts operate on divisive territory, which is extended by their presentation of the female body as a terrain on which they map gendered, racial and/or religious violence alongside masochistic pleasure and desire.

Both novels make use of the pornographic and entwine it with high culture, particularly opera and classical music, but *The White Hotel* spans from the early 1900s until 1941 and explicitly represents the historical murder of 33,771 Jewish and Roma people at the Babi Yar Massacre on the 29th and 30th September 1941.[2] In contrast, Jelinek's semiautobiographical novel is set in contemporary society, almost forty years after National Socialism. Her references to Nazism are more subtly conveyed through relationships characterized by mastery and cruelty, such as the abrasive approach of Erika Kohut, the eponymous piano player, towards her students. Erika's relationship with her students echoes her relationship with her mother and pupil/lover, Walter Klemmer, though in these personal relationships her position is reversed and she adopts the subordinate role.

The question of adaptation brings out further contrasts between these two novels. In 2001, Jelinek's text was successfully adapted into the critically acclaimed feature film *La Pianiste* (*The Pianist*, 2001) by Austrian film-maker Michael Haneke, while *The White Hotel* is yet to be filmed despite the rushed promise 'soon to be a major movie'[3] on the 1982 paperback version. In *Bleak Hotel* (2008), Thomas describes the seductions and disappointments of Hollywood, most notably the legal and contractual procedures that have halted the process of adaptation up to this point. However, he also recognizes that the varying styles of each of the seven sections present practical difficulties for film adaptation.

The prologue of *The White Hotel* introduces Thomas's fictional Sigmund Freud through a series of letters and the remainder of the novel is divided into six chapters: 'Don Giovanni', a pornographic poem, written between the staves of Wolfgang Amadeus Mozart's opera, followed by 'The Gastein Journal', a reformulated version of the previous chapter. These chapters are presented as documents written by Lisa Erdman, a woman of Jewish descent on her father's side but who adopts her mother's religion, Christianity, and hides her Jewish heritage. The third chapter, 'Frau Anna G', is written from the perspective of a fictionalized Freud and mimics his case-study style, particularly those found in *Studies on Hysteria* (*Studien über Hysterie*), co-authored with Josef Breuer in 1895. This section analyzes the material from the previous two chapters as Freud links Lisa's hysterical symptoms — pain in her left ovary and breast, terrifying hallucinations during sex with her anti-Semitic husband, and shortness of breath — to an unacknowledged attraction to women and the repressed knowledge that her mother had an affair with an uncle. The fourth chapter, 'The Health Resort', is written in realist prose and documents Lisa's life after her analysis, though also includes memories and allows the reader access to truths which are absent from her analysis with Freud, somewhat undermining his authoritative assessment and diagnosis. Chapter five, 'The Sleeping Carriage', reveals Lisa's symptoms as prophetic of her future murder at Babi Yar, during which a Nazi officer rapes her using a bayonet, thus furthering the critique of Freud's lineal reasoning that Lisa's hysteria was rooted in the past. The final chapter, 'The Camp', imagines an afterlife for the victims of Babi Yar, a kind of Promised Land filled with milk and honey, though also containing reminders of the preceding traumas.

Controversially, 'The Health Resort' not only fictionalizes the Babi Yar massacre, but also borrows and adapts the testimony of Dina Pronicheva, the sole survivor of the events.[4] With this in mind, the first two pornographic chapters, 'Don Giovanni' and 'The Gastein Journal', present difficulties in and of themselves. Both describe sexually explicit scenarios using imagery and language that contains and veils Thomas's later representation of the genocidal crimes at the Babi Yar ravine. As well as this, these fantasies take place in a dream-like setting against a backdrop of deadly disasters that also anticipate the penultimate chapter — floods, fires, landslides, for instance.

The interest shown by both David Lynch and David Cronenberg[5] might have provided the ingenuity and expertise to tackle the aesthetic questions raised by the heterogeneity of Thomas's novel. According to Thomas, however, Cronenberg believed *The White Hotel* to be 'too literary a novel to film'.[6] The ultimate failure of this film project points at the fundamental difficulty of adapting *The White Hotel* for the screen. Thomas himself remarked that the widely varying styles of each chapter present a particular and 'serious challenge for a film maker'.⁷ Firstly, this paper examines Thomas and Jelinek's interlacing of erotic or sexual imagery — particularly masochism — with traumatic histories; second, I address the question of adaptation and translation by offering a close reading of Jelinek's novel and Haneke's film version in order to track the transformation that the novel undergoes, especially the anti-romantic plot of the film. Lastly, these aspects are related to the peculiarities of genre in *The White Hotel* in relation to a hypothetical adaptation.

## Sexual Hierarchies

When the Swedish Academy awarded Jelinek with the Nobel Prize in Literature, Knut Ahnlund famously quit his membership of the same institution, for he thought her writing was 'unenjoyable, violent pornography'.⁸ Indeed, Jelinek *de*-eroticizes the erotic, employing tropes and scenes belonging to the genre while simultaneously stripping them of eroticism in order to suggest their relation to violence and oppression. In contrast, Thomas's descriptions of sexuality that appear in Lisa's confessional writings have been described as ranging from the 'banal, to a lush romantic intensity, with a remarkable precision of imagery [that] is seductive, frightening, and beautifully alive'.⁹ Susanne Kappeler, however, writes 'it is inconceivable [...] that he [i.e. the author] should believe that linking sexual violence with the holocaust was a profound, original artistic achievement'.¹⁰ While Kappeler's assessment is compelling within her overall argument in *The Pornography of Representation*, my alternative reading challenges the contention that the juxtaposition of sexuality and Nazi terror in *The White Hotel* necessarily trivializes the events portrayed, and will be discussed later in greater detail. (In the present volume, Thomas Wynn encounters a similar dilemma in the context of the Marquis de Sade's *120 Days of Sodom*. Despite its representations of extreme sexual violence, the text is meant to create arousal.)

*The Piano Player*, as a decisively feminist text, belongs to a tradition of women's writing in which authors utilise tropes of victimisation in order to explore their own position under patriarchy — akin to Sylvia Plath, Ingeborg Bachmann and Anne Sexton, to name a few examples. In this respect, Jelinek conflates feminine and masculine gender roles with the dichotomies masochism/sadism, victim/perpetrator, and Jew/Nazi. For instance, allegories of music are traditionally female, but in Jelinek's text it chokes Erika like poison gas.¹¹ Likewise, when Walter makes his way to Erika's apartment in order to rape her, he describes it as 'a gruesome act of annihilation'¹² ['[ein] grausame[s] Vernichtungswerk'].¹³ Additionally, Walter fulfils the stereotypical image of a Hitler Youth: with blond hair, blue eyes, and a sporty physique, and his appearance is repeatedly contrasted with Erika's feebleness and her Jewish looks.

*Die Klavierspielerin* also contains what may loosely be described as a confessional trope: a letter, written by Erika to Walter, describing her masochistic wishes. In her letter, she asks: 'please hit me, with the back of your hand too, slap my face when we're alone'[14] ['schlage mir bitte, auch mit dem Handrücken, fest ins Gesicht, wenn wir miteinander allein sind'].[15] Through her masochistic demands, Erika seems to embody the male masochist, exemplified in the work of Leopold von Sacher-Masoch. In contrast to female masochism, which is naturalised within Freudian discourses, male masochism tends to be considered in performative terms.[16] Despite its scenarios of torture in Sacher-Masoch's works, the desires of the tyrannical woman remain unspoken and subordinated to the wants of the male masochist, hence endowing it a high degree of performative agency. By inverting the female role in the founding text of masochism, Jelinek brings out its essential truth: while the female despot may appear to have power, she is merely responding to the sexuality of her male partner. By attempting to usurp the masculine privilege of active desire, the truth and problem of so-called female masochism is also revealed, namely that this form of masochism is characterised by passivity and accessibility, rather than active pleasure-seeking or desire.

Erika's requests both attract and repel Walter, who wonders 'whether she has gone totally overboard. He pokes at her: has sex driven her completely out of her mind?'[17] ('ob sie jedes Maß verloren hat. Er klopft bei ihr an, ob sie erotisch vollkommen außer sich geraten sei').[18] This comment is in line with the many ironic references to Freudian catchphrases, e.g. the characterisation of women as 'the eternal riddle' ('[d]as ewige Rätsel').[19] While Jelinek uses familiar pornographic phrasing, there is also a comic, ironic element. For instance, upon reading 'that she's supposed to stick her tongue in his behind when he mounts her'[20] ['daß sie ihm die Zunge in den Hintern stecken muß, wenn er rittlings auf ihr sitzt'],[21] Walter is bewildered: '[He] is sceptical about what he reads, he blames it on the poor lighting. A woman who plays Chopin so marvellously couldn't possibly mean that'[22] ['[Er] bezweifelt sehr, was er liest, und schiebt es auf schlechte Beleuchtungsverhältnisse. Die Frau kann es so nicht gemeint haben, die derartig Chopin spielt'].[23] His consternation underlines the constructed division between intellectual and sexual (or sexualized) women, while simultaneously highlighting the absurdities of this dichotomy. By using Walter as an intermediator for the letter, i.e. not allowing readers direct narrative access to it, the erotic trope of confession is somewhat de-eroticized. As well as this, the method also draws attention to the role of male-interpretations of women's writing and speech, as the loss of control that the letter signifies when Erika hands it over to Walter highlights the power imbalance between the two, suggesting Walter's more powerful position in determining his and her role in the scenario.

Various scholars have read Thomas's text as a critique of Enlightenment values,[24] aligning the novel with the arguments put forward in Theodor Adorno and Max Horkheimer's *Dialectic of Enlightenment* (1944), which connects the bureaucratic efficiency of Nazism with the Enlightenment 'virtue' of Pure Reason. Lisa's poem exemplifies this reading, while also drawing on the potentially erotic trope of confession. During her therapeutic treatment for 'hysteria', Lisa's self-revelation is framed as confessional in numerous ways — perhaps most clearly through the crucifix she wears around her neck, and her acknowledgment that, in her fantasies, the figure of the priest represents Freud, her analyst. With this in mind, Lisa's writings to Freud are doubly confessional: as a male-written text, Lisa's erotic poem and prose in *The White Hotel* ventriloquize feminine sexuality and desire in much the same way as other fictional male-written erotic confessions, e.g. John Cleland's *Fanny Hill* (1748) and Felix Salten's *Josephine Mutzenbacher* (1906).

Simultaneously, it also pertains to Michel Foucault's conception of the medicalized confession within sadomasochistic hierarchies: the power (im)balance between the confessant and priest or analyst supports and replicates broader socio-political power structures that produce knowledge through coercion or violence. Since this knowledge is implicitly sexual, Victorian discourses on sex must be considered as a form of *ars erotica*. Indeed, Thomas's novel illustrates this conception of *knowledge as power* as Freud's 'presentation of his patient's erotic writings differs considerably depending on the audience: to his colleague Hanns Sachs, he offers the manuscript with something approaching a wink'.[25] This observation suggests the potentially erotic function of the patient's sexual landscape for the analyst, and chimes with Foucault's point that this form of erotica legitimizes patriarchal forms of prurience through the medical discourses surrounding it, re-inscribing 'the procedure of confession in a field of scientifically acceptable observations'.[26]

By situating Lisa's 'confession' between the scores of Mozart's *Don Giovanni*, an opera which typifies patriarchal machismo, Thomas meta-fictionally alludes to the dramatization of the holocaust, while also framing the desire of the protagonist as contained and constrained by masculinist discourses. Freud's mastery over her narrative is emphasized in the chapter entitled 'Frau Anna G'. Alternatively, the placement of Lisa's fantasies within Mozart's opera may also suggest a counter-narrative to the brute sexuality of the opera, which is subsequently mirrored in the imagery of her poem. As Marie-Luise Kohlke points out, just as the violence of the sexual imagery is recycled in Thomas's representation of Lisa's death at Babi Yar, the 'Camp' chapter also echoes descriptions from Lisa's erotic writings. In particular, the imagery of Lisa's miraculously lactating breasts. In this respect, the 'sexual tenor of the final chapter is consoling and regenerative [...]. From implicit death wish, sexuality is transformed into an affirmation of life and humanity'.[27]

In this light, the novel portrays the struggle against Nazism and the hierarchies of science to equal parts. Indeed, the rhapsodic love-making in the fantasized hotel is interrupted by a rock of flint smashing through the window, signifying the forceful intrusion of culture into the womb-like pre-symbolic space. While on the one hand the text reproduces the dichotomies female/male, nature/culture, Eros/Thanatos, and masochism/sadism, it also demonstrates how these constructed opposites create and libidinize violence. Within these binaries, psychoanalytic and medical discourses belong to the masculine — to culture, Thanatos and sadism. Lisa's poetic description of an imagined encounter with Freud's son exemplifies this point: 'his thrumming fingers filled| me with a great gape of wanting [...]|| I was split open| by your son, Professor'.[28] The masochistic pleasure of Lisa's encounter is apparent in the language: the pleasure of penetration reformulated as feeling split open. This phrasing also reminds us of Lisa's therapy, where her psyche is 'split open' by Freud, as well as the ultimate destruction of her body at Babi Yar. With this in mind, the figure of Freud's son in the fantasy is ambiguous, referring both to Freud's actual son and to psychoanalysis at large, Freud's brainchild. The erotic confession and self-revelation function as means to link patterns of patriarchal social and sexual oppression, which is endemic to science and epitomised in the horrors of violent excess.

### Voyeurism and Complicity

By gendering and sexualizing victimisation and violence, and conflating Jewish and female victimisation with masochism and pleasure, Thomas's narrative risks promoting the 'dangerous claim that the Jews of Europe were a masochistic people',[29] thereby problematically implying Lisa's complicity with the violence wrought against her. Jelinek, like Thomas, raises issues of consent and complicity. For instance, when Walter forcibly enters Erika's apartment and then rapes her, while repeatedly citing the letter she wrote. This point is also raised when the narrator meditates on the relationship between circus animals and their tamer, asking: 'does the former wild beast and present-day circus animal love its tamer? Perhaps, but this is not obligatory. Each urgently needs the other'[30] ['Liebt das ehemalige Tier der Wildnis und jetzige Tier der Manege seinen Dompteur? Es kann möglich sein, doch es ist nicht obligat. Der eine bedarf des anderen dringend'].[31] However, while questions of victim complicity are raised, the text queries the discourses that create such dynamics, particularly the 'construction of hysteria, through its chronicling of Erika's pathological symptoms and its revelation, the rape scene'.[32] In this respect, *Die Klavierspielerin* also interrogates essentialist ideology that naturalizes female and Jewish masochism, instead employing narrative cues to demonstrate the internalisation of sexist and anti-Semitic discourses.

Consider the following description of Erika, for example: 'Erika feels solid wood in the place where the carpenter made a hole in any genuine female [...] and the rot is still spreading'[33] ['Erika hat ein Gefühl von massivem Holz dort, wo der Zimmermann bei der echten Frau das Loch gelassen hat [...] und die Fäulnis schreitet voran'].[34] In this passage, the rot is rooted in her female-ness. However, the constructed nature of this association is also highlighted through the reference to the (male) carpenter, locating the power of the gaze and the construction of feminine identities in masculinist discourses. Additionally, the novel's ending depicts Erika stabbing herself impotently in the shoulder, carrying traces of Kafka's *The Trial* (*Der Prozess*, 1925) in which Joseph K. (referred to mostly as K.), the central figure, is climactically executed by his tormentors: 'the hands of one of the gentleman were laid on K.'s throat, while the other pushed the knife deep into his heart and twisted it there, twice'[35] ['an K.s Gurgel legten sich die Hände des einen Herrn, während der andere das Messer ihm tief ins Herz stieß und zweimal dort drehte'].[36]

Likewise, Erika thinks that 'the knife should dig into her heart and twist around'[37] ['[d]as Messer soll ihr ins Herz fahren und sich dort drehen'].[38] The similarity between Kafka and Jelinek's respective finales, as well as referrals to Erika as 'K.' within the text, create associations between *The Piano Player* and *The Trial*. Kafka's novel is often read as an exploration of 'Jewish guilt' and the limits of freedom,[39] thus this intertextuality further conflates female and Jewish masochism and shame. Ultimately Erika impotently stabs herself in the shoulder before walking home, potentially suggesting Erika's failure to fully embody the masculine role of tortured artist.

The above points are explored further when Erika visits a peep show — a setting that reproduces the erotic trope of voyeurism in a commercial context. Surrounded by the otherwise exclusively male clientele, Erika enters a booth, which smells of disinfectant, and her gloves remain on as she examines a sperm-encrusted tissue. By observing such details, Jelinek presents the scenario as a dry, clinical, and sterile performance. Exposing the contrived eroticism of the peepshow constitutes part of Jelinek's critique of the commodification of sexuality and how pornography shapes sexualities, limiting the possibilities of the erotic through the processes of mass production. At the peepshow, Erika is spectator and director at the same time: 'curtains up for Erika, who can be seen in the wings pulling the wires'[40] ['Vorhang auf für Erika, wie sie hinter der Bühne die Fäden zieht'].[41] The first object of her gaze 'makes a tiny o with her mouth'[42] ['[macht] mit dem Mund ein kleines o'],[43] the next performer: a 'dragon lady with dyed red hair thrusts her chubby backside into view'[44] ['[e]ine rotgefärbte Drachenlady schiebt jetzt ihre leicht fettliche Rückseite ins Bild'],[45] eventually showing 'her alleged cellulite'[46] ['ihr[e] vermeintliche Zellulitis'].[47] The description of the women on stage are primarily characterized by artificiality and guilt. They have synthetic hair colours, one pulls at her nipple as if it were rubber, underlining the interchangeability and commodification of women as sex objects. The alleged cellulite points to the criminality and guilt attached to women within patriarchal dialectics.

As the only female client, Erika inhabits a typically male position in line with the rest of the novel as, repeatedly, the protagonist acts as voyeur. For instance, she spies on couples using her dead father's binoculars, and also uses his shaving mirror to examine her own vagina. This exemplifies Jelinek's Lacanian contention that women, doubly alienated upon entry into the patriarchal symbolic and language, conceive of themselves as Other. However, Erika's position as a consumer also frames her as the puppet master in this scenario, gazing at the performers who are dehumanized by language.

The description of the o-shaped mouth hints at the literary tradition of masochist pornography: most notably, Anne Desclos's *The Story of O* (*Histoire d'O*, 1954).[48] Desclos's narrative was written under the pseudonym 'Pauline Réage' in response to her lover, Jean Paulhan, who claimed that no woman could write like de Sade. Through this connection, Jelinek hints at the exclusion of authentic feminine voices in erotic discourse, as we are often in a position of writing *against* patriarchal forms of erotica, while using language and images seeped in masculinist configurations of the body.[49] Scrawled on the wall of Erika's booth are the words 'St. Mary drunken whore'[50] ['St. Maria besoffene Hure'].[51] By referring to the Judeo-Christian virgin/

whore dichotomy in the setting of the peepshow, Jelinek's critique of visual and narrative pornographic discourses points at the sexual politics of phallocentrism that reduces and divides women in this respect. Rather than isolating and demonizing pornography as if it exists in a vacuum, Jelinek presents porn as merely another medium through which the same reactionary versions of womanhood are (re)imagined, (re)presented, and (re)constructed.

A description of Erika, while she watches the peepshow, consolidates these points:

> Erika watches very closely. Not in order to learn. Nothing stirs or moves within her. But she has to watch all the same. For her own pleasure. Whenever she feels like leaving, something above her energetically presses her well-groomed head back to the pane, and she has to keep looking. She is off-limits to herself.[52]
>
> [Erika schaut ganz genau zu. Nicht um zu lernen. In ihr rührt und regt sich weiter nichts. Doch schauen muß sie trotzdem. Zu ihrem eigenen Vergnügen. Immer wenn sie fortgehen möchte, drückt etwas von oben ihren gutfrisierten Kopf energisch wieder gegen die Scheibe, und sie muß weiterhin blicken. Die Drehscheibe, auf der die schöne Frau sitzt, fährt im Kreis herum. Erika kann nichts dafür. Sie muß und muß schauen. Sie ist für sich selbst tabu.[53]]

What is distinct about this scene is the *absence* of pleasure; despite Erika's attempts to capture the supposed eroticism of the peepshow, she is merely a spectator to lust and desire. Erika keeps her gloves on throughout the show, signifying a lack of engagement with her surroundings. The force compelling her to remain in her seat is, arguably, the same that brought her there: a desire to explore a sexual subjectivity, which is then stunted and left unsatisfied by the poverty of avenues available to her. The ontological concerns implied through the marionette analogy also reflect the text's broader interest in language and ventriloquism, represented by Erika's preferred mode of expression — the piano. Within the novel this art form is presented as colonized by a male lineage of composers (Schubert, Beethoven, Bach), providing a metaphor for the two-fold alienation of women within specifically *patriarchal* language.

## Adaptation: the Anti-Romance

Formally, Haneke's critically acclaimed French-language adaptation remains faithful to Jelinek's narrative thrust: both share the same characters in the same or similar situations that follow a corresponding order. However, the adaptation and translation conjures (ironic) stereotypical associations with French romance, although the setting of the film is still Vienna. Given Jelinek's interest in twisting and adapting commonplace phrases or words as a way to complicate our understanding of the roles her characters embody, Haneke's translation of the title deserves our scrutiny.

Joachim Neugroschel's English rendering (2004) already tampered with its innuendo: although the literal translation would read 'The Piano Player' — or 'The Female Piano Player', as the gender is implied by the article and suffix — he opts for *The Piano Teacher*. While hinting at a lacklustre career as a pianist, Neugroschel's title nonetheless prioritizes Erika's role in relation to others (as the term teacher implies a student), rather than focusing solely on Erika and her mode of expression. Jelinek's original phrasing is already unusual given that the titular piano player is, in fact, a pianist and professor at the renowned Vienna Conservatoire. By opting for the title *Die Klavierspielerin*, as opposed to 'Die Pianistin', Jelinek reduces Erika's profession to the hobby of a dilettante, but also suggests a lack of creativity. Referring to Erika as a 'piano player' implies a lack of mastery: she is a figure who plays a tune which is determined by another. This subtle difference signifies the text's concern with ventriloquism. The poetic, rhyming quality of 'Klavierspielerin' creates a kind of mirroring or merging effect between the two components of the phrase: Klavier/spielerin (piano/player), which within the text is tantamount to language/ woman. Spieler/in can also mean 'actor' in German, alluding to performativity, in particular the lack of authenticity in Erika's position as an artist — an identity not fully available to her due to her womanhood. Commenting on his adaptation of Jelinek's novel, Haneke states that he 'left the German title of the book not quite as it is, to give her [i.e. Erika] more dignity'.[54] The clumsiness of the German title, however, contains an important strand of the narrative, most notably Erika's stunted and failed development as an artist. After all, Jelinek's text 'perverts the genre of the Künstlerroman'[55] by linking this failure to her sex and her relationships.

Aside from such recalibrations, Haneke adapts and compresses the narrative in numerous ways. For example, when Erika is about to visit a cinema showing S&M porn,[56] the camera follows her with Schubert's Piano Trio No.2 playing over the shot. The speed and rhythm of the piano is *adagio* and Erika's movements and thoughts appear incorporeal and lofty. Then she enters the porn booth and, for a few seconds, the music and porn are synchronized. This scene presents problems and challenges for Haneke who is renowned for his love of on-screen screens. How to reproduce scenes with pornographic aesthetics without aligning with the filmic practices he seeks to critique? In the novel, Jelinek is able to puncture the sexual imagery with humour, irony and Erika's irritated thoughts, pleasures and feelings. Arguably, the explicit hard core porn that the audience is shown contradicts the polemic against pornographic representation and cinematic voyeurism. However, as Juliet Wigmore points out, Haneke draws a distinction between obscenity and pornography, the former constituting that which is unacceptable — Erika's desires, for instance — and the latter a reformulation of the obscene into a consumer product. For Wigmore, Haneke's film is 'in consonant with the effects of the pornographic description in the novel, which are filtered through the narrator's distanced, often ironic perspective'.[57] Indeed, the shock induced by this scene also raises questions regarding the audience. As Erika is presented to us as a kind of perverse case-study, the *mise-en-abyme* works to query *our* spectatorship.

In the novel, Erika's pleasure is marked by an urgent desire to urinate. For instance, when spying on a Viennese prostitute with a Turkish client, the narrative voice explains: 'certain organs labor in the spectator, and she can't control them: they work double-time or even faster. Strong pressure on her bladder, an irksome disturbance that overcomes her whenever she gets excited'[58] ['Irgendwelche Organe in ihr arbeiten plötzlich, ohne daß sie es kontrollieren kann, in doppeltem Tempo oder noch rascher. Ein starker Druck auf der Blase, ein lästiges Leiden, das sie immer überkommt, wenn sie sich aufregt'].[59] When she finally does urinate, the narrator explains: 'She ponders nothing — no cause and no consequence. She relaxes her muscles, and the initial patter turns into a gentle, steady running'[60] ['Sie erwägt nichts, keine Ursache und keine Folgerung. Sie läßt Muskeln locker, und es wird von einem anfänglichen Prasseln zu einem sanften, stetigen Rinnen'].[61] While unconventional, the release conveyed is compatible with conceptions of orgasm: emptying out, clarity, and relaxation — the 'petite mort'. But these associations are so reliant on access to Erika's thoughts that in *La Pianiste* her pleasures are somewhat lost. While the viewer is shown Erika urinating, it is neither highlighted to the same degree as the novel, nor does it have quite the same sexual associations.

In addition to such infidelities, Haneke's adaptation also accentuates features of the text in a way that strengthens his critique of normative and generic romance. In the novel, Erika and Walter's first sexual encounter follows a violent act of sabotage whereby she, out of jealousy, puts broken glass into a female student's coat pocket. Afterwards, Erika hides in the staff toilet, but Walter follows her. The narrator explains:

> These two lead performers intend to put on a love scene, completely private, no extras, no walk-ons, only one lead under the leaden heaviness of the other lead. In accordance with the occasion, Erika instantly gives herself up as a person. A present wrapped in slightly dusty tissue paper.[62]

> [Diese beiden Hauptdarsteller wollen nun eine Liebesszene aufführen, ganz unter sich, ohne Statisten, nur der eine Hauptdarsteller, schwer belastet, unter dem anderen Hauptdarsteller. Gemäß dem Anlaß gibt sich Erika als Person sofort auf. Ein Geschenkartikel in leicht angestaubter Seidenpapierverpackung.][63]

The description of grimy toilets, in conjunction with the references to performance, exposes the generic conventions of romance as clichés, while also adding an element of disgust to the scene. In the film, the tiled floor of the toilet is spotlessly clean. The lovers look at one another and then kiss passionately for around thirty seconds before sinking to the floor together in what is a romantic scene. Indeed, the image of the lovers embracing on the floor is also used for the cover of Neugroschel's 2004 translation and the DVD. The impression of this scene is deliberately misleading and illustrates Haneke's engagement with, and manipulation of, romantic tropes that jar with the narrative — particularly the climax — of the film. However, moments later, the scene changes: no passionate embraces or sounds of the lovers kissing. Instead, the camera shows Erika's back as Walter stands at arms-length and struggles to get an erection. The *mise-en-scène* — the gleaming white cleanliness of the staff toilets — now mirrors the sterility of the scenario and, implicitly, the reused and recycled tropes of mainstream romance.

Like Jelinek, Haneke also delivers his critique of patriarchal configurations of female speech, as brought forward by the case histories of psychoanalysis. When Erika presents Walter with her letter, she sits quietly on the sofa while Walter, from his armchair, reads her letter and asks if she is mentally ill, thereby perfectly rendering the stereotypical postures of patient and analyst. However, while Haneke presents a stark 'feminist treatise about how strident female sexuality is taboo and punishable',[64] Jelinek places greater interest on historical cycles of domination and submission. For instance, the clientele of the peepshow are repeatedly referred to as Turks. Haneke indeed presents men of stereotypically southern Mediterranean appearance, but the portrait is less distinct. Jelinek reminds readers of mutual tensions between native Austrians and Turks, ranging from the *Battle of Vienna* (1783) to contemporary conflicts with migrant workers. These points are arguably less relevant to Haneke. Moreover, *La Pianiste* glosses over the relationship of Erika's parents. Her mother's oppressive presence and the psychological decline and death of her father, whose presence haunts the narrative, manifest the binary components of the war generation: that of victim and perpetrator. Through these 'losses of translation', Haneke's focus on Erika's 'perversions' comes at the expense of the broader socio-political context.[65]

### Non-Adaptation and Narrative Promiscuity

Thomas's kaleidoscope of genres proves more difficult to contain or separate than Jelinek's text. In addition to the pornographic depictions of sex and equally vivid portrayals of violence, his incorporation of Dina Pronicheva's testimony attaches another dimension of controversy. The promiscuous style of *The White Hotel* works towards a critique and evaluation of ethics and representation, and calls into question the possibility of ethical witnessing. For instance, there is Thomas's depiction of bystanders whose 'faces were pressed to the windows, looking down on the dense mass of migrants. Some looked sorry for them, but others laughed and jeered'.[66] Readers/audiences of tragic histories are — at best — driven by a desire to understand and acknowledge the pain of others. Nonetheless, this scene implicates the reader, putting her into the place of either a masochistic viewer, over-identifying with the characters in search for some kind of catharsis, or using a sadistic gaze, forming part of Thomas's meditation on representation.[67] This imagery and concern with spectatorship resonates with the concerns of Jelinek's text and Haneke's film, described above.

In addition, references to film, photography and newspaper articles illustrate and exacerbate Lisa's traumatic experiences. For example, she traces back the initial onset of her symptoms to a bragging letter written by her husband, a prosecution lawyer. To her great horror, she learns that his rhetorical abilities were used to enforce a man's death penalty.[68] As well as this, there are several references to the crimes of real-life murderer Peter Kürten, who was charged with nine counts of murder in 1931. In *The White Hotel*, these crimes are documented in the press in lurid detail and greatly torment Lisa.[69] The gratuitous details in the press mirror, to some extent, the horrific descriptions in 'The Sleeping Carriage' chapter, continue the text's problematisation of representation. Kürten's sensationalized crimes seem to overshadow the suffering of the victims, whose pain is lost through a disproportionate focus on Kürten's perversities.

References to film further highlight the mediated nature of our understanding of cruelty: during the massacre, 'no one could have imagined the scene, because it was happening. In spite of the shouts [...] Lisa heard nothing. As in a silent film.'[70] Moreover, in the 'Camp' chapter, the inhabitants watch 'badly made documentaries', one of which refers back to the murderer Peter Kürten, though Lisa has forgotten why she recognizes the name.[71] These instances exemplify the narrative preoccupation with sensationalized trauma and the alienating effects of reproductions of tragedy, while also chiming with Michael Berry's assertions that 'by the end of the twentieth-century, the ways people imagine, contextualize and conceive of violence and war has become increasingly dictated by television, film and the mass media'.[72] By situating media portrayals of trauma in a narrative that seeks to represent a massacre, Thomas self-reflexively comments on his own narrative. These references also form part of Thomas's critique of prescriptive generic containment with regards to some representations of trauma: by adhering to conventions of genre — whether documentary, true crime, or historical fiction — the events described risk reduction to depersonalized products for consumption. For film makers in particular, representing the holocaust, as well as other instances of historical trauma, represents challenges as this medium is so closely entwined with pleasure, voyeurism and fetishism. With this in mind, filmic holocaust representations run the risk of merely sensationalizing trauma and profiting from the painful stories they want to share.

The translation of traumatic histories into language challenge conceptions of 'truth', not because *forms* of representation are impossible — novels like Thomas's contest such claims — but, rather, a satisfactory and comprehensive documentation of the events defies possibility. The people who experienced them cannot testify. *The White Hotel* exemplifies this problem by drawing heavily — almost word for word — on Pronicheva's account. Thomas argues that as the sole survivor of the massacre, she is

> the truthful voice of the narrative at that point. [...] It could not be altered. The time for imagination was before [the massacre]; and, in my novel, after. Imagination [...] is exhausted in the effort to take in the unimaginable.[73]

While both *Die Klavierspielerin* and *The White Hotel* merge truth and fiction in ways that disrupt generic boundaries, the categorization of *Die Klavierspielerin* as semiautobiographical and Thomas's use of Pronicheva's testimony contain different ethical implications. Jelinek is, among other things, seeking to represent a sense of her subjectivity as it is connected to constructed ideas of sex, race and culture, and, as such, is free to represent herself however she chooses. In contrast, Thomas's adaptation of testimony jars with discourses regarding holocaust narrative, which posit that fact and fiction should be distinguishable. As a non-Jewish, English writer, Thomas intrudes into the territory of holocaust testimony in order to make a broader point regarding representation.

In her discussion of *The White Hotel*, Rebecca Scherr highlights the unconventional decision to place sexuality at the forefront of holocaust narrative. Given that Nazi discourses and practices 'conspired to strip the individual of any means towards imagining oneself a being, human and sexual',[74] the absence of sex characterizes most examples of survivor testimony. For Scherr, Thomas's startling prose comes at the expense of 'sexualizing and trivializing one survivor's testimony of Babi Yar'.[75] According to James Young, Thomas appropriates Pronicheva's 'voice *as a style*, a rhetorical move by which he would impute to his fiction the authority of testimony without the authenticity of actual testimony.'[76] There are clear ethical implications here as 'Thomas's novelistic twist on this testimony brings Dina's experiences into the realm of fiction — a dangerous move in our era of Holocaust deniers, who claim the Holocaust itself is a conspiracy perpetuated through narrative and photographic fiction.'[77] Pronicheva's testimony constitutes *evidence*, not entertainment, and therefore its truthfulness and accuracy as recounted are integral components, but its use in Thomas's novel blurs the testimony/fiction divide.

Thomas's failure to provide his reader with a cue to mark the beginning and end of Pronicheva's account, which he has also adapted, is certainly problematic. However, Lisa's subconscious is not only fused with Pronicheva's, it also merges with the 'hysterical' women analyzed by Freud, framing Lisa as a link between two discourses (psychoanalysis and Nazism), therefore positioning Nazism as part of a continuity of violence. While Kappeler argued that Thomas's libidinization of Nazism is incompatible with ethical representation, Kohlke points toward the aesthetic quality of the novel's counter-erotics: the inclusion of sexuality 'reminds us of the human body's vulnerability to potential violation as well as pleasure, which we all share.'[78] In other words, the implicit vulnerability of intimate scenarios may have the effect of (re)humanizing the subject, encouraging engagement by disallowing readers to characterize victims purely by their victimisation, i.e. their relationship to their oppressor. By giving access to the tactile sensitivities and pleasures of the body, as well as exposing the reader to descriptions of corporeal pain, Thomas disturbs the generic constraints that risk the symbolic petrification of people who are victimized.

## Speculative Conclusions

As mentioned in my introduction, David Cronenberg stands among the directors linked to the non-making of *The White Hotel*. Arguably, this director already made numerous attempts of adapting this novel — every time focussing on isolated chapters. His 1996 adaptation of J. G. Ballard's *Crash* (1973)[79] bears a strong thematic resemblance to 'Don Giovanni' and 'The Gastein Journal' chapters of Thomas's novel, given Thomas and Cronenberg's shared concern with Freudian formulations of the sex and death drives. Additionally, the film's predilection for formal repetition frames it as a Sadeian text: first, the viewer sees the sex scenes, and then s/he hears them recounted by the characters, with the aim at prolonging their pleasure, 'echoing de Sade's maxim that "the sensations communicated by the ear are the most enjoyable and have the keenest impact"'.[80] Thomas utilizes a similar method of repetition. In 2011, Cronenberg adapted John Kerr's *A Most Dangerous Method* (1998),[81] which depicts the triangular relationship between Sabina

Spielrein, C. G. Jung and Freud, focusing particularly on the sadomasochistic power imbalance in the relationship between analyst and analysand. Spielrein and Jung's love-affair recalls Thomas's 'Frau Anna G' chapter. While not overtly sexual as in Cronenberg's film, Freud's son is the sexual object of Lisa's fantasies, and the pseudonym 'Anna G' also reminds the reader of Freud's daughter, Anna Freud, suggesting a thinly veiled desire between the two. Moreover, in the therapy sessions Freud displays quasi-sadistic tendencies.[82] In these two films, Cronenberg has adapted material akin to three chapters from Thomas's text.

Roman Polanski can also be counted among the hypothetical directors of *The White Hotel*. *The Pianist* (2002), an adaptation of Wladislaw Szpilman's memoirs from the Warsaw ghetto,[83] corresponds somewhat to the 'Sleeping Carriage' chapter due to its filmic re-formulation of testimony, and Jeff Kanew's *Babi Yar* (2003) recounts and represents the same genocidal atrocity described in the novel.[84]

These examples show that the content of the individual chapters poses little difficulty for adaption. Instead, it is the idiosyncratic combination and merging of genres that creates a problem for film makers. It is precisely the blending of genres that accounts for the difficulty of filmic representation. While for Kappeler and Scherr the generic peculiarities — in particular the unification of pornography with holocaust testimony — seem to trivialize the tragedy Thomas seeks to represent, it is exactly this integration which accounts for its difficulty to film. Without denying the problematic fusing of holocaust memory with, in Scherr's words, 'sexy memory',[85] the generic juxtapositions also constitute an obstacle to filmic exploitation. This fusing can therefore also suggest complexity, rather than triviality, mirroring the problems implicit in trying to represent such traumas without reducing them to a particular genre. Whereas Jelinek makes a formal commitment to presenting a damning view of heteronormativity, cruelty and the cycles of repression and sadism, Thomas's metafictional techniques and pluralistic combination of tenderness with pornography, and testimony alongside fiction proves a disquieting challenge to filmmakers.

## Bibliography

ANDREAS-SALOMÉ, LOU. *The Erotic*, trans. by John Crisp (New Brunswick, NJ: Transaction Publishers, 2012).

BETHMAN, B. L., *Obscene Fantasies: Elfriede Jelinek's Generic Perversions* (PhD dissertation University of Massachusetts Amherst, 2009) <http://scholarworks.umass.edu/open_access_dissertations/86/> [accessed 17 July 2016].

BERGER, JAMES, *After the End: Representations of Post-Apocalypse* (Minneapolis, MN: University of Minnesota Press, 1999).

BERRY, MICHAEL, *A History of Pain: Trauma in Modern Chinese Literature and Film* (New York, NY: Columbia University Press, 2008).

BOWLES, DANIEL, *The Ends of Satire: Legacies of Satire in Post War Germany* (Berlin: De Gruyter, 2015).

BROWNING, MARK, *David Cronenburg: Author or Film-Maker* (Chicago, IL: University of Chicago Press, 2007).

BRUNETTE, PETER, *Michael Haneke* (Chicago, IL: University of Illinois Press, 2010).

CROSS, RICHARD K, 'The Soul is a Far Country: D. M. Thomas and *The White Hotel*', *Journal of Modern Literature*, 18.1 (Winter 1991), 19–47.
FOUCAULT, MICHEL, *The Will to Knowledge: The History of Sexuality 1*, trans. by Robert Hurley (London: Penguin, 1998).
GRISSEMANN, STEFAN, 'Österreich im Herbst', in *Haneke/Jelinek Die Klavierspierin: Drehbuch, Gesprach, Essays* (Vienna: Sonderzahl, 2001), pp. 167–74.
HAMMERSCHLAG, SARAH, *The Figural Jew: Politics and Identity in Postwar French Thought* (Chicago, IL: University of Chicago Press, 2010).
HANEKE, MICHAEL, *La Pianiste* (Kino International, 2001).
HART, LYNDA, *Between the Body and the Flesh: Performing Sadomasochism* (New York, NY: Columbia University Press, 1998).
HUTCHEON, LINDA, *A Poetics of Postmodernism: History, Theory, Fiction* (New York, NY: Routledge, 1998).
JELINEK, ELFRIEDE, *Die Klavierspielerin* (Hamburg: Rowohlt, 2015).
—— *The Piano Teacher*, trans. by Joachim Neugroschel (London: Serpent's Tail, 2010).
KAFKA, FRANZ, *Der Prozeß* (Norderstedt: Books on Demand, 2015).
—— *The Trial*, trans. by David Wyllie (New York, NY: Dover Publications, 2009).
KAPPELER, SUSANNE, *The Pornography of Representation* (Cambridge: Polity Press, 1986).
KOHLKE, MARIE-LUISE, 'Sublime Violations: Trauma Literature, Violence and Counter-Erotics', in *Sexual Politics and Desire of Belonging*, ed. by Nick Rumens and Alejandro Cervantes-Carson (Amsterdam: Rodopi, 2007), pp. 220–48.
LEVINE, GEORGE, 'No Reservations', *The New York Review of Books* (28 May 1981) <http://www.nybooks.com/articles/1981/05/28/no-reservations/> [accessed 17 July 2016].
OJUMO, AKIN, 'Cannes Ordinaire', *The Guardian* (20th May, 2001) <https://www.theguardian.com/film/2001/may/20/cannes2001.cannesfilmfestival> [accessed 17 July 2016]
SCHERR, REBECCA, 'The Uses of Memory and the Abuses of Fiction in Holocaust Fiction and Memoir', in *Other Voices* 2.1 (February 2000), <http://www.othervoices.org/2.1/scherr/sexuality.php#N1> [accessed 17 July 2016].
SCHLIPPHACKE, HEIDI, *Nostalgia After Nazism: History, Home and Affect in German and Austrian Literature and Film* (Lewisburg, PA: Bucknell University Press, 2010).
SHEILS, BARRY and JULIE WALSH, 'Tragedy and Transference in D. M. Thomas's *The White Hotel*', *Psychoanalysis and History*, 15.1 (2013), 69–89 <http://dx.doi.org/10.3366/pah.2013.0122> [accessed 25 April 2015].
THOMAS, D. M., *Bleak Hotel* (London: Quartet Books, 2008).
—— *The White Hotel* (Harmondsworth: Penguin, 1982 [orig. 1981]).
—— *The White Hotel* (London: Phoenix, 2004).
YOUNG, JAMES, *Writing and Rewriting the Holocaust: Narrative and the Consequences of Interpretation* (Indiana, IN: Indiana University Press, 1988).
WIGMORE, JULIET, 'Sex, Violence and Schubert. Michael Haneke's *La Pianiste* and Elfriede Jelinek's *Die Klavierspielerin*', in *Processes of Transposition: German Literature and Film*, ed. by Christiane Schönfeld and Hermann Rasche (Amsterdam: Rodopi, 2007), pp. 293–306.

## Notes to Chapter 10

1. Andreas-Salomé, Lou. *The Erotic*, trans. by John Crisp (New Brunswick, NJ: Transaction Publishers, 2012), pp. 63–64.
2. See Bruce J. DeHart, 'Babi Yar Massacre', in *Atrocities, Massacres, and War Crimes: An Encyclopaedia*, ed. by Alexander Mikaberidze, 2 vols (Santa Barbara CA: ABC-Clio 2013), I, 50
3. See D. M. Thomas, *The White Hotel* (Harmondsworth: Penguin, 1982 [orig. 1981]).

4. Pronicheva related her memoirs to Anatoly Kuznetsov who published it under a pseudonym: A. Anatoli, *Babi Yar: A Document in the Form of a Novel* [orig. Бабий яр. Роман-документ], trans. by David Floyd (London: Jonathan Cape 1970).
5. Thomas, D. M. *Bleak Hotel* (London: Quartet Books, 2008).
6. Ibid., p. 98.
7. Ibid., p. 15.
8. Quoted in Heidi Schlipphacke, *Nostalgia After Nazism: History, Home and Affect in German and Austrian Literature and Film* (Lewisburg, PA: Bucknell University Press, 2010), p. 68.
9. Levine, George, 'No Reservations', *The New York Review of Books* (28 May 1981) <http://www.nybooks.com/articles/1981/05/28/no-reservations/> [accessed 13 October 2016].
10. Kappeler, Susanne, *The Pornography of Representation* (Cambridge: Polity Press, 1986), p. 92.
11. See Jelinek, *Die Klavierspielerin*, p. 32.
12. Jelinek, *The Piano Teacher*, p. 277.
13. Jelinek, *Die Klavierspielerin*, p. 302.
14. Ibid., p. 229
15. Ibid., p. 267.
16. See Lynda Hart, *Between the Body and the Flesh: Performing Sadomasochism* (New York, NY: Columbia University Press, 1998).
17. Jelinek, *The Piano Teacher*, p. 233.
18. Jelinek, *Die Klavierspielerin*, p. 271.
19. Jelinek, *Die Klavierspielerin*, p. 78.
20. Jelinek, *The Piano Teacher*, p. 231.
21. Ibid. p.269.
22. Jelinek, *The Piano Teacher*, p.230.
23. Jelinek, Die Klavierspielerin, p.269.
24. See Linda Hutcheon, *A Poetics of Postmodernism: History, Theory, Fiction* (New York, NY: Routledge, 1998); James Berger, *After the End: Representations of Post-Apocalypse* (Minneapolis: University of Minnesota Press, 1999).
25. Richard K Cross, 'The Soul is a Far Country: D. M. Thomas and *The White Hotel*', *Journal of Modern Literature*, vol.18.1 (Winter 1991), 19–47 (p. 25).
26. Michel Foucault, *The Will to Knowledge: The History of Sexuality 1*, trans. by Robert Hurley (London: Penguin, 1998), p. 65.
27. Marie-Luise Kohlke, 'Sublime Violations', in *Sexual Politics and Desire of Belonging*, ed. by Nick Rumens and Alejandro Cervantes-Carson (Amsterdam: Rodopi, 2007), pp. 220–48 (p. 239).
28. D. M. Thomas, *The White Hotel* (London: Phoenix, 2004), p. 9.
29. Barry Sheils and Julie Walsh, 'Tragedy and Transference in D. M. Thomas's *The White Hotel*', *Psychoanalysis and History*, 15.1 (2013), 69–89 (p. 77).
30. Jelinek, *The Pianoplayer*, p. 113.
31. Jelinek, *Die Klavierspielerin*, p. 130.
32. Daniel Bowles, *The Ends of Satire: Legacies of Satire in Post War Germany* (Berlin: De Gruyter, 2015), p. 114.
33. Jelinek, *The Piano Player*, p. 56
34. Jelinek, *Die Klavierspielerin*, p. 62.
35. Franz Kafka,. *The Trial*, trans. By David Wyllie (New York, NY: Dover Publications, 2009), p. 165.
36. Franz Kafka, *Der Prozeß* (Norderstedt: Books on Demand, 2015), p. 175.
37. Jelinek, *The Piano Teacher*, p. 285.
38. Jelinek, *Die Klavierspielerin*, p. 335.
39. See Sarah Hammerschlag, *The Figural Jew: Politics and Identity in Postwar French Thought* (Chicago, IL: University of Chicago Press, 2010), p. 87.
40. Jelinek, *The Piano Teacher*, p. 58.
41. Jelinek, *Die Klavierspielerin*, p. 64
42. Jelinek, *The Piano Teacher*, p. 59.
43. Jelinek, *Die Klavierspielerin*, p. 65.

44. Jelinek, *The Piano Teacher*, p. 60.
45. Jelinek, *Die Klavierspielerin*, p. 64.
46. Jelinek, *The Piano Teacher*, p. 60.
47. Jelinek, *Die Klavierspielerin*, p. 65.
48. Pauline Réage, *L'histoire d'O* (Paris: Éditions Pauvert, 1954).
49. In her later novel, *Lust* (1989), Jelinek considers the masculinist pornographic tradition more directly, but in *Die Klavierspielerin*, too, her critique is apparent.
50. My own translation, K. J.
51. Jelinek, *Die Klavierspielerin*, p. 66.
52. Jelinek, *The Piano Teacher*, p. 59.
53. Ibid, p. 65–66.
54. Michael Haneke quoted in Peter Brunette, *Michael Haneke* (Chicago, IL: University of Illinois Press, 2010), p. 89.
55. B. L. Bethman, *Obscene Fantasies: Elfriede Jelinek's Generic Perversions* (PhD dissertation University of Massachusetts Amherst, 2009) <http://scholarworks.umass.edu/open_access_dissertations/86/> [accessed 17 July 2016].
56. *La Pianiste*, dir. Michael Haneke (WEGA, 2002).
57. Juliet Wigmore, 'Sex, Violence and Schubert. Michael Haneke's *La Pianiste* and Elfriede Jelinek's *Die Klavierspielerin*', in *Processes of Transposition: German Literature and Film*, ed. by Christiane Schönfeld and Hermann Rasche (Amsterdam: Rodopi, 2007), pp. 293–306 (p. 302).
58. Jelinek, *The Piano Player*, p. 148.
59. Jelinek, *Die Klavierspielerin*, p. 169–70.
60. Jelinek, *The Piano Player*, p. 153.
61. Jelinek, *Die Klavierspielerin*, p. 174.
62. Jelinek, *The Piano Player*, p. 180.
63. Jelinek, *Die Klavierspielerin*, p. 208.
64. Akin Ojumo. 'Cannes Ordinaire', *The Guardian* (20 May, 2001) <https://www.theguardian.com/film/2001/may/20/cannes2001.cannesfilmfestival> [accessed 17 July 2017].
65. Narrative 'faithfulness' isn't necessarily a pre-requisite for the successful adaptation of a text, and indeed, while 'faithful' on the surface, Haneke brings his own concerns to his retelling. For a detailed and enlightening discussion of this point, and for Haneke's views on adaptation, see Stefan Grissemann's 'Österreich im Herbst', in *Haneke/Jelinek* Die Klavierspielerin: *Drehbuch, Gespräch, Essays* (Vienna: Sonderzahl, 2001), pp. 167–74.
66. Furthermore, as Barry Sheils and Julie Walsh note, the use of the word *anagnorisis* twice within Thomas's novel, combined with its punning relation to 'Anna G neurosis', encourages readings that posit the text as an exploration and complication of the relationship between representation and ethics through the weaving of tragic reality with tragic theatre. See Sheils, 'Tragedy and Transference', p. 75.
67. Of course, empathy need not automatically be masochistic, but the consumption of novels, a form traditionally associated with entertainment and pleasure, dealing with the holocaust or other historical traumas begs the question of reader motivation and blurs the divide between ethical witnessing and reading for, perhaps unconscious/unacknowledged, (masochistic) pleasure.
68. Thomas, *The White Hotel* (2004), p. 177.
69. Ibid., p. 159.
70. Ibid., p. 215.
71. See ibid., p. 229.
72. Michael Berry. *A History of Pain: Trauma in Modern Chinese Literature and Film* (New York, NY: Columbia University Press, 2008), p. 320.
73. James Young, *Writing and Rewriting the Holocaust: Narrative and the Consequences of Interpretation* (Bloomington, IN: Indiana University Press, 1988), p. 55.
74. Rebecca Scherr, 'The Uses of Memory and the Abuses of Fiction in Holocaust Fiction and Memoir, *Other Voices*, 2.1 (February 2000), <http://www.othervoices.org/2.1/scherr/sexuality.php#N1> [accessed 17 July 2016].

75. Ibid.
76. Young, *Writing and Rewriting the Holocaust*, p. 56.
77. Scherr, 'The Uses of Memory and the Abuses of Fiction in Holocaust Fiction and Memoir'.
78. Kohlke, 'Sublime Violations', p. 243.
79. J. G.Ballard, *Crash* (London: Cape, 1973); *Crash*, dir. David Cronenberg (The Movie Network & Telefilm Canada, 1996).
80. Mark Browning, *David Cronenberg: Author or Film-Maker* (Chicago, IL: University of Chicago Press, 2007).
81. See *A Dangerous Method*, dir. David Cronenberg (Recorded Picture Company, 2011); John Kerr, *A Most Dangerous Method* (New York, NY: Knopf, 1993).
82. For instance, during a therapy session Lisa's pains become greatly increased when talking about her godson: 'they were so severe that she begged to be allowed to go home. I was not prepared to let her go without attempting to find the cause of this sudden deterioration' (Thomas, *The White Hotel* (2004), p. 118).
83. See Władysław Szpilman, *Śmierć miasta* [*Death of a City*] (Warsaw: Wiedza, 1946).
84. See *Babi Yar*, dir. by Jeff Kanew (Central Cinema Company Film, 2003).
85. Scherr, 'The Uses of Memory and the Abuses of Fiction in Holocaust Fiction and Memoir'.

CHAPTER 11

# From Literary Contact to Cinematic Intimacy: Patrice Chéreau Meets Hanif Kureishi

*Juliette Feyel*

When addressing the debate about the distinction between eroticism and pornography, it is not uncommon to come across Claude Tapia, who contrasts 'good' and 'bad' taste.[1] According to Tapia, pornography portrays sex in a base, ugly and dirty manner, whilst eroticism would sublimate it through refinement and aesthetics. This aesthetic judgement, however, is becoming increasingly blurred by the rise of the 'porn chic' vogue. A recent *France Culture* radio broadcast discusses the democratization of sexual practices that used to be considered marginal or deviant, such as bondage and S&M.[2] In the last decades, the marketing of sex toys has altered their image substantially;[3] today, even mainstream celebrities like Gwyneth Paltrow advise their followers on which sex toys they should buy.[4] Similarly, the fashion designer Sonia Rykiel hosts a cosy boudoir dedicated to women's pleasure in Saint-Germain, an upmarket district of Paris. Sex shops appear not to be viewed as 'dirty' any more. This would support Andrea Dworkin's notion that 'erotica is simply high-class pornography; better produced, better conceived, better executed, better packaged, designed for a better class of consumer.'[5]

Another criterion often used is whether sex is implicitly or explicitly depicted, the former having access to distribution channels unimaginable for the latter. Yet again, the psychological thriller *Don't Look Now* (dir. Nicolas Roeg, 1973) includes what appears to be an unsimulated sex-scene, and *9½ Weeks* (dir. Adrian Lyne, 1986) and *Basic Instinct* (dir. Paul Verhoeven, 1992) also became box-office hits despite kinky scenes ranging from clichéd depictions of homosexuality to bondage and S&M. While the adjective 'pornographic' hardly applies to these productions, D. H. Lawrence's argument comes to mind when considering heated debates about whether the sex scenes were simulated or real. Whenever such a 'dirty little secret'[6] is discussed, something hypocritical enters the discourse. It hides under the appearance of respectability and endeavours to produce a sharp and delightful thrill. As a result, implicit sex can be more obscene than explicit sex.

This definition relies on the response of the audience, and cultural idiosyncrasies make it difficult to draw the line. Take recent French directors such as Bertrand Bonello, Jacques Nolot, Catherine Breillat, Bruno Dumont, and Jean-Claude Brisseau: is it because she is French that the academic Martine Beugnet enthusiastically praises what she calls a 'cinema of sensation', for it has 'the ability to reach a spectator's mind through the intelligence of the affective'?[7] By contrast, the American critique James Quandt articulates his distaste for the 'New French Extremity',[8] which he accuses of exploiting graphic sex in order to attract attention. This cultural difference appears to be taken for granted by Susan Sontag in her essay 'The Pornographic Imagination'. Despite their graphic content, Sontag champions the works of Marquis de Sade, Georges Bataille, and Pauline Réage by identifying them with a long and distinguished tradition of high literature.[9]

In order to move beyond the moral relativism inherent to such debates, I propose a definition that appears useful in this context. In his essay *Eroticism* (*L'Erotisme*, 1957),[10] Bataille contrasts our usual, day-to-day state of individuality with the domain of eroticism. The latter implies contact and communication, and dissolves the calm and orderly state of everyday reality. Eroticism puts the subject into question by relating it to violence and a transcending force beyond corporeal limits. It makes us participate in the grand flux of universal expenditure, an experience that brings us close to death — to the 'little death.' (See Julia Boog-Kaminski and Kathrin Emeis's article in the present volume.)

After Bataille, Jacques Lacan draws much inspiration from this dichotomy between everyday and exceptional states of mind. He reinterpreted Sigmund Freud, whose theory encountered an impasse when dealing with the death-drive, a principle opposed to the pillar of psychoanalysis, the pleasure principle. How can a subject so eagerly seek an experience at odds with the search for the pleasure principle, i.e. the ego's imaginary sense of coherence? In *Seminar VII*, Lacan rephrased Freudian theory and posited that whilst the *ego* seeks a sense of control, the *id* and *superego* command it to *jouissance* — a concept encapsulating the meaning of enjoyment, bliss, but also of loss and expenditure.[11]

In this regard, Roland Barthes uses the same dichotomy as Lacan, but he applies it to the experience of reading literature:

> Text of bliss: the text that imposes a state of loss, the text that discomforts (perhaps to the point of a certain boredom), unsettles the reader's historical, cultural, psychological assumptions, the consistency of his tastes, values, memories, brings to a crisis his relation with language.[12]
>
> [Texte de jouissance: celui qui met en état de perte, celui qui déconforte (peut-être jusqu'à un certain ennui), fait vaciller les assises historiques, culturelles, psychologiques, du lecteur, la consistance de ses goûts, de ses valeurs et de ses souvenirs, met en crise son rapport au langage.[13]]

Drawing on Barthes, I will use the term 'pornography' to designate the titillating artefact that pleases and confirms the ego through conventional representations of sex, whereas 'the erotic' will refer to texts and films that put convention into question. To support my point, I will compare the 2001 film *Intimacy* directed by

Patrice Chéreau, starring Mark Rylance and Kerry Fox, with the 1998 novella that it is based on, written by Hanif Kureishi and bearing the same title. (I will refer to the film by the French title, *Intimité*, the novel by the English title, *Intimacy*.) Drawing this parallel will help examine how a multi-faceted translation, as a process of carrying something from one place to another, impacts a storyline. Indeed, the plot was actually carried from one language to another and then back again, as Chéreau read the novella in a French translation, worked with Anne-Louise Trividic on a script in French and then translated it back into English for the actors. The story was carried from one culture to another, from one medium to another, from one single writer to a team, including director, director of photography, script-writers, actors, editors. Chéreau put the challenge very bluntly: 'Later I thought, what can these two strangers, a gay Frenchman and a straight British-Indian make together, if anything?'[14] This comparison will offer the opportunity to reflect on what happens when eroticism crosses borders.

### Explicit, not Pornographic

One of the common points between Chéreau and Kureishi is their rejection of embellishment when portraying sex. In Britain controversies around *Intimité* were raised by the thirty-five minute scene of explicit sex and the fellatio performed by Kerry Fox. Hence, in numerous interviews Chéreau and Fox defended the artistic value of such images; they generally underlined the film's authenticity and realism with regards to love relationships. Fox argues: 'Patrice and I talked about how it would be good to do an extremely truthful film about a sexual relationship, about how we'd never seen a film like that.'[15] In another interview, Chéreau protests:

> Just because 35 minutes of this film is about intimacy it should not be reduced to a film about sex [...]. Sex is the way to communicate at the beginning. I just wanted to show how beautiful it could be. [...] This is not about sex. Watching these people doesn't arouse me. They are completely ordinary.[16]

It is noteworthy that the official posters in France and Britain evoked totally different expectations from the audience. The French poster shows the two protagonists looking at each other in the eye, surrounded by a blurred crowd of indifferent people; it lays stress on their connection, as the man bends forward to kiss the woman. In contrast, the UK distribution exploited the scandalous aura surrounding the film, shaping the viewer's expectation in a very different manner than in France: the protagonists are naked and lying on the floor, the woman has her back to the man, her face averted, the man has one hand on her hip, the other hand clasping her by the hair. A comment crosses the poster in bold letters: 'the most controversial film of the year'.

Although writers are not normally under as much commercial pressure to promote their work, Kureishi was forced to justify himself following accusations that *Intimacy* was a means to take revenge on his former wife, whom he had left for a younger woman in remarkably similar circumstances as those described in the novella. Because of the publication of an angry article written by his sister about the writer's tendency to exploit his family's privacy, *Intimacy* has been suspected of the same misdeed. Moreover, he was attacked for writing the character Jay's cynical comments about women, to which the writer answered: 'I've never had any desire to be good, [...] I don't like goodness particularly. I like passion.'[17]

The novelist was disappointed that critiques did not pay more attention to the formal, literary experiments of this book. And in effect, commentators like Frederick Luis Aldama[18] and Ruvani Ranasinha[19] were disappointed not to find the postcolonial issues and social commentaries of his earlier period writings. Given the number of unflattering statements about women, they also qualified his recent turn towards middle-aged and middle-class male psychological preoccupations as indulgent and morally dubious. But Kureishi repeats, every time he is criticised: 'The truth is, everything we really desire is either forbidden, immoral or unhealthy, and, if you're lucky, all three at once.'[20]

Chéreau was also accused of misogyny, as he also used Kureishi's short story 'Nightlight' (1997) to explore his interest in the anonymous dimension of the sexual encounters between protagonists. Some disliked this impersonal interaction and judged it unrealistic.[21] For example, Kristina Nordstrom, who runs the *Women Filmmakers Symposium in Los Angeles*, claimed:

> Of course no woman would be attracted to sex like that. [...] The sex in the movie all involves the bottom of the ninth inning. A woman would be turned off by a man who doesn't spend time being tender and sweet, and showing that he cares for her. There's no foreplay. She walks in, they rip off each other's clothes, and a few seconds later, they're in a frenzy. Any woman would know that this movie was directed by a man.[22]

Here, Nordstrom presupposes a discrete female desire that finds its natural expression within the courtly love etiquette. Her thinking is informed by Dworkin and Linda Williams[23] who pointed at the misogynistic representations at work in pornographic artefacts. And indeed, wordless sex is a typical feature of pornography in which the plot is minimal and sexual scenes are only tenuously connected by inept dialogues. The focus of 'Nightlight' and *Intimité*, however, lies somewhere else; the man feels increasingly attached to the mysterious woman who comes to visit him every Wednesday and this emerging bond bewilders him. 'Nightlight' triggered Chéreau's imagination when he read: 'If sex is how you meet and get to know people, what does he know of her?'[24] So relational psychology is the major preoccupation of both Kureishi and Chéreau. While their protagonists share a strictly sexual relationship without socially engaging with each other, when they begin to speak, it is already too late; their tacit bond is broken. We can also note that in the novella, as well as in the film, the majority of the dialogues occur when an argument is taking place, as if words were bound to bring about conflict, lies and misunderstandings, as if only the body could speak the truth. Chéreau argues:

> That's how the story was: two unknown people. So we decided, "What can you learn about someone when making love to them?" That was really interesting to direct. The sex became a language — a dialogue and they are talking.[25]

Interestingly enough, *Intimacy* is not so graphic, especially when comparing it with books written by bestselling authors such as Maxim Jakubowski and Alessandra Torre, for example. The tropes of pornographic literature insist on the formidable size of the man's organ, the insatiable thirst of the beast-like woman for being penetrated, stretched out and flooded by huge quantities of fluid, a metaphor of the male's unlimited power to fill and content her.[26] But in *Intimacy*, a sense of crudeness stems from a crafty use of language that does not rely on visual descriptions. An impression of transgression is conveyed by the way the writer combines concision, rhythm, and contrasted language registers:

> I should have gone out with her [*i.e. Susan*] for six months. Or maybe a one-night stand would have been sufficient. But I wasn't ruthless enough, and I didn't know what I wanted.
> *I begin to rub and pull my prick.*
> How long will she dislike me? A few months? Years? These partings or abandonments can cut deep[.][27]

The phrase in italics produces a break in many ways: a diegetic break, since his reflection on his moribund marital relationship is interrupted by a rapid, unexpected reference to the concrete origin of enunciation. The present irrupts within the past, the body in language. Visually the sentence is isolated between two longer paragraphs; the statement is short, straight-forward, and the monosyllable "prick", with its explosive consonances, is emphasised both by an alliteration with 'pull' and the trochaic rhythm laying a very strong emphasis on the final crude word. Yet the self-doubt of the last paragraph seems at odds with the implicit macho attitude of the text.[28] Further on, the masturbatory act is told in present tense and first person singular, to fully represent Jay's internal viewpoint. Tactile sensations are also left aside, Jay only states 'I am running through my library of stimulating scenes',[29] which gives way to a series of vague allusions to grotesque episodes. The reader is brought to guess — literally between the lines — the moment of climax through a simple note: 'That should do it. Christ. Yes.'[30] Although the passage is unequivocal, the absence of visual details is striking; the full act remains entirely unsaid. Kureishi is probably more shocking because he reveals the most secret, selfish and shameful desires of a middle-aged man, who is distressed by his own decline and eager to grab any little piece of pleasure while he still can.

In the film *Intimité*, two naked bodies are staged in full intercourse but the technique is completely different from extremely codified hard-core movies, as brought forward by the industry's biggest production company, *Vivid Entertainment*. In such films, undressing and changes of postures are cut out; poses facilitate close-ups on genitals, often from a low angle; colours are saturated; the soundtrack is a mix of grunts and groans, and binary-rhythmic music.

Chéreau's style also contrasts with Sam Taylor-Johnson's erotic romcom *Fifty Shades of Grey* (2015). Here, the protagonists slowly take each other's clothes off, allowing some lingering close-ups on the man's athletic torso and shoulders; the woman remains half-dressed in chic lingerie and shots focus on the man's hands caressing and kissing her neck and stomach. Eye-level, medium two-shots prevail and the figures appear from the side in a dim back-light. Languorous, sensual music contributes to the aestheticization of the whole. While *Vivid* movies end after the 'money shot',[31] sex scenes in *Fifty Shades of Grey* are dominated by foreplay. The former genre invites the viewer to identify with the alpha male hero, and the latter reaches out to aficionados of female romantic drama. The intention to arouse is similar, except that one type of pornography relies on exaggeration (size, prowess, accumulation), while the other type focuses on attenuation (concealment, ellipsis, idealization).

In contrast, Chéreau's thirty-five minute sex scene is filmed in one long shot with no music and hardly any sound apart from a few sighs. The two white bodies are filmed from a high angle, crawling toward each other and intermingling their arms and legs, set against the background of a stained carpet in the dim light of a winter morning that comes piercing through the window in a basement. Like Kureishi, Chéreau doesn't try to embellish sex. Instead, *Intimité* focuses on the bashful, gradual approach of one hand toward another's skin, and the apprehensive yet desirous gazes. Facial expressions inform us about the characters' conflicting feelings, which are not always blissful. There are clumsy moves, trials and errors; postures change when they are felt to be uncomfortable. Both bodies remain in full sight with no fetishistic use of close-ups, none of their physical defects are concealed. All of this gives a sense of vulnerability and precariousness that differs from the emphasis on power and beauty specific to pornography. The collaboration of Chéreau and Kureishi addresses the failure of cinema to capture intricacies of feeling:

> Patrice and I talked about keeping the camera close to the bodies; not over-lighting them, or making them look pornographically enticing or idealized. It will be a sexuality that isn't sanitized, symbolized or bland, that isn't selling anything. The point is to look at how difficult sex is, how terrifying, and what a darkness and obscenity our pleasures can be.[32]

Both novella and film were less shocking for their explicitness than they were for their common rejection of the exaltation and embellishment that underlie the conventions of the pornographic genre. In other terms, they questioned the habits of the readers and viewers by displaying the darker zones of the erotic psyche.

### Translator, Traitor

Beyond his stance about the representation of real sex, Chéreau has not always been entirely faithful to Kureishi's work. Part of this is due to the different constraints that apply to different media. When the two authors had their preliminary meetings, they 'decided early on that *Intimacy* was too internal, and, probably, too dark, to make a film — a conventional film, that people might watch — on its own.'[33]

In effect, the plot of *Intimacy* stretches over a few hours and does not provide much action or suspense. The opening sentence demonstrates that Jay has already made up his mind about abandoning his family. The rest of the text, although it involves contradictory options, should not mislead us; Jay hesitates less than he struggles with guilt. It has often been stated that his reproaches regarding Susan's capability as a professional woman, partner and mother were shamefully unfair and could only result from his own resentments and feelings of inadequacy facing a woman of the post-feminist era. But the character acknowledges his selfishness and cowardice, as well as the disastrous consequences of his resigning his fatherly responsibilities. He admits that his search for Susan's responsibility in their break up is an attempt to alleviate his bad conscience. Subsequently, the 155 pages of the novella present us with the internal circumlocutions of a man's bad faith and cynical attempt at justifying a rather pathetically mundane situation — a middle-aged man seeking one last bit of gratification in the arms of a young woman out of fear of aging: 'I think I have become the adults in *The Catcher in the Rye*.'[34]

Chéreau used many situations in *Intimacy* in order to flesh out Jay's character through flashbacks. But a feature film needs to have a beginning and an end. 'Nightlight' provided him with a starting point: an enigma, the mystery around the Wednesday woman, which then needed to be resolved in the second part of the film. Halfway through the film, according to an original idea of Trividic, there is a shift of viewpoint, where the chaser becomes the pursued. We are now to discover Claire's background and daily life, as well as its parallels with Jay's past existence. Like Jay, her early artistic aspirations were disappointed, and like him she is unhappily married and has a young son who looks up to her. But, contrary to him, she will never leave her family. The conditions of cinematic reception forced the script-writers to transform a fragmented, achronological narrative into a more traditional linear plot.

Chéreau rendered the internal debates that form the substance of the novella by adding new characters, the confidants Ian (Philippe Calvario) and Betty (Marianne Faithful). The ensuing discussions grant viewers access to the protagonists' thoughts. This addition can be regarded as a simple device to adapt a text for the screen. This cannot be said of another addition, Claire's husband Andy (Timothy Spall). The part of Andy is based on Asif in Kureishi's novel. He represents the faithful husband and disapproves of Jay's considerations over leaving his family. Asif says: 'But marriage is a battle, a terrible journey, a season in hell and a reason for living...'[35] Andy pronounces the same sentence in the second half of the film, when Jay tries to destabilize and humiliate him. But its meaning changes dramatically from the book to the film. Kureishi's character embodies the typical conservative *pater familias*, a model of moderation and a firm believer of concessions in a couple, since he adds: 'You need to be equipped in all areas, not just the sexual.'[36] By contrast, Andy is madly in love with his wife and seems to emotionally depend on her, as he claims that she brought him back to life. Whereas Kureishi's narrator derides Asif, as much as Jay's Indian father, for sticking to conventional, old-fashioned ways, Chéreau provides Andy with an aura of poignant distress as he gives up on his claim to Claire's exclusivity. Such a modification goes beyond the mere search for a cinematic equivalence: Chéreau seems to use Kureishi's material in a way that re-orients its significance.

## Two Cultures

As a testimony to the meeting of two cultures, the result of Chéreau's adaptation of *Intimacy* is a hybrid piece of work, which the French found very English and the British very French. Chéreau claimed that he was inspired by a certain rawness he perceived in English cinema, something that to him pervaded Kureishi's writing. For the French audience, *Intimité* conjures British social realism as exemplified by directors like Ken Loach, Mike Leigh, and Stephen Frears, who collaborated several times with Kureishi. Chéreau portrays the working-class areas of London, without omitting several typically English realia (red bus, terraced-house, pub, black cab). Chéreau was attracted to the acting style of English actors: 'I wanted to meet English actors, because everyone knows the level of the British actors is really high. It was a dream to work with them.'[37] Furthermore, he described them as 'being incredibly real, a lot more than their French counterparts.'[38] In turn, the British were more inclined to link Frenchness with an interest in crude sex and a predilection for long philosophical discussions:

> The script is excessively talky, but the characters don't just talk. They rail and rant and squabble, at the slightest excuse and at a hyperdemonstrative pitch that is an established convention in French psychological realism, but one that seems alien to British acting styles outside TV soap.[39]

After his first viewing of the film, Kureishi wrote 'Filming *Intimacy*', an essay documenting his encounter with Chéreau. Throughout the essay, the writer insists on establishing himself on equal footing with the director. Despite all the praise, one cannot help noticing a certain regretful tone. His lack of involvement in the production itself triggered a feeling of being dispossessed: 'I generated ideas for him to use, alter or throw away, as he liked — trying not to become too possessive of them.'[40] In brief, Chéreau's translation was an appropriation of Kureishi's material, a reconfiguration of it that ends up serving a totally different artistic purpose. Kureishi's work freed and nurtured Chéreau's, who despite his fidelity to the book's components, brought the story into his own personal themes and concerns. By inventing a sequel to *Intimacy* and 'Nightlight', it is as if Chéreau has absorbed Kureishi's creation into a larger master-project.

In light of Bataille's definition of eroticism, Chéreau and Kureishi find different approaches to putting the subject into question. While Kureishi offers us an argument in the form of an internal monologue, Chéreau stages the debate and also interjects his own responses. It is as if the director had engaged the writer's text with the attitude of a listener who, like the Athenian demos in ancient theatre, wishes to respond to the central protagonist's argument. In the film, when Jay hides his bewilderment by adopting a dismissive attitude toward the woman who comes to him every Wednesday for sex, the addition of Ian's character is more than a mere device for helping Jay articulate his feelings. Ian contributes his own points of view. Performed by Philippe Calario, whose English is strangely pervaded by French turns of phrase and who, notwithstanding his apparent homosexuality, may bear a slight physical resemblance to Chéreau (brown-haired pale man, squarish face), Ian's character seems to be a spokesman for the director:

> You know when you're with someone, there's only a very short time when you can really give each other things for free, with neither of you having to ask... because later on, all you do is make demands of each other. Perhaps the only difference between her and all the rest is that she's asking you for nothing.[41]

Moreover, the development of Claire's viewpoint brings another contradictory statement into relief. In the last scene, she finally explains: 'Who should I have been to keep everyone satisfied... just to come, and see a man, and bury myself in his arms because I wanted to?'[42] An anonymous sexual relationship is the solution she has found to fit together both her family duties that force her to answer for her actions and need for passion, abandonment, and oblivion.

Watching the film with the book in mind creates a dialogue, which reflects, as if in a mirror, a man's dilemmas about sexuality from the viewpoint of a gay man and a woman. The adaptation of a solitary creation into a project involving intermediaries and interpreters gave birth to a dialogical piece of art, a polyphonic staging of stances. Kureishi and Chéreau's divergent views on eroticism are also apparent through the evolution of the male protagonist from the book to the film. Jay appeared in *Intimacy* as an ageing man, troubled with a sense of impending impotence:

> How weak the arc of my urine is, and how I strain to send a respectable semicircle into the pan. Even when my boys were tiny, and those round little worms, their penises, were no thicker than a cable, the arc of their urine had a magnificent velocity. With me there is always a sticky mess on the floor. Dad had prostate cancer. They stuck metal and plastic instruments through the opening of his prick.[43]

The abrupt imaginary association between the capacity to urinate and to be erect is regarded as an ineluctable decline along a direct line from youth to decrepitude. Jay's vengeful onanistic use of Susan's most expensive anti-ageing cream is a symbolical protest against their inescapable evolution into a middle-aged middle-class couple, a life fiercely defended by all the representatives of order: his parents, Asif, Susan, and the therapist they consult. Haunted by a sense of oppression, Jay's departure rests on the tenuous hope of rekindling his capacity for wanting and being wanted. And yet, nothing guarantees that he will find what he thinks he is searching for:

> I know love is dark work; you have to get your hands dirty. If you hold back, nothing interesting happens. At the same time, you have to find the right distance between people. Too close, and they overwhelm you; too far and they abandon you. How to hold them in the right relation?[44]

In *Intimacy*, Jay uses sex in order to keep women at the right distance. He resents Susan's sexual disinterest in him as a lack of love, as he asks 'Is it too much to want a tender and complete intimacy?'[45] At the same time, he fears intimacy: 'Whenever I was with a woman, I considered leaving her. I didn't want what I wanted.'[46] In the film, Jay is a lot more decisive about what he wants and, after an afternoon spent waiting desperately for Claire, he decides to ruin the life she keeps away from him. There is a lot of wickedness in Jay when he provokes Andy and tries by all means to destroy the idyllic delusion that the pathetic cheated husband clings to.

In Chéreau's version, Jay is torn apart by the feeling that someone else is close to Claire. Abandoning the economy of gift, of tacit, impersonal agreement, Jay opts for knowledge and control. He goes one step further and crosses the border separating the real world from the naked presence into that of possession. Jay as a character evolved from a man in fear of not being able to be wanted (Kureishi) to the crisis of a man realizing that he wants more than his lover (Chéreau). Jay is impeded by fear in both cases, fear of not overcoming the pleasure principle (Kureishi) and fear of losing oneself with a stranger and the subsequent relinquishment (Chéreau).

Kureishi's characters suffer from the bad conscience of having crossed the line separating convention from desire. In contrast, Chéreau's characters grab and cling unto each other's bodies, as if it were a question of survival. Yet paradoxically, both *Intimacy* and *Intimité* leave us with an ambiguous ending: the seemingly euphoric ending of the novella appears bitterly ironic, for it is unclear whether the scene told in the second person is actually happening or if it is Jay's mental anticipation of his reconciliation with Nina. Moreover, other ominous signs suggest that this relationship is bound to bring disappointment as Jay mentions several pitiful divorced men, too. The melancholic ending of the film, with David Bowie's song 'The Hotel' as a soundtrack playing as Claire and Jay both go their own way, leaves room for hope. Have the characters understood something that will help them love better in the future? Translated from one artist to another, the discussion of sexual relationships reaches a much more optimistic conclusion in the film.

As a result of this change of tone and atmosphere, one can also note a shift of genre. Kureishi's narrator is stuck in a dilemma because he considers only one possible alternative to his present situation. Two models are rigidly presented as antagonistic in his mind:

> Both he [*i.e. Father*] and Mother were frustrated, neither being able to find a way to get what they wanted, whatever that was. Nevertheless they were loyal and faithful to one another. Disloyal and unfaithful to themselves. Or do I misunderstand?[47]

And if he cannot embrace the old-fashioned marital model involving effort and self-abnegation, it is because he belongs to the wrong generation:

> Susan, who is four years younger than me, thinks we live in a selfish age. She talks of a Thatcherism of the soul that imagines that people are not dependent on one another. In love, these days, it is a free market; browse and buy, pick and choose, rent and reject, as you like. There's no sexual and social security; everyone has to take care of themselves, or not. Fulfilment, self-expression and "creativity" are the only values.[48]

In a consumerist age, in which one focuses solely on the age and physical beauty of people to measure their value as human beings, love can only be enthralled by fear. Romantic love no longer provides a retreat from capitalism. Instead, its ruthless, competitive, and profit-seeking culture has started to inform partners' decisions. Kureishi also mentions in passing that his Jay is of Asian descent, just like him. Autobiography aside, this could point towards the feeling of a generation all the more estranged from their parents as they, as children of immigrants, had to go through a particularly deep acculturation in order to identify with the British middle-class of the eighties. This would demonstrate that Kureishi did not completely give up the social preoccupations that are characteristic of his most famous novels.

Although Chéreau belongs to the same generation, his film does not display the same social perception. In the French man's view, Jay can only be a divorcee impoverished by the money he gives to his ex-wife and children. London appears a dilapidated city, full of people in precarious situations, lonely, alcoholic. Yet brutality comes only from the attitude of people towards one other. If they do not manage to accept the gift of intimacy for what it is, if they try to control it — and to this extent, Jay's mistake may appear as a reworking of the myth of Eros and Psyche — it goes away. The social novel is turned, through Chéreau's appropriation, into a more universal fiction, closer to the genre of tragedy. For Chéreau these seemingly ordinary people with their shabby lives hide inner worlds of drama and passion.

Interestingly, although he felt somehow excluded from the film project, Kureishi does not seem to hold a grudge against Chéreau, rather seduced by the filmmaker's personality:

> He is certainly less impatient and bad-tempered than me. He goes out more than I do. He is more decisive. [...] In the end, I am not sure what it is that my imagination likes to do with him, but just looking at Patrice, or hearing his voice on the phone, cheers me up; he makes me want to be a better artist.[49]

Although Kureishi is keen on pointing out that he does not admire the director 'too much', he implies knowingly or unknowingly that their encounter as artists was 'not unlike the couple at the beginning of the film'.[50]

## Conclusion

*Intimacy* offers an opportunity for a unique kind of cinematic adaptation and two-way translation of a piece of literature. The story travels several times between the author and two script-writers, across different languages, and amongst different cultures. Kureishi and Chéreau both agree that there is a truth about relationships and intimacy that can only be captured by the portrayal of raw sex, without adding any commentary. To address straight-forwardly the reality of eroticism is not intended to arouse the audience, but rather to invite them to reflect on what eroticism reveals: the struggle in which intimate relationships are entangled out of fear of intimacy. Without hiding behind long speeches, such intimacy manifests itself in sex, where the lovers expose themselves to the other's gaze.

As a stage director, Chéreau is notorious for his highly personal way of interpreting classic plays and operas. He does not prove his loyalty through a selfless hommage to a writer's words. Under his direction, Kureishi's work becomes the starting point of a polyphonic play in which various characters debate the reasons for relational difficulties. Kureishi's Jay seems incapable of finding intimacy with any woman, because of his self-centredness and fear of crossing the border separating two individualities. By contrast, Chéreau starts off where the border is already crossed and Jay starts to suffer from depending on a stranger. He tries to restore the realm of domesticated pleasure with his demands on this woman, by means of which he lets *jouissance* (in the sense Lacan and Barthes give to the term) evade their relationship. Eroticism, that is real intimacy, finally appears out of reach for Kureishi's post-Thatcherite, disenchanted anti-heroes. In Chéreau's film, however, the genuine erotic encounter of two naked bodies is a furtive, glowing chance of surviving the ennui of everyday life.

## Bibliography

ALDAMA, FREDERICK LUIS, '*Intimacy* by Hanif Kureishi' (review), *Callaloo*, 22.4 (1999), 1097–1100.
BARTHES, ROLAND, *The Pleasure of the Text*, trans. Richard Miller (New York, NY: Farrar, Straus and Giroux, 1975).
BATAILLE, GEORGES, *Eroticism*, trans. by Mary Dalwood (London: Marion Boyars, 1962).
BEUGNET, MARTINE, *Cinema and Sensation: French Film and the Art of Transgression* (Edinburgh: Edinburgh University Press, 2007).
BROWN, MICK, 'Hanif Kureishi: A Life Laid Bare', *Telegraph*, 23 February 2008, <http://www.telegraph.co.uk/culture/books/3671392/Hanif-Kureishi-A-life-laid-bare.html> [accessed 1 August 2016].
CHUNG, GABRIELLE, 'Here Are Some Gwyneth Paltrow's Favourite Sextoys', *Celebuzz*, 10 May 2016 <http://www.celebuzz.com/2016-05-10/gwyneth-paltrow-goop-sex-toys/> [accessed 22 July 2016].
DARKE, CHRIS, 'Truly, Madly, Explicitly', *The Guardian*, 1 July 2001, <https://www.theguardian.com/film/2001/jul/01/features> [accessed 25 July 2016].
'Director Defends Intimacy', *BBC News*, 15 February 2001, <http://news.bbc.co.uk/2/hi/entertainment/1171719.stm> [accessed 1 September 2016].
DWORKIN, ANDREA, *Pornography: Men Possessing Women* (New York, NY: Plume, 1989).
EBERT, ROGER, 'Stimulation Is The Real Issue of *Intimacy*', *www.rogerebert.com*, 11 February 2001, <http://www.rogerebert.com/festivals-and-awards/stimulation-is-the-real-issue-ofintimacy> [accessed 25 July 2016].
GENETTE, GÉRARD, *Figures II* (Paris: Seuil, 1969).
*Intimité*, dir. by Chéreau, Patrice (Téléma Productions, 2001).
KAHN, SYLVAIN, 'Les nouveaux territoires de l'érotisme', *France Culture*, 15 June 2016 <http://www.franceculture.fr/emissions/planete-terre/les-nouveaux-territoires-de-l-erotisme> [accessed 9 August 2016].
KAUFMAN, ANTHONY, 'Interview: Night Lights; Patrice Chéreau Probes *Intimacy*', *Indiewire*, 16 October 2001 <http://www.indiewire.com/article/interview_night_lights_patrice_chereau_probes_intimacy> [accessed 25 July 2016].
KIMBLE, LINDSAY, 'Yes, Gwyneth Paltrow's Goop Recommends a $15,000 Gold-Plated Sex Toy', *People*, 10 May 2016 <http://people.com/movies/gwyneth-paltrows-goop-shares-favorite-sex-toys/> [accessed 11 Oct 2016].
KUREISHI, HANIF, 'Filming *Intimacy*', *Prospect Magazine*, 20 February 2001 <http://www.prospectmagazine.co.uk/features/filmingintimacy> [accessed 25 July 2016].
—— *Intimacy* (London: Faber & Faber r, 1998).
—— *Love in a Blue Time* (London: Faber & Faber, 1997), p. 78.
—— *The Last Word* (London: Faber & Faber, 2015).
LACAN, JACQUES, *The Seminar of Jacques Lacan, Book XVII: The Other Side of Psychoanalysis*, ed. Jacques-Alain Miller, trans. Russell Grigg (New York, NY: W. W. Norton, 2007).
LAWRENCE, D. H., *Pornography & Obscenity* (London: Faber & Faber, 1929).

NORTIER, VIVIANE, 'Patrice Chéreau en toute *Intimité*', *La Dépêche du Midi*, 17 March 2001 <http://www.ladepeche.fr/article/2001/03/17/176774-patrice-chereau-en-toute-intimite.html > [accessed 25 July 2016].
QUANDT, JAMES, 'Flesh & Blood: Sex and Violence in Recent French Cinema', *Artforum*, 1 February 2004, <https://artforum.com/inprint/issue=200402&id=6199> [accessed 25 July 2016].
RANASINHA, RUVANI, *Hanif Kureishi* (Tavistock: Northcote House, 2002).
RIGOULET, LAURENT, 'Dans l'*Intimité* de Chéreau', *Libération*, 22 March 2000, <http://next.liberation.fr/culture/2000/03/22/dans-l-intimite-de-chereau-a-londres-et-en anglaispatrice-chereau-tourne-l-adaptation-d-un-livre-de_320518> [accessed 25 July 2016].
ROMNEY, JONATHAN, 'Dodgy Sex Goes the Way of All Flesh', *Independent*, 29 July 2001 <http://www.independent.co.uk/arts-entertainment/films/reviews/intimacy-patrice-chereau-119-mins-18-9276505.html> [accessed 25 July 2016].
SONTAG, SUSAN, *Styles of Radical Will* (London: Secker & Warburg, 1969).
WILLIAMS, LINDA, *Hard Core: Power, Pleasure, and the 'Frenzy of the Visible'* (Berkeley, CA: University of California Press, 1989).

## Notes to Chapter 11

1. See Claude Tapia, 'L'érotisme au cinéma', *Connexions*, 87 (2007), 43–64.
2. Sylvain Kahn, 'Les nouveaux territoires de l'érotisme', *France Culture*, 15 June 2016, <http://www.franceculture.fr/emissions/planete-terre/les-nouveaux-territoires-de-l-erotisme> [accessed 9 August 2016].
3. See Andrea Dworkin, *Pornography: Men Possessing Women* (New York, NY: Plume, 1989), p. 11.
4. See Lindsay Kimble, 'Yes, Gwyneth Paltrow's Goop Recommends a $15,000 Gold-Plated Sex Toy', *People*, 10 May 2016 <http://people.com/movies/gwyneth-paltrows-goop-shares-favorite-sex-toys/> [accessed 11 Oct 2016].
5. Dworkin, *Pornography: Men Possessing Women*, p. 11.
6. D. H. Lawrence, *Late Essays and Articles* (Cambridge: Cambridge University Press, 2004), p. 243.
7. Martine Beugnet, *Cinema and Sensation: French Film and the Art of Transgression* (Edinburgh: Edinburgh University Press Ltd, 2007), p. 178.
8. James Quandt, 'Flesh & Blood: Sex and Violence in Recent French Cinema', *Artforum*, 42.6 (2004), 126–32.
9. See Sontag, Susan, *Styles of Radical Will* (London: Secker & Warburg, 1969), pp. 35–73.
10. See Georges Bataille, *Eroticism*, trans. Mary Dalwood (London: Boyars, 1962).
11. See Jacques Lacan, *The Seminar of Jacques Lacan Book XVII: The Other Side of Psychoanalysis*, ed. Jacques-Alain Miller, trans. Russell Grigg (New York, NY: W. W. Norton, 2007), p. 18.
12. Roland Barthes, *The Pleasure of the Text*, trans. Richard Miller (New York, NY: Hill & Wang, 1975) p. 14.
13. Roland Barthes, *Le Plaisir du texte* (Paris, Seuil, 1973), p. 12
14. Hanif Kureishi, 'Filming Intimacy', *Prospect Magazine* (20 February 2001) <http://www.prospectmagazine.co.uk/features/filmingintimacy> [accessed 25 July 2016].
15. Chris Darke, 'Truly, Madly, Explicitly', *The Guardian*, 1 July 2001, <https://www.theguardian.com/film/2001/jul/01/features> [accessed 25 July 2016].
16. [Anon.], 'Director defends *Intimacy*', *BBC News*, 15 February 2001, <http://news.bbc.co.uk/2/hi/entertainment/1171719.stm> [accessed 1 September 2016].
17. Quoted in Mick Brown, 'Hanif Kureishi: A Life Laid Bare', *The Telegraph*, 23 February 2008, <http://www.telegraph.co.uk/culture/books/3671392/Hanif-Kureishi-A-life-laid-bare.html> [accessed 1 August 2016]
18. See Frederick Luis Aldama, '*Intimacy* by Hanif Kureishi' (review)', *Callaloo*, 22.4 (1999), 1097–1100.

19. See Ruvani Ranasinha, *Hanif Kureishi* (Tavistock: Northcote House, 2002), p. 19.
20. Kureishi, Hanif, *The Last Word* (London: Faber, 2015) p. 275.
21. For a discussion of the effect or verisimilitude resulting from its plausibility within genre constraints, see Gérard Genette, *Figures II* (Paris: Seuil, 1969), pp. 71–99.
22. Qutoed in Roger Ebert, 'Stimulation Is The Real Issue of *Intimacy*', www.rogerebert.com, 11 February 2001, <http://www.rogerebert.com/festivals-and-awards/stimulation-is-the-real-issue-of-intimacy> [accessed 25 July 2016].
23. See Linda Williams, *Hard Core: Power, Pleasure, and the 'Frenzy of the Visible'* (Berkeley, CA: University of California Press, 1989), p. 30.
24. Hanif Kureishi, *Love in a Blue Time* (London: Faber and Faber, 1997), p. 78.
25. Anthony Kaufman, 'Interview: Night Lights; Patrice Chéreau Probes *Intimacy*', *Indiewire*, 16 October 2001 <http://www.indiewire.com/article/interview_night_lights_patrice_chereau_probes_intimacy> [accessed 25 July 2016].
26. See Williams, *Hard Core*, pp. 112, 176, and 178.
27. Hanif Kureishi, *Intimacy* (London: Faber, 1998), p. 107. [*My italics, J.F.*]
28. See Aldama, '*Intimacy* by Hanif Kureishi', p. 1097.
29. Kureishi, *Intimacy*, p. 109.
30. Ibid., p. 111.
31. In hard-core pornography, this trope designates the end of a sex scene. According to Williams, it 'most perfectly embodies the profound alienation of contemporary consumer society.' Williams, *Hard Core*, p. 107.
32. Hanif Kureishi, 'Our Beautiful Project', *The Guardian*, 31 January 2001 <https://www.theguardian.com/film/2001/jan/31/artsfeatures.fiction> [accessed 14 September 2016].
33. Ibid.
34. Kureishi, *Intimacy*, p. 146.
35. Kureishi, *Intimacy*, p. 33.
36. Ibid., p. 43.
37. Quoted in Kaufman, 'Interview: Night Lights; Patrice Chéreau Probes *Intimacy*'.
38. Viviane Nortier, 'Patrice Chéreau en toute *Intimité*', *La Dépêche du Midi*, 17 March 2001 <http://www.ladepeche.fr/article/2001/03/17/176774-patrice-chereau-en-toute-intimite.html> [accessed 25 July 2016].
39. Jonathan Romney, 'Dodgy Sex Goes the Way of All Flesh', *Independent*, 29 July 2001 <http://www.independent.co.uk/arts-entertainment/films/reviews/intimacy-patrice-chereau-119-mins-18-9276505.html> [accessed 25 July 2016].
40. Kureishi, 'Our Beautiful Project'.
41. *Intimité*, dir. by Patrice Chéreau (Téléma Productions, 2001).
42. Ibid.
43. Kureishi, *Intimacy*, p. 85.
44. Kureishi, *Intimacy*, p. 94.
45. Ibid., p. 77.
46. Ibid., p. 81.
47. Ibid., p. 58.
48. Ibid., p. 69.
49. Kureishi, 'Our Beautiful Project'.
50. Ibid.

CHAPTER 12

# Adapting *Jing Ping Mei*, Serializing Sex: Hong Kong's Pornographic Serial Melodrama

*Jianqing Chen*

*Jin Ping Mei* (金瓶梅), translated to English as *The Plum in the Golden Vase,* is probably the most notorious Chinese pornographic novel. Lengthy and explicit descriptions of sex garnered the novel a notoriety in China akin to John Cleland's *Fanny Hill* (1748) in English literature. Under the pseudonym Lanling Xiaoxiao Sheng 兰陵笑笑生, 'The Scoffing Scholar of Lanling', the book was created and disseminated in the late Ming Dynasty (1368–1644), extended to more than 100 chapters and 2,923 pages in the photo-facsimile of the original wood-block, and involves over fifty characters.[1] Although the novel is enormous and complex, the core story tells the rise and fall of the polygamous household of a hypersexual and corrupt merchant named Ximen Qing 西门庆 through chronicling the illicit, sexually transgressive daily life and the domestic struggles among Ximen Qing and his six wives. The book title *Jin Ping Mei* takes its name from the three central female characters who form the nucleus of the plot — *Jin* from Jinlian 金莲, 'golden lotus', *Ping* from Ping'er 瓶儿, 'vase', and *Mei* from Chunmei 春梅, 'spring plum'.[2] The book ends with the disintegration of the household and the death of all the main characters as retribution for their sexual excess and squalor.

Although *Jin Ping Mei* is widely recognized by the general public, it is a book more heard of than read. As Ding Naifei summarizes, there are two *Jin Ping Mei* in terms of space of circulation and readership: the full version reserved in the secret library and archived for the purposes of collection and research, only accessible to the literati, and the abridged version circulated among the general public, fragmented and expurgated.[3] According to Ling Hom Lam and Dahlia Porter's study, there were both expensive photolithographic editions which maintained the novel's fullness and coherence for the purpose of repeated analysis and appreciation, and cheap illustrated editions of *Jin Ping Mei*, popular commodities that catered to sequential reading.[4] Therefore, in addition to the more cultivated mode of reading which featured intensive reading, revision and commentary, the novel was also read in an extensive and desultory way by middle-and low-brow urbanites in leisure for pleasure. The former developed into a field of academic study known as Jinology (金学 *jinxue*) and the latter constituted the popular erotic imagination and pornographic consumption.

The loss of the complexity and explicitness of the original text is undoubtedly disappointing. However, it offered Hong Kong porn directors the freedom to imagine and reinterpret the original stories in variety of film adaptations. Many *Jing Ping Mei* films were produced in Hong Kong cinema from the 1970s to the present, before and after the establishment of the three-tiered rating system in 1988. Li Hanshiang 李翰祥, a film auteur famous for high art historical drama, contributed six versions: *The Golden Lotus* (金瓶双艳) in 1974 was the first, followed by *Wu Song* (武松) in 1982, *Golden Lotus: Love and Desire* (金瓶风月) in 1991, *The Amorous Lotus Pan* (少女潘金莲) in 1994. These films were promoted as *fengyue* (风月) films, a euphemism for romantic affairs and sexual frolicking depicted via a hazy aesthetic. Besides Li's films, there is also *New Jin Ping Mei* (新金瓶梅, 1996), directed Tan Ming 谭铭, *The Forbidden Legend Sex & Chopsticks Part I* (金瓶梅1, 2008) and *Part II* (金瓶梅2: 爱的奴隶, 2009), directed by Qian Wenqi 钱文锜, and the *New Jin Ping Mei 3D* (新金瓶梅3D, 2016), directed by Chung Kai Cheung 钟继昌. All films have been categorized and thereby disparaged as the third-tier porno films.

Although these *Jin Ping Mei* films are expensively made and popular among spectators, they are overlooked by Hong Kong film historians. In fact, to the contrary of martial art films, another mainstay of Hong Kong cinema which have been overly researched and celebrated by film scholars, pornographic films, although they pervade Hong Kong cinema, are generally ignored, denied and even intentionally purged when historicizing Hong Kong cinema. In her article 'Porn Power: Sexual and Gender Politics in Li Han-Hsiang's *Fengyue* Films', Hong Kong film scholar Yau Ching 游静 laments the large amount of pornographic *fengyue* films Li made after his return to Shaw Studios in the 1970s.[5]

Separate from film critics and scholars who shunned the entire discussion of pornographic films because of their artistic vulgarity and moral depravity, literary scholars show more openness and inclusiveness as they begin to incorporate the study of erotica into research. Scholars believe that even if the pornographic elements are 'ugly' and 'bestial', in Hu Shi's 胡适 words,[6] they are useful and socio-historically informative if read in a 'correct way'. In his *A Brief History of Chinese Fiction* (中国小说史, 1930), Lu Xun 鲁迅 points out that readers tend to ignore the serious social message and artistic achievement of *Jin Ping Mei* because of its pornographic elements. He writes that it shows a profound understanding of his times and contains an unmatched variety of human interests.[7] David Roy, the novel's most recent translator into English, regards the book as an example of adherence to an alternative moral philosophy — the philosophy of Xunzi 荀子 which claims that human nature is basically evil and if allowed to reach its full expression without the conscious moulding and restraint of ritual, it is certain to lead the individual astray.[8] There are also interpretations that treat eroticism as an evil of ancient Chinese society in the private sphere; or alternatively as a celebration of a humanist, individualist instinct.[9]

Despite the variety of discourses, discussions have remained on the level of moral evaluation and aesthetic appreciation, functioning in destigmatizing the erotic book. No matter whether they bypass the erotic passages or celebrate them, a consensus is reached that the highly detailed sexual descriptions are indecent. The focus of the debate then hinges on the social-stylistic effects of the erotic passages — that is, whether the lascivious paragraphs contaminate and annihilate the whole book. No efforts are given to formal analysis of the sexual descriptions. No one tends to question why the novel was deemed so obscene.

The two *Jin Ping Mei*, with regards to intertextuality and intermediality in particular, are the topic of this paper. Different from those literary film scholars who intuitively label sexual representation as infamy, I aim to examine erotic passages from the novel and adaptation of sex scenes in pornographic films. I argue that *Jin Ping Mei* as a book develops a unique literary form, which hybridizes highly-embellished descriptive language and ribald vernacular expressions to represent sexual activity. In film adaptations, while the elaborated erotic texts are transformed into sex scenes in the form of *chungong* pictures (春宫图), the unrefined colloquium becomes a narrative mode driven by gossip and overhearing in order to deliver moral judgments. The conjunction of graphic sexual representation and a morality-centered narrative mode thus makes *Jin Ping Mei* films unique hybrids of pornography and melodrama.

### Flowery erotic passages

Sexual description in *Jin Ping Mei* the novel is characterized by astoundingly poetical refinement and rhetorical flourish. The writer not only throws in all kinds of literary forms — including poems, lyrics, couplets, aphorisms, quotations and etc. into the narrative — but also piles up minute descriptions of material objects from garments, jewelleries and accessories to sex toys and medicine. The erotic passages are usually verbose, excessively composed of rarely-used characters to delineate the surroundings into detail. The outdoor backyard garden or the indoor boudoir are two common intercourse venues. An excerpt of the most juicy grape-arbor-sex-scene in Chapter 27 is a salient example:

> Ximen Qing thereupon stood up, took off his *jade-colored silk tunic*, hung it over the balustrade, and went over under the flower trellis beside the juniper hedge on the west side of the peony bed to relieve himself.
> By the time he returned, the woman had already unrolled *the cool bamboo mat* and positioned the pillow and quilt to her satisfaction. She had stripped herself so that not a stitch of silk remained on her body, above and below, and was reclining face-up on the mat, wearing *scarlet shoes* on her feet, and cooling herself with *a white silk fan* [...].
> [E]xhilarated by the wine, he took off his own clothes, above and below, sat down on a cool *porcelain taboret*, and started out by titillating her [*pistil of flower*] with his toe. [...] He then took off the woman's red embroidered shoes, unwound her foot bindings, and amused himself by using them to suspend her two feet from the grape arbor overhead, so that she looked just like "*A Golden Dragon extending Its Claws.*" As a result:

> Her vagina was greatly distended,
> Her "*Red Hook*" was completely exposed, and
> Her "*Chicken Tongue*" protruded from within.
>
> Ximen Qing started out by stooping over her and placing his *jade chowrie handle* inside the mouth of her vagina, thus demonstrating the position known as "*Inserting the Arrow Upside Down*."[10]
>
> [这西门庆起身,脱下玉色纱縂儿,搭在栏杆上,迳往牡丹畦西畔[...],小净手去了。回来,妇人又早在架儿底下,铺设凉簟枕衾停当,脱的上下没条丝,仰卧于衽席之上,脚下穿着大红鞋儿,手弄白纱扇儿摇凉。西门庆走来,看见怎不触动淫心。于是剩着酒兴,亦脱去上下衣,坐在一凉墩上。先将脚指挑弄其花心[...]; 一面又将妇人红绣花鞋儿,摘取下来戏,把他两条脚带解下来,拴其双足,吊在两边葡萄架儿上如金龙探爪相似。使牝户大张,红钩赤露,鸡舌内吐。西门庆先倒覆着身子,执麈柄抵牝口,卖了个倒入翎花,一手据枕,极力而提之,提的阴中淫气连绵如数,鳅行泥淖中相似。][11]

The narrative of Ximen Qing and Jinlian's carousal is interspersed with a depiction of the views, the furnishings and the decor of the backyard garden. The rarely-used Chinese characters are carefully placed in order to indicate the specific physical shape and craftsmanship of the objects. The Chinese characters are generally in complicated and flamboyant configuration, decorated by components indexing the texture and colour. The Chinese character 簟 *dian* (bamboo mat) indicates the material, bamboo, with the bamboo-radical 竹 *zhu* on the top. Similarly, the radicals 土 *tu* (earth) and 纟 *si* (silk) signify that the materials of the 墩 *dun* (porcelain taboret), and 縂 *xuan* (silky tunic). The colour spectrum is rendered by adjectives, such as 'jade-colored', 'white', 'scarlet', and by place nouns, for example 'flower trellis' and 'grape arbor'. The depiction of the environment does not simply mimic the material world. Instead, the verbal performance reappraises and refigures the real world. That is to say, the description of the environment, with its distinct mood and style, carefully circumscribes sex acts in space-time. It is a natural space-time of sexual fantasy, free from the social order and political problems.

Besides the environmental depiction, the description of sex also features euphemistic reference to sexual organs and metaphorical description of sex acts. The penis is named 麈柄 *zhubing*, which translates into English as 'jade handle', while the female genitals are metaphorically referred to as 'the budding pistil of a flower', 'red hook', and 'chicken tongue'. Sex positions and acts are vividly sketched as 'Inserting the Arrow Upside Down' or 'The Old Monk Ringing the Bell'. These metaphors for sexual organs and acts are organic, with frequent reference to animals and plants. These organic metaphors blur the boundary between the descriptions of the external environment and the unfolding of sex acts. The women's fair body echoes the white silk fan in her hand, while her exposed 'red hook' matches the red embroidered shoes on her feet. Therefore, instead of assuming a unilateral relation between human bodies and the natural environment by saying that the human bodies are adorned by ornaments that borrow from the animal and plant world, it is more appropriate to conclude that the human body and the environment are reciprocally determined and constituted. Similar to the environmental descriptions which create a certain poetic ambience of languor, romance and eroticism, the metaphors for sexual organs and acts endow the female body, the desired object, with great allure as well as idealizing and liberalizing sexuality as a primitive vitality. Any possible discomfort or revulsion towards a lecherous man and woman is therein temporarily suspended.

The descriptive passage seems prolonged and distracting, especially after being extended by English translation. Literary scholars, overwhelmed by the excess of minute descriptions that serve little novelistic function, often resort to the study of seventeenth-century print culture to find justification. They argue that tedious details are driven by an '"encyclopaedic" impulse', which is 'an effect of commodification of knowledge'.[12] 'The plot is just an excuse' for 'random jotting, curiosity display, showy erudition and leisure distraction', and among which 'any discovery of aesthetic correspondence can only be an accident'.[13] This socio-economically based study reveals some truths beyond the reach of textual analysis. Nonetheless, attributing such description to idiosyncratic and contingent factors prevents further study of the style of description. Whether the emergence of aesthetic style is accidental or not, this flowery language is able to narrate sexual activity with decency, while ensuring the savouring of sexual stimulation and pleasure. Neither dull anatomic vocabulary nor ribald vernacular can achieve this effect.

### Chungong *pictures and seriality*

In the process of film adaptation, ornate descriptions in the novel are visualized and transformed into pornographic tableaux by virtue of *chungong* pictures. They depict sex acts for the purpose of arousal and instruction in erotic relations between sexes. The term *chungong* (春宮) is comprised by the words 'spring', a euphemism for sex, and 'palace', indicating the aristocratic origin of this graceful artistic style. Literary sources tell of emperors during the pre-Tang period who commissioned their court artists to paint erotic murals in the chambers where they engaged in copulation with their teams of concubines.[14] (For an in-depth study of *chungong* pictures, see Jie Guo's article in the present volume.)

Multiple examples demonstrate *Jin Ping Mei* pornographic films' reference to *chunggong* visual traditions. In the third episode of *New Jin Ping Mei*, for example, Ximen Qing and Ping'er have sex in a study room surrounded by *chungong* pictures. The montage shows that they change sex positions according to the pictures. In another film, *Golden Lotus: Love and Desire*, there is also a scene that explicitly shows Ximen Qing and Li Ping'er engaging in sex acts after being aroused by reading several pages of a *chungong* album. The woman continues to browse erotic pictures while the man penetrates her. The *chungong* album functions during both foreplay and intercourse as a sex toy. Even when the films do not show the pictures directly, they still allude to the erotic visual tradition by imitating the same sexual positions depicted in them. For example, in a sex scene in *Golden Lotus: Love and Desire*, a maidservant assists Ximen Qing and Li Ping'er's sexual intercourse by lying under the woman's lower back, serving as cushion to lift her up (see figures 12.1 & 12.2).

Similarly, *The Forbidden Legendary Sex and Chopsticks II* contains a sex scene featuring Ximen Qing and Jinlian's coitus on a swing in the backyard. This also follows a pattern derived from *Chungong* pictures (see figures 12.3 & 12.4):

ADAPTING *JING PING MEI*, SERIALIZING SEX 191

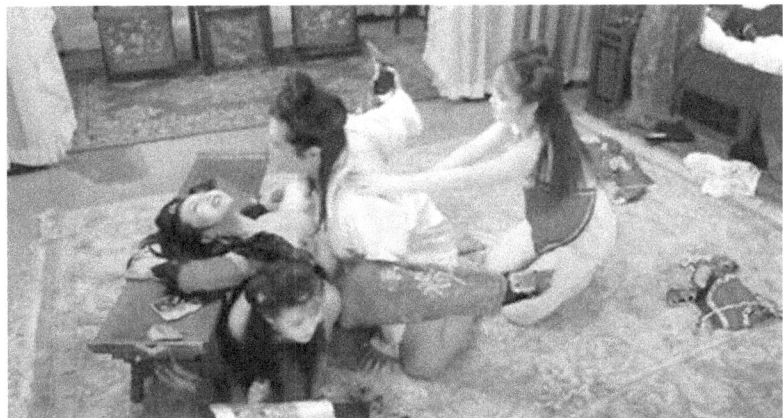

FIG. 12.1. Film still from *Golden Lotus: Love and Desire*.

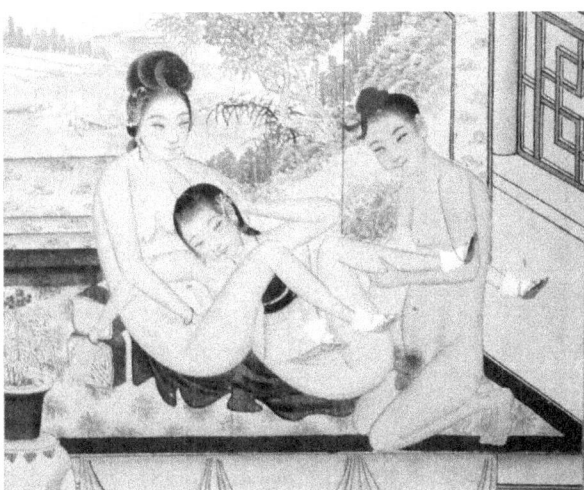

FIG. 12.2. 'Spring Picture' [19th century], Wikimedia Commons, <https://commons.wikimedia.org/wiki/File:18XX_Spring_Picture_03_anagoria.JPG> [accessed 10.10.2016].

*Chungong* visual traditions and erotic logics facilitate the translation of descriptive language into the frames. Stationary shots create pornographic tableaux imitating *chungong* pictures. These simple static tableaux frame and fix erotic acrobatics in a space crowded with sexually connotative iconographies. Compared with the prolonged sex scenes in Western porn films, the sex scenes in *Jin Ping Mei* films are generally abbreviated and segmented. Lasting only a matter of minutes, the brief montages capture the sex positions and the changes of positions to bracket the whole process, tantalizing the spectators rather than leading to orgasm. Meanwhile, the visual orchestration of décor and furniture within frames enrich the shortened sex process and manifest what is omitted in time. Exquisitely carved canopy beds, beautifully painted tiles and carpets and collections of objects with erotic designs create spaces pervaded by erotic motifs and symbols. Food and fruits on a table, a

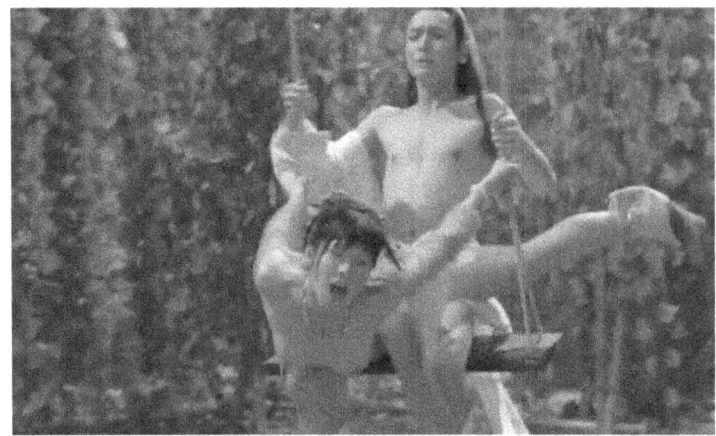

Fig. 12.3. Film still from *The Forbidden Legendary Sex and Chopsticks II*.

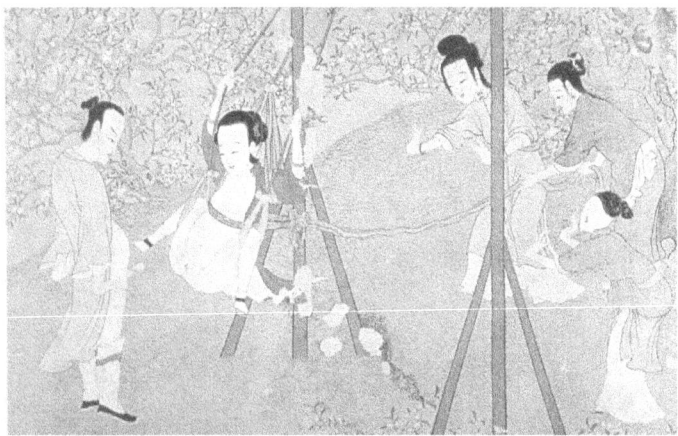

Fig. 12.4. *Qingdai mixi tu* (清代秘戏图, *Qing dynasty secret play picture*), Wikimedia Commons, <https://commons.wikimedia.org/wiki/File:Qinger001.jpg> [accessed 10.10.2016].

washbasin on the floor or clothes scattered at the foot of the bed leave traces of what happened before intercourse, extending the narrative timeline backwards. In this sense, narrative time is not simply curtailed, but condensed and spatialized by the room setting. Instead of fading away as the narrative goes on, emotion and impulse are stored and accumulated architecturally in fixed objects.

Excitement is intensified as sex is serialized, stringed together one scene after another in sequence, just as *chungong* pictures were commonly compiled in an album. As the lyric from *Jin Ping Mei* exemplifies, 'the names of the position are twenty-four in numbers, each one designed to arouse the lust of the beholder'.[15] The ensemble of sex scenes provides a kaleidoscope of coital techniques. Different from American portrayal of sex acts emphasizing orgasmic release, the pleasure of the sex scene serial seems to lie in tasting of the diversity of acts and prolonging intercourse. The final release, understood as a moment of loss, is deferred indefinitely.

Pornography is rarely considered to be a serial phenomenon. As Susan Sontag writes in her essay 'The Pornographic Imagination', repetition in pornography is fatigue, the perfect form of pornography should be compressed and feature non-interchangeable personages.[16] Even Sara Schaechek who considers seriality the basic structure in organizing sex acts in pornography, cannot deny that repetitiousness risks making pornography boring.[17] One possible reason for the perceived dullness of repetitive sex acts concerns Western pornography's obsession with explicitness. Modern Western culture has generated a *scientia sexualis* nurtured by the desire to present more detailed explorations of measurable and scientific truth of sexuality.[18] Based on this, the pleasure of Western hard-core pornography lies in what Linda Williams called the 'frenzy of the visible', that is the maximal visibility of the secret places of human bodies as well as the whole intercourse process ending with male ejaculation, the 'money shot'.[19] Western moving image pornography thus invites audiences to go through the whole process of labouring along with the performers so as to reach powerful orgasms. Long takes and close-ups are applied to discover more and more anatomical knowledge, unobservable to the naked eye. In this sense, the degree of sexual pleasure pivots on the extent of epistemic seeing. It is not surprising, then, that Western pornography privileges the single, fully-articulated sex scene.

However, according to Foucault, there is another procedure for producing sexual pleasure, mainly existing in the East and more ancient societies: *ars erotica*. This tradition understands sex as a secret art. In *ars erotica*, the truth of sex is drawn from pleasure itself and relies on the repeated practices of accumulated experience. The immediacy and generality of sexual knowledge, the two presuppositions of *scientia sexualis*, are questioned in *ars erotica*. No matter how smart a person is, it is almost impossible for him/her to have full control over his/her body immediately. Like other body art (i.e. dancing or martial arts), the mastery of sexual skills requires repetitious practice. No matter how extensive one's sexual knowledge is, it can neither exhaust individual differences nor reach universal truth, due to the inevitable limitations of human knowledge. *Ars erotica* suggests a return back to personal erotic practices and experience to understand sexuality. As Foucault articulates,

> pleasure is not considered in relation to an absolute law of permitted and the forbidden, nor by reference to a criterion of utility, but first and foremost in relation to itself; it is experienced as pleasure, evaluated in terms of its intensity, its specific quality, its duration, its reverberations in the body and the soul[.][20]

Fragmented sex scenes trigger spectators' memory of their own experiences, doubling the sensuality caused by moving images of sex with their own recalled sensual experience. Although the binary is not absolute according to Foucault, the distinction between *scientia sexualis* and *ars erotica* dismisses the general assumption that inexplicit sexual representation is erotica and explicit representation is pornography. Instead, different understandings of sexuality and mechanisms of producing pleasure operate from behind, as it were. (For a more critical evaluation of Foucault's distinction, see Joshua Mostow's article in this volume.)

The Western style, which privileges the single fully-articulated process of phallocentric thrusting, is just one among many models of sexual representation. *Jin Pin Mei* films, even if not explicit in the Western sense, ensconce themselves within pornography — not eroticism, not soft-core pornography. Or even, with their omission of phallic depiction and focus on the female face and body in the onscreen depiction of sex, *Jin Ping Mei* films declare an alternative erotic logic and style that reformulate multiple demarcations — soft-core versus hard-core, or erotica versus pornography — usually based on the degree of visibility, and challenge the androcentric gender hierarchy reinforced by phallocentric discourse and display of sex.

## Vulgar vernacular pillow talk

In *Jin Ping Mei*, the flowery depiction of sex acts is also strangely intertwined with coarse vernacular conversation. In Hollywood films, sex talk is generally used to temper the graphic display of sex. In her discussion of Hollywood sex talk, Linda Williams notifies that American films remain visually reticent but verbally abundant in the new post-Code era, since they seem more comfortable talking about carnal knowledge then showing it.[21] In contrast, in *Jing Ping Mei*, sex talk is the primary source of obscenity. Jinlian's words in Chapter 27 after Ximen Qing's tantalizing foreplay provides a salient example:

> Her starry eyes grew dim,
> and she moaned incessantly,
>   inarticulately calling out, "My Big-dicked Daddy! What are you up to? Go all the way in and be done with it. The itch in the clitoris of the cunt of this whore of yours has entered the marrow of her bones. Take pity on me and let me off for now."
>   In the mouth of this whore no expression, no matter how unspeakably obscene, was left unsaid[.][22]

> [那妇人在枕畔朦胧星眼, 呻吟不已, 没口子叫:「大玑玐达达, 你不知使了甚么行子, 进去又罷了。淫妇的毯心子痒到骨髓里去了, 可怜见饶了罢。」淫妇口里碜死的言语都叫了出来[。]][23]

Ximen Qing often calls Jinlian 小油嘴 *xiao you zui* ('little oil lips') for daring to use the shameless language no other women dares to speak. She unscrupulously calls herself 'this whore of yours' and her partner 'Big-Dicked Daddy' during sexual intercourse to vent her sexual desire and pleasure. Tearing apart the refinement painstakingly built up by flowery depiction, filthy talk stimulates every inch of the reader's nerve and encroaches on readers' restraint. This is because language taboos are broken down not only by the context and connotation, but also by Chinese characters' blunt depiction. In terms of the scurrilous context and connotation, the word 达达 *dada*, meaning 'daddy', adds to the erotic passage a sense of perversion when used by Jinlian and other wives to address Ximen Qing during sexual intercourse. In terms of Chinese characters' blunt depiction, 玑玐 *jiba* and 毯 *bi*, the vulgar vernacular referring to the penis and vagina, imitate the look of sexual organs with the radical 毛 *mao* on the left side signifying pubic hair in front of genital area.

Since these Chinese characters are replaced by other homonyms with less sensational shapes in modern Chinese language, the modern reader feels even more startled when encountering these unequivocal pictographs. Vulgar Chinese characters punctuate the flow of the passage as they tend to pop out and attract more attention with their rare and shocking configuration. These obscene words still manage to stimulate readers even during the most desultory pleasure-seeking reading.

### Voyeurism, overhearing and moral schemes

The inclusion of vulgar vernacular within sex scenes probably derives from the novel's special kinship with popular oral entertainment,[24] or even more basically, the genre's root in hearsay and gossip as 小说 xiaoshuo, the Chinese term for novel which literally means 'small talks', suggests. Paize Keulemans explains how dirty pillow talk, together with eavesdropping and gossip, function as productive narrative forms driving the narrative of sexual transgression.[25] Pillow talk, like small tentacles, extends from the sexual senses to the rest of narrative, bringing sex scenes into the fabric of the film.

This sound-driven narrative device is preserved and adapted in the *Jin Ping Mei* films. As vague sexual murmurs and moans in the films replace the clear dirty talk in the book, the acoustic elements usually appear in tandem with more visually explicit voyeurism. A world and time is thus built up to proliferate the onscreen sex, and more importantly, to work through the moral conundrums concerning sexual pleasure and social taboo.

In addition to stimulating pleasure via third-party observation, overhearing and voyeurism multiplies sex acts and narratives to embrace more and more characters. When the voyeur is female, usually the maid, the master will invite her to join in. A sex scene in *The Golden Lotus: Love and Desire* shows that Jinlian calls her maid to join in after discovering her hiding behind the curtain and snooping. If it is an illicit sex act and happens to be seen by a malicious voyeur, usually a man other than Ximen Qing, this sex act will lead to another act since the new sex act functions as trade-off to seal the mouth of the malicious voyeur. Overhearing and voyeurism create an endless narrative flow. This narrative flow is by no means a linear unravelling. Rather, it creates a large constellation which integrates different people, places, events and information in a seemingly chaotic though trackable way. It is the spatialization of temporality, or in other words, the spatial imaginary of 'spread' and 'sprawl'.

The expansion of narrative and the involvement of numerous characters functions not only for the sake of orgiastic permutations, since characters are not sex-driven stereotypes who can be interchanged. These characters, no matter how minor, are unique figures endowed with special personas, family roles and social status. The entirety of these characters constitutes an extensive sex-related network, a world that orbits around Ximen Qing's family.

Because of overhearing and voyeurism, the world of these films, despite the abundance of sex, is not a 'pornotopia'[26] free of social responsibility and restrictions.

The performers' outrageous and outlawed sex acts — adultery for instance — are aware of their scandalous nature. Voyeurism and eavesdropping, while eliciting the transgressive pleasure of the onscreen voyeur and spectators who share his/her point-of-view, automatically involves moral judgment of the people peeped upon. Once their secret is exposed, moral punishment will follow. The unfolding of narrative gradually shows how sex talk and vocalizations during the illicit acts flow beyond the closed chamber, passing through windows, spreading out of the yard, climbing over the high walls, running from one month to another in gossip, and finally reaching Ximen Qing. In the films *Golden Lotus: Love and Desire*, while Ximen Qing commits adultery with his neighbour, a series of high pitched sexual moans reach him. After suspecting that the sexual sounds come from his fifth wife, he decides to trace the sound. A series of crosscuttings shows him climbing over the wall and approaching his wife's room and his wife's sex acts with a maidservant. Overhearing and voyeurism bridge different narrative spaces, bring different narrative threads together, and drive the narrative to follow a winding path. But Ximen Qing is not the only eavesdropper, in *The Golden Lotus* jealousy also drives Jinlian to spy on her husband (see figure 5).

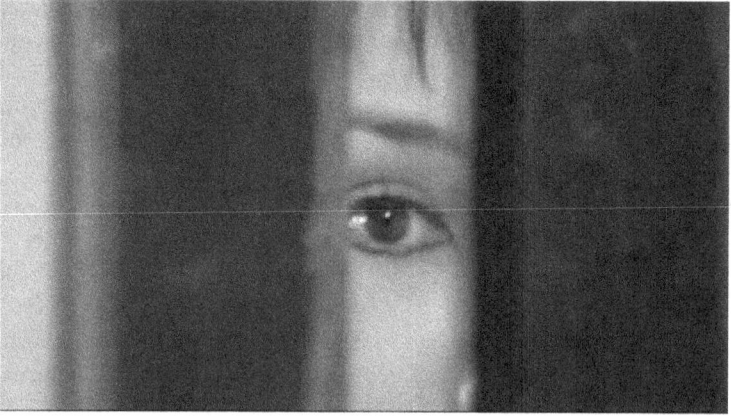

Fig. 12.5. Film still from *The Golden Lotus*

The scandal-and-gossip-oriented narrative thus creates a loose flow, which gives time for subtle changes to take place and latent perniciousness to take shape before final moral judgment at the end. It also entails twists and turns, reworking the knotty moral problems that cannot be solved once and for all. As a result, in the slow and erratic progress of the serial melodramatic narrative, moral legibility is thoroughly considered and moral ambiguity is meticulously negotiated, unlike the tight and linear narratives characterizing classical tragedy and feature length films.

The duality of sex acts and the narrative content leading to sex justifies calling these films 'pornographic melodrama'. The term melodrama I am using here by no means refers to a certain type of work displaying sentiment exceeding the bounds of good taste, but the evolving mode of narrative crucial to the quest for a hidden moral legibility and the establishment of moral good in the world where traditional imperatives of truth and morality have been violently questioned.[27] One might think that the two forms, pornography and melodrama, are quite opposite, as melodrama maintains a strong articulation of good and evil often absent in Western pornographic traditions where, as Stephen Marcus put it, it is 'always bedtime' — the ideal time and space that legitimates fantasies of seducing and being seduced by the other.[28] However, the Chinese tradition, as epitomized by the *Jin Ping Mei* book and films alike, juxtaposes the celebration of sexual pleasure and the perils of sexual obsession, creating tension between the contradictory forces of fear and pleasure, spontaneity and responsibility, victimization and vilification, without either reconciling or cancelling one or another out. Moral norms providing for family stability are consistently at war with transient sexual ecstasy.

This struggle becomes even more radical if we bring together different moral claims in different versions of *Jin Ping Mei* films. As the story keeps retelling itself, moral attitudes vary as female characters change. They are either portrayed as the victims of patriarchal society or scheming villainesses who commit numerous seductions and murders, either as lustful sluts with unsatisfied sexual appetites or as a liberated woman fighting for love. Each *Jin Pin Mei* film is an iteration, a repetition with difference, that self-reflexively rephrases the limits of the old versions and generates new possibilities. Every version, while also standing alone, contributes a special facet or layer, collaboratively building up the narrative complexity, characters' psychological depth and moral conflicts of the whole *Jin Ping Mei* story, making the story an ever more enigmatic sexual event.

## Conclusion

In *Dream of the Red Chamber* (红楼梦 *Hong Lou Meng*, 1759/1791–92), the author Cao Xueqin 曹雪芹 introduces a mystical item: 风月宝鉴 *feng yue bao jian*, translated as 'mirror of voluptuousness'. This mirror is used to heal the disease of a lustful man Jia Rui 贾瑞, caused by his unfulfilled forbidden love for his sister-in-law. The mirror is double-sided, but one should only gaze at the back side to cure one's illness. Following the instructions, Jia Rui looks at the mirror from its back side where he sees a skeleton. Scared by the skeleton, the sick man turns the mirror over to look at its front side and sees his seductive sister-in-law. After masturbating to this image repeatedly, he dies of consumption.

This double-sided mirror of voluptuousness, with one side reflecting one's sexual fantasy and the other side serving as moral admonition, serves as an apt symbol for the contrapuntally conflicted pornographic serial melodrama. Linda Williams uses Denis Diderot's *Indiscreet Jewels* (*Les Bijoux Indiscrets*, 1748) as an allegory for the knowledge-pleasure of sexuality.[29] In Diderot's phantastic dialogue, a magic ring makes the genitals speak and thereby emblematizes Western porn's quest for a *sciencia sexualis* that produces a definitive truth. In contrast, the Chinese mirror addresses the double nature of sex: it can not only arouse, satisfy and incite, it can also disgust, bore, and intimidate. A sex act not only stands on its own for its distinctive mechanisms and experience, but implicates hidden social bonds.

Pornographic serial melodrama presents the volatility and dialectics of sexuality, not simply pleasure.

## Bibliography

*I. Printed sources*

CAHILL, JAMES, 'Chinese Erotic Painting', jamescahill.info (personal website) <http://jamescahill.info/illustrated-writings/chinese-erotic-painting/preface-and-introduction#_ftnref> [accessed 10.10.16].

DING, NAIFEI, *Obscene Things: Sexual Politics in Jin Ping Mei* (Durham: Duke University Press, 2002).

FOUCAULT, MICHEL, *The History of Sexuality: An Introduction*, trans. by Robert Hurley (New York, NY: Pantheon, 1978 [orig. 1976]).

HU, SHI 胡适, 'Da Qian Xuantong Shu' (答钱玄同书 [Letter to Qian Xuantong]), in *Wen Cun* (文存) (Beijing: Waiwen chuban she, 2013).

HSIA, C. T., *The Classic Chinese Novel: A Critical Introduction* (Ithaca, NY: Cornell University Press, 1996).

*Jin Ping Mei Cihua* (金瓶梅词话 [The Plum in the Golden Vase: Novel and Verse]), ed. by Yun Jian 允键, 3 vols (Taipei: Zeng ni zhi wen hua shi ye you xian gong si, 1980).

KEULEMANS, PAIZE, 古柏, 'Jin Ping Mei Zhongtan: Cong Liuyan Dao Chouwen' (金瓶梅重探:从流言到丑闻 [Scandalous Writing: Gossip, News and Rumors in 'Jin Ping Mei']), *Beijing Daxue Zhongguo guwenxian yanjiu zhongxin jikan* (北京大学中国古文献研究中心集刊 [Peking University Ancient Chinese Literature Research Centre Journal]), 11 (2010), pp. 268–80.

LAM, LING HON and DAHLIA PORTER, 'Hybrid Commodities, Gendered Aesthetics, and the Challenge of Cross-Cultural Comparison: A Response to Moretti's "The Novel: History and Theory"', *Literature Compass*, 7.9 (2010), 900–11.

LU, XUN 鲁迅, *Zhongguo Xiaoshuo Shilüe* (中國小說史略 [A Short History of Chinese Fiction]), in *Collected Works*, 4 vols (Taipei: Tangshan chubanshe, 1989).

*The Plum in the Golden Vase*, trans. by David Tod Roy, 5 vols (Princeton, NJ: Princeton University Press, 2006).

SCHASCHEK, SARAH, *Pornography and Seriality: The Culture of Producing Pleasure* (New York, NY: Palgrave Macmillan, 2014).

SONTAG, SUSAN, 'The Pornographic Imagination', in *Style of Radical Will* (London: Secker & Warburg, 1969).

WILLIAMS, LINDA, 'Film Bodies: Gender, Genre, and Excess', *Film Quarterly*, 44. 4 (1991), 2–13.

—— *Hard Core: Power, Pleasure and the "Frenzy of the Visible"* (Berkeley, CA, University of California Press, 1989).

—— *Playing the Race Card: Melodramas of Black and White from Uncle Tom to O. J. Simpson* (Princeton, NJ: Princeton University Press, 2001).

—— *Screening Sex* (Durham: Duke University Press, 2008).

YAU, CHING, 'Porn Power: Sexual and Gender Politics in Li Han-hsiang's Fengyue Films', in *As Normal as Possible: Negotiating Sexuality and Gender in Mainland China and Hong Kong (Queer Asia)*, ed. by Yau Ching (Hong Kong: Hong Kong University Press, 2010), pp. 113–32.

## II. Film sources

*The Amorous Lotus Pan* (少女潘金莲) dir. by Li Han-shiang 李翰祥 (Lin Hop Production Company, 1994).

*The Forbidden Legend Sex & Chopsticks Part I* (金瓶梅1), dir. by Qian Wenqi 钱文锜 (My Way Film Company, 2008).

*The Forbidden Legend Sex & Chopsticks Part II* (金瓶梅2:爱的奴隶), dir. by Qian Wenqi 钱文锜 (My Way Film Company, 2009).

*The Golden Lotus* (金瓶双艳), dir. by Li Han-shiang 李翰祥 (Nippon Herald Films, 1974).

*Golden Lotus: Love and Desire* (金瓶风月) dir. by Li Han-shiang 李翰祥 (Jin Kao Yun Film Company, 1991).

*New Jin Ping Mei* (新金瓶梅), dir. by Tan Ming 谭铭 (King's Entertainment, 1996).

*New Jin Ping Mei 3D* (新金瓶梅3D), directed by Chung Kai Cheung 钟继昌 ([production company?], forthcoming 2016].

*Wu Song* (武松), dir. by Li Han-shiang 李翰祥 (Shaw Brothers, 1982).

## Notes to Chapter 12

1. See David Tod Roy, 'Introduction', in *The Plum in the Golden Vase*, trans. by D. T. R., 5 vols (Princeton, NJ: Princeton University Press, 2006), I, pp. xvii–xlviii.
2. 'Golden lotus' is a euphemism for women's small bound feet, an erotic attribute in imperial China. The other names also have sexual connotations.
3. See Ding Naifei, *Obscene Things: Sexual Politics in Jin Ping Mei* (Durham: Duke University Press, 2002), pp. 33–35.
4. See Ling Hon Lam and Dahlia Porter, 'Hybrid Commodities, Gendered Aesthetics, and the Challenge of Cross-Cultural Comparison: A Response to Moretti's "The Novel: History and Theory"', *Literature Compass*, 7.9 (2010), 900–11 (p. 902).
5. See Yau Ching, 'Porn Power: Sexual and Gender Politics in Li Han-hsiang's Fengyue Films', in *As Normal as Possible: Negotiating Sexuality and Gender in Mainland China and Hong Kong (Queer Asia)*, ed. by Yau Ching (Hong Kong: Hong Kong University Press, 2010), pp. 113–32 (p. 104).
6. See Hu Shi 胡适, 'Da Qian Xuantong Shu' (答钱玄同书, Letter to Qian Xuantong), in *Wen Cun* (文存) (Beijing: Waiwen Chuban She, 2013), p. 51.
7. See Lu Xun 鲁迅, *Zhongguo Xiaoshuo Shilüe* (中國小說史略, *A Short History of Chinese Fiction*), in *Collected Works*, 4 vols (Taipei: Tangshan chubanshe, 1989), III, 187.
8. See Roy, 'Introduction', pp. xxiv–xxvii.
9. See Ding Naifei, *Obscene Things*, pp. 18–33.
10. *The Plum in the Golden Vase*, II, 144. [In my rendering, I will use Pinyin spelling for the names (Roy uses Wade-Giles). In the case of terms like 鸡舌 *jishe*, I use a literal translation, 'chicken tongue' instead of 'clitoris'. Unless otherwise stated. all emphases are my own. J. C.]
11. *Jin Ping Mei Cihua* (金瓶梅词话 *The Plum in the Golden Vase: Novel and Verse*), ed. by Yun Jian 允键, 3 vols (Taipei: Zeng ni zhi wen hua shi ye you xian gong si, 1980), I, 407–08.
12. Lam, 'Hybrid Commodities', p. 904.
13. Ibid.
14. See James Cahill, 'Chinese Erotic Painting', jamescahill.info (personal website) <http://jamescahill.info/illustrated-writings/chinese-erotic-painting/preface-and-introduction#_ftnref> [accessed 10.10.16].
15. *The Plum in the Golden Vase*, I, 271.
16. See Susan Sontag, 'The Pornographic Imagination', in *Style of Radical Will* (London: Secker &Warburg, 1969), pp. 62–63.
17. Sarah Schaschek, *Pornography and Seriality: The Culture of Producing Pleasure* (New York, NY: Palgrave Macmillan, 2014), p. 2.
18. See Michel Foucault, *The History of Sexuality: An Introduction*, trans. by Robert Hurley (New York, NY: Pantheon, 1978 [orig. 1976]), p. 63.

19. See Linda Williams, *Hard Core: Power, Pleasure and the 'Frenzy of the Visible'* (Berkeley, CA, University of California Press, 1989), pp. 8–9.
20. Foucault, *The History of Sexuality*, p. 57.
21. Linda Williams, *Screening Sex* (Durham: Duke University Press, 2008), p. 11.
22. *The Plum in the Golden Vase*, II, 148.
23. *Jin Ping Mei Cihua*, I, 409.
24. C. T. Hsia. *The Classic Chinese Novel: A Critical Introduction* (Ithaca, NY: Cornell University Press, 1996), p. 154.
25. See Paize Keulemans 古柏, 'Jin Ping Mei Zhongtan: Cong Liuyan Dao Chouwen' (金瓶梅重探:从流言到丑闻 [Scandalous Writing: Gossip, News and Rumors in 'Jin Ping Mei']), *Beijing Daxue Zhongguo guwenxian yanjiu zhongxin jikan* (北京大学中国古文献研究中心集刊 [Peking University Ancient Chinese Literature Research Centre Journal]), 11 (2010), 268–80.
26. Williams, *Hard Core*, pp. 174–82.
27. See Linda Williams, *Playing the Race Card: Melodramas of Black and White from Uncle Tom to O.J. Simpson* (Princeton, NJ: Princeton University Press, 2001), pp. 10–23.
28. See Linda Williams, 'Film Bodies: Gender, Genre, and Excess', *Film Quarterly*, 44. 4 (1991), 2–13 (p. 10).
29. See Williams, *Hard Core*, pp. 1–3.

# INDEX OF NAMES AND TEXTS
❖

*120 Days of Sodom* 13–27, 106 n. 12

Adorno, Theodor W. 71, 76 n. 31, 157
Agamben, Giorgio 46
Ahnlund, Knut 156
Aldama, Frederick Luis 175
d'Alembert, Jean le Rond 93
Andreas-Salomé, Lou 154
Antenhofer, Christina 107
Ariwara no Narihira 128
St. Augustine 2

Badiou, Alain 44–52, 58, 61
Baker, Nicholson 66, 70–73
Bakhtin, Michail 96
Ballard, J. G. 166
Barad, Karan 49–51, 61
Barber, Stephen 46, 52, 65
Barthes, Roland 3, 15, 66, 73, 91, 140, 149–50, 173, 183
Basile, Giambattista 95
Bassnett, Susan 3
Bataille, George 65 n. 65
  *Eroticism* 141–43, 148, 150, 173, 179
  *Madame Edwarda* 5, 141, 144–47
  *Tears of Eros* 141, 147–49
Benjamin, Walter 3, 151 n. 20
Bennington, Geoffrey 15
Berry, Michael 165
Bersani, Leo 49
Beugnet, Martine 173
Blei, Franz 33
Boccaccio 5
*Book of Rites* 92
*Book of Songs* 99
Brancart, Auguste 34–36, 40, 42
Briod, Blaise 95, 108
Brun, Catherine 53
Buñuel, Luis 52, 60
Burroughs, William 65 n. 65

Cahill, James 113
de Carlowitz, Aloïse Christine 95
Carlyle, Thomas 95, 108
*Carnal Prayer Mat* 1–2, 7, 91, 98–102, 110–12, 114–20
Carter, David 21
*Catharine II.* 79, 82–84, 85, 87, 89 n. 31

Catullus 97
Chéreau, Patrice 174–83
Chino, Kaori 133–35
Chong, Kai Cheung 187, 190
Cinderella 85, 95, 128
Cleland, John 158, 186
Clunas, Craig 110, 112
Cole, Peter 30
*Confessions* 2, 102
Croissant, Doris 135
Cronenberg, David 155, 166–67

Damrosch, David 5
Derrida, Jean-Jacques 2, 102
Desclos, Anne 72, 160, 173
Diderot, Denis 93, 197
Ding, Naifei 186
Don Giovanni 155, 158, 166
*Dream of the Red Chamber* 114, 120, 122 n. 20, 197
Dworkin, Andrea 4, 15–16, 172, 175
Dworkin, Craig 45

Eco, Umberto 3
*Éden Éden Éden* 43–50
Eliade, Mircea 2
Ellis, Havelock 125
Erlmann, Veit 96
*Essentials of Medicine* 126–28
Evans, Martin 50

*Fanny Hill* 158, 186
Felski, Rita 18, 27
Feng, Zhi 95
Fenves, Peter 95, 100
*Fifty Shades of Grey* 4, 7, 47, 79, 84–87, 151 n. 1, 176–77
Fink-Eitel, Hinrich 125
Flint, Larry 4, 41
Fludernik, Monika 140, 142
Foucault, Michel 5, 125–26, 134–35, 140, 149, 158, 193
Fox, Graham 45
France, Peter 13–14
Freud, Sigmund 155, 157–59, 166–67, 173
Furedi, Frank 15

Gnüg, Hiltrud 5

Goethe, Johann Wolfgang:
  *Roman Elegies* 91, 96–98, 101–03
  *Sorrows of Young Werther* 79–82, 84–85, 87, 89 n. 25
  *Wilhelm Meister* 91, 93–96
Gutting, Gary 135, 137 n. 5
Guyortat, Pierre 143
  *Éden Éden Éden* 43–50
  *Tomb for 500, 000 Soldiers* 43–61

Hanan, Patrick 1, 98–100, 108 n. 64, 110, 112–13, 115
Haneke, Michael 155–56, 161–64, 170
Hardy, Thomas 86
Harman, Graham 103
Harper, Donald 126
Hegarty, Paul 147
Heidegger, Martin 103
Heinse, Wilhelm 96
Herder, Johann Gottfried 93, 96, 103
*History of a Libertine* 110–13
Homer 3, 23
*Hong Lou Meng* 114, 120, 122 n. 20, 197
Horkheimer, Max 157
ter Horst, Eleanor 96
*House of Holes* 66, 70–72
Huang, Martin 116
Hunt, Lynn 5
Husserl, Edmund 103
Huston, Nancy 117

Idema, Wilt 114
Illouz, Eva 75 n. 15, 78, 82, 84–85, 151 n. 1
*Intimacy* 174–83
Ishigami, Aki 124 n. 64
*Ishimpō* 126–28

Jacobson, Roman 101
James, E. L. 4, 7, 47, 79, 84–87, 151 n. 1, 176–77
Jelinek, Elfriede 154–57, 159–67, 170
*Jin Ping Mei* 5, 110, 112, 116, 120, 122 n. 3, 186–98
*Josephine Mutzenbacher* 158
Jullien, François 2, 12

*Kama Sutra* 5
Kant, Immanuel 93, 106 n. 12
Kappeler, Susanne 156, 166–67
Kawabata, Yasunari 71
Keane, Webb 18, 20
Kendall, Stuart 50, 57
Kendrick, Walter 3
Kennedy, A. L. 66–70, 72–73
Keulemans, Paize 195
Kohlke, Marie-Luise 158, 166
Kronhausen, Eberhard & Phyllis 36
Kuhn, Franz 99–100

Lacan, Jacques 160, 173, 183

Lam, Ling Hon 186
Lambert, José 3
*Lascivious History of Hailing* 110–13, 119
Lawrence, D. H. 6, 172
Lefevere, André 3
Li, Han-shiang 186
Li, Yu 1–2, 7, 91, 98–102, 110–12, 114–20
Ling, Xiaoqiao 113
*Lotus Sutra Painted on Fans* 129–35
Luhmann, Niklas 75 n. 2, 78–79, 82, 87
Luke, David 96–97
Lynch, David 115

Marcus, Steven 37, 40, 197
Marks, Laura 60
de Mirabeau, Honoré Gabriel Riqueti 36
Mishima, Yukio 147
de Musset, Alfred 36
*My Secret Life* 35

Neugroschl, Joachim 161–63
Nordstrom, Kristina 175

Onfray, Michel 15
Ono no Komachi 128
*Original Bliss* 66–70, 72
Ovid 9, 97

Parrault, Charles 95
Pavlov, Ivan 101–02
Pevear, Richard 116
*Piano Player* 154–57, 159–67
*Pillow Book* 6, 129, 134
Plato 76 n. 26, 92
*Plum in the Golden Vase* 5, 110, 112, 116, 120, 122 n. 3, 186–98
Polanski, Roman 167
Porter, Dahlia 186
Pronicheva, Dina 155, 164–66, 169 n. 4
Pym, Anthony 14, 16–17

Qian, Wenqi 187
Quandt, James 173

Ranasinha, Ruvani 175
Réage, Pauline 72, 160, 173
Richardson, Samuel 1
Rimbaud, Arthur 143
Robyns, Clem 3
Roche, Charlotte 5
*Roman Elegies* 91, 96–98, 101–03
*Rou Pu Tuan* 1–2, 7, 91, 98–102, 110–12, 114–20
Rousseau, Jean-Jacques 2, 102
Roy, David 187

von Sacher-Masoch, Leopold 79, 82–85, 87, 89 n. 31, 157

de Sade, Donatien Alphonse François  1–2, 4, 6, 23, 33, 44–45, 57, 65 n. 65, 93, 106 n. 12, 143–44, 146, 152 n. 40, 160, 166, 173
   *120 Days of Sodom*  13–27
   *Juliette*  2
Salten, Felix  158
Scherr, Rebecca  165–67
Schönfeld, Eike  72
Seaver, Richard  15–16, 22–23
Sei, Shōnagon  6, 129, 134
Shattuck, Roger  15
Sontag, Susan  4–5, 14–17, 72, 140–42, 152 n. 40, 173, 193
*Sorrows of Young Werther*  79–82, 84–85, 87, 89 n. 25
Spivak, Gayatri Chakravorty  18–19, 21, 27
Steinberg, Leo  132
Steiner, George  18
*Story of O***  72, 160, 173
*Story of the Western Chamber*  114
Stroessen, Nadine  38
Surya, Michel  50, 147, 151 n. 23 & 27

*Tale of Genji*  6, 132–34, 138 n. 29
Tan, Ming  187, 190
Taylor-Johnson, Sam  176–77
Thomas, D. M.  154–59, 164–67
Tibullus  97
Tissot, Samuel  1–2
Titzmann, Michael  38
Toba, Sōjō  131

*Tomb for 500,000 Soldiers*  43–61
Toury, Gideon  3
Trividic, Anne-Louise  174, 178
Tymoczko, Maria  14

*Unofficial History of the Embroidered Couch*  110, 114, 120

*Venus in Furs*  85
Venuti, Lawrence  14
Voegelin, Salomé  92
Volokhonsky, Larissa  16
Voß, Johann Heinrich  3

Wainhouse, Austryn  15, 22–23
'Walter'  35
*White Hotel*  154–59, 164–67
Wigmore, Juliet  162
*Wilhelm Meister*  91, 93–96
Williams, Linda  175, 185 n. 31, 193–94, 197

*Xi Xiang Ji*  114
Xunzi  92–93, 100, 103, 187

Yang, Wuneng  95
Yau, Ching  187
Yeh, Catherine Vance  135

Zhang, Longxi  2, 11 n. 7

# SUBJECT INDEX

❖

animals 44–57, 61, 146, 159, 176, 189

BDSM 54, 60, 85–86, 151 n. 1, 172, 185
bestiality 49
Bildungsroman 36, 71, 162

capitalism 46, 48–49, 51, 61, 79, 84, 86, 151 n. 20, 181
*chungong* 111, 119, 122 n. 17, 130, 188–92
Confucianism 1, 92, 106 n. 9 & 10, 112
cross-dressing 135
cultural difference 1–6, 34, 36–38, 40, 44, 47, 72, 87, 92–93, 96–99, 126–34, 148–49, 179, 193–94

death drive 148, 150, 158
dildo 22, 34, 36, 38–39, 71, 114, 172, 188, 190

ekphrasis 1–2, 35, 110–20, 129
Enlightenment 1, 33, 92–93, 152, 157
erection 37, 147, 163, 180
Eros vs. Thanatos 148, 150, 158
erotica:
　vs. pornography 21, 33, 160, 172, 187, 193
　for sexual arousal 1–2, 35, 110–20, 122 n. 20, 129
ethics 13–15, 18, 103, 112, 164, 170

death drive 148, 150, 158

holocaust 154–56, 158–60, 165–67, 170 n. 67
homosexuality 35–36, 47, 123, 121 n. 1, 172, 174, 179–80

impotence 37, 102, 163, 180

masturbation 1–2, 5, 22, 25, 46–47, 100, 108 n. 64, 176, 180, 197
'money shot' 176, 185 n. 31, 193
mysticism 64 n. 35, 96, 142–49

onomatopoeia 70–71, 94–95, 98–100
oral sex 174
orgasm 9, 100–01, 113, 126, 146, 163, 191–93

patriarchy 156–61, 163, 197
pornography 13, 66–68, 70–73, 77 n. 34, 156, 160–62, 167, 175, 177, 185 n. 31, 188, 193–94, 197
　as consumer good 33–41
　as opposed to eroticism 3–4, 91, 97, 172–73, 193
postcolonialism 43–61, 175

post-humanism 44–45, 51, 57, 61, 64 n. 32

queer 48–51, 61, 63 n. 13

rape 15, 152 n. 40, 46, 55, 59–60, 155–56, 159
romantic love 45–47, 54, 59, 69, 75 n. 15, 79–80, 94, 120, 133, 156, 163, 177, 181
Romanticism 96

sadomasochism 47, 57, 154, 158, 162, 164, 167, 172
shoe fetish 94–96, 102, 107 n. 20, 108 n. 45, 189
*shunga* 122 n. 17, 130
sound 91–103, 106 n. 9, 115, 119, 163, 177, 195–96

threesome 40, 98–100, 119–20, 145, 191, 196
torture 36, 148–49, 153 n. 80
toys 22, 34, 36, 38–39, 71, 114, 172, 188, 190
translation:
　Chinese to English 94–95, 98–100, 111–16, 119–20, 188–89, 194
　Chinese to German 99–100
　and cultural difference 1–6, 34, 36–38, 40, 44, 47, 72, 87, 92–93, 96–99, 126–34, 148–49, 179, 193–94
　English to 51 languages 78
　English to German 68–70, 72–73, 80–83
　ethics of 13–16, 155–56, 165–66, 170 n. 66
　English to French 174
　French to English 17–26, 43–45, 47, 53, 55–60, 143–46, 148
　French to German 36–40, 70
　from image to text 190–92
　from text to film 161–65, 178–79, 161–63, 166–67, 175–82, 186–88, 190, 195–97
　from text to image 132
　German to 5 languages 94–95
　German to English 80, 96–98, 101–02, 156–57, 159–62
　Japanese to English 126, 128–29, 131–32
　re-translation 36–40
　theory of 1–3, 5, 14–15, 17–18, 27

violence 1, 18–21, 27, 43, 45–48, 50–58, 61, 68, 141–43, 148, 154–59, 164–65, 173
voyeurism 98–100, 116–20, 145, 148–49, 160–65, 195–96

'the West' vs. 'the East' 5, 12, 125, 193–94

wordplay 70–73, 148

www.ingramcontent.com/pod-product-compliance
Lightning Source LLC
Chambersburg PA
CBHW082245220526
45469CB00009B/2880